Keynes and Marx

MANCHESTER
1824

Manchester University Press

PROGRESS IN POLITICAL ECONOMY

Series editors: Andreas Bieler (School of Politics and International Relations, University of Nottingham), Gareth Bryant (Department of Political Economy at the University of Sydney), Mònica Clua-Losada (Department of Political Science, University of Texas Rio Grande Valley), Adam David Morton (Department of Political Economy, University of Sydney), and Angela Wigger (Department of Political Science, Radboud University, The Netherlands).

Since its launch in 2014, the blog Progress in Political Economy (PPE) – available at www.ppesydney.net/ – has become a central forum for the dissemination and debate of political economy research published in book and journal article forms with crossover appeal to academic, activist and public policy related audiences.

Now the Progress in Political Economy book series with Manchester University Press provides a new space for innovative and radical thinking in political economy, covering interdisciplinary scholarship from the perspectives of critical political economy, historical materialism, feminism, political ecology, critical geography, heterodox economics, decolonialism and racial capitalism.

The PPE book series combines the reputations and reach of the PPE blog and MUP as a publisher to launch critical political economy research and debates. We welcome manuscripts that realise the very best new research from established scholars and early-career scholars alike.

Keynes and Marx

Bill Dunn

MANCHESTER UNIVERSITY PRESS

Published by Manchester University Press
Oxford Road, Manchester M13 9PL
www.manchesteruniversitypress.co.uk

British Library Cataloguing-in-Publication Data is available

ISBN 978 1 5261 5490 3 hardback
ISBN 978 1 5261 7177 1 paperback

First published by Manchester University Press in hardback 2021

This edition published 2023

Typeset by Newgen Publishing UK

Contents

Figures

Tables

Acknowledgements

This book has developed over several years and through many conversations. I owe particular thanks to my colleagues and to students in the Department of Political Economy at Sydney University. Many thanks to all at Manchester University Press, in particular the series editors, and to the anonymous referees. I am very grateful to Luke Finley for his copy-editing.

Some of the conceptual arguments were developed in a paper presented to the Trans-Pennine Working Group of the Conference of Socialist Economists, Manchester, in 2016. Earlier versions of the material that became Chapter 6 were presented in papers delivered to the 2016 conferences of Work, Employment and Society and of Historical Materialism, London. Earlier versions of the material now in Chapters 7, 8 and 9 was presented in papers delivered in 2016 at the University of Kingston and in 2017 at the Conference of Historical Materialism, Sydney. I am very grateful for the opportunity to present these papers and to all the participants for their comments and criticisms. The book is an expanded version of an article which appeared in *Global Society*: 'On the Prospects of a Return to Keynes: taking Keynes's political philosophy seriously' (Dunn 2018). I am grateful to the editors and the anonymous referees.

My greatest thanks to Carmen Vicos, for help with the manuscript and with so much more.

Introduction: towards a critical but constructive appraisal of Keynes's thought

There are good reasons to revisit Keynes. The global financial and economic crisis of the 2000s punctured some of the hubris around unrestrained markets. The coronavirus crisis again confirmed that governments could mobilise resources to counter both the disease and economic contraction. Keynesian ideas regained credibility and found new audiences. Much of what Keynes said in the 1930s seems to fit: against austerity, about economic uncertainty, about money and financial assets, about income inequality and effective demand, about the need for balance in the international economy. There is widespread anger at the results of the global economy's 'neo-liberal' turn of recent decades and at post-crisis responses in which apparently Keynesian measures have been quickly abandoned. For conservative politicians and orthodox economists, Keynes remains a demon to be exorcised but for many others he again represents the hope of a return to a gentler and more socially responsible form of capitalism.

Rejecting the too-common characterisation of Keynes as either hero or villain, this book aims to develop a constructive, left-wing critique. It argues that there is an enormous amount to be learnt from Keynes but there are also problems with his analysis: problems with what he says, with his economic 'model' and with what he leaves unsaid, with the way in which he looks at the world and what he therefore leaves unanalysed.

Some of the problems can be overcome by reworking Keynes's insights on Marxist foundations, and doing this also helps to develop a richer Marxism. This proposition will horrify more dogmatic followers of both Keynes and Marx, who have seldom been on speaking terms (Tsuru 1994). Keynes himself was brutally rude about Marxism, dismissing it as 'illogical and dull' (*Collected Writings*, Volume IX: 285; the *Collected Writings* are hereafter cited using 'CW' with the volume number, e.g. CWIX: 285). Some of Keynes's followers can be more sympathetic (Cottrell 2012) and several 'post-Keynesians' are happy to acknowledge Marxist insights on class and dynamic

1

change. But they typically insist that these insights can only thrive when grafted onto a Keynesian stem.

From the Marxist side, there have been useful engagements with Keynes but these are both rather rare and tend to fall into one of two camps. On the one hand, there are polemical hatchet-jobs. Marxists can outdo Keynes for invective and dismiss him as just another bourgeois economist, at best a subtler apologist for capitalism than the mainstream he purports to criticise (Eaton 1951). Keynes, according to Meek, 'precisely because he was a *bourgeois* thinker, succeeded only in substituting a new collection of illusions for an older collection which had become a little shop soiled' (1956: 129). To mention Keynes or Keynes's followers without suitably derogatory epithets is revisionist back-sliding, is to be an inconsistent socialist (Mattick 1971).

On the other hand, some Marxists promise a happy marriage. Harcourt argues that 'when Marx and Keynes examined the same issues in the capitalist process, they came up with much the same answers' (2004: 3). For Sweezy, Keynes's writings cannot be challenged either in terms of their 'logical consistency ... or on the basis of Marxian analysis of the reproduction process' (cited in Linder 1977: vol. 1, 261). Foster and McChesney go further, claiming that 'Marx figures centrally in Keynes's analysis' (2012: 51). Now Marx and Keynes were saying much the same thing. Particularly in the aftermath of the 2007–09 economic crisis, many Marxists and Keynesians offered broadly similar explanations and could unite against economic orthodoxy, against both the theory and the austerity policies. As with Keynes, the crisis also renewed interest in Marx, with several mainstream commentators admitting Marx's renewed relevance. Moreover, the Marx that some of these accounts rediscovered, with a stress on income inequality and problems of insufficient investment and consumer demand, could sound remarkably Keynesian (Roubini 2011, Magnus 2011, Gray 2011).

It is argued here that none of these approaches is satisfactory. The importance of strategic alliances and respectful dialogue should not mean airbrushing out significant differences. A dogmatic parochialism can exaggerate, but there are substantial impediments to a comfortable embrace. Marx and Keynes had very different worldviews. Marx's historical materialism, if never the structural determinism of opponents' caricature, is a materialism. It gives at least some analytical priority to questions of social relations of production, in particular to these social relations of production over individuals' perceptions. Keynes's epistemology is not always clear or consistent but, as will be argued below, he often broadly articulates an idealist individualism, which severely limits his break with the mainstream. If Keynes's economics involved some reconnection between theory and the real world, with which the marginalist mainstream had appeared to lose all contact, his ideas can reasonably be characterised as an attempt to save a theoretical system that for Marxists would be better broken up for scrap. Keynes's politics remained in many respects conservative. All sorts of methodological and political differences therefore caution against combination by the method of mixing-and-stirring. Similarly, there are reasons to be cautious of a congenial division of labour, which cedes production to Marx while taking from Keynes 'a theory of money, the elements of a theory of employment, and an emphasis on practical economic policy' (Hodgson 1982: 233). Simply adding Marx and Keynes together seems liable to foster a fragile eclectic hotchpotch, ultimately less convincing than the sum of its parts. Much hangs on the nature of any prospective combination.

Marx's engagement with his classical forebears provides inspiration. As Foley puts it, Marx 'wants to find the kernel of truth in the knowledge constructed by others. His criticism is in this sense positive' (1986: 2–3). Marx recognises the importance of the classical economists' 'science', incorporating their innovations but going beyond them. Marx's attitude was far from one of outright rejection and often involved socialising and reworking earlier concepts, most obviously the labour theory of value he found in Smith and Ricardo. Even what Marx called vulgar political economy was not necessarily absolutely wrong. Marx accepted as a matter too obvious to need lengthy explanation that there were laws of supply and demand. Their explanation of price variations merely said nothing about the more important anterior questions of the levels around which prices varied. He had different priorities.

Similarly, it is argued here that even where Keynes's general 'model' or 'system' remains unsatisfactory, he discusses theoretical issues with which Marxists can potentially engage productively. Keynes makes important theoretical innovations and his insights into time and uncertainty, the motivations of investment, the role of consumption, the persistence of unemployment, the nature and role of money, and the establishment of interest rates all seem worth incorporating into any modern critical political economy. Keynes may have held a naively optimistic view of state capacities, but here too his identification of the fundamental fact of state involvement and its economic importance should also force Marxist political economy to more fully incorporate an analysis of what states can and cannot achieve. At the very least, Keynes addresses issues of vital importance which Marxists have tended to neglect. What follows therefore attempts to do two things. First, it suggests that Keynes's critique can and should be radicalised (and at the same time made more realistic and useful). Second, so reinterpreted, there is much that these Keynesian insights can add to Marxism, at least as it is normally understood. Keynes says useful and important things which should be incorporated into any Marxist understanding of the world. Perhaps, going back to Marx, it might be possible to advance to the areas of Keynes's enquiries without needing Keynes himself as a guide. However right in principle, my simple pragmatic response is that it is unobvious that Marxists have followed such paths. It is worth looking to see what can be discovered by following Keynes's trail, while surveying the country through Marxist lenses.

Questions of analytical priority are often crucial. A bit more will be said about this in later chapters but the first point is simply the fact that both Marx and Keynes do prioritise analytically. But their priorities are different. Marx begins with assumptions about the reality of both a physical and social world which works behind the backs of those involved. In modern jargon, he rejects methodological individualism, even if some Marxists insist otherwise (Roemer 1982, Elster 1985). However, a prioritising of social being and of social structures over individual intentions and actions does not require a flip into methodological collectivism. Structures and agents are mutually interdependent, for Marxists as for many others (Weber 1930, Callinicos 1989a, Arrow 1994, Lawson 1997, Onuf 1997). But the relationship need not be assumed symmetrical. It is entirely possible for there to be interdependent but asymmetrical relations. The moon and the earth orbit their common centre of gravity but this is closer to the earth than the moon, so that talking about the moon's orbit around the earth is often a useful first approximation. To recognise interrelation does not require a relapse into liberal eclecticism, as if not only did everything influence everything else but also everything were equally analytically important. It remains not only possible but necessary, whether consciously or otherwise, to prioritise.

Marx identifies how he proposed to do this, notably in the *Contribution to the Critique of Political Economy* (1970) and in the introduction to the *Grundrisse* (1973), where he sets out an analytical ordering suggesting a movement from the abstract and general to the more concrete and specific. There is an articulation between different levels of abstraction, and provisional 'truths' established at one level can be used but also tested and potentially modified in relating them to the more concrete evidence at the subsequent levels. Marx never completed promised subsequent volumes, and *Capital* never goes far beyond the most abstract of levels (Rosdolsky 1977, but see Lapides 1992, Pradella 2014). *Capital* introduces core concepts like value and exploitation, which in turn can provide the background against which more concrete investigations can be set, but the implication is that a Marxism which sticks too closely to the study of nineteenth-century texts remains limited. It was clear for Marx that subsequent levels are informed by what is established before without being narrowly determined by them and that each level has a distinct, irreducible moment of its own.

The reason for repeating this here is that the distinction between different levels of analysis allows that particular insights of mainstream social science can often be seen as not absolutely wrong but wrong in so far as they are presented as absolutes. Laws of supply and demand, psychological characteristics, the power of the nation-state, are at best partial and one-sided but become potentially useful once understood within the context of exploitation, accumulation and dynamic change: once put in their proper analytical place.

Much of Keynes's work can be reconceived in this light. One important implication, which will be emphasised in what follows, is that Keynes's general theory is rather less general than he claims (Hodgson 2004). He bases this claim for generality primarily on the grounds that his theory incorporates the 'special case' of the classical theory in the manner that Einstein's general relativity incorporates special relativity but also the earlier Newtonian vision he was transcending. The analogy fails because, unfortunately, 'one cannot say that Newtonian economics is good enough for practical purposes' (Galbraith 1996: 20). Keynes himself admits the point, insisting that classical theory 'is not incomplete in the sense it deals with a special case rather than the general case. I maintain that as a theory it applies to no case at all' (CWXIII: 593). But Keynes remained largely a critic from within, in order to show that orthodoxy failed on its own terms (Chick 1983, Hillard 1988). Even his most penetrating insights can remain quite limited attacks on particular marginalist assumptions. As Marxist critics were quick to point out, this means there are important respects in which Keynes's system, for example in its individualism and lack of dynamism, represents a regression in relation even to pre-Marxist classical political economists like Smith and Ricardo.

But we do not advance or retreat evenly on every front, and there are areas where Keynes's analysis addresses issues which either the level of abstraction of *Capital* or the concrete historical development of capitalism leave relatively neglected in Marx. The suggestion here is therefore that there is much in Keynes with which it is worth critically engaging, but that there cannot be a simple combination of Marx and Keynes or a simple division of labour where they do different jobs according to taste – Marx on production, Keynes on money; Jewish on Saturday, Christian on Sunday. So the attempted Marx–Keynes synthesis here differs from others. Many of the existing combinations seem to be affected on relatively narrow, technical grounds. Most have been attempted by critical Keynesians, aware (as above) that they are appropriating Marxist intuitions into a Keynesian social ontology. Robinson (1964), for example, perhaps the most 'Marxist' of Keynesians, is simply dismissive of value theory, implying that Marxists should decommission their theoretical weapons before there can be any meaningful engagement. The suggestion here is that any synthesis would work better the other way around; that Keynes's insights require critical embedding into a broader socioeconomic context than his own approach allows. A Marx–Keynes synthesis would require different and specifically Marxist starting points. Keynes's arguments should be taken seriously but often need to be critically reworked, his concepts socialised, placed within the context of exploitation and dynamic change.

There is also a practical problem in arguing for a dialogue between Marx and Keynes in that few from either tradition bother reading, far less understanding, the other. A particular challenge in engaging with Keynes is that he appears to present an army of different adversaries. Keynes himself 'abandoned ideas as ruthlessly as he was eager to acquire new ones' (Balogh 1976: 67). He has been subject to widely different interpretations. Dostaler writes of Keynes that:

> as an economist, he appears, at one extreme, as an orthodox neoclassical economist and, at the other, as one who breaks completely with classical orthodoxy to outline a new theoretical horizon. In politics, he is judged to be a conservative elitist by some and a crypto-communist by others. The kaleidoscope evinces even more colours in philosophy, where the same man is considered by different people to be a rationalist, a realist, an empiricist, an idealist, a positivist, and even an existentialist. (1996: 14)

There is no agreed interpretation, with matters not helped by Keynes's own penchant for 'raising the dust' and polemical exaggeration. Some followers insist that Keynes's system stands or falls as a coherent whole (Kicillof 2018) while others happily cherry-pick. A relatively thorough and sympathetic engagement with Keynes's work is therefore a prerequisite for any serious Marxist critique.

The next three chapters accordingly try to explain where Keynes was 'coming from'. Chapter 1, on Keynes's life and times, suggests that Keynes's ideas need to be understood in the context of his own social circumstances. He was an avowed member of the 'enlightened bourgeoisie', disdaining boorish proletarians. His perspective was also almost always specifically British. Keynes explicitly invokes a 'Scotch and English' (he was never fond of the Welsh) tradition of humane science, naming 'Locke, Hume, Adam Smith, Paley, Malthus, Bentham, Darwin, and Mill, a tradition marked by a love of truth and a most noble lucidity, by a prosaic sanity free from sentiment or metaphysic, and by an immense disinterestedness and public spirit' (CWX: 86). Sadly, if Britain's past provided most of Keynes's heroes, by the time Keynes was writing, its present looked less inspiring. He lived through times of Britain's relative decline, when its educated bourgeoisie could no longer expect to rule the world. The spectre of communism, and by the 1930s of fascism, haunted Europe while Britain was challenged and surpassed, particularly by the US. Within Britain, the inter-war period became one long economic stagnation. The complacency of laissez-faire practice and liberal free-market economics rang hollow. Keynes grappled with the increasingly unignorable failures of the market and the reality of state intervention. The very fact that Keynes identified with his class and national interests set him apart from the sham universalism of the liberal mainstream. At the same time, he always kept one foot inside the inner circle. Intellectually he shared many of the mainstream's assumptions. Personally, he served as a government official rather than just an academic economist and would befriend most of the prime ministers of the day.

Chapter 2 examines Keynes's philosophy, stressing what it describes as an inconsistent idealism and individualism. From his student days, Keynes was profoundly influenced by the conservative British philosopher G.E. Moore. Primarily an ethicist, Moore rejected a crude Benthamite utilitarianism, a rejection which Keynes would continue to celebrate, not least for inoculating him against socialism. For Keynes 'it was this escape from Bentham, joined with the unsurpassable individualism of our philosophy, which has served to protect the whole lot of us from the final *reductio ad absurdum* of Benthamism known as Marxism' (CWX: 446). Moore emphasised private intuition as the means to know what was good but, admitting areas of uncertainty, he suggested that in practice we need to fall back on convention as a guide. Keynes would be more willing to challenge convention, but at the cost of elevating the power of intuition of at least some individuals. Meanwhile, and in some tension with this, Keynes's own work on probability established that there were areas of genuine uncertainty, where it is impossible to know, impossible to know even probabilistically, or even to order one thing as more likely than another. To degrees which remain disputed, this thinking about probability and uncertainty would continue to inform Keynes's mature economics. At the very least, time becomes important and it becomes impossible to assume that people always make what with hindsight might be reckoned rational utility-maximising decisions. This becomes fairly devastating for the principles and pseudo-scientific pretensions of mainstream economics. Conversely, Marxists can point to the limits of individualism in Keynes's thought and emphasise capitalist imperatives, which make some outcomes much more likely than others, and posit capitalist instability, as a source of uncertainty. But at the same time, and as developed in later chapters, capital involves an ineliminable element of guesswork: of firms' guessing how competitors will behave and of guessing aggregate economic performance, of people really acting, making a difference in ways which qualify any vision of either capitalists or workers as mere victims of conditions beyond their choosing.

Chapter 3 turns to Keynes's politics. His political philosophy owed most to Edmund Burke, a deeply conservative figure but an intelligent conservative who admitted the need for change if the greater horrors of revolutionary upheaval were to be avoided. In terms of Keynes's practical politics, he was a long-standing member of the British Liberal Party, often a very active member. This was the historical party of British capitalism but by the twentieth century was both broad and divided. Keynes was somewhere on the centre-left of the party. He had much in common with the leftist 'New Liberals', some of whose economic proposals anticipate Keynes. At the same time, Keynes could be dismissive of both their economics and their more radical reform proposals. He was also deeply critical of a conservative wing of the Liberal Party, which he thought barely distinguishable from the Conservatives. As in many things, there was a pragmatism to Keynes's politics and an advocacy of a 'middle way'. Initially he supported Asquith, the liberal imperialist, but he then threw in his lot with Lloyd George's reforming agenda of the 1920s. More generally, Keynes's politics was characterised by an advocacy of state intervention to manage the market economy, to 'save capitalism from itself', in Hobsbawm's phrase (Wattel 1986: 3). Mann (2017a) has recently characterised a broad tradition going back to the French Revolution and to Hegel as 'Keynesian' in the sense that it acknowledges this need for the state to transcend liberalism, or in order to achieve a more sustainable liberalism. Mann is sympathetic to this project, but it is possible to acknowledge the important reality of state intervention and the intellectual challenge this represents to economic orthodoxy, while also being sceptical of Keynes's optimism about state capacities or benign oversight.

Chapter 4 considers economics before Keynes. Rather than attempting a general history of economic thought, it considers three themes, in order to understand Keynes's later economics. First, it discusses his relation to the older (pre)classical tradition. Keynes selects his opponents carefully. He defined them as 'classical' in an original way. In a footnote to the first page of the *General Theory* he writes that:

> 'The classical economists' was a name invented by Marx to cover Ricardo and James Mill and their *predecessors*, that is to say the founders of the theory which culminated in the Ricardian economics. I have become accustomed, perhaps perpetuating a solecism, to include in the 'classical school' the *followers* of Ricardo, those, that is to say, who adopted and perfected the theory of Ricardian economics, including (for example) J.S. Mill, Marshall, Edgeworth and Prof. Pigou. (1973: 3)

Keynes then sometimes refers to the predecessors like Smith as 'pre-classical'. This categorisation allows Keynes to ignore much of what would more normally be understood as the classical tradition, while selectively recovering important insights, for example about effective demand and economic aggregates. Keynes also expresses sympathy with the labour theory of value, but he interprets this more in the sense of an accounting device than as the epistemological basis for political economy as it had been for Marx. Other key questions for the older classical tradition, around economic growth and the origins of profit, remain safely buried in the graves dug for them by the marginalist revolution in the 1870s. Differences of wealth and income matter to Keynes, but these are conceived in individual rather than class terms. Keynes associated the classics particularly with an acceptance of the quantity theory of money and with an acceptance of 'Say's Law'. Keynes defined the latter in terms of supply creating its own demand and rejected this because, amongst other things, money matters, money is not 'neutral', and this undermines the standard version of the quantity theory which sees changes in the quantity of money translated into equivalent changes in prices. For Keynes, money was instead first a unit of account but also a store of value, with the implication that monetary decisions could matter profoundly to the wider economy.

Second, Chapter 4 discusses marginalism, particularly as Keynes encountered it in the work of Jevons and Marshall. Marginalists made important arguments about economic efficiency and individual utility, which continue to inform mainstream economic thinking. Keynes accepts much of this worldview and his method of exposition in the *General Theory* is often marginalist and Marshallian, even as he makes very powerful criticisms of particular claims, notably around the operation of labour markets.

Third, the chapter considers the development of Keynes's own critique of the economic mainstream prior to the *General Theory*. Although Keynes later described himself as having been 'classical' when he wrote these earlier works, his two major economic books also make important innovations. The *Tract on Monetary Reform*, published in 1923, amongst other things, is deeply critical of the gold standard and depicts moderate deflation as a greater evil than moderate inflation. Keynes is already bitterly critical of mainstream complacency and the idea that in the long run the market will sort things out, will eventually return the economy to a happy equilibrium. It is here that Keynes famously objects that '[i]n the long run we are all dead' (1923: 65). The *Treatise on Money*, published in 1930, is long and sometimes obscure, designed to establish Keynes's professional standing. In some respects, it nevertheless reaches further than the *General Theory*, attempting a sweeping, dynamic depiction of the relation between money and the wider economy. It is here that Keynes develops his famous paradox of thrift, in which individually rational decisions can sum to a disastrous economic and social whole.

Chapter 5 risks a summary of the *General Theory*. This is risky because the *General Theory* is a notoriously difficult and disputed book, still subject to rival interpretations. Drawing particularly on Chick (1983), Sheehan (2009) and Kicillof (2018), the chapter concentrates on sketching Keynes's alternative 'model', which shows how it becomes entirely possible for the economy to reach an 'equilibrium' with unemployment. Rather than beginning with assumptions of full employment, Keynes sees the volume of employment and the national income as 'dependent variables' – dependent, that is, on the propensity to consume, on what he calls the schedule of the marginal efficiency of capital and on the rate of interest (1973: 245), with the rate of interest itself determined independently of savings and investment by liquidity preference and the supply of money from the central bank. The general theory is treated as adopting a substantially 'static' or 'stationary' approach (Kregel 1976). In this, Keynes mirrors the orthodoxy but shows how orthodox assumptions of market 'clearing' become unsustainable. The chapter inevitably leaves important themes under-investigated. In particular, it stresses, with Keynes, that while 'money enters into the economic scheme in and essential and peculiar manner, technical monetary details fall into the background' (1973: xxii). Discussions of money and finance are substantially deferred until Chapters 7, 8 and 9.

The subsequent chapters shift focus towards a critical appropriation of Keynes's insights. Chapter 6 concentrates on unemployment. It argues that Marx's general analysis of capitalism, and several arguments around the specifics of unemployment, remain effective points of departure. Not least, unemployment is a political achievement *for* capital, not the economic anomaly it is for Keynes. Marx's analysis of unemployment, however, remains underdeveloped. It is suggested that although Keynes's language and method, couched in substantially individual and static terms, can appear profoundly problematic, the idea of 'unemployment equilibrium' can be a useful heuristic device. Decisions are made in real time, at moments at which there are 'given' levels of capital and of unemployment, which can reasonably be depicted as being in a temporary balance, from which there is no internal imperative to move. Keynes insists that the future is uncertain and all social actors, including firms, are really guessing at what is likely to succeed. There is no reason to assume these guesses sum around what Keynes's classical opponents might see as some ideally rational mean, and it often makes sense for firms to accumulate at less than any theoretical maximum, to invest and to recruit workers only slowly and reluctantly. Keynes's attack on the mainstream also shows how a simplistic supply-side model in which demand looks after itself is inadequate and in doing so also provides a useful reminder to Marxists to investigate the specific moments of other social relations, of finance and consumption, rather than reducing these to straightforward determinants of accumulation. Keynes also (despite some controversy) develops the idea of 'frictional unemployment' which begins in the mainstream as a device for explaining away the troubling reality of market imperfections. Keynes moves beyond the mainstream apologia towards explanation of such frictions. But it is possible to go further. Keynes's emphasis on markets and the downward stickiness of wages, which he shares with the mainstream, limits his critique, but once capital's dynamism and its inherent spatial and temporal heterogeneity are acknowledged, the idea of friction can be worked harder. 'Imperfections', of physical and political geography, of power and institutional conservatism, pervade capitalist markets, producing slow and partial adjustments, between sectors of capital and more broadly between firms, economic activities and across space. The chapter finally returns to politics and to states, never Keynes's benign overseers but also irreducible to the imperatives of capital or the market. Unemployment is always political and never simply an economic phenomenon.

Chapter 7 discusses money and, in a somewhat similar vein to the previous chapter on unemployment, it argues that there are problems and lacunae in Marxists' understanding which an engagement with Keynes can help to address. In particular, it identifies three areas where a constructive critical appropriation of Keynesian insights potentially enriches Marxist monetary analysis. First, for Marx, money is a social relation not a thing, and Marxists have reasonably prioritised money as a measure of value as socially necessary labour time. However, precisely because it is a social relation, that measure should be recognised as inherently imperfect. Historical materialism can also recognise that money also has specific material properties, which reflect but also influence capitalist social relations. This discussion then draws on and extends Keynes's discussions of money's properties, which can be more or less adequately met by different material forms. Second, money matters. It cannot simply be 'read off' from developments in the wider economy and has at least some real effects on that economy, which need to be reintegrated analytically. Keynes quite mistakenly accuses Marx of accepting the quantity theory and Say's Law, but Marx's dismissal of these was somewhat summary and the details of Keynes's critique usefully highlight the ineliminable importance of money for the real economy and suggest that even if better conceived as a second-order effect, Marxist analyses of capital accumulation need to incorporate the specific monetary moment. Third, while Marx recognised the importance of hoarding, his analysis remained sketchy and its implications have seldom been investigated. An engagement with Keynes's crucial concept of liquidity preference, extended and understood as a social and institutional phenomenon, can enrich Marxist monetary analysis.

Chapter 8 continues the discussion of the previous chapter, now considering profit and interest. Marx, following the older tradition of classical political economy, saw interest rates as ultimately determined by profit rates. This remains a valid starting point against an apparently almost exclusive determination by financial variables in Keynes, but there are variations in interest rates hanging on much more contingent relations and there is a real financial moment, the product of both state and private financial agency, which needs to be critically investigated. Interest rates at least react back and need to be reincorporated into an understanding of the determination of profit rates. In particular, the active and changing role of both state and private financial institutions needs to be investigated.

Chapter 9 focuses on the real but constrained monetary power of states and other institutions in greater historical concreteness. In *Capital*, the level of abstraction at which Marx was working meant that he said relatively little about states or international relations. This implies that insufficiencies in Marx's own analysis of money might be seen less as aberrations or mistakes than as something that follows from his avowed method of movement from the abstract and general to the concrete and specific. But that movement needs to be made. The need to investigate concretely the monetary capacities of states becomes particularly important in a world of non-commodity money. States do, as Keynes insisted, have at least substantial monetary power. Positing states within an inter-state and essentially global capitalist system also helps to undermine a crude state/market or exogenous/endogenous distinction, while historical reflections show how states and state forms profoundly influenced changing monetary relations and the development of capitalism. Very brief historical sketches highlight the importance of institutions, particularly of states, in changing monetary relations and of these in changing broader relations of capital accumulation.

Chapter 10 looks at the practice of Keynesianism after Keynes. Keynes died in 1946 so never lived to see the long period of prosperity which became associated with his name. Particularly in rich countries, the post-war decades to the mid-1970s were ones of uniquely stable and consistent growth. It is this period and its successes, at least as much as the *General Theory*, which few people read and fewer understood, that gave meaning to the term 'Keynesianism' and cemented Keynes's reputation. There is then an irony in that the policies pursued by the governments of leading countries followed Keynes's ideas in at most the broadest of senses. While Keynes helped to establish an acceptance of the legitimacy of government intervention, in boom time there was little need for most of the specific policies Keynes developed during the Great Depression. At an international level, the Bretton Woods monetary system contained strongly anti-Keynesian elements while the two most successful post-WWII national economies, Japan and West Germany, had anti-Keynesian policies imposed upon them by post-war settlements. When economic crisis hit in the 1970s, many states turned to what looked more like Keynesian fiscal responses. Amongst other things, these produced high levels of inflation while only much more provisionally helping to restore conditions of economic growth. The perceived failures helped to open the door to the reassertion of the old economic orthodoxy, sometimes dubbed 'neo-liberalism', while many Keynesians started to reconsider whether what had come to be known as Keynesianism did indeed follow Keynes's prescriptions.

Chapter 11 turns to the development of Keynesian theory after Keynes. This book is about Keynes rather than Keynesianism and it does not claim to do justice to the diversity of the subsequent thought. Marx's comment, late in life, that 'All I know is that I am not a Marxist' might equally apply. Indeed, at a meeting in 1944, Keynes similarly claimed 'I was the only non-Keynesian there' (cited in Dostaler 2007: 253). There is a vast and contradictory diversity of putatively Keynesian thought, with little agreement on even how to categorise it. The chapter distinguishes three strands, arguing that despite major differences there are common limitations in an incomplete break with economic orthodoxy. The mainstream 'neo-classical Keynesian synthesis' explicitly advocates reconciliation. It accepts Keynes's identification of the importance of economic aggregates and takes this to say that there is a specific 'macroeconomic' realm, within which government and government intervention matters but which can be studied as a thing apart. Governments have tools with which to manipulate interest rates and make trade-offs between unemployment and inflation, but such a Keynesianism loses any sense of a broader critique. Amongst other things, 'macroeconomics' allowed the reconstitution of the old economic orthodoxy as 'microeconomics', which could proceed as if the Keynesian revolution had never happened.

A second strand is distinguished here in its emphasis on 'market imperfections'. For 'new-Keynesians' this implies that the mainstream claims of market efficiency need not hold. It can lead to some profound criticisms of conventional thinking and crude pro-market policy proposals. For example, Stiglitz, the 'godfather' of New Keynesianism (Mott 1989), opposed the International Monetary Fund (IMF) structural adjustment programmes and austerity in the aftermath of the 2007–09 crisis. But similar arguments can also be read as saying that the appropriate solution is to get rid of the market 'imperfections', to make the world shape up to the faulty neo-classical theory. Eliminating government and labour interference often become particularly pressing concerns. This section also discusses an ostensibly distinct and often hostile 'post-Keynesian' current, whose adherents are more likely to reject such political conclusions. This tradition is more likely to study corporate monopoly alongside labour unions and to acknowledge 'class struggle'. Rather like the new-Keynesians, however, their key

focus remains on 'imperfect competition' and the marginalist models therefore implicitly remain the ideal.

At this point I need a brief digression. Almost all professional economists
to whom I have mentioned that I am writing a book about Marx and Keynes
assume that means that I am actually writing a book about Michael Kalecki.
Of the few who I have been able to persuade that I am in fact writing a book
about Marx and Keynes, almost all assume that I should instead be writing
a book about Kalecki. I therefore need to make clear that while I have no
objection to anyone who wishes to write such a book, this is not it. (There
are already good accounts; see e.g. Lopez and Assous 2010.) Kalecki was an
important economist, who said some similar things to Keynes. Unlike Keynes,
he was familiar with Marx's work and often used Marxist language. I hope
the reasons for looking at Marx and Keynes become clear in the following
pages, and it is hard to compare the efficacy of one project against another
without first doing them both. Some problems with Kalecki's views will be
discussed briefly in Chapter 11 but there are reasons why, despite ostensible
similarities with Marx, he is not the focus of this book. First, Kalecki's original
'anticipation' of Keynes was couched as an explanation of business cycles.
Keynes's analysis, in contrast, is original in its depiction of unemployment
equilibrium, unemployment precisely as a stable rather than a temporary or
cyclical phenomenon. There is a strong case for arguing that business cycles do
not exist (Hoover 2012), and for Marxists the idea is problematic, suggesting
the economy goes round and round, rather than lurching ungainly onwards.
Second, as above, Kalecki's arguments often involve claims of monopoly and
imperfect competition. These are indeed real and important phenomena, but
in taking perfect competition as the antithesis, these ideas align with the mainstream in seeing deviations from some idealised capitalism as both the analytical and normative basis for critical theory (Mott 1989, Shaikh 2016). Keynes,
too, can be guilty of this, but ideas of imperfect competition play a much more
limited role in his thinking (Harcourt and Sardoni 1996). In any case, the
problems of capitalism do not lie only in its imperfections. Third, Kalecki has
relatively little to say about money, perhaps where Keynes is most interesting
and where Marxists have most to learn (Sawyer 1996). Fourth, Kalecki has
little to say about uncertainty, where Keynes also says original, interesting and
important things from which Marxists can learn.

Meanwhile, as Chapter 11's third strand, other post-Keynesians go back
particularly to the *General Theory*'s chapter 12 and do emphasise uncertainty, not least to challenge the epistemological foundations of mainstream
economic thinking. Economic unpredictability becomes a recurring theme.
This is an important insight, but as discussed in Chapter 3, there are questions
about how far it can be pushed without descending into analytical nihilism
or reducing political economy to questions of individual psychology. It is

argued that even as a radical critique, post-Keynesian thinking on uncertainty often remains oriented towards the mainstream. Much as with the identification of market imperfections, this has the effect of reinforcing the mainstream as the centre of the analytical universe. Whether aiming at constructive dialogue or at more or less profound deconstruction, a more radical, positive political economy requires different starting points.

Finally, this book's Chapter 12 considers the anti-Keynesian turn since the 1970s and the prospects for a return. A conventional reading sees a radical turn against Keynesian policy in the 1970s, particularly in the US and UK. Initiated under Democratic and Labour governments but forcefully consolidated under Reagan and Thatcher, an increasingly open, competitive and financialised international environment soon saw other countries following suit. Keynesianism as university economics beat an ignominious retreat. This chapter's discussion qualifies this view. Many of the practices which had come to characterise rich-country economies in the 1950s and 1960s endured. Government spending fell at most modestly and, despite many attacks on the most vulnerable, the welfare state remained largely intact. 'Automatic stabilisers', the rise in welfare payments and fall in taxation in times of slump, remained powerful. In short, rich-country economic practice in the early twenty-first century looked more like that of the 1960s than the 1920s. In many poorer countries, too, despite decades of liberalising policies, states remained highly interventionist. There were, however, major economic reorganisations, with corporate restructuring and financialisation weakening the national bases of political economy. The advantages of going back to Keynes were repeatedly raised in the aftermath of the 2007–09 global financial crisis (GFC), and the policy responses to it appeared to confirm the ability of states to intervene effectively, even if this involved the rescue of the rentier class rather than Keynes's preferred euthanasia. More radical Keynesians insisted the responses were insufficiently Keynesian and denounced the rapidity of their abandonment for austerity as 'madness'. The continuation of liberal policies, however, found powerful backers and a powerful rationale in class and international competition. Similarly, the environmental crisis saw powerful demands for 'green Keynesianism' or a 'Green New Deal', but these faced substantial obstacles at both national and international levels. On the basis of the earlier analysis, the chapter evaluates the prospects of a return to Keynes in light of Keynes's own philosophy and politics and the changed conditions of the global economy. It suggests that Keynes's own caution militates against any easy adoption of the sort of policies he prescribed and that he provides at most an incomplete guide in terms of how effective reform policies might be forged. Once again, it is argued that Keynes says much that is useful, but that it is necessary to go further.

This book is primarily an engagement with theory. Its themes, however, are not simply a matter of academic interest. The revival of Keynes raises pressing political questions about how the left should relate to demands for reform. There are grounds for common struggle, for example on the questions of financial regulation and of redressing income inequality and addressing unemployment. The period labelled 'Keynesian', from the end of WWII until the 1970s, confirms that capitalism can be reformed, but the conditions and the struggles that produced that period are not themselves easily reproduced and there are reasons to be sanguine about the prospects of a return to Keynes. This is not to preclude the possibility of reform and better policy but to advocate a careful evaluation of the possibilities and the suitability of different strategic ideas. This book hopes to contribute to such strategic thinking.

1

Keynes's life and times

Introduction

This chapter cannot detail Keynes's life. There are probably already more biographies than are strictly necessary, including many good ones. Skidelsky's (1983, 1992, 2000) huge three-volume study seems particularly authoritative and is raided liberally in what follows. The purpose of this book is to discuss Keynes's theories, but ideas make better sense in the context of the life and times of the people who articulate them. In Keynes's case, both the life the times are extraordinary and despite Keynes's individual brilliance, there is a particularly strong case for seeing him as a product of and spokesperson for his class and nation.

Keynes's thinking was shaped during times of remarkable social and economic upheaval. Following an age of apparent stability and complacent British imperial hegemony, the period from 1914 to 1945 was one of drastic change. This 'Thirty Years' War' (Dowd 2004) saw the end of the *belle époque*, of 'liberal' capitalism and of peace within the imperialist heartlands. Western capitalism descended into the Great Depression and sharpened class struggles. The Russian Revolution and the rise of an apparently viable socialist alternative became widely attractive, not least to many of Keynes's Cambridge contemporaries, and contrasted with the rise of fascism and nationalism, which culminated in a Second World War even more destructive than the First. A liberal economics based on enlightened self-interest in which, by assumption, neither states nor unemployment existed made sense neither as theory nor ideology, and Keynes became the most prominent of many economists trying to articulate a more realistic theory, a theory which would better describe capitalism but also better defend it. By the end of this period, Keynes had become both the world's most famous economist and a leading player in the negotiations to shape the post-WWII order, now a world where the US had displaced Britain as the dominant power.

17

The chapter's title follows convention by putting the life first, but the content prioritises the turbulent times to highlight how Keynes's life (1883–1946) spanned this extraordinary age. Imperfectly and with some overlap, the chapter is divided chronologically into four parts, from 1883 to 1914, to 1929, to 1939 and to 1946, reasonably marking stages in Keynes's intellectual and political career.

The *belle époque* and its demise (1883–1914)

Keynes was born into a world of affluent complacency. British capitalism seemed unthreatened either at home – Chartism was a distant memory – or abroad – industrial and military superiority could see off resistance in the colonies with murderous efficiency. The British Navy, in particular, protected the Empire from European challengers.

Keynes would later articulate this pre-war world with typical panache. Acknowledging that even then most people had worked hard and long for little reward, Keynes consoled himself that 'anyone at all exceeding the average' could escape to a life of comfort:

> The inhabitant of London could order by telephone, sipping his morning tea in bed, the various products of the whole earth, in such quantity as he might see fit, and reasonably expect their early delivery upon his doorstep; he could at the same moment and by the same means adventure his wealth in the natural resources and new enterprises of any quarter of the world, and share, without exertion or even trouble, in their prospective fruits and advantages; or he could decide to couple the security of his fortunes with the good faith of the townspeople of any substantial municipality in any continent that fancy or information might recommend. He could secure forthwith, if he wished it, cheap and comfortable means of transit to any country or climate without passport or other formality, could despatch his servant to the neighbouring office of a bank for such supply of the precious metals as might seem convenient, and could then proceed abroad to foreign quarters, without knowledge of their religion, language, or customs, bearing coined wealth upon his person, and would consider himself greatly aggrieved and much surprised at the least interference. (CWII: 6–7)

With hindsight, it is easy to see that this order was already disintegrating. A process of relative economic decline had set in. The dynamism of Britain's mid-nineteenth-century industrial revolution had given way to much slower growth, even between 1873 and 1896 to what was known at the time as the 'Great Depression' (before this term later came to be more commonly associated with the conditions of the 1930s). Social and political changes were underway. Parliamentary reform in 1884 extended the electoral franchise to about 28 per cent of Britain's adult population, incorporating middle-class men and many better-off working-class 'householders' (Punnett 1994). By the end of the decade, mass unions were being built, no longer just amongst skilled workers. The year of Keynes's birth had seen the founding of socialist parties: the Social Democratic Federation – the first British Marxist party – and the reformist Fabian Society. Both of these would remain small, but they were influential in the early days of the Labour Representation Committee, forerunner of the Labour Party, which began to stand candidates in parliamentary elections, winning its first two seats in 1900 and by 1910 holding forty-two, a minority of some substance. Resistance to British rule in Ireland increased and the British Liberal Party under Asquith, the old-school free-trade imperialist, became increasingly open to Irish home rule and to social reforms at home. Women's disenfranchisement met growing opposition both within parliament and from the suffrage movement beyond. This was, however, still a world lacking any general presumption in favour of democracy, and much of the British ruling class continued as if the old ways would endure. Free trade met some Tory opposition but was not seriously challenged. The gold standard remained an article of faith. British elites largely still assumed their rule and their rules were assured.

Meanwhile, other countries were catching up and overtaking Britain. By 1913, the US was already richer in both absolute and per capita terms. Germany was not far behind (Maddison 2003). At the outbreak of war, Germany's military spending was already more than 20 per cent greater than Britain's (Russett 1985). These competitors were also succeeding through more openly illiberal means. Germany had abandoned its brief experiment with free trade in the 1870s. The US never made such an experiment. By the early years of the twentieth century, mass socialist parties were well established in several European countries.

Such changes still lay ahead from the world of privilege and prejudice into which Keynes was born. Both of Keynes's parents were from affluent, religiously non-conformist backgrounds. Davis argues that Keynes inherited and would retain 'Victorian notions of individual commitment to the public good' and to 'utopian thinking' (1994: 171, 172). His mother would be the first woman mayor of Cambridge. His father, wealthy from the family's gardening business, was himself a lecturer in political economy at Cambridge University, later becoming a university bureaucrat (Skidelsky 1983). Eminent economists and philosophers shared the dinner table of Keynes's youth, while the slightly less eminent were hired as private tutors well into Keynes's adulthood, ensuring his smooth ascent through Eton and its associated college, King's Cambridge. Keynes's genius would be intensively cultivated. Keynes Senior did fret that quadratic equations and

lengthy Latin prose were harsh for a boy of nine, but he encouraged his son
with regular beatings and occasional whippings (Moggridge 1992: 26).

Keynes took a degree in mathematics. At university, he became a member
of an elitist private, invitation-only, men-only club called the 'Apostles',
whose other members included the philosophers Moore and Russell as
well as a few fellow undergraduates including Strachey, Keynes's long-time
friend and some-time lover. Keynes was particularly influenced by Moore's
philosophy, as will be discussed in Chapter 2. He also became a member of
the informal 'Bloomsbury Group', which has been seen as the Apostles' artistic London extension. At Cambridge, Keynes also joined the Liberal Club
and the Union, and he would become a leading member of both (Dostaler
1996, Moggridge 1992).

Keynes's serious interest in economics began slightly later. He started
reading Marshall's *Principles* in late June 1905 'and in July discovered
Jevons, "one of the minds of the century"' (O'Donnell 1989: 14). Soon,
he was writing to Strachey that 'I find Economics increasingly satisfactory,
and I think I am rather good at it. I want to manage a railway or organise a
Trust, or at least swindle the investing public. It is so easy and fascinating to
master the principles of these things' (cited in Skidelsky 1983: xxiii).

On leaving university in 1906, Keynes joined the Civil Service. To his
disappointment he came only second in the exams, a failure he attributed to
his greater knowledge of maths and economics than his examiners. Second
place meant he missed out on his preferred Treasury posting, instead going
to the India Office. There (that is, at the Office in London; he never went
to India), Keynes began working seriously on money and, amongst other
things, wrote a paper advocating a paper currency, because less would go
into hoards than gold (Moggridge 1992: 225), an important theme to which
he would return. His first book would be published in 1913 on *Indian
Currency and Finance*. By then he had resigned from the Civil Service to
accept a scholarship at Cambridge, which he won at the second attempt
in 1908 for a thesis on probability – ideas he would continue to develop
and would finally publish in 1921. He was also able to take up an economics lecturing position, newly created by a University Board chaired by
his father (Skidelsky 1983: 185). Cambridge, and Cambridge University,
would remain at the centre of Keynes's life, albeit later shared with London
and with a variety of official and unofficial government roles.

Like the vast majority of Eton's and Cambridge's academically successful,
Keynes understood himself to be part of a ruling, intellectual elite. More
than most, Keynes's experiences would have confirmed every early prejudice. As Harrod, Keynes's friend and early biographer puts it, '[n]o one
in our age was cleverer than Keynes, nor made less attempt to conceal it
... He had never ceased to believe that the well-being of society depended

on the strong, clear thinking of the few' (1951: 644, 646). Keynes would become a close personal acquaintance not only of major intellectual figures like Russell and Wittgenstein but also of almost every major politician in Britain of the first half of the twentieth century, very close, at different times, to Asquith, Lloyd George and Churchill.

Keynes was a complex character, seeing himself as an iconoclast while accepting the privileges and sharing many of the prejudices of his time and place. He 'chaperoned' his sister as what he termed a 'hired rough' on suffrage marches (Moggridge 1992: 169) but appears never to have challenged the exclusion of brilliant women like Robinson from the Apostles. He deplored 'medieval' attitudes towards sex questions while his private letters talked lightly of raping young men. He could be an appalling snob, who could alienate even his closest friends. Strachey described him as a 'malignant goblin' (Skidelsky 1983: 204), Woolf as 'sensual, brutal, unimaginate' (Skidelsky 1992: 15). He could be famously mean, the paucity of wine on offer at his Sussex country house outraging his Bloomsbury friends. But he could also be exceedingly generous, subsidising and working enormously hard for people and causes he deemed worthy: Kings College, his Cambridge theatre, the Arts Council, and for the release of colleagues Sraffa and Singer, deemed enemy aliens and interned during WWII.

Keynes was also a nationalist and a racist. This needs some translation into the perspective of a more enlightened twenty-first century where (at least amongst readers of books like this) such views have become less acceptable. Racism and nationalism were ancient prejudices, almost background assumptions of Keynes's times and class. The nationalism is relatively straightforward. Although Keynes saw himself as cosmopolitan, his outlook was resolutely British. Much as people may think of other people's religions, he thought of nationalisms other than British nationalism as rather silly and parochial. He simply accepted that Britain and the Empire were somehow 'right', though not in everything, and he could write about the superiority of American financial and monetary management (Keynes 2011). He could support Irish home rule, assumed of course to continue within the Empire (Moggridge 1992: 191). But Britain was right in a more general, perhaps even moral sense. Britain and the British Empire were run by right-minded people rather like Keynes himself, and he appears to have been genuinely confused and upset that American left-liberals saw Britain as the arch-imperial power and looked at it unfavourably even compared with Japanese expansionism (Skidelsky 2000).

Keynes's racism was a more curious mixture. He disliked the Chinese but had a patronising fondness for Black Americans. He quite liked Germans but was never keen on the French. He had an antipathy towards the Welsh, particularly at one time as embodied by Lloyd George, 'this goat-footed bard, this half-human visitor to our age from the hag-ridden magic and enchanted woods of Celtic antiquity' (CWX: 23). But for Keynes there were worse things than the Welsh: 'I'm not sure that I wouldn't even rather be mixed up with Lloyd George than with the German political Jews' (CWX: 384). If unexceptional for a man of his class and time, Keynes's anti-Semitism, which he made little attempt to conceal, can still be shocking. He found Einstein acceptable, although he reports their meeting with gently mocking amusement, seeing him as 'a naughty Jew-boy, covered in ink, pulling a long nose as the world kicks his bottom; a sweet imp, pure and giggling' (CWX: 382). Less acceptable were 'the other kind of Jews, the ones who are not imps but serving devils, with small horns, pitch forks, and oily tails. It is not agreeable to see a civilisation so under the ugly thumbs of its impure Jews who have all the money and the power and the brains' (CWX: 383–4). Chandavarkar (2000) sees the anti-Semitism as offset by Keynes's support for Zionism, particularly his significant role in committee preparing the ground for the 1917 Balfour Declaration. The ideas may, of course, be complementary, perhaps attested by Keynes's advocacy of offers to the Nazis to arrange the emigration of German and Austrian Jews. Supporters prefer not to dwell on this anti-Semitism and a 'shameful – and puzzling' (Moggridge 1992: 611) preface to the 1936 German edition of the *General Theory* where Keynes recommended his ideas as 'more easily adapted to the conditions of a totalitarian state' (1973: xxvi). To say that Keynes's views were the product of the time and unexceptional should not excuse them, and there were already anti-racist, internationalist currents and political movements of which Keynes was well aware and which he distrusted.

But this does not make Keynes some sort of proto-fascist. Indeed, as Skidelsky insists, and despite Keynes's long-standing pro-German feelings, he 'loathed the Nazi regime, never visited Germany after 1933, and never drew attention to the successes of Hitler's economic policies – a commendable feat of self-denial in the circumstances' (2000: 28). Now Keynes made a point of praising 'the prophets of the ancient race – Marx, Freud, Einstein' (CWXXVIII: 21). Similarly, Keynes had been politically close to Mosley when Mosley was in the Labour Party and when he first broke from it, but he would have nothing to do with the British Union of Fascists. And while he was a long-standing advocate of eugenics, in 1943 he did finally resign 'as vice-president of the Malthusian League in protest against the decision of its Council to urge the government to take steps to restrict the fecundity of the poor – a policy of which he had approved as a young man, but which now struck him as grossly insensitive in the light of Hitler's eugenic experiments' (Skidelsky 2000: 168).

Keynes's politics will be discussed in more detail in Chapter 3. They are not entirely consistent but, as in most things, Keynes favoured a 'middle way'. The point here is to emphasise where Keynes was coming from, whence his political philosophy and critical economics. The comfortable world described in the passage cited above, where an Englishman, very explicitly a man, could naturally travel and buy shares without let or hindrance, while equally naturally having a servant to do the legwork, was soon to be more radically challenged.

In this context, it is worth stressing that the liberalism of nineteenth-century British capitalism was an illusion. In Marx's phrase, capitalism came into being 'dripping from head to toe, from every pore, with blood and dirt' (1976: 926). It was built on money made in the slave trade and slavery. It was dominated by giant companies and exported at gunpoint. Indeed, the individualist assumptions of what would become standard economics emerged precisely in the age of the robber barons and the new imperialism. Such an economics fitted the worldview of big capitalists and bureaucrats, including economics professors. Success was conveniently attributable to the survival of the fittest. Even before Keynes, and before WWI, state practices seldom followed free-market prescriptions, but times of peace and prosperity allowed the prejudices to persist relatively unchallenged. 'Peace, progress, a stable social order: these could never again appear so feasible as they did in the England of the prosperous between 1870 and 1914' (Lekachman 1967: 53). The war and its aftermath brought major changes and challenged old ways of thinking.

War and peace (1914–29)

Few people anticipated the horrors of the First World War. The nineteenth-century liberal view, which Keynes later criticised (CWXXI: 233–51), and which was repeated shortly before the war by both the liberal Angel and the Marxist Kautsky, had come close to saying that war was now precluded. The interlocking interests of capital in the leading countries meant 'ultra-imperialism' in Kautsky's phrase and the 'peaceful' carve-up of the world. Socialist parties warned of war and threatened to stop it, but opposition crumbled once hostilities were declared. Across Europe, the war was initially popular. The ensuing hardships, conscription and mounting casualties soon undermined the general enthusiasm. By the time of the Armistice in November 1918, there had been something of the order of fifteen million military and civilian deaths. Britain experienced nothing like the revolutionary ferment of Russia or Germany but the war profoundly shook the old certainties.

Keynes himself was 'summoned' to the Treasury early in 1915, where his good work for the rest of the war earned him the honour of Companion of the Order of the Bath, Third Class (Tily 2019). He rose quickly from an initially junior position, one of his early responsibilities being 'the acquisition of scarce foreign currencies [w]here his nerve and mastery became legendary' (Lekachman 1967: 22). Most of the Bloomsbury Group opposed the war from the start, and Keynes's role in government distanced him from many of his friends. He was making new connections, becoming a regular at the Asquiths' and social occasions at 10 Downing Street (Moggridge 1992). Keynes now literally walked the corridors of power, and this can reasonably be seen as conditioning his worldview and his economics. He would move easily between his Whitehall and Cambridge circles and became brilliantly adept at shifting the tone of his writing for different audiences. He became a very effective journalist and populariser of economic ideas, while for his academic peers he seems to have enjoyed being deliberately difficult. The rulers of the day, however, were seldom far from the front of his mind. For Keynes, things could be better if only rulers could be persuaded to take good council, particularly his own.

Keynes initially thought the war was justified. With the introduction of conscription, however, he registered as a conscientious objector. As a Treasury official he faced no personal danger of being sent to the front, so this was an idiosyncratic but highly principled gesture against what he saw as an illiberal infringement of individual freedom. As the war dragged on, like that of many others, Keynes's general attitude also changed. By December 1917 he was writing privately that 'I work for a Government I despise and for ends I think criminal' (cited in Skidelsky 1983: xxiv).

There was also no hiding the organised character of the war economy. In times of pre-war prosperity, capitalism's illiberal character could be discretely ignored. Success could be attributed to liberal values, free markets and free trade. Now government intervention drove production. Policy recognised that workers had power which needed to be bought off. Legislation in 1918 included 'prohibiting wage cuts for a period of six months, and establishing further Trade Boards, Joint Industrial Councils and an Industrial Court' (Clarke, P. 1988: 199). Unemployment insurance became 'almost universal', including 'non-contributory benefits' (Clarke, P. 1988: 200). Free trade and the gold standard (the strict link between the pound and a weight of 113 grains of gold) were suspended. Access to precious metals could hardly be allowed to dictate the war economy and, of the leading powers, the US alone remained on gold.

Joining the war only in 1917, the US had earlier begun lending to Britain and France, helping to sustain those countries' war efforts but in the process running up huge debts which then informed the Versailles Conference and the 'Carthaginian Peace' imposed on Germany. President Wilson came with his fourteen-point plan for a post-war world of international cooperation but was unwilling to forgive allied debts, and the British and French in turn demanded reparations from Germany. By this time, Keynes had become the principal Treasury representative. He saw the negotiations first hand and was contemptuous both of the leading participants and of the final Treaty. Keynes's *Economic Consequences of the Peace* (1919; CWII) made his fame, and his peace with Bloomsbury.

The *Economic Consequences* introduces several themes which will recur in Keynes's later works. First, the book is informed by what might be called an 'inconsistent idealism'. This is an idealism not in the sense that Keynes has in mind a better, ideal world, although that is probably also true. Rather, he stresses intentions and ideas as the primary motor of change. Skidelsky writes about how Keynes attributed the disastrous Treaty 'to two things – the inadequacy of the statesmen's ideas, and the inadequacy of their characters' (1983: 386). In the published version he largely spared Lloyd George, his former boss, from his harshest criticisms. But he was scathing of the other participants. Keynes does acknowledge domestic pressures, for example on Wilson, the economic drivers of British and French demands for reparations, and the potentially adverse consequences for future borrowing of any debt write-off. But it remains possible to 'appeal to the generosity of the United States' (CWII: 93) and Keynes's main explanation for Wilson's behaviour remains his foolishness. '[I]t was harder to de-bamboozle this old Presbyterian than it had been to bamboozle him' (CWII: 34). At least in the desperate post-war situation, 'the power of ideas is sovereign' (CWII: 158–9). Or, as Keynes would write shortly afterwards, the turn of events in Europe 'will not be the work of the doctrines of Marx, nor of the disciplined force of international labour, but of the timid and short-sighted wags and stupid heads of its own conservative leaders' (CWXVIII: 84). The case for the decisive role of individuals and ideas is probably as strong here as ever; the players were singularly influential and the conjuncture unique. That opportunity lost, Keynes put more emphasis on the role of public opinion and his sequel, the *Revision of the Treaty* (CWIII), while still focused on elite guidance, also 'contained a clearer statement of Keynes's views of the role of public opinion in politics. As he saw it, reform and change were the products of discussion through which public opinion was formed and guided' (Moggridge 1992: 370).

Second, although formally most of Keynes's economic analysis remains mainstream, the *Economic Consequences* is already concerned with the relations between production and consumption and has a vision of what Keynes would later term the 'declining marginal propensity to consume'. Before the war, 'society was so framed as to throw a great part of the increased income into the control of the class least likely to consume it' (CWII: 11). The labouring classes are 'compelled, persuaded, or cajoled' while the capitalists 'call the best part of the cake theirs' (CWII: 11–12). This enrichment of the already rich was acceptable only on the tacit assumption that capitalists' greater share of wealth would be invested not consumed (CWII: 12). This explicit framing in terms of class disappears from much of Keynes's later economic writing, but concerns with the economic consequences of distribution would remain crucial.

Third, Keynes opposes inflation. There would soon be significant qualifications to this, and conservative critics of Keynes and defenders of 'sound' money have latched on to these qualifications. Keynes would later allow that moderate inflation was less damaging than deflation but never more than that. Keynes never repudiated his warnings against 'debauching the currency' and the 'menace of inflationism' (CWII: 148, 157).

Fourth, there is an important sense of tension between domestic policy possibilities and international relations. The *Economic Consequences* also sets a precedent in Keynes's analysis being quintessentially British. As Schumpeter would later note, 'Keynes's advice was in the first instance always English advice, born of English problems even where addressed to other nations. Barring some of his artistic tastes, he was surprisingly insular, even in philosophy, but nowhere so much as in economics' (2003: 274). The world economy may have been ill served by Versailles, but it was overwhelmingly Britain's problems with which Keynes was concerned. He describes particularly how the imbalances, implicit in the German need to pay reparations, would impact on Britain's exports and its gold reserves and domestic economy. The connections between domestic and international monetary relations would be a recurring theme.

Fifth and finally, Keynes proposes reforms to avoid a worse fate. The great powers ended the war in 1918 at least in part before the war was ended for them by the Russian method. In his rasher moments and letters to friends and family, Keynes's disdain for the old world shows him sympathetic to radical change. At Christmas 1917 he could write:

> the turn things have now taken, probably means the disappearance of the social order we have known hitherto. With some regrets I think I am on the whole not sorry. The abolition of the rich will be rather a comfort and serve them right anyhow. What frightens me more is the prospect of general impoverishment. (cited in Moggridge 1992: 280)

By May 1919 his reaction to Versailles meant that 'with such a Peace as the basis I see no hope anywhere. Anarchy and Revolution is the best thing that can happen, and the sooner the better' (cited in Moggridge 1992: 312). But Keynes's more considered writing in the *Economic Consequences* took radical change more as a warning, took it more in Lampedusa's sense that things needed to change if they were to stay the same (de Cecco

1989, Rosanvallon 1989). The dangers were of capitalists' own making. It is capitalists who 'allow themselves to be ruined and altogether undone by their own instruments, governments of their own making and a Press of which they are the proprietors' (CWII: 150). If a Marxist might put it slightly differently, at least one Marxist was deeply impressed. For Lenin, Keynes's conclusions were all the 'more powerful, more striking, and more edifying' for the fact that they came from an 'avowed bourgeois ... English philistine' (cited in Turner 1969: 9). Lenin accordingly gave instructions to the state publishing house 'to publish quickly (with abridgements)' (cited in Turner 1969: 9). For Keynes, however, capitalists' errors could and must be corrected if the world was to avoid the 'serious menace of Spartacism' (CWII: 107).

The threat soon receded. Even in Britain, post-war workers' militancy had briefly challenged the old order. In this context, the Treasury and the Bank of England soon squeezed the life out of a brief post-war economic boom, inducing mass unemployment which helped to squeeze the life out of labour. Keynes supported this. In February 1920 he advocated raising the bank rate, to 10 per cent if necessary, to break the boom. Keynes would later change many of his economic views, but as late as 1942, he affirms 'that I should give today exactly the same advice as I gave then, namely, a swift and severe dose of dear money, sufficient to break the market' (CWXVII: 185). Keynes by no means rejected monetary policy or its use for deflationary ends when circumstances dictated. But in Britain, once the brief boom was broken, there would be no return to prosperity and no 'roaring twenties'. Severe unemployment continued throughout the decade, with the level only briefly, in 1927, dropping below 10 per cent (Davidson 2009: 11). By this time, the pre-war complacency was long gone. The Liberal Party was ruinously split by Lloyd George's illiberal wartime coalition with the Conservatives, and Labour had become the official opposition. Keynes struggled to sustain his pre-war optimism. 'Progress is a soiled creed black with coal dust and gunpowder, but we have not discarded it. We believe and disbelieve, and mingle faith with doubt' (CWXVII: 448). Keynes already advocated a 'middle way'.

As the stagnation dragged on, Keynes (like many other economists) became increasingly dissatisfied with the traditional prescriptions. Wartime restrictions had been dismantled, the Bank of England reasserted its autonomy, and the 'Treasury View', insisting on the priorities of sound money, balanced budgets and austerity in recessionary conditions, held firm. Even as more interventionist experiments were attempted in other countries, British policy orthodoxy insisted that the only legitimate tools involved controlling credit, saving, investment and the spread of information (Dostaler 2007: 189). Keynes had opposed the inflationary boom but now equally feared the deflationary contraction which again 'brought Britain to the "verge of revolution"' (Skidelsky 1992: 133). The old liberal mantras of balanced budgets, sound money and the sufficiency of automatic market mechanisms looked increasingly hollow. By 1924 Keynes was insisting 'I bring in the State; I abandon *laissez-faire*' (CWXIX: 228–9).

To this purpose, by the end of the decade, Keynes threw his intellectual and rhetorical powers behind Lloyd George's campaign for public works, not least in the 1929 election. Old antipathies were forgiven, if not forgotten. Keynes co-authored a pamphlet with Hubert Henderson, *Can Lloyd George Do It?*, arguing that '[t]he whole of the labour of the unemployed is available to increase the national wealth. It is crazy to believe that we shall ruin ourselves financially by trying to find means for using it' (CWIX:120). This was breaking with the economic mainstream, but that mainstream was also shifting. Keynes and Henderson cite the authority of Pigou, who would become an important foil of Keynes's attack in the *General Theory*. For orthodoxy, public works schemes had the advantage over dole payments because the latter prevented wages falling as much as they might otherwise have done (Robinson and Eatwell 1973: 47). Of course, a fundamental reason why by this time Lloyd George could not 'do it' was that the Liberal Party was a largely spent force. The election campaign was unsuccessful. The Liberals made modest gains, but won just 59 of 615 seats. MacDonald's Labour Party won 287 and formed a minority government.

Keynes had also argued against Britain's return to the gold standard, already in 1923 denouncing gold as a 'barbarous relic' (1923: 138). The argument for gold was an old one, with Hume's 'specie flow mechanism' suggesting that it assured automatic adjustments; trade deficits lead to gold outflows, reducing economic activity, which then reduces imports, and thence the deficits. Surpluses are similarly self-correcting. The simple mechanism allows the market to work its magic. Gold appeared to have served Britain well for almost a century from 1821 to 1914 (or for two centuries, if we neglect the Napoleonic hiatus from 1797). Keynes shared neither the faith in 'automatic adjustment' nor the disregard 'of social detail, [which] is an essential emblem and idol of those who sit in the top tier of the machine' (CWIX: 224). Britain rejoined the gold standard in 1925 at the pre-war parity with the dollar but productivity had risen much more slowly in Britain than in the US. Meanwhile France had rejoined gold at a much lower rate. So the pound was effectively overvalued in relation to its major competitors. British exports, British industry and, importantly, British mining were chronically uncompetitive. In 1925 Keynes spoke against the return to gold at a dinner party organised by Churchill, the chancellor of the exchequer. He was supported by McKenna, chairman of the Midland Bank and himself a former chancellor (Clarke, P. 1988: 39). Churchill rejected their advice, much later admitting the return to gold was 'the biggest blunder of his life' (cited in Clarke, P. 1988: 41). Keynes's spelled out his arguments under the polemical title of the *Economic Consequences of Mr Churchill*. The chancellor responded graciously, inviting Keynes to join his private dining club, which Keynes accepted with alacrity.

Back on gold, reducing wages appeared the only way to increase British competitiveness. Keynes's argument included a discussion of why this was difficult to achieve. Wages (and rents and profits) are 'sticky', slow to respond to the imperatives of the market (CWIX: 228, Dimand 2019a). This was, of course, a social and political rather than simply an economic process, and soon came to a head in proposed cuts to miners' pay and in the confrontation which became the General Strike. Keynes argued instead for 'a "social contract" by which all wage-earners would be asked to accept a 5 per cent reduction in money wages and all dividend holders a 1s[hilling] increase in income tax' (Skidelsky 1992: 204). When the unilateral wage cuts, and therefore also the strike, went ahead Keynes accordingly blamed it on 'muddles' (Moggridge 1992: 447). He wrote that 'my feelings, as distinct from my judgment, are with the workers' (Skidelsky 1992: 251). That judgement, however, remained that 'Liberals of all complexions agreed that the General Strike was not within the limits of constitutional action, that it must be defeated' (Harrod 1951: 375). Existing wage rates and the gold standard were unsustainable. However, in the aftermath of the strike's defeat, it soon became clear that even the cuts' imposition did little to improve Britain's trade position, let alone establish prosperity. Orthodox economic thinking, of course, insisted on still more wage cuts. Keynes's arguments against this were now more political than economic. In 1929 he wrote that a 'drastic reduction of wages in certain industries, and a successful stand-up fight with the more powerful trade unions might reduce unemployment in the long run ... If any party stands for this solution, let them say so' (cited in Clarke, P. 1988: 77). To cut wages so deeply was 'a dangerous enterprise in a society which is both capitalist and democratic' (Keynes 2011: volume 2, 385).

Keynes himself continued to prosper. He not only wrote about money but made money in large amounts, speculating particularly successfully on commodity markets (Skidelsky 1992, Moggridge 1992). His books and his journalism made him famous. In an early celebrity wedding, in 1925 he married Lydia Lopokova, a famous Russian ballerina. He was also gaining status as a professional economist. Editor of the *Economic Journal* as early as 1912, he needed a major academic work to consolidate his reputation and in 1930 published the vast *Treatise on Money*. By then, of course, the world economy had taken a deeper turn for the worse.

The Great Depression (1929–39)

The US and much of continental Europe had enjoyed an economic boom
in the late 1920s, but optimism was shattered by the Wall Street crash of
October 1929. The crash's effects rapidly spiralled outwards from the US;
employment fell and international trade collapsed (Kindleberger 1973).
Around the world, countries abandoned the gold standard. The Great
Depression had begun. It would continue almost throughout the 1930s,
with economic recovery only finally achieved with rearmament and the descent into WWII. As Marxists pointed out, '[t]he old fairy stories about the
virtues of capitalism left to itself no longer deceived many people' (Eaton
1951: 11). Keynes's own attempts to make sense of the economy and the
failings of mainstream economics in the *Treatise on Money* and the *General
Theory* will be discussed in Chapters 4 and 5. This section emphasises
how the world of depression, class struggle and international competition
forced a rethink, first by policy-makers and then by theorists who began to
catch up.

The extraordinary US boom of the 1920s had a real material basis in the
expansion of mass production, most obviously in the 'Fordism' of the auto-
industry. The country became a major net exporter. Gold flowed in, feeding
the boom, which turned into euphoria and bubble. For Keynes:

> The leading characteristic was an extraordinary willingness to borrow money
> for the purposes of new real investment at very high rates of interest – rates of
> interest which were extravagantly high on pre-war standards, rates of interest
> which have never in the history of the world been earned, I should say, over a
> period of years over the average of enterprise as a whole. This was a phenom-
> enon which was apparent not, indeed, over the whole world but over a very
> large part of it. (CWXIII: 345)

In 1929, pessimism took over. Initially, as the depression spread, many
governments, including Hoover's Republican administration in the US,
broadly followed conventional laissez-faire advice, to let it be, to do
nothing. Soon, however, they were provoked into what had previously been
considered illegitimate if not impossible responses. As will be discussed in
Chapter 6, for neo-classical economics, unemployment could only reflect
people's rational preference for leisure over work at the available wage
rate. Other than such 'voluntary' unemployment, only a modicum of 'frictional' unemployment was allowed as people moved from one occupation
to another. Again, bizarre as it might now seem, for Keynes's mainstream
opponents, state intervention attempting to alleviate unemployment and
economic depression was not simply objectionable and expensive – it could
not work. Anything the state did, by definition, was less efficient than the

market and so would divert resources, reducing economic activity and employment. While these sorts of ideas did, and still do, provide grounds for endless intellectual games amongst professional economists, in the changed circumstances of the 1930s they became useless either as ruling ideology or as a guide to policy. What was happening went far beyond anything explicable as frictional or voluntary unemployment. 'Vast numbers of men were *despairingly* unemployed' (Shackle 1972: 167). The depression itself and the social protest it provoked provided a spur to intervention. The slump also intensified international competition, protectionism and the drive to war. As Lee writes, 'it was hard to do all that and still avoid big budget deficits' (1989: 147).

The US witnessed a particularly remarkable transformation. Levels of workers' organisation and militancy had been close to negligible in the 1920s but, rather than falling as had often happened in previous economic slumps, now militancy revived. Already during the 1932 presidential campaign, Roosevelt reported an exchange with 'an old friend who runs a great western railroad. "Fred," I asked him, "what are people talking about out here?"... "Frank," he replied, "I'm sorry to say that men out here are talking revolution"' (cited in Boyer and Morais 1977: 272). The subsequent rising of the unions in the auto-industry is most famous, but the sit-down strikes also involved 'hospital workers, trash collectors, gravediggers, blind workers, engineers, prisoners, tenants, students and baseball players' (de Angelis 2000: 52). New York's hotel workers and the teamsters in Minneapolis fought famous strikes.

Galbraith describes the reforming policy response as conservative, in the sense that 'without it capitalism would surely not have survived' (1986: 55). The US New Deal, however, also represented a symbolic rejection of the previously dominant attachment to laissez-faire. Keynes gushed in an open letter to Roosevelt in 1933: 'You have made yourself the trustee for those in every country who seek to mend the evils of our condition by reasoned experiment within the framework of the existing social system' (cited in Dostaler 2007: 80). The experience of the New Deal was a messier struggle than is sometimes remembered. Cuts at state and local level often undermined increases in federal spending. The Supreme Court ruled the National Recovery Administration unconstitutional in 1935, state minimum-wage laws were also rejected, and only a watered-down Agricultural Adjustment Act was finally allowed to pass in 1938 (Allen 1968). But there were real changes, and the level of government intervention rose. The crisis, which had seen a cascade of bank failures, also prompted much more rigorous financial regulation (Galbraith 1995).

In other countries too, governments were being pushed into action. The Nazis in Germany prioritised rearmament but also oversaw a more general increase in government spending, economic planning and regulation. Other authoritarian regimes also implemented what, with hindsight, can look much like Keynesian policies (Aldcroft 1993). Boyer (1986) argues that the New Deal and Schacht's policy in Germany particularly influenced the French Popular Front government, while Sweden probably provides the closest anticipation of Keynes's proposals, with government spending used directly as a demand stimulus (Gourevich 1989). Without attempting a world tour of reform, there was a huge variety of state-led economic experiments, which in many countries extended to substantial nationalisations, notably of mines and railways (Clarke, S. 1988). Of course, outside the capitalist bloc, and for all that the USSR was descending into Stalinist brutality, forced industrialisation appeared to overcome the irrationality of booms and slumps and the problems of mass unemployment. It appealed as an attractive model to many of Keynes's Cambridge contemporaries and to Fabian socialists like the Webbs. It added to the legitimacy of state economic intervention. Many of the policies which would later be associated with Keynes were already being tried (Mattick 1971: 114).

Many of the ideas which would become associated with Keynes also began to be articulated in a variety of more or less coherent forms and in various places, notably by Kalecki in Poland and Myrdal and Lindahl in Sweden. There were others derided as monetary cranks, like Foster and Catchings, but also Keynes's colleagues (both friends and rivals) at Cambridge like Robertson and Kahn. Dostaler writes: '[i]n short, these ideas were in the air' (2007: 256). Keynes's innovations were substantial but, like many lesser thinkers, he exaggerated the revolutionary nature of his own ideas. Keynes wrote to Shaw:

> To understand *my* state of mind, however, you have to know that I believe myself to be writing a book on economic theory which will largely revolutionise – not, I suppose, at once but in the course of the next ten years – the way the world thinks about economic problems. (CWXIII: 492)

If Keynes had the advantage for posterity 'that *The General Theory* was published at the right time and in the right place and language' (Dostaler 2007: 256), he had the disadvantage of living in a country that was slow to change. Partly because the 1920s had been so bad, Britain's decline in the 1930s was relatively mild, but even as the depression deepened, the government broadly followed conventional advice. Spending did increase, but the 'Treasury View' broadly held until 1941. In 1930, the Bank of England still expressed its remedial preferences for cuts in wages and social services, a shift in taxation 'to bear less heavily on profits', for 'rationalisation' and a Calvinistic outlook (Clarke, P. 1988: 136). In 1931 Keynes too still favoured restoring confidence through a 'sound' budget, postponing social service expenditure and stopping 'abuses of the dole', although he did think the Labour government went too far, mocking Snowden: 'the first Socialist Chancellor is also the last adherent of true blue *laissez-faire*' (cited in Clarke, P. 1988: 165, 220).

Even the British Labour government had to be seen to be concerned with unemployment and accordingly appointed committees, the Macmillan Committee and the Economic Advisory Council (EAC). Keynes was influential on both these and the tenor of their findings was interventionist, but their influence on policy remained slight. An alternative 'May committee' in February 1931 instead recommend big cuts of £96m and tax rises £24m. For Keynes these proposals were 'not fit for publication; – they are not even fit for circulation to the EAC' (cited in Moggridge 1992: 523). Keynes had long rejected any idea that nothing could or should be done to counteract depression.

His own ideas were evolving. Keynes is rightly associated with public works through which state spending (and government debts) could invigorate a depressed economy but he also continued to argue for other policies, particularly for low and decreasing interest rates and for restrictions on finance. Later this would extend to advocating 'the euthanasia of the rentier' (1973: 376). Keynes's penchant for a dramatic phrase contrasts with his pragmatic policy preferences. As earlier, 'I bring in the state; I abandon laissez-faire, [but] not enthusiastically' (CWXIX: 228–9). Keynes's support for state intervention was always qualified. It involved particular forms of direction rather than state ownership, which in most circumstances he opposed. There is therefore continuity in Keynes's fight for a centre ground, for improving capitalism, so saving it from more radical change. As will be discussed in Chapter 3, Keynes is self-consciously a liberal in the sense of supporting only 'minimal' state intervention, but now sees that the necessary minimum rising to higher levels than his neo-classical counterparts countenanced. So while contesting conventional policy prescriptions and neo-classical economics, Keynes also sees his middle way as rescuing economics from the twin horrors of Marxism and a non-mathematical 'institutional' approach (Hansen 1953: 4). Crucially, Keynes rejects both the idea shared by Marxists and the pro-capitalist economist Schumpeter that crises were inevitable and the idea shared by (some) Marxists and mainstream economists that once in a crisis, policy was ineffective. Keynes has more faith in a state-supported system, insisting that capitalist prosperity and stability could be restored (Eaton 1951, Pilling 1986, Minsky 2008).

The depression also changed international relations and attitudes towards trade and the gold standard. The US, which had been inching towards freer trade, now imposed sharply higher tariffs. Even in Britain, free trade and the gold standard finally came under strain. In the *General Theory*,

Keynes would support mercantilist policies, including the achievement of trade surpluses, which would imply a fiercely competitive strategy. By definition, not every country can achieve surpluses. He also argued, however, that the implementation of his domestic policy ideas would mean that '[i]nternational trade would cease to be what it is, namely, a desperate expedient to maintain employment at home by forcing sales on foreign markets and restricting purchases, which, if successful, will merely shift the problem of unemployment to the neighbour' (1973: 382–3). Eichengreen (1984) has summarised Keynes's apparently shifting attitude towards trade in terms of a consistent prioritising of full employment. Restricting trade could be seen as a more politically achievable goal than restricting foreign investment (Radice 1988), while some restrictions were necessary if public works schemes were to succeed. Without them, spending would lead to spiralling budget and balance-of-payments deficits. Keynes wrote of protection: 'I am sure it is radically unsound, if you take a long enough view, but we cannot afford always to take long views' (cited in Moggridge 1992: 511).

As above, Keynes had opposed the return to gold. By the 1930s he largely accepted it as a *fait accompli*, but the problems soon came to a head, the crisis taking a deeper turn in Britain with a run on sterling in 1931. By August, Prime Minister MacDonald and a few leading colleagues famously abandoned Labour to join with Conservatives and Liberals in a National Government. The Sterling Crisis became sharper, particularly with the 'Invergordon Mutiny', a strike by British sailors, resisting pay cuts. Faced with this, in September, the government suddenly abandoned the gold standard, allowing the pound to fall (Ereira 1981).

Here it seems worth repeating a famous little story that a leading Labour politician bemoaned that when they had been in office 'nobody told us you could do that'. The story is reported by, amongst many others, Kindleberger (1973), Eichengreen and Cairncross (1983), and Runciman (2014). With just slightly different phrasing, Kindleberger attributes the line to Tom Johnson; Runciman and many others attribute it to Sidney Webb. The story's beauty lies in its demonstration of how monetary affairs become naturalised. We assume that because the economy works in a particular way, this is how it must continue to work. The gold standard was an ancient and venerable institution which had come to be taken for granted. Similarly, today it is easy to think of existing international financial arrangements, the 'floating' currency regime, as almost natural and inevitable. A few developing-country governments might try to interfere with the free market in international currencies but common sense, supported by any number of academic papers, tells them they do so at their peril. The story nags at our conscience with the idea that what is, does not have to be. Unfortunately, the story is almost certainly untrue.

The different names being cited should ring alarm bells, and all the references trace back either to Skidelsky (1968) for the Johnson story, or to Taylor (1965) for the Webb version. There the trail runs cold, more than thirty years after the event, with neither of these (eminent) authorities providing any further evidence or reference. More fundamentally, the story is implausible because the question of whether or not Britain should remain on gold was a live political issue at the time. The country had only returned to gold six years earlier, prompting Keynes's much-read *Economic Consequences of Mr Churchill*, attacking precisely this policy. Keynes wrote to MacDonald just before the formation of the National Government that it was 'now nearly *certain* that we shall go off the existing gold parity at no distant date' (CWXX: 591). Amongst others, Bevin, the ultimate Labour insider, who sat with Keynes on the Macmillan Committee, had continued to see leaving gold not simply as an option but as the primary economic policy objective (Moggridge 1992). Leading Labour figures were very close to these debates. I cannot locate Lord Sidney on the day the gold link was broken, but his wife Beatrice Webb was at Keynes's country house in Tilton and reportedly unhappy that the economist was 'too agitated and elated to care to be cross examined' (cited in Moggridge 1992: 528). Hutton reports Keynes 'chuckling like a boy who had just exploded a firework under someone he doesn't like' (cited in Skidelsky 1992: 397). Unfortunately, the idea that breaking the link with gold never crossed the minds of leading Labour insiders seems implausible, and we should look elsewhere to explain their quiescence. Keynes would have attributed policy conservatism mainly to a lack of imagination, or to plain obtuseness, but powerful interests in Britain supported sound money, a strong pound and austerity.

The abandonment of gold at least eased the economic constraints and the pound's fall eased Britain's balance-of-payments difficulties. Low interest rates, precluded while trade deficits had to be covered by attracting money into the country, became a possibility and helped a modest economic revival, notably with something of a boom in private house-building (Skidelsky 1992). But across the world, mass unemployment had become the norm. Keynes's colleagues, notably including Pigou (1933), continued to theorise it as largely an anomaly, which could be explained away within the standard economic framework. By contrast, Keynes, particularly in the *General Theory*, put employment at the forefront of his rethinking of economic theory. The book was published in 1936, and was soon widely reviewed and translated. It is a difficult, academic text, whose influence is contested, as will be discussed in Chapter 10. But at least in North America, even before the war, avowedly Keynesian economists sat in or close to government, and elsewhere too, several governments began to follow something resembling what would later be seen as Keynesian policies.

Rearmament, the Second World War and the post-war world
(1939–46)

In Britain, policy was slow to change. From 1937 rearmament began to provide an economic stimulus, but it would be two years into war itself before the British Treasury's insistence on traditional remedies, on austerity and balanced budgets, would finally be shattered. For the first time, the 1941 budget was explicitly concerned with the macroeconomy, not just the government budget (Moggridge 2019). By then Keynes had assumed a semi-official post as 'advisor to the Chancellor of the Exchequer, a position he held until his death' (Patinkin 1987: 38). He was again firmly ensconced in the corridors of power and directly influencing policy.

Keynes opposed the build-up to war, broadly supporting Chamberlain's policy of appeasement but advocating a firmer, more active stance. He criticised a 'paralysis of will … [w]e just rearm a little more, grovel a little more, and wait and see … Our power to win a war may depend on increased armaments. But our power to avoid a war depends much more on our recovering that capacity to appear formidable, which is a quality of will and demeanour' (CWXVIII: 102, 104). Keynes had a particular disdain for what he saw as contradictory socialist arguments opposing both appeasement and rearmament. Still in early 1939, he thought that Hitler was bluffing (Hardeen 2019).

As rearmament at last brought economic recovery, by 1937 Keynes turned his attention from unemployment to inflation. This became a bigger issue with wartime mobilisation. Keynes now addressed different economic problems to those of the depression and his policy prescriptions changed accordingly. In 1940 Hayek, the arch-liberal, was so reassured by Keynes's *How to Pay for the War* that they now agreed on the economics of scarcity 'even if we differ on when it applies' (cited in Skidelsky 2000: 56). Some of Keynes's allies were less impressed. Kahn, probably Keynes's closest collaborator and nearest co-thinker, objected to Keynes's concentration on preventing inflation and instead advocated a policy emphasis on speeding up labour mobilisation (Skidelsky 2000). Keynes's '"fiscal theory" of war finance was put forward explicitly as an alternative to physical planning of resources' (Skidelsky 2000: xix). New situations require new policies, but Keynes's attitudes appear to have shifted back much closer to those he had previously challenged.

Keynes now wrote:

> There are in these matters deep undercurrents at work, natural forces, one may call them, even the invisible hand, which are operating towards equilibrium … I find myself more and more relying for a solution for our problems on the

invisible hand which I tried to eject from economic thinking twenty years ago. (cited in Skidelsky 2000: 460, 470)

Skidelsky writes '[h]is more radical followers attributed his growing conservatism to the malign influence of his Treasury associates. Naturally enough everyone is influenced by his immediate associations; and there is some substance to the charge that Keynes "went native"' (2000: 140). By September 1941 Keynes could add director of the Bank of England to his official appointments (Moggridge 1992). The revisionism, however, should not be exaggerated, and Keynes broadly supported the Beveridge report, establishing the bases of Britain's post-war welfare state – although here too Keynes thought Beveridge too ambitious and, with Robbins, one of his old adversaries, was able to whittle down some of the proposals (Moggridge 1976).

As so often, Keynes was fighting on many fronts. Even in poor health, he also became increasingly preoccupied with questions of international post-war reconstruction, from as early as 1942 advancing plans for a new British–US-led world order (CWXXV). He would become the principal British negotiator at the conference held at Bretton Woods in New Hampshire in 1944, which gave its name to the post-war monetary system. Keynes's initial proposals maintained an 'extreme (if not ludicrous)' hope of a fairer international system which would equally punish surpluses and deficits (Flanders 2019: 68). Even as Keynes clung to unrealistic visions of Britain's importance, his own plans increasingly acknowledged the realities of US leadership (CWXXVI). There was, of course, real negotiation before the conference, which then involved a deal in which the US also needed Britain. Where they could, Keynes and his US counterpart, White, would agree in private, sometimes before taking apparently rival texts to the 'monkey-house' of the other forty-two countries' representatives (Skidelsky 2000: 345). The US, however, had by this time become unambiguously the leading power, and the outcomes broadly reflected US plans. These were not necessarily antithetical to those of powerful interests within Britain. Helleiner (1994), for example, reinterprets the deal as one between American and London high finance. However, Keynes remained over-optimistic about his powers of persuasion, notably in his hopes for American financial generosity towards Britain. He also remained, to put it frankly, deluded about Britain's relative position in the world, hoping that Britain and the Empire would be able to control the post-war institutions. Instead, the International Bank of Reconstruction and Development (or World Bank) and the IMF awarded votes like commercial businesses, according to their participants' contributions, guaranteeing the US the most votes and an effective veto over policy changes.

The international system and Keynes's attitude towards it will be discussed in more detail in Chapter 10, but it becomes a considerable stretch to see the resulting Bretton Woods regime as Keynesian in any straightforward way. Both the institutional structures and their practices differed markedly from those that Keynes advocated. The regime contained significant 'anti-Keynesian' biases. Where Keynes wanted to achieve stability through systems that penalised both surplus and deficit countries, Bretton Woods forced adjustments, through devaluation and contractionary domestic policies, only onto those with deficits. There would be imperatives for deficit countries to adjust their currency pegs downwards but no parallel compulsion for surplus countries to adopt expansionary domestic policies or increase their currency values – an asymmetry which would finally prove crucial to the system's unravelling. Of course, in 1944 and for many years to come, the US would be the major surplus country, and the appealing logic of Keynes's argument was insufficient to win US agreement. Pilling writes, 'Keynes' proposals were listened to with apparent respect but White's plan was the one adopted. Here was living refutation of Keynes' notion that ideas were more powerful than vested interests' (1986: chapter 5, 7).

The agreements did nevertheless facilitate a much higher level of international coordination than seen in the pre-war world, and Keynes welcomed them on this basis. He would glowingly endorse the deal in recommending it to the British House of Lords, where he now sat as a Liberal peer. He saw the agreement as much better than nothing. Amongst other things, Keynes welcomed the acceptance of 'capital controls', restrictions on the movement of money across borders, allowing states to prioritise national economic policy objectives, even if the US would not limit such movements across its own borders.

From the late 1930s Keynes was in poor health and suffered a series of heart attacks. Even assuaged by his considerable wealth, his relentless work no doubt hindered any full recovery. He would not live to see the prosperous times which became widely associated with his name. In April 1946 he suffered a final, fatal heart attack. His life was celebrated with pomp and ceremony in a service at Westminster Abbey. Skidelsky's summary seems fitting.

> That Keynes should be mourned in death by a governing class he had often derided, and enfolded by a religion whose tenets he had dismissed as 'hocus-pocus,' was not inappropriate. Keynes's world had been that of the British Establishment, at no time more than in the last six years of life. He was tethered to it by upbringing, inclination, aptitude, language and, above all, by his Englishness. (Skidelsky 2000: 473)

This world profoundly shaped Keynes's thinking, which the subsequent chapters will attempt to scrutinise.

Conclusion

Keynes's relatively short life was a remarkable personal triumph. He achieved wealth and fame. What would have mattered more to Keynes, he became accepted as the pre-eminent economic authority and his ideas became influential. Those ideas, or what people took as those ideas, would subsequently be claimed across a broad political spectrum. It should not be surprising that he was honoured by the British ruling class. Keynes's iconoclastic style and acerbic wit could exaggerate his hostility to established wealth and power and to established economic thinking. As this chapter has argued, his perspective was always that of the British bourgeoisie, albeit of what he saw as its enlightened branch. At the same time, Keynes offered the hope that capitalism, wisely managed, could be both more just and more efficient. Many socialists became Keynesians. Already during his life, people were taking different things from Keynes, stimulating controversies that still flourish. The following chapters reconsider Keynes's ideas, particularly with a view to what the left should make of them.

2

Keynes's philosophy

Introduction

This chapter and the next discuss Keynes's philosophy and politics, particularly with a view to how they influence his economics. The division of these chapters is somewhat arbitrary, and some of the material inevitably leaks between them. Broadly, however, this chapter introduces Keynes's philosophy, the next his politics, including his views of the state and the inter-state system.

Probably more than any major economist since Marx, Keynes thought deeply about political and philosophical issues. He was a sophisticated thinker, close intellectually as well as personally to several leading philosophers of the age. He was particularly strongly influenced by Moore, and wrote one major work, the *Treatise on Probability*, which operates at the intersection of mathematics, logic and philosophy. There is controversy about the influence of this early work, and of Keynes's philosophical thought in general, but there are clearly connections between his philosophy, his politics and his mature economics (Fitzgibbons 1988, O'Donnell 1991, Tabb 1999).

It will be argued that Keynes never develops an entirely coherent overall philosophy. This undermines grander claims for a 'Keynesian economic system' and for the generality of the general theory. Keynes develops profound insights, which he does not always follow through, and makes philosophically provocative statements from whose implications he pulls back. An apparently individualist idealism and questions about the basis of knowledge might, if pushed to their (il)logical conclusions, appear radically incompatible with a genuinely critical political economy. More positively, however, these ambiguities enable the adoption or appropriation of Keynes's insights in a way that a more rigorously internally consistent system might preclude. In particular, Keynes is right that individuals act in the face of real uncertainties and that this has important economic implications.

I hope what follows accurately represents Keynes's philosophical thinking. It should be stressed, however, that professional philosophers and professional Keynes-ologists hold different, even radically divergent, interpretations. The purpose of this chapter is less to uncover what Keynes really thought than to identify important lines of his thinking, and their implications.

The first section begins with a commentary on Moore, to whom Keynes's ethics and epistemology owed most. For Moore, doubts about the consequences of action narrow the space for legitimate politics and he falls back on convention as a guide. The second section discusses how, for Keynes, an individualist intuitionism also substantially derived from Moore is nevertheless able to go further. Keynes has more confidence in the ability of at least some human minds to directly perceive both normative and positive truths and potential paths towards informed social action. However, the individualist idealism on which this hangs is not rigorously secured and, as the third section continues, it also sits uncomfortably with an acceptance of the idea of 'organic unity'. The fourth and final substantive section turns to Keynes's own major philosophical contribution and his views of time and uncertainty. Keynes raises both general epistemological questions and important issues of how the economy should be understood. For Keynes, our confidence in prediction diminishes the further we peer into the future. All this has devastating consequences for mainstream approaches and mathematical formalism. Amongst other things, it also raises awkward questions, taken up in subsequent chapters, about how social action can be justified and how either economic theorists or state policy-makers avoid falling into the same epistemological holes towards which Keynes points.

Moore's philosophy

Keynes's philosophy owed most to Moore, who is now little known and therefore needs some introduction. Moore was ten years Keynes's senior, already a prominent philosopher and charismatic member of the Cambridge Apostles when Keynes arrived. Moore's philosophy was formed out of an engagement with two locally influential alternative traditions, neo-Hegelianism and pragmatism. On the one hand, Moore rejected what he perceived as the neo-Hegelians' radical holism and idealism (both of which much amplified anything in Hegel). This meant that their idealism was accordingly general rather than individual, 'constituted by our mind, *qua* a participation in the eternal consciousness' (Passmore 1968: 59). Moore refused to dissolve the parts into the whole or their relations (1993: 85). He is certain 'that the common-sense view of the world – which he sets out in some detail – is true; he knows, for example, that there are living human beings with whom he can communicate' (Passmore 1968: 210). At the same time, Moore continues to reject individualism at a methodological level. It is wrong 'when it is supposed, that, if one part of a whole has no intrinsic value, the value of the whole must reside entirely in the other parts' (1993: 236). Indeed, it is quite possible that things 'perfectly worthless in themselves, are yet constituents of what is far from worthless' (1993: 255). Moore gives an example of appropriate punishments of crime. On the other hand, against the pragmatists, for Moore the metaphysical, understood in opposition to 'the natural' (1993: 261), is an important realm of truth and existence. '[T]his is particularly obvious with regard to truths like "Two and two are four," in which the objects, about which they are truths, do not exist' (1993: 162). Moore's criticisms of both the neo-Hegelians and the pragmatists are often telling.

His positive account is less convincing. Moore was primarily an ethicist. He thought knowledge of what was 'good' was available directly without reference to anything else. Good is like yellow, 'a simple notion, just as "yellow" is a simple notion' (1993: 59). Yellow and good are recognisable but cannot be discovered from other properties of the world. Any attempt to define goodness, or to explain it in terms of something else, ends up either in circularity or in what Moore condemns as the 'naturalistic fallacy' (1993: 22). A thing cannot be good because it is normal. A hedonist utilitarianism does not make sense. 'Mill tells us that we ought to desire something … because we actually do desire it' (1993: 125). The other properties in terms of which goodness is defined must turn out to be 'absolutely and entirely the same with goodness' (1993: 62). Instead, 'the fundamental principles of Ethics must be self-evident' (1993: 193). Ultimately, to know reality, whether 'good' or 'yellow', Moore falls back into a judgement of an 'intuitional kind' (1993: 130). Moore's vision, as Davis puts it, is of a 'non-social private intuition' (1994: 18).

Below, it will be argued that Keynes accepts much of this. Moore, however, appears to retreat. MacIntyre asks:

> [H]ow, then, do we recognize the intrinsically good? The only answer Moore offers is that we just do. Or put this another way: Moore's account could only reach the level of intelligibility if it were supplemented by an account of how the meaning of good is learned. (1967: 252)

Moore invokes 'common sense' as the guide, this involving, amongst other things, a wonderfully Victorian English aversion to sexual pleasure (1993: 146) while valuing 'certain states of consciousness, which may be roughly described as the pleasures of human intercourse and the enjoyment of beautiful objects' (1993: 237). MacIntyre writes that Moore 'exclude[s] all the values connected with intellectual inquiry and with work. Moore's values are those of a protected leisure, though it is in what he excludes rather than in what he does value that the parochial and classbound character of his attitudes appear' (1967: 256).

Keynes shares Moore's stress on affection and aesthetic enjoyment as the principal goods. While not completely dismissive of material wants, he sees them largely in the negative, as things which can be overcome (O'Donnell 1991: 12). No Benthamite, let alone Marxist, egalitarianism is sustainable. 'We used to regard Christians as the enemy, because they appeared as the representatives of tradition, convention and hocus pocus. In truth it was the Benthamite calculus based on an overvaluation of the economic criterion, which was destroying the quality of the popular Ideal' (CWX: 446).

But if Keynes shares the aesthetic values, there is more divergence in terms of how to reconcile recognising good with doing good. Moore again falls back on convention. Here faith in *a priori* intuition is insufficient and established wisdom provides a guide. There might, in principle, be instances where the established rule is not the best course of action, but even now Moore asks, '[c]an the individual ever be justified in assuming that his is one of these exceptional cases? And it seems that this question may be definitely answered in the negative' (1993: 211). 'If we *knew* that the effect of a given action really would be to make the world, as a whole, *worse* than it would have been if we had acted differently, it would certainly be wrong for us to do that action' (Moore, cited in Baldwin 1993: xxvii). The problem is that we cannot know. Our knowledge is insufficient to be confident in the consequences of our actions, particularly as these reverberate 'throughout an infinite future' (Moore 1993: 202). 'Accordingly it follows that we never have any reason to suppose that an action is our duty: we can never be sure that any action will produce the greatest value possible' (1993: 199). Whatever our distrust of convention, individual judgement is outweighed by the probability that such judgement is misplaced. Even if it were right and 'we can clearly discern that our case is one where to break the rule is advantageous, yet, so far as our example has any effect at all in encouraging similar action, it will certainly tend to encourage breaches of the rule which are not advantageous' (1993: 212). There seems to be no escape from the solid test of long experience. It is easy to see why Skidelsky characterises Moore as an old-fashioned, churchgoing conservative (1992: 50).

Keynes remained torn by his "favourite dilemma"; the potential discrepancy between being good and doing good and his doubts about the consequences of action, discussed below, accentuate a preference for being over doing; for motives over consequences (Davis 1994, Fitzgibbons 1988). Keynes, however, was less respectful of tradition than Moore, and this was predicated on a stronger conviction that intuition allowed breaking with convention, at least in certain circumstances (CWIX: 447–8). But, as will be

	Individualism	Organic Unity
Idealism		Neo-Hegelianism
	Moore/Keynes	[Hegel]
Realism		[Marx]
	Empiricism - Pragmatism	

Figure 2.1 Idealism and realism vs individuals and wholes in Moore and Keynes

discussed below, if intuition pushes against some of Moore's conservative conclusions, it does so at the cost of amplifying an idealist elitism.

Re-reading Moore's *Principia Ethica* in 1906 'convinced Maynard all over again that it was "the greatest work on philosophy ever written"' (Skidelsky 1983: 173). In 1938 Keynes reaffirms his mature adherence to it 'fundamental intuitions' (CWX: 444). His early 'religion ... remains nearer the truth than any other that I know ... It was a purer, sweeter air by far than Freud cum Marx. It is still my religion under the surface' (CWX: 442). This memoir has been questioned as an accurate recollection of his earlier beliefs (Davis 1994), and Keynes's philosophical thinking changed. But there were continuities, and the intuitionist epistemology and the uncertain consequences of action would become recurring themes. Keynes adopts Moore's views with qualifications and omissions but broadly follows his half-steps away from neo-Hegelian idealism and organic unity, and from pragmatism's realism and individualism. Figure 2.1 attempts to summarise the relations, adding a parenthetical Marx and Hegel on grounds of plausibility.

Idealism and individualism

This section highlights the enduring importance of an individualist idealism in Keynes's thought, even as he hedges both the individualism and the idealism.

Keynes repeatedly emphasises the priority of ideas. *The Economic Consequences of the Peace* insists that 'the power of ideas is sovereign' (CWII: 158–9). Later, 'superstition', 'prestige' (CWIV: 132) and the quality of argument (CWIX: 285) become important economic variables. Keynes writes that 'we can be saved by the solution of an intellectual problem, and in no other way' (CWXIII: 492). Most famously, the *General Theory* insists:

[T]he ideas of economists and political philosophers, both when they are right and when they are wrong, are more powerful than is commonly understood. Indeed the world is ruled by little else ... I am sure that the power of vested interests is vastly exaggerated compared with the gradual encroachment of ideas. (Keynes 1973: 383)

Keynes concludes 'soon or late, it is ideas, not vested interests, which are dangerous for good or evil' (1973: 384). In this last formulation, Keynes's 'not' is without qualification. Elsewhere there are ambiguities, but Keynes appears consistently idealist at least in the sense of prioritising ideas over material interests.

Also, in common with Moore, Keynes's idealism was typically of an individualist bent, underpinned by psychology. The *General Theory* insists that a 'decision to consume or not to consume truly lies within the power of the individual; so does a decision to invest or not to invest' (1973: 65). We also then learn that '[e]ffective demand is made up of the sum of two factors based respectively on the expectation of what is going to be consumed and on the expectation of what is going to be invested' (CWXIII: 439). Individual entrepreneurs are the (flawed) heroes of Keynes's narrative in the *General Theory*, with their investment decisions hanging on a willingness 'to take a chance' over and above 'cold calculation' (Keynes 1973: 150).

There are qualifications and controversies about whether Keynes accepts individualism at a methodological level. Notions of 'organic unity' discussed below, which he also takes from Moore, suggest not. The individualist idealism, however, seems to inform Keynes's notions of probability as subjective rather than objective. 'There is no direct relation between the truth of a proposition and its probability. Probability begins and ends with probability' (1921: 356). He endorses Paley's sentiment that 'although we speak of communities as of sentient beings ... nothing really exists or feels but *individuals*' (CWX: 449). In Keynes's economics, an apparent acceptance of individualist premises resonates with, and appears to be reinforced by, his engagement with the mainstream on its own terms (Dobb 1956). For Keynes, changes in the expectations of change are themselves the key cause of change (1973: 152, Davis 1994: 138). As Coddington argues, Keynes appears to be suggesting that 'beliefs change erratically without corresponding changes in their basis in conditions ... [and this] leads to autonomous variations in the aggregate of expenditure resulting from investment decisions' (1983: 53).

O'Donnell writes that '[t]o the question, "Where do correct ideas come from? Do they drop from the skies? Are they innate in the mind?" ... Keynes's response would have been that they are Platonic forms discovered by the intuitive power of the mind' (1989: 90). Again, Keynes follows Moore in suggesting that knowledge is available directly through private intuition, just

as neither yellow nor good can be discovered from other properties of the
world. As Davis comments, the human mind appears to have 'some special
non-sensory, cognitive facility for apprehending this relation' (1994: 20).

But not all minds are equal, and Keynes's partial break with convention only makes sense if some intuitions are privileged over others. As
Skidelsky writes, differences of opinion must stem either from differences in
the questions or from differences in facilities of perception. Moore stressed
differences in the questions. Keynes was less egalitarian and tended to
emphasise differences in faculties. '[S]ince people's intuitions differ, this doctrine rapidly degenerates into the claim that some intuitions are privileged –
that is, that the expert in intuition should be on top' (Skidelsky 1992: 407).
This justifies an elitist politics, discussed in the next chapter, and Keynes's
enduring faith in enlightened thinking and intellectual leadership. He insists
that '[i]nsufficiency of cleverness, not of goodness is the main trouble'
(CWXXVII: 384). This appears to allow the necessary leap of faith by
which economists and wise governments may transcend both Moore's conservatism and Burkean objections to policy reorientation, again as discussed
in the next chapter.

There are, however, several reasons to be cautious. Keynes acknowledges there are limits to intuitionism as a basis of practical knowledge,
and he does not defend his understanding in detail. In his otherwise enthu-
siastic account, O'Donnell admits that 'Keynes's epistemology clearly
suffers shortcomings. Its intuitionist component ... has now been generally
abandoned' (1989: 333). Later, Keynes even describes absolute intuition as
'hardly a state of mind which a grown-up person in his senses could sustain
literally' (cited in Hillard 1988: 4).

The interpretation of Keynes's thought as an individualist idealism therefore needs to be qualified. If Keynes is an idealist, this does not involve a
deep-rooted ontological idealism, and (like Moore) Keynes is instead clearly
a realist in the sense of accepting that an external social and physical reality
exists. Even some of Keynes's 'idealist' assertions reported above make clear
that he recognises such an exterior reality, in some more or less ill-defined
relation with individuals' ideas. When Keynes says of his early beliefs that
'[n]othing mattered except states of mind, our own and other people's of
course, but chiefly our own' (CWX: 436), this implicitly recognises worldly
matters but chooses to disdain them. Keynes's reflections on the classical
'Ricardian' victory make particularly clear that he recognised ideas and
material interests as intertwined.

> That its teaching, translated into practice, was austere and often unpalat-
> able, lent it virtue. That it was adapted to carry a vast and consistent logical
> superstructure, gave it beauty. That it could explain much social injustice and

apparent cruelty as an inevitable incident in the scheme of progress, and the attempt to change such things as likely on the whole to do more harm than good, commended it to authority. That it afforded a measure of justification to the free activities of the individual capitalist, attracted to it the support of the dominant social force behind authority. (1973: 33)

Keynes's ironic tone notwithstanding, there is little here to trouble a Marxist. Keynes stresses the relative importance of ideas but within an essentially interactionist understanding. Lawson writes that although 'Keynes does ascribe significant powers of *a priori* reasoning to individuals … throughout his total contributions he is explicit that such *a priori* thought is considered always to be open to constant modification and correction through continual interaction with experiences of the real world' (1988: 56). Keynes even writes that '[i]t may be possible, a hundred years hence, to investigate … the influence of railways on morality' (Helburn 1991: 47). The final section of this chapter will discuss Keynes's views on uncertainty in more detail but will argue that Keynes always thought at least some aspects of the external world were more or less knowable and had more or less influence on consciousness. For Coddington, Keynes is then only making 'an opportunistic but mild flirtation with subjectivism' (1983: 62). There were at least realist and materialist facets to Keynes's thinking. The implication, of course, is that we cannot simply choose to leap from what is to what might be, to a preferred political economy.

Keynes's individualism is also qualified. The next section turns to the question of parts and wholes, but in several places Keynes seems to abandon individualism and to privilege wholes. In *The End of Laissez-Faire*, Keynes writes that '[t]he purpose of promoting the individual was to depose the monarch and the church; the effect – through the new ethical significance attributed to contract – was to buttress property and prescription. But it was not long before the claims of society realised themselves anew against the individual' (CWIX: 273). If Davis (1994) is right and the mature Keynes becomes increasingly influenced by Wittgenstein's language philosophy, this would also support a social rather than individual construction of knowledge. The *General Theory* often discusses rules and conventions, and this undermines a straightforwardly individualist psychology (Davis 1994).

So again there are ambiguities. It seems clear that Keynes accepted some form of interactionist epistemology, affording some priority to ideas over material circumstances and to individuals over social structures, but with the nature of the interaction left open. The implication is that while Keynes is right to insist that individuals and their ideas matter, right even that at certain conjunctures their influence can be decisive, he provides few grounds for evaluating the limits and possibilities of action. He tends to bracket his economic variables as either indeterminate or hanging on individual psychology, without identifying how we might get into the heads of the actors. Expectations become important, but we never know 'why people expect what they expect' (Schumpeter, cited in Skidelsky 1992: 577). Keynes occasionally invokes Freud, for example in explaining gold fetishism (1923: 132), but also claims universal psychological laws almost wholly without reference to, or knowledge of, the psychological literature (Hodgson 2004). Revisiting Keynes's categories as more open social constructions might make them more plausible but might also allow them to be worked harder and made more amenable to empirical testing.

Organic unity

It was suggested above that Keynes's individualism and idealism were qualified, never established with epistemological care. They contrast with a professed faith in organic unity, even a privileging of wholes. This stress on organic unity can also be traced to Moore (1993), and by 1938 Keynes also claims it as part of his early beliefs (CWX: 436). Alternatively, Winslow argues that after writing the *Treatise on Probability* Keynes 'explicitly abandons atomicism in favour of organicism as the metaphysical description appropriate to the moral sciences generally and in economics particularly' (cited in Rotheim 1988: 87). In 1933 Keynes writes:

> We are faced at every turn with the problems of organic unity, of discreteness, of discontinuity – the whole is not equal to the sum of the parts, comparisons of quantity fail us, small changes produce large effects, the assumptions of a uniform homogenous continuum are not satisfied. (CWX: 262)

This has several implications for Keynes's politics and his economics. As above, any idealism becomes qualified. Ideas, social structures, even structures as material as railways, are mutually constitutive. Conversely, this interactionist view means that economics could not be viewed 'objectively', like a natural science.

> I also want to emphasise strongly the point about economics being a moral science. I mentioned before that it deals with introspection and with values. I might have added that it deals with motives, expectations, psychological uncertainties. One has to be constantly on guard against treating the material as constant and homogeneous. It is as though the fall of the apple to the ground depended on the apple's motives, on whether it is worth while falling to the ground, and whether the ground wanted the apple to fall, and on mistaken calculations on the part of the apple as to how far it was from the centre of the earth. (Keynes CWXIV: 300)

Such an interdependence is at the heart of Keynes's wariness of mathematical precision and formal mathematical presentation in preference for 'ordinary discourse' where 'we can keep "at the back of our heads" the necessary reserves and qualifications' (1973: 297). Keynes recognises at least an in-principle social interdependence (CWXIV: 11–12).

O'Donnell (1989), amongst others, goes much further and sees the importance of aggregates in Keynes's economics as predicated upon a deeper epistemological acceptance of organic unity. Keynes can depict individuals as social beings and, as above, the *General Theory* often acknowledges the importance of rules and conventions. O'Donnell reads Keynes's reinstatement of the importance of economic aggregates and his repeated emphasis on fallacies of composition in a similar way. The *General Theory* is explicitly concerned with the whole economy, and Keynes identifies this aggregation as a secondary sense in which his theory is general (1973: xxii). Keynes's key variables – the marginal efficiency of capital and liquidity preference – are aggregates. But as 'schedules' they are still conceived as aggregates of individual decisions. Perhaps most strikingly, Keynes is explicit that the 'classical case', which is a resolutely individualist case, comes into its own in conditions of full employment. It is then unobvious that fallacies of composition and aggregation refute individualism methodologically. Modern new-Institutionalist economics and game theory, for example, suggest otherwise. O'Donnell writes that '[t]he principle of atomism or methodological individualism was applicable in some situations, and the principle of organic unity in others' (1989: 177). If this points to a methodological muddle, it does re-emphasise that Keynes was not a consistent individualist. At least implicitly, there is some more or less vaguely understood relation between individuals and society, between agency and structure. As will be discussed in the next chapter, Keynes's aggregates are also almost always conceived in national terms, introducing important ambiguities about the 'whole', about the relations between individuals, nations and the global economy.

Significantly, Keynes also writes, 'I myself was always an advocate of a principle of organic unity through time, which still seems to me only sensible' (CWX: 436). As will be seen below, Keynes depicts the future as unknowable, but organic unity through time suggests continuity as well as change (Lawson 1997), and Fitzgibbons (1988: 49) sees Keynes as involved in a lifelong struggle to reconcile the two. Potentially, this can reinforce a conservative Burkean 'principle of prudence' (Shionaya 1991: 21) but, going beyond Moore, there may be some bases for making informed prediction and thence for choosing between alternatives. De Carvalho writes:

> [A]lthough in the strictest sense the world changes continually, for practical purposes there is enough continuity in social processes to allow some space

to the principle of induction. This certainly was Keynes's view not only in the *Treatise on Probability* but also in *The General Theory*. (1988: 79)

This anticipates problems discussed in the next section.

Keynesian uncertainty and its implications

This section discusses Keynes's views on probability and uncertainty. Davis (2019) suggests that only here does Keynes go far beyond Moore. The implications of Keynes's views on probability and uncertainty for his economics have been much contested, but they also have serious consequences for any political philosophy, for any optimism about judicious state intervention and appropriate policy reorientations.

Keynes makes one of the 'first serious attempts to grapple with the logical foundations of probability' (Chow and Teicher 2012: xi). He raises important issues about the limits of knowledge in general and particularly about prediction. Using language anticipating that employed to describe his economic theory as 'general', Keynes argues for an expanded system 'to cover all forms of rational argument, including those whose conclusions were accompanied by doubt, uncertainty or incomplete entailment' (O'Donnell 1989: 30).

> As soon as mathematical probability ceases to be the merest algebra or pretends to guide our decisions, it immediately meets with problems against which its own weapons are quite powerless. And even if we wish later on to use probability in a narrow sense, it will be well to know first what it means in the widest. (Keynes 1921: 6)

For Keynes, some belief is secure. 'The highest degree of rational belief, which is termed *certain* rational belief, corresponds to *knowledge*'. (1921: 10) Some 'propositions, in which our rational belief is both certain and direct, are said to be *self-evident*' (1921: 17). We are back with Moore and intuition, and with sensations of 'yellow', from which we can pass directly to knowledge of yellow (Keynes 1921: 12). Some areas remain unruffled by scepticism and doubt.

Often, however, there is only more or less reliable evidence of the truth of a proposition, and '[p]robability is the study of the grounds which lead us to entertain *rational* preference for one belief over another' (Keynes 1921: 97). Often there is not even that. Keynes distinguishes between areas where it is possible to assign a numerical value, as in 'aleatory' or dice-game probability, and those where it is only possible to ascribe ordinal values of one thing being more likely than another. But there is also an important distinction between these two situations and those where judgement is impossible.

A lack of certainty – say, knowing there is a fifty/fifty chance of something occurring, or that the chance of cloudy weather exceeds the chance of rain – is not to be confused with unquantifiable 'uncertainty' in Keynes's sense. This is the class where we simply have no basis for judgement (Lawson 1988: 46).

It is this category which leads to interesting and challenging epistemological questions. Achieved outcomes provide no guarantee of the likelihood of those events having happened, let alone of their recurrence (Keynes 1921: 243). Moreover, the compass of uncertainty expands as we look into the future. The *General Theory* briefly refers to the earlier work on probability, and Keynes shortly afterwards affirms:

> By 'uncertain' knowledge I do not mean merely to distinguish what is known for certain from what is only probable. The sense in which I am using the term is that in which the prospect of a European war is uncertain, or the price of copper and the rate of interest twenty years hence, or the obsolescence of a new invention, or the position of private wealth owners in the social system in 1970. About these matters there is no scientific basis on which to form any calculable probability whatever. We simply do not know. (CWXIV: 113–14)

Keynes then describes how a 'practical theory of the future' is 'based on so flimsy a foundation, it is subject to sudden and violent changes. The practice of calmness and immobility, of certainty and security, suddenly breaks down. New fears and hopes will, without warning, take charge of human conduct' (CWXIV: 114). This is a vision where 'sensible decision makers "know" it will always be impossible to possess at any future date a complete list of prospects' (Davidson 2009: 109).

Even 'softer' interpretations of these insights have fairly devastating consequences for mainstream economic thinking. The whole point of entrepreneurship, as Shackle (1972) argues, is to make economic decisions, which actively change the economy and shape the future. Conventional models based on rational individual 'robot decision makers', 'cannot explain the essential creative function of entrepreneurial behaviour in a Keynes-Schumpeter world, where the reality is transmutable' (Davidson 2009: 113). Crucially, the concept of utility collapses; if the future is unknowable, it becomes meaningless to invoke a utilitarian calculus which discounts future pleasures against the present (Skidelsky 1992). People can never reliably ascertain their interests (Mattick 1971). Much of econometric modelling also becomes deeply suspect. Davidson contrasts Keynes's approach with the 'ergodic axiom' where 'the outcome at any future date is the statistical shadow of past and current data' (2009: 31). In Keynes's vision, 'the future is ontologically uncertain' (Davidson 2009: 101). Decisions at one time destroy the environment in which they themselves were made. Already in

Keynes's *Probability*, the 'hope, which sustained many investigations in the course of the nineteenth century, of gradually bringing the moral sciences under the sway of mathematical reasoning, steadily recedes' (1921: 349). In a warning that would also inform his mature economics, 'it is possible, under cover of a careful formalism, to make statements, which if expressed in plain language, the mind would immediately repudiate. There is much to be said, therefore, in favour of understanding the substance of what you are saying *all the time*, and of never reducing the substantives of your argument to the mental status of an x or y' (Keynes 1921: 19, footnote). Contrary to its repeated aspirations, economics can never become physics (CWXIV: 300).

More radical 'post-Keynesians', in particular, then see uncertainty as the key to understanding Keynes's economic innovation (Dow 1996). The concepts of the *Treatise on Probability* can be translated into the economics of the *General Theory*. 'The "unknown" probabilities of the *Treatise* became the "irreducible" uncertainty … The concept of "weight of argument" is roughly translatable into the "state of confidence"' (Skidelsky 1992: 87). For Shackle, 'insurmountable lack of knowledge, or the expense of gaining knowledge, lie at the root of liquidity preference' (1972: 216, Chick 2019). All of this informs depictions of the dynamic and unpredictable character of the economy and challenges assumptions of stability and the essentially static representations of mainstream economics.

As will be discussed in Chapter 11, for some of Keynes's followers, wilder readings of uncertainty go much further, appearing to undermine all bases of knowledge and rational social action and, at least by implication, all bases for economic theory, including Keynes's own. Instead of harmonious equilibrium, we have a theory of disorder (Davidson 2009, Shackle 1972). Events are not replicable and no historical process of statistical learning is possible (de Carvalho 1988). This fairly quickly becomes a position of 'analytical nihilism' (Coddington 1983), a term used critically but which its advocates like Shackle accepted (Bateman 1987). Uncertainty becomes *the* big variable, the tidal wave which obliterates the rest of the economic landscape. If all this provides a remarkable and seldom acknowledged anticipation of postmodernism, it seems the innovation more of post-Keynesian followers than of Keynes himself.

For Keynes, there are clearly large areas of social and economic life where risks are unquantifiable (Dow 2019), and the descent into a pervasive radical uncertainty seems hard to square with his political practice or the bulk of his writing (Bateman 1987). Coddington argues that 'even the most cursory acquaintance with the facts of his life show that he was not reduced to the state of puzzled indecision that a wholehearted adoption of such [sceptical] standards would entail' (1983: 58–9). Keynes apparently accepts the existence of many economic situations which are ergodic and where rational decisions and probabilistic risk apply. There remains space for inductive principles (de Carvalho 1988). Keynes depicts 'individuals [as] much more similar than they are dissimilar in their reaction to news' (1973: 199) and clearly believed that some beliefs are relatively well founded, at least in the short run. Other interpreters accordingly detect a more social but a more conservative version of uncertainty underpinning Keynes's mature economics (Davis 1994, Sheehan 2009).

The distinctions between different timespans become particularly pertinent, and Keynes's scepticism about our knowledge of the more distant future encourages his emphasis on the short run. People do form expectations, at least *as if* these had some rational basis. In the short run, in particular, people can often fall back on current experiences and convention as a guide to action (Keynes 1973: 50, 162, 199; see also Bateman 1987, Coddington 1983, Dostaler 2007). Kregel argues that uncertainty is ever-present but 'different assumptions could be made about the constancy of expectations and their effect on the system' (1976: 211). 'The relative importance of long- and short-period expectations are thus given varying weight in the General Theory' (Kregel 1976: 212). Keynes first assumes that long-period expectations are given. He knows that they actually shift but, even while acknowledging that the long-term propensity may itself be subject to change, he is 'locking up' this effect analytically (Kregel 1976: 212). Kregel sees this as an essentially Marshallian procedure (Kregel 1976: 222), one of partial rather than general equilibrium, a distinction discussed in Chapter 4. Despite its 'rather confusing mix' (Kregel 1976: 212), Keynes's method allows him to examine what is likely to occur when short-term expectations are disappointed, without affecting long-term expectations (Kregel 1976). Keynes envisages entrepreneurs making successive revisions of short-term expectations in the light of experience (1973: 50). As will be discussed in Chapters 5 and 6, there are valid analytical reasons for Keynes's use of a short-run equilibrium analysis, but it comes with problems. Amongst other things, it means that for the vast majority of the *General Theory*, much that is dynamic and changeable in capitalism is simply accepted as 'given'. The uncertainty-reducing emphasis on the short run narrows the gap with the economic mainstream.

In still tamer readings of uncertainty, expectations appear to become just another variable, introduced into what otherwise remains an essentially orthodox framework. They can be treated as just another independent variable amongst others, just one factor understood to lie behind liquidity preference, which can be fed into suitable equations (Clarke, P. 1988).

If we decline to go the whole nihilist hog, it therefore becomes germane to ask what makes some knowledge more or less secure. In Keynes's presentation uncertainty can appear to be random, divorced from any consideration of the economic imperatives that make some outcomes and some decisions more likely than others. Coddington argues that in the *General Theory*, expectations appear 'as autonomous influences that come in from outside, not as elements that are moulded in the course of the process that is being analyzed' (1983: 88). Davis, by contrast, insists that Keynes's view was that 'uncertainty is ultimately a social relation' (1994: 108) but, in contrast to some of Keynes's own earlier criticisms of economic orthodoxy (CXIX: 285), his mature economics leaves any social content largely implicit. There is little sense of power relations or ideology as he depicts individuals in competitive markets, with little social structure within or beyond the national economy (Dowd 2004, Galbraith 1995). In its disregard for such issues, Keynes's economic analysis again converges with the mainstream and contrasts with the dynamic assumptions with which Marxists work from the beginning and which some radical Keynesians like Robinson (1966) have accepted as a better starting place. Capitalist competition generates imperatives, compels certain behaviours if firms are to survive, while it is specifically the unruly character of capitalism which generates so many of the uncertainties (Kincaid 2006, Shaikh 2016).

Even the long run may not be radically uncertain in Keynes's sense. At the risk of excessive literalism, his own examples bear a brief reflection. If we extrapolate the World Bank (2016) data for the price of copper from 1960 to 1995 over the subsequent twenty years, they can 'predict' a 2015 price of $3391 per metric tonne. A simple regression analysis even provides stat-istical confidence levels and would support a claim to be 99 per cent certain that the price would lie somewhere between $2500 and $4051. By 2015 the price actually stood at $6295. This confirms Keynes's scepticism and reminds us of the folly of so much econometric prediction. There was a quite unanticipated commodities boom after 2003 (Wray 2008). Such results, however, hardly confirm radical uncertainty. At an order-of-magnitude level, the price was quite predictable. We were unlikely to be buying copper at a few cents or several millions of dollars per tonne. Similarly, interest rates have continued to fluctuate but, at least for the leading countries which were the focus of Keynes's attention, within rather narrow parameters. The case of European war is somewhat different, and the binary makes it both essentially non-quantifiable and untestable. Yet for a statement written in 1937, Keynes's claim that the prospects of war were radically unknowable is startling. It is surely at least possible to identify developments making war more or less likely, tending to increase or decrease political tensions. Some rival confident predictions of peace or war counsel caution, but we are hardly dealing with radical indeterminacy. Lawson recalls Keynes's warning in *Probability*: the fact that some probability relations that may not be known by everyone 'must not be allowed to carry us too far' (1988: 43).

According to Keynes, '[w]e are merely [*sic*] reminding ourselves that human decisions affecting the future, whether personal or political or economic, cannot depend on strict mathematical calculation' (Keynes 1973: 162). There are also many passages where Keynes makes clear, that he believed there to be long-run, secular trajectories (Mattick 1971).

There are therefore ambiguities about the status of uncertainty in Keynes's work and the uses to which it is put. But even qualified versions point towards accentuated problems of how to justify appropriate social action in specifically Keynesian terms. Our lack of knowledge of the future can mesh with Burke's conservative political philosophy, to which Keynes acknowledges considerable debts. As discussed in the next chapter, Keynes's own references to Burke emphasise the conservative potential of a maxim that we should not endure current hardship for uncertain future gains. It will be suggested that the principle is susceptible to a more radical inversion, but there is at least an ostensible problem. 'If there *is* uncertainty, then the best motives for action could be either to follow the social rules (Moore) or to follow an intuitable duty (Keynes)' (Fitzgibbons 1988: 93). As the previous section suggests, neither option is satisfactory. Only stronger versions of idealism and elitism allow change to be effected simply by a rational policy rethink. As will be discussed in the next chapter, Keynes leaves government largely unexamined, but even in his own terms, rather implausibly high levels of competent intuition seem necessary to avoid problems whereby elite decisions must 'be based on beliefs the epistemological foundations of which are more or less flimsy' (Coddington 1983: 50–1). It seems plausible that state intervention can reduce uncertainty. Large institutions, whether firms or states, can and must plan in ways quite foreign to the neo-classical vision of individual utility maximisation and market competition. But the philosophical argument would appear to leave states vulnerable to the same intrinsic uncertainties. If market actors do not know the future, it is unclear how states, or the bureaucrats within them, might attain privileged knowledge.

Conclusion

It would be unreasonable to expect Keynes to resolve ancient philosophical problems about the limits of our knowledge, about the relation between wholes and parts, structures and agents, ideas and material circumstances. That he is concerned with these issues puts him on an altogether higher plane than most economists, to whom they never occur or who seize on a crude methodological individualism as if it were a truth universally acknowledged. It was also one of Keynes's great strengths that he was willing to change his mind as he grappled with these issues and their economic implications. The ambiguities and apparently different positions in Keynes's writings nevertheless leave problems in interpreting his economics, including the *General Theory*, where the philosophical underpinnings are left largely tacit (Gerrard 1988: 148). Keynes does claim have written a *general* theory, and it is reasonable to examine it, and to criticise it, as such.

As Mann writes, Keynes, like Hegel before him, claims to identify universals which are actually specifics, which mirror 'the white, masculine, colonialist, and bourgeois world in and to which they spoke' (2017a: 47). Keynes appears to emphasise individuals, to engage with the mainstream on its own terms, but then stresses the social construction of mores. It also turns out that the individuals on whom Keynes will focus are not just any individuals but bourgeois individuals, entrepreneurs and financiers. Workers have little agency, while the state appears as unexamined saviour. Keynes invokes uncertainty as an explanatory variable but never 'chases it down', leaving it open to radical interpretations which would undermine all economic theory, including Keynes's own, but also leaving open questions of exactly how this sits with parallel invocations of predictable, conventional behaviour and Keynes's confidence in intuition and wise policy. If this means that Keynes ultimately fails to provide a satisfactory closed 'system', that he is only inconsistently idealist, individualist and indeterminist, this inconsistency allows rather than precludes the critical appropriation of his insights.

3

Keynes's politics

Introduction

Keynes was intensely political. He was an activist, a populariser of economic ideas, an influential Treasury official, and seldom for long out of touch with the prime minister of the day. Fitzgibbons argues that he 'developed his political theories long before his economics, and the principles of his economics reflected his politics rather than the other way around' (1988: 54–5). It is probably not a simple either/or but for Keynes, economics was never a neutral scientific endeavour, and it makes sense to understand his economics in the light of his political views. He wants to develop a more realistic theory, but even his most abstract work is oriented to providing a better guide to policy. Keynes can be seen as writing in the 'advice to princes' tradition, offering a better guide for rulers of the existing system.

As usual with Keynes, there are ambiguities and his political stance is contested. Ostensibly this is odd because, although Keynes says some different things, he fairly consistently occupies a space bounded on the one hand by British liberalism, broadly understood to involve support for individual social and economic freedom, and on the other hand by a conservatism drawn particularly from Burke. Keynes bequeathed no single summary of his views, but his political writings are extensive and he was an almost lifelong member of the Liberal Party. Moreover, the space between Burkean conservatism and British liberalism is not as broad as might be imagined, with many leading liberals of the nineteenth century acknowledging similar debts. As Keynes writes admiringly of Asquith, '[h]is temperament was naturally conservative. With a little stupidity and a few prejudices dashed in he would have been Conservative in the political sense also' (CWX: 38–9). The next section will discuss what Keynes took from Burke, and the following one his avowedly liberal politics. Of course, these relatively conventional political stances in no way invalidate Keynes's many powerful criticisms of liberal orthodoxy in economic theory. It will also be argued that even invocations of Burke have, or can be given, a radical twist; Burke suggests we should not countenance immediate evils for uncertain future gains, but we might equally say we should not tolerate present evils for fear they might incur contingent future costs. This discussion, however, anticipates an important secondary purpose of this chapter, which is to argue that the 'left' should be wary of any straightforward appropriation of Keynes.

The third section accordingly discusses O'Donnell's (1989) claim that Keynes was a socialist. Keynes is sympathetic to certain strands of socialist thought within and outside the British Labour Party and he did at one point describes himself as occupying the 'extreme left of celestial space' (CWIX: 309). The term 'socialism' has become extremely flexible and it is possible to incorporate elements of Keynes's thought under such an umbrella. But overall this is misleading. While there are undoubtedly radical aspects to his thought, Keynes is better understood as a pro-capitalist, not a socialist thinker.

As the fourth and final section continues, Keynes brings in the state, but in a quite consistently liberal way in that he still conceives the requisite level of state intervention as being minimal, albeit while raising the bar. Keynes is right to point out that states do act, and that by acting they can improve national and social well-being. As Mann (2017a) has argued, Keynes stands within a long-standing tradition going back to the French Revolution and Hegel, which sees the state as necessary to achieve liberal objectives, that a more thoroughgoing or dogmatic liberalism would destabilise. However, Keynes remains naively optimistic about the state's capacities to act in the general interest, and he retains an elitist, anti-democratic rather than socialist, conception of how and what states should do. A specifically British, but also more broadly a national rather than international or global, orientation also informs and limits Keynes's political economy.

Burke and conservatism

This chapter begins with Burke, Keynes's earliest obvious political influence, and it identifies the persistence of at least a 'small c' conservatism. As Fitzgibbons argues, '[a]lthough Keynes's policies were liberal, his political theory was drawn from an outlook typically associated with traditional conservatism and the old Right' (1991: 131). Keynes read Burke while still at school, and bought the *Complete Works* with the aid of prize money (Skidelsky 1983). As above, Keynes wrote no substantive statement of his political views, but Skidelsky reports that such a treatise on 'The Political Doctrine of Edmund Burke' had been part of his early plans (1992: 57). Keynes's later writings often acknowledge debts to Burke and, although sometimes obscured by Keynes's iconoclastic language, he repeats many of 'Burke's political positions: simultaneously conservative and liberal, free-trader and imperialist, opposed to the French Revolution and for the English revolution' (Dostaler 1996: 19; see also Helburn 1991, Skidelsky 1983, 2013). Keynes also shares Burke's elitism, in some respects amplifying it. He endorses a greater degree of change than Burke would have countenanced, but his advocacy of a 'middle way' and his stress on the need for balance in economic and social life and in adjusting to changes can all be understood in Burkean terms. There is a recognition of the need to conserve even in Keynes's harsh criticisms of mainstream economics and the economic practices of his day.

Burke sometimes couches his opposition to change in terms of its affront to the king and established religion, a language uncongenial to Keynes. There is, however, a more serious argument about action and its consequences which Keynes would consistently endorse. Burke (1955) argues that current suffering cannot be justified by uncertain future gains. Contrasting the horrors of the French Revolution with Greek tragedy, Burke writes of 'a principal actor weighing ... in the scales hung in a shop of horrors – so much actual crime against so much contingent advantage' (Burke 1955: 92). Anticipating the arguments of Popper (1944) and Hayek (1947) about the uncertain consequences of social action, prophecy and grand plans are illegitimate, only piecemeal reforms ever justified. Burke insists on respect for tradition: '[w]e procure reverence to our civil institutions on the principle upon which nature teaches us to revere individual men: on account of their age and on account of those from whom they are descended' (Burke 1955: 39). He elaborates. 'Merits are confirmed by the solid test of long experience and an increasing public strength and national prosperity' (Burke 1955: 66).

Keynes agrees about the insecurity of future gains, the importance of convention, and the knowledge preserved by existing institutions. The young Keynes writes that '[w]e shall do well, as Burke says, to avail ourselves of the general bank and capital of nations and of ages. It is out of this that arises that class of actions commonly known as duties' (cited in O'Donnell 1989: 110). As late as 1940, Keynes still argues that '[c]ivilisation is a tradition from the past, a miraculous construction made by our fathers ... hard to come by and easily lost' (cited in Skidelsky 2000: 68). National prosperity would also remain a crucial yardstick.

Similar Burkean principles are at work in Keynes's questioning of the 'long run' as a suitable basis for economics, his cautious reformism and disdain for Marxism. He condemns the 'purposive man' who 'does not love his cat, but his cat's kittens; nor, in truth, the kittens, but only the kittens' kittens, and so on forward for ever to the end of catdom' (CWIX: 330). The principle is at work in Keynes's criticisms of the Versailles Treaty (Helburn 1991), in his opposition to the Bolshevik 'experiment' in Russia and in his attitude to the threat of war. Here, against his moderate-left collaborators on the *New Statesman and Nation*, Keynes supports British rearmament but also a peace policy, close to the official line of appeasement.

> It is our duty to prolong peace, hour by hour, day by day, for as long as we can. We do not know what the future will bring, except that it will be quite different from anything we could predict. I have said in another context that it is a disadvantage of 'the long run' that in the long run we are all dead. But I could have said equally well that it is the great advantage of 'the short run' that in the short run we are still alive. Life and history are made up of short runs. (CWXVIII: 62)

Keynes shares Burke's cautious pragmatism and fear of upheaval. Some of Keynes's more radical proposals can be interpreted in similar vein. He questions the sanctity of private property where private interests threaten general stability. He is deeply critical of unproductive rentiers and a 'feudal' hereditary principle because they undermined entrepreneurial dynamism (CWIX: 299). As discussed below, Mann has recently interpreted Keynes and Keynesianism in a Hegelian sense, as a liberalism qualified by prior interests in preserving capitalism and civilisation from revolution and the threat of revolution which poverty legitimises (Mann 2017a). Despite the different Burkean or Hegelian philosophical underpinnings, the conclusions are similar. Keynes rejects 'classical' economics and the economic practices of his day, at least in part because he thought them unsustainable and socially and economically destabilising.

Burke is also an unapologetic elitist. Writing in the context of the French Revolution, he maintains that '[t]he abuses of power by great men in history are minor compared to the present outrages' (1955: 53). Conversely:

> The occupation of a hairdresser or of a working tallow-chandler cannot be a matter of honour to any person ... Such descriptions of men ought not to suffer oppression from the state; but the state suffers oppression if such as they, either individually or collectively are permitted to rule. (1955: 56)

Keynes has a bit more sympathy with the French Revolution, but he expresses similar elitist sentiments in both national and class terms. He disdains the 'boorish proletariat' for 'the intelligentsia who, with whatever faults, are the quality in life and surely carry the seeds of all human advancement' (CWIX: 258). The correct economic solutions, in particular, 'will involve intellectual and scientific elements which must be above the heads of the vast mass of more or less illiterate voters' (CWIX: 295). As sympathetic biographers acknowledge, Keynes 'never lost hope that morality and the permeation of ideas could be relied upon to disseminate enlightened thinking' (Brittan 2006: 182). 'He was and would always remain convinced that only an intellectual elite, of which he undoubtedly considered himself a gifted member, could understand the complex mechanisms of economics and politics' (Dostaler 2007: 89). What Hall characterises as a 'trickle-up model' (1989a: 8) means that Keynes believes he could win round his opponents and to alter state policy. 'He believed in the supreme value of intellectual leadership, in the wisdom of the chosen few' (Harrod 1951: 331–2). Enlightened elites should rule.

Keynes was accordingly at most a qualified supporter of democracy. Fitzgibbons writes that 'Keynes agreed in principle with Burke that there is no right to universal suffrage, and that the people only have a right to good, but not necessarily representative government' (1988: 170). For Keynes, '[t]here is no very great *a priori* probability of arriving at desirable results by submitting to the decision of a vast body of persons, who are individually wholly incompetent to deliver a rational judgement on the affair at issue' (cited in Helburn 1991: 42). Keynes's qualified defence of democracy is predicated specifically on its limited character. 'In the first place, whatever the numerical representation of wealth may be, its power will always be out of all proportion; and secondly the defective organisation of the newly enfranchised classes has prevented any overwhelming alteration in the preexisting balance of power' (cited in O'Donnell 1989: 282).

With Burke, Keynes acknowledges problems of how any one individual or group of individuals could justify change and their judgement of its efficacy against the judgement of others. For Keynes, however, the elitism and the intuitionist philosophy he derives from Moore push against the conservative conclusions according to which we must always fall back on existing institutions. Confidence in elite judgement can outweigh any simple acceptance of social convention. He thought that 'Burke's timidity was often extreme to the point of absurdity' (O'Donnell 1989: 281). If this still provides scant grounds for a theory of political action, Burke also articulates ideas from which Keynes draws more critical lessons.

First, and in Burke very briefly, while 'the very idea of the fabrication of a new government is enough to fill us with disgust and horror' (1955: 35), a 'state without some means of change is without the means of its conservation' (1955: 24). So the facility to change is necessary and there is a pragmatism even to Burke's conservatism. Keynes sees Burke identifying as 'one of the finest problems in legislation, to determine what the State ought to take upon itself to direct by the public wisdom and what it ought to leave, with as little interference as possible, to individual exertion' (cited in CWIX: 288). As will be discussed in the final section of this chapter, Keynes both embraces the general point and applies it more specifically.

Unfortunately, for Keynes there are practical difficulties. 'Material poverty provides the incentive to change precisely in situations where there is very little margin for experiments' (CWIX: 294). Reform is needed precisely to avoid a worse fate but may be hard to achieve. Keynes's views on uncertainty and an inherent lack of knowledge of the future seem to amplify a judicious Burkean caution.

Second, what begins as a tentative and pragmatic accommodation to change in Burke might alternatively allow, even insist upon, quite radical reorientation. Burke's argument about the relation between present suffering and what future gains may or may not achieve seems amenable to an inversion whereby we reject present suffering in the name of only contingent future gain. A similar logic allows that current hardship cannot be justified in the name of (uncertain) future advantages. We should presumably seize current advantage or eliminate hardship at the expense of only contingent future privation. Skidelsky goes so far as to describe this as 'the bedrock of Keynesian economics' (*Washington Post* 9 May 2013). Keynes seldom explicitly frames his economic arguments in this way, but such a rationale might be discerned behind at least some of his proposals. For example, he writes:

> I would not discard an expedient which would be of material benefit over the next five years merely because it meant that our level of life twenty years hence would be a little lower than it might have been, if we had been more austere now. Moreover, too much austerity might upset the apple-cart. (CWXIII: 196)

It would be worth spending our way out of crises, even at the cost of running up debts, the consequences of which are unknown. Of course, Keynes is confident (perhaps more confident than his own epistemology really justifies) that the prosperity to which spending would bring a return would mitigate any future hardship against which the present amelioration of suffering needs to be weighed. Such an argument, however, would insulate Keynes's proposals from more trenchant 'liberal' criticisms. It might also be possible to push the principle further, even to revolutionary conclusions which would have been anathema to Burke and probably to Keynes. Current evils should be stopped even if we cannot know the repercussions of stopping them.

Varieties of liberalism

In some tension with the Burkean influences discussed above, Keynes almost always identifies with liberalism and the British Liberal Party. His economics would reach conclusions which challenged many liberal shibboleths, but it comes from within rather than without the liberal economic tradition.

Keynes was typically socially and politically liberal in the broader sense of the term. As an educated bourgeois, and like his Bloomsbury friends, Keynes is much more 'socially liberal' than much of contemporary British society and in this he can reasonably depict himself as being to the left also of several labour-movement figures, amongst whom puritanical and Catholic traditions ran deep. He believed on sex questions that the 'state of the law and of orthodoxy is still medieval – altogether out of touch with civilised opinion and civilised practice and with what individuals, educated and uneducated alike, say to one another in private' (CXIX: 302). This liberalism did not extend to drinking or gambling and he supported banning alcoholic spirits (CWIX: 303), although presumably not the fine wines he preferred and sold cheap at his Cambridge theatre. Chapter 1 mentioned Keynes's racial prejudices but he was not suggesting these should be legislated, and in that sense he remains liberal.

The rest of this section briefly concentrates on Keynes's political practice, his avowed political liberalism. This changed over the years, in part reflecting the changing nature of the Liberal Party and the changing circumstances in which it operated, particularly the relative decline of Britain's national economy. It also reflects Keynes's pragmatic desire to speak strategically to the powerful. When the Liberals lost power in the country, with little hope of regaining it, Keynes lost interest in the party.

Keynes was a more or less lifelong member of the British Liberal Party. He joined on 'going up' to Cambridge and soon became a leading member of the university Liberal Club. Although he always declined invitations to stand for parliament, Keynes campaigned actively, speaking and publishing in support of Liberal election campaigns, particularly in the 1920s. He was active in the Liberal summer schools and by 1927 he and Henderson had direct responsibility for Liberal Party economic policy (Clarke, P. 1988). From 1942 he sat on the Liberal benches in the House of Lords.

There are, however, many sorts of liberal and there is no agreement on how to categorise Keynes (Fitzgibbons 1988). The Liberal Party was broad and divided. It was the historical party of British capitalism, and Keynes initially sided with Asquith, the liberal imperialist. As mentioned in Chapter 1, in the 1920s and at the cost of his personal friendship with Asquith, he switched allegiance when Lloyd George put plans for state spending to combat unemployment at the centre of his campaign. His alliance with Lloyd George would be short-lived and the belated publication in 1933 of Keynes's reflections on Lloyd George at Versailles, tactfully omitted from the 1919 original, re-opened old hostilities. Lloyd George's memoirs in turn depicted Keynes as 'an entertaining economist whose bright but shallow dissertations on finance and political economy, when not taken seriously, always provide a source of innocent merriment to his readers' (cited in

Clarke, P. 1988: 289). Keynes became particularly critical of more conservative elements within the party and of a clinging to outdated principles
'set on old-fashioned individualism and *laissez-faire*' (CWIX: 300). He even
'sympathise[d] with Labour in rejecting the idea of cooperation with a party
which included, until the other day, Mr Churchill and Sir Alfred Mond, and
still contains several of the same kidney' (CWIX: 310).

If this set him against more conservative elements, Keynes also kept his
distance from the party's 'left'. There is some ambiguity here, and both
Clarke (P. 1988) and O'Donnell (1989) see Keynes's economics as developing
within, and seeking to modernise, the left-wing 'New Liberalism', associated
with people like Hobhouse, Hobson and Muir. There are some similarities
in their economic diagnoses, particularly in identifying problems of insufficient demand and in their political outlooks, opposing socialism and class
warfare but finding common ground with 'ordinary and moderate labour'
(Clarke, P. 1988: 80). The New Liberals' reform proposals, however, tended
to go much further than Keynes would countenance. Famously, Hobson
objected to Britain's imperialist project, which Keynes never questioned, but
in domestic policy too the New Liberals often advocated quite extensive
nationalisation, for example of mines and railways, the control of trusts
and cartels, more social spending, more social provisions like minimum
wages and more progressive taxation (Skidelsky 1992). Their diagnoses
of structural economic problems also contrast with Keynes's insistence
that economic evils stem primarily from 'risk, uncertainty, and ignorance'
(CWIX: 291). For Keynes these different origins allow different remedies
and that appropriate state policy could substantially overcome the difficulties (Skidelsky 1992). By 1925, Keynes was also worrying that the left's ill-
advised attempts to democratise the Liberal Party were undermining what
had hitherto been its sufficiently autocratic management (CWIX: 295–6). He
was only in a qualified way towards the left of the party, insisting that 'the
class war will find me on the side of the educated *bourgeoisie*' (CWIX: 297).

Of the Liberals' rivals, however, Keynes was more hostile to the
Conservatives than Labour, and as the Liberal Party went into decline,
Keynes proposed alliances. He identifies socialists within the Labour Party,
whose 'company and conversation ... many Liberals today would not
find uncongenial' (CXIX: 309). Having overseen the Liberal takeover of
The Nation in 1923, his decision in 1931 to merge the paper with *New
Statesman* 'symbolised the fact that historic Liberalism had run its course'
(O'Donnell 1989: 320). Keynes now advocates a broader alliance of 'progressive forces', which he identified in both the Liberal and Labour parties
but also beyond. He finds in the Mosley of 1930 a particularly attractive
combination of 'British socialism, bred out of liberal humanitarianism,
big business psychology, and the tradition of public service' (O'Donnell

1989: 323). By 1934, the Liberal Party 'lay in ruins' and Keynes refused to provide financial support in the following year's election when for the first and only time he voted Labour (Skidelsky 1992). Keynes's tentative support for Labour did not extend to the 1945 election, where he 'view[ed] with great alarm a substantial victory by either of the major Parties' (Keynes CWXVIII: 210). In the event, following Labour's famous win, and despite misgivings, Keynes agreed to continue as advisor to the new chancellor, Dalton, his former student.

A left-wing Keynes?

In contrast to the interpretation here of Keynes's politics as an amalgam of liberalism and Burkean conservatism, O'Donnell (1991) insists that Keynes was a socialist. He rightly points out that 'socialism' is a broad term and certainly not the preserve of Marxism. Many socialists of a reformist, social-democratic hue have subsequently subscribed to some version of what came to be called Keynesianism. This, however, is no argument about what Keynes himself believed. So although there are quotable passages which allow Keynes to be read as a socialist, it will be suggested that this is hard to square with the general tenor of his politics.

As above, Keynes's social liberalism puts him to the left of several labour leaders in important respects. At a personal level, his Bloomsbury friends were mainly further to the left, several at least sympathetic to Marxism and Keynes was happy to include the Marxist Dobb in his Cambridge inner circle. His economics put him to the left of many policies of the Labour governments of the 1920s, particularly of Snowden, the Labour chancellor, whom Keynes seems to have held in particular disdain.

Keynes is critical of crude individualism. 'The world is *not* so governed from above that private and social interests always coincide. It is *not* so managed here below that in practice they coincide. It is *not* a correct deduction from the principles of economics that enlightened self-interest always operates in the public interest' (CWIX: 287–8). Keynes deplores the 'paradox of poverty in the midst of plenty' (1973: 30). He favours at least a greater degree of equality than he found in Britain in the 1930s and argues that 'it follows that, the sum of the goods of each part of a community being fixed, the organic good of the whole is greater the more equally the goods are divided amongst the parts' (1921: 320). Keynes even occasionally accepts the label of 'socialism'.

As seen in Chapter 1, his frustration with WWI and the Versailles Peace see him making radical, even apparently revolutionary statements in his private letters. More moderately, he spoke to the Cambridge Union with

Sidney Webb, supporting 'collectivist socialism' as both inevitable and desirable (Moggridge 1992: 19). In conversation in the *New Statesman* he argued that:

> the question is whether we are prepared to move out of the nineteenth century laissez-faire state into an era of liberal socialism, by which I mean a system where we can act as an organised community for common purposes and to promote social and economic justice, whilst respecting and protecting the individual – his freedom of choice, his faith, his mind and its expression, his enterprise and his property. (CWXXI: 500)

The inclusion of freedoms of enterprise and property already suggest this is at least a peculiar vision of socialism. Any attribution of socialism to Keynes needs to be seriously qualified.

Elsewhere Keynes is explicit that the institutional foundations of Western civilisation, the only foundations on which 'personal life can be lived', are not socialist but 'the Christian Ethic, the Scientific Spirit and the Rule of Law' (cited in Skidelsky 2000: 51). Keynes argues that '[t]he political problem of mankind is to combine three things: economic efficiency, social justice, and individual liberty' (CWIX: 311). Social justice enters the picture for Keynes, as it does for socialists, sometimes in an acknowledged awkward relation with individual liberty, but for Keynes both tend to be subservient to economic efficiency (Peden 2006). Therefore, unemployment is bad, at least primarily, because it is wasteful of resources. Excessive inequality is bad because it involves unproductive consumption and waste. On the other hand, wage cuts, even amongst the poorest, may be entirely justified if (and the qualification is important) they restore profits and growth. Keynes is therefore not in favour of equality for its own sake. 'I believe that there is a social and psychological justification for significant inequalities of income and wealth, but not for such large disparities as exist today' (1973: 374).

Individual liberty also tends to trump social justice, as witnessed in Keynes's rather gushing praise for Hayek's *Road to Serfdom*. 'I find myself in agreement with virtually the whole of it; and not only in agreement with it, but in deeply moved agreement' (CWXXVII: 385). Hayek's book, and Keynes's reaction, need to be understood in the context of fascism and Stalinism in the 1940s, but, as will be argued below, there is agreement that there should be as much market freedom and as little state interference as possible, only disagreement about where to draw the line. Keynes defends the prices system, seeing '[t]he abolition of consumers' choice in favour of universal rationing [a]s a typical product ... of Bolshevism' (cited in Skidelsky 2000: 68).

Keynes's abhorrence of Marxism has an almost pathological intensity. While he barely glanced at Marx's works, he denounces a 'doctrine so illogical and dull' (CXIX: 285). 'Leninism is the faith of a persecuting and propagating minority of fanatics led by hypocrites' (CWIX:257). The Bolshevik revolution was 'the fruit of some beastliness in the Russian nature – or in the Jewish nature – or in the Russian and Jewish natures when, as now, they are allied' (CWIX: 270). Keynes joined the red-baiting of Labour around the fraudulent Zinoviev letter in the 1924 election (Dimand 2019b). He also disliked trade union leaders and remained consistently unimpressed by pro-working-class politics. In early 1926, a time of extraordinary income inequality (Piketty 2014: 316), he opposes the self-interest of trade unions: 'once the oppressed, now the tyrants, whose selfish and sectional pretentions need to be bravely opposed' (CWIX: 309).

Keynes's reaction to Marxism and to the Russian Revolution seem to be informed by the perceived civilisational threat they posed. This is the substance of Mann's (2017a) interpretation linking Hegel and Keynes, although Keynes's reaction to the Russian Revolution is very different to Hegel's initial welcoming of the French. As even the relatively radical younger Keynes writes in condemnation of Versailles, '[i]f we aim deliberately at the impoverishment of Central Europe, vengeance, I dare predict, will not limp. Nothing can then delay for very long that final civil war between the forces of reaction and the despairing convulsions of revolution, before which the horrors of the late German war will fade into nothing' (CWIII: 169). Both Keynes and Hegel advocate more state involvement in the economy as a means to preclude such catastrophe. Mann accordingly dismisses depictions of Keynes as a socialist as 'idiotic', the alternative reality of the Tea Party and the *Daily Telegraph* (2017a: 64).

The next section says more about Keynes's attitude towards the state. He favoured more intervention, as have many socialists, and indeed a venerable tradition equates the state with socialism in a relatively unproblematic way. It was an association made by Lassalle, Marx's adversary in Germany in the nineteenth century, and it was made by the Fabians in Keynes's day. The equivalence also suited the propaganda of both East and West in the post-WWII Cold War era, and opponents of both socialism and Keynesianism have been quick to tar them with the same brush. The common usage perhaps establishes a certain synonymity between 'Keynesianism', 'socialism' and 'statism', but it implies that socialism had existed across millennia, from ancient slave societies to many of the monarchies and war economies of the modern world. It is surely necessary at least to add supplementary criteria. The extent to which Keynes brought in the state was relatively modest, while the existence of this much broader tradition in favour of state intervention, going back at least to Hegel, confirms that it is not a specifically socialist commitment.

Keynes, the state and the inter-state system

This section makes four points. First, very briefly, it argues that Keynes is right to identify states as important economic actors. This ostensibly banal observation is a challenge to the economic mainstream which (then and now) often proceeds as if there were no state. Marxists might also do well to take notice; the state acts in ways not reducible to the market's (or capital's) imperatives. Second, Keynes's vision of state intervention remains essentially liberal. Intelligent liberals have long recognised the need for some state intervention, while seeking to keep this to a minimum. Keynes substantially shares this outlook, merely conceiving the necessary minimum at a higher level than contemporaries like Hayek. Third, Keynes brings in the state as *deus ex machina* (Sweezy 1956, Balogh 1976, Linder 1977), benign and disinterested. In common with Mann's recent characterisation of a broad tradition of Keynesianism going back to Hegel (maybe even to Plato), but now in contrast to harder-line liberals like Hayek, Keynes views the state as an essentially benevolent institution, capable of overcoming the turbulence of civil society. This is deeply problematic. Fourth, Keynes's specifically national vision also limits the profundity of his insights, not least his reassertion of the importance of economic aggregates. The relevant economic whole is ultimately global, it is more than the sum of its national parts, and the capitalist world-system profoundly limits and conditions state capacities.

Bringing in the state

Keynes's economics recognises the importance of the state. He was responding to real changes in the world and the growth of states which had occurred from the late nineteenth century. Of course, long before Keynes, chancellors of the Exchequer and Treasury secretaries, even those convinced by mainstream economic ideas, presumably acted on the assumption that their actions had economic repercussions and that they might even do some good. The growth of state activities nevertheless made an analytical exclusion increasingly implausible. The World War and the activist responses to the Great Depression would further increase the scale of state intervention, forcing itself into a reluctant economic consciousness.

Economic theory without the state was something of an intellectual game, irrelevant to the real world. Keynes begins the *General Theory* by insisting that he made fewer assumptions than neo-classical orthodoxy and this made his ideas applicable to 'the economic society in which we actually live' (1973: 3). Markets could not be assumed to produce equilibrium and full employment, while the increasing reality of state intervention made a real and often positive difference to the working of the capitalist economy. Keynes's analysis had clear implications that both monetary policy and direct intervention in the 'real' economy could have significant effects with beneficial consequences.

As obvious as this might now seem, even the simple acknowledgement of the economic role of states becomes an enduringly vital challenge to the economic mainstream, which still substantially assumes that there are markets but no states and that these markets work efficiently to maximise individual and social well-being. Economic theory without the state becomes an unreal and unconvincing apologetics for capitalism. For Marxists, by contrast, it is axiomatic that states act, and act in the interests of capital. But that too says little about what states do, and why and how this changes.

Keynes's qualified liberalism

Keynes both theorised the effects of state action and wanted the state to take more responsibility for economic management than either neo-classical economists or British politicians in the 1920s or 1930s thought appropriate. However, there is an important sense in which this advocacy of greater state intervention fits within, rather than challenging, a broader liberal tradition. It can be seen as still advocating a 'minimal state'. Keynes merely raised the necessary minimum. Socialistic thoughts may appear elsewhere in Keynes but not in his vision of the state, which remains elitist, undemocratic and inegalitarian.

As Keynes's dispute with Hayek made clear, even the hardest-line liberals accept that the capitalist or market economy needs some state intervention. Keynes agreed with the principle. As he wrote to Hayek, 'I did not say that you should not be *attached* to the price system. (I share your attachment.) I said you should not be *deceived* by it' (CWXXVI: 297). Keynes thought 'a rightly directed individualism was the best guarantor of *personal liberty* and *the variety of life*' (O'Donnell 1989: 297). He maintained that '[i]n all ages private property has been an essential element in liberalism – a bulwark against the State and a stimulus to comfort and culture (CWXXI: 500). Keynes insisted 'I am in favour of retaining as much private judgment and initiative and enterprise as possible' (CWXXI: 240). The question is therefore always a matter of degree. Once again we find Keynes's vision of the state informed by Burke. 'We cannot therefore settle on abstract grounds, but must handle on its merits in detail what Burke termed "one of the finest problems in legislation, namely to determine what the State ought to take upon itself to direct by public wisdom, and what it ought to leave, with as little interference as possible, to individual exertion"' (CWIX: 288). 'In the details of the balance between liberty and the state, Keynes departed from Burke, but the principle of a balance was accepted' (Fitzgibbons 1988: 166). For Keynes, '[t]he important thing for government is not to do things which individuals are doing already, and to do them a little better or a little worse; but to do the things which at present are not done at all' (CWIX: 291). So, as Skidelsky puts it, Keynes 'brought in the State to redress the failings of society, not because he loved it, but because he saw it as the last resource' (Skidelsky 1992: xv). Particularly where the free market provoked profound instability or revolt, it could not be left alone. State intervention is justified because the claims of poverty and the threat to civilisation trump an abstract liberalism. There are situations where 'nothing can preserve the integrity of contract between individuals, except a discretionary authority in the State to revise what has become intolerable' (Keynes 1923: 56). As things fell apart in the 1930s, some of Keynes's statements imply that the necessary minimum level of state intervention had become very high.

Most famously, the *General Theory* ends by advocating a 'somewhat comprehensive socialisation of investment' (1973: 378). This has been widely and differently interpreted, but it is worth noting that it is investment, not 'the instruments of production', which Keynes wants to 'socialise'. The socialisation of investment is proposed as necessary because Keynes believes that falling returns on investment will eventually tend to make entrepreneurs unwilling to take the necessary risks. Private investment and thence employment will dry up. As usual, Keynes sees his proposals as a necessary minimum and posits them against alternative forms of planning and nationalisation which would involve a far greater state encroachment on the prerogatives of the market (Winch 1989: 109). Keynes also had a soft spot for coordination through employers' associations, local and semi-autonomous bodies like the Port of London Authority, and what might now be called 'quangos', but his support was conceived as a pragmatic rather than a principled response, recognising that atomistic competition could be destructive and seeking various ways to reduce it. Keynes remained liberal in believing there should be only as much ntervention as necessary and that only certain forms were acceptable.

Keynes particularly advocates greater state control of finance, and he avours this with some choice phrases about the euthanasia of the rentier. gain this is tied to his economic analysis, not least his rejection of the idea at market forces automatically bring everything into equilibrium through djustments in the interest rate. Financial operators, notably through the speculative demand for money, can push up the interest rate, creating a discentive to 'real-economy' entrepreneurs to invest. Control of money and interest rate by an independent central bank could maintain the flow of ds to industry and avoid the perils of market volatility, arbitrary influ- by politicians and demands for democratic control. Similarly, Keynes advocates public works – primarily as a politically necessity, though he does also see them as relatively efficient compared with dole payments which pay people for not working. Such schemes 'work' in the sense of provoking investment where the private sector is unwilling to venture. The 'crowding out' argument is invalid; public works can add to national wealth and their costs can be redeemed when the economy returns to prosperity. Keynes always saw such direct interventions as a temporary expedient and, as seen in Chapter 1, he was quick to switch back from state spending to fighting inflation when the economy turned upwards.

Mann draws parallels with Hegel to reconceive Keynesianism as 'the liberalism of those who (however reluctantly) acknowledge in the arbitrary inequity of poverty the continued historical legitimacy of revolution' (2017a: 204). Facing poverty as an inescapable fact, and animated by the threat of revolution, 'something must be done' (2017a: 7). It is necessary to 'rein in' the economic problem (2017a: 56). Keynesianism therefore becomes a qualified liberalism, but an unqualified liberalism is unsustainable. 'The closer liberalism comes to laissez-faire purity, the more likely it is to implode' (Mann 2017a: 171).

Mann's Keynesianism, which therefore goes back to the French Revolution and forward to many modern thinkers, 'rejects both dogmatic individualism á la Locke and essentialist collectivism á la Bodin' (2017a: 49). Instead it involves 'simultaneous cancellation and preservation of the two previous moments in a new if not-necessarily-stable unity' (2017a: 49). Such a dialectic will be familiar to readers of Hegel, and it is a reasonable if more contestable claim to make of Keynes. Mann also sees the Hegelian/Keynesian state accomplishing new tasks required by liberal capitalism. Civil society now creates disruptive tendencies with the potential to produce a 'radically transformed social order' (Mann 2017a: 50). This is Mann's key argument and the point of Keynesianism's fundamental disjuncture with conventional liberalism. The French Revolution provides the vital well-spring, and Keynesianism is conceived particularly as a response to Robespierre and the Terror. The failure to deliver an 'honourable poverty', in Robespierre's phrase, 'gives birth to the ruinous "rabble"' (Mann 2017a: 46). It is this menace 'of popular rejection of the existing order' and the 'liberal capitalist anxiety' it provokes that informs Mann's understanding of Keynesianism (2017a: 84). It is 'the liberalism of those who (however reluctantly) acknowledge in the arbitrary inequity of poverty the continued historical legitimacy of revolution' (2017a: 204). 'Keynesianism … would never have emerged without a revolutionary past to endlessly haunt it' (2017a: 7). Robespierre, and Hegel after him, saw all other rights as subordinate to the right to basic necessities (2017a: 94). Life and happiness are prior to freedom (2017a: 126, 148).

It seems clear, however, that at least for Keynes, the concern is less with the plight of the poor themselves than that they might become insubordinate. Before WWI, 'employment was, of course, substantially below full employment, but not so intolerably below it as to provoke revolutionary changes' (1973: 308). For Mann, Keynesianism is the result of the 'historical experience of revolution, because the shadow of revolution – revolutionary terror in particular – animates it, gives it momentum, and constantly reinvigorates it' (2017a: 72). Keynesianism's contemporary revival, evidenced particularly in the interest in Piketty's (2014) *Capital in the Twenty-First Century*, similarly attests to the severity of the current legitimisation crisis (Mann 2017a).

Only the state has the answer. Drawing analogies with Marx's famous transformation by capital of money, through commodity production, into more money, M-C-M', Mann characterises the Keynesian dialectic of illiberal liberalism's transformation through the state to liberal freedom: L-S-L' (2017a: 386). In particular, Keynesian political economy becomes a 'post-revolutionary pharmaceutical science of government, crucial to the process of legitimation' (Mann 2017a: 28).

Keynesianism does therefore sit somewhat uncomfortably within the liberal tradition. Hegel describes how the free market produces processes requiring 'regulation to bring it back to the universal, and to moderate and shorten the duration of those dangerous convulsions to which its collisions give rise, and which should return to equilibrium by a process of unconscious necessity' (cited in Mann 2017a: 166). Amongst other things, Keynesianism therefore rejects the 'logic behind modern liberal democracies' institutionalized neglect of injustice in favour of endless fretting over the legitimacy of the means by which it might be redressed' (2017a: 188). Mann interprets this neglect as the product of an unfortunate Kantian victory according to which questions of who shall be free are superseded by questions of how, of 'acceptable paths from unfreedom to freedom' (2017a: 187). In a sense, Keynesianism becomes a more consistent liberalism, rejecting this supersession, by prioritising practical conservative questions of acceptable means, over liberalism's substantive questions.

For both Hegel and Keynes there is then an important sense that their political philosophy is necessarily conservative, accepting the need for change precisely to prevent more substantial civilisational catastrophe. Many harder-line liberals would accept the basic principle. Hayek explicitly did so in his exchanges with Keynes. Others, including Friedman, acknowledge the same point. As above, Keynes's political philosophy owed much to Burke's intelligent conservatism, similarly haunted by the fear of revolution and acknowledging the need for change to avert catastrophe and for state intervention to secure it: a 'state without some means of change is without the means of its conservation' (Burke 1955: 24). By the 1920s, even most of

Keynes's intellectual opponents in practice also endorsed government intervention to alleviate unemployment.

Keynes's benign state

Unfortunately given its importance to his economics, Keynes provides no theory of the state, and his understanding of the potential for effective state intervention remains hugely optimistic. This has serious implications for any subsequent evaluation of whether his economic ends are achievable, both in the sense of whether the policies he advocates would have their desired effects but also in the sense of whether or not they are likely to have the support of powerful vested interests necessary to see them achieved. Keynes's own closeness to leading British political figures no doubt coloured his judgement. He was in a rare position to influence decisions and to appreciate politicians' stupidity when they failed to take his advice.

Skidelsky depicts Keynes's vision of the state as substantially Platonic: one of wise rulers providing benevolent guidance (1992: 543). Or as Moggridge puts it, Keynes always maintained '[t]he philosopher king's assumption of knowing what was best for the public' (1976: 135). An intellectual aristocracy was needed to run national affairs (Dostaler 2007). Keynes countered Hayek's insistence that increasing state intervention paved the 'Road to Serfdom' by insisting that '[m]oderate planning will be safe if those carrying it out are rightly oriented in their own minds and hearts' (XXVII: 387). For Keynes, the state must be run by experts and protected from democracy.

Mann again finds parallels with Hegel and his idea of a universal class, whose 'capacity to undertake this role is attributable to political economy, the science of modern government' (2017a: 181). What is required is the 'peaceful "disorganization of civil society", ... under the guise of much wiser, more pragmatic and experienced "*hommes d'état*"' (2017a: 173). As Mann writes, we are simply invited to assume that 'proper stewardship and appropriate institutions' are at hand. 'The question of political agency – outside the 'universal class' of enlightened technocrats managing the state apparatus, at least – never arises and need not concern us' (2017a: 364). Mann concludes that for Keynesianism, '[h]ope is only possible when the separation [of politics and economics] is acknowledged as legitimate, when the poor consent to their poverty. Without it, the economic seeps into politics, and all bets are off' (2017a: 370).

Any failure to provide wise leadership is, of course, no accident. Without denying that there can be stupid policy, that governments would be better advised by Keynes than by many counsellors before and since, this optimistic vision at least needs qualification.

Keynes himself had earlier been deeply critical. Still scarred by the experience of Versailles, in the *Revision of the Treaty* he insisted, 'only individuals are good, and all nations are dishonourable, cruel and designing'
(CWIII: 127). As Marx's (1975) early writings against Hegel insist, the state
had sectional interests of its own which preclude it being seen as standing
'above' society. Marx's later depictions of the state as simply a capitalist
executive may be a polemical first-order approximation, but even conservative modern public choice theory (e.g. Tullock 1987) accepts that politics
and government rest on vested interests rather than abstract principles or
wise council. As Dowd writes, Keynes's economics involves a systematic
'neglect of any examination of power and politics' (2004: 131). Keynes's
focus on market failures and what might be done about them means he
overlooks the many state failures, while simultaneously reinforcing the
illusion of a separation of state from society.

As mentioned in the previous chapter, it is hard to see how Keynes's own
epistemology allows the state or even its wisest advisors to overcome the
fundamental problems of uncertainty he identifies. There is no telos to capitalism, making particular policies objectively 'better'. Even if we imagine
that there could be some consensus of ends, Keynes's own views undermine the ability of policy-makers to discern the means of achieving them.
Keynes seems to abandon the problems of uncertainty and non-ergodicity in
jumping to the uncertainty-reducing capacity of states. The state can hardly
have privileged access to the unknowable probabilities of future events
(Fitzgibbons 1991). Of course, this is not to deny that state intervention
provides a degree of conscious oversight, within a single national economy,
unavailable to competing capitals. That intervention, however, remains
much more of a contested social achievement than Keynes acknowledges,
with state power also profoundly limited within an essentially anarchic
international context.

The illusion of national interests

Keynes is acutely aware that particular states operate within an international
system which constrains them. From his writing on the Versailles Treaty
and its consequences to his efforts to shape the post-WWII world, Keynes
is concerned, for example, with the effects of trade and capital movement
and the potential tensions between national interests and general ones. Even
while still a defender of liberal order and free trade, the younger Keynes
could recognise his 'favourite dilemma', an ethical incommensurability
between being and doing good, playing out at the international level. French
currency devaluation involved being bad but doing good – policies Britain
might do well to ape (Harrod 1951: 394–5). The *Tract* and *Treatise* discuss

international monetary arrangements extensively and how these limit state capacities.

Keynes's vision, however, is substantially one of separate national political economies and separate national states interacting 'at arm's length'. Keynes's economic aggregates, the important secondary sense in which his theory is *general* (1973: xxii) – aggregates for investment, the marginal efficiency of capital, the rate of interest, liquidity preference, the quantity of money, the volume of employment, the propensity to consume – are all conceived in national terms. This understanding did much to establish modern economic common sense, providing a significant stimulus to the production of better national economic data, encouraging a process that beyond the US had previously been underdeveloped (Eatwell 1986, Rosanvallon 1989). This very data collection, however, reinforces a particular national way of looking at the world. The nation (perhaps for Keynes even the British nation) remains the focus of analysis and the appropriate level of aggregation, reifying the nation-state as the appropriate unit of analysis.

On the one hand, this downplays divisions within countries. 'Through aggregation, struggle is subsumed, hidden and flattened out' (de Angelis 2000: 24, Negri 1988). Keynes's specifically national conception leaves state power (but only that) above individuals (Pilling 1986, Mattick 1971). On the other hand, Keynes's aggregates only run to national boundaries; so there are two distinct sets of relations. There are national economic relations, then there is an international system built on national foundations. The recent literature on 'globalisation' has shown how claims of state retreat can then hang on exaggerated understandings of how states were once effective containers of economic relations (MacLean 2000), an understanding which owes much to Keynes. The level of society is that of the nation-state, on which other states impinge, but 'externally', as it were. Keynes's challenge to individualism therefore remained ultimately a national not a genuinely social one. This nation-centrism also introduces a methodological problem similar to assuming individually rational action. Much as individuals are actually social beings, so states are shaped by domestic social relations and by inter-state competition and capital accumulation at a global scale. Keynes's treatment leaves the state quarantined beyond the level of economic analysis, perceived as exogenous to, rather than as something to be integrated within, the economic system understood as a whole.

All of this accords with broader criticisms of Keynes's politics, a politics which is place-bound, 'Western' and even specifically British, concerned with providing enlightened advice to rulers, to improve the running of the economy in order to preserve rather than radically transform the established order.

Conclusions

Keynes's politics were complex and any simple designation is potentially misleading, but they seem best understood as a qualified liberalism. This is a liberalism in that it prioritises individual freedom, in society (and in this Keynes was more consistent than many who claim the term) and in the economy. However, it is a liberalism which is qualified by Burkean conservatism, respectful of tradition and wary of radical reform. It is also qualified by a greater willingness than shown by most liberals to admit the failures of laissez-faire and to invoke the state as the agent of their solution, even as the state remains substantially a liberal state, open to enlightened and disinterested management, as something external to the economy rather than as something shaped in the process of contested social and economic relations.

As Chapter 12 will discuss, even as modern mainstream microeconomics has reasserted the irrelevance of the state to economic analysis, much of Keynes's advice continues to inform public policy. The previous chapters, however, have suggested that the power of ideas is articulated with social interests and the power of Keynes's economic thinking is correspondingly limited by what it says – and also what it does not say, what Keynes assumes – about the state and its capacities.

4

Economics before the *General Theory*

Introduction

This chapter introduces economics as Keynes encountered it and then how his own work before the *General Theory* begins to break from orthodoxy.

Keynes depicts almost all his predecessors, at least those he considered worth discussing, as 'classical' economists. He acknowledges that this stretches the concept, but it allows him to include not just 'Ricardo and James Mill and their *predecessors* ...[but also] the *followers* of Ricardo' (1973: footnote 3). His understanding therefore includes the later marginalist or 'neo-classical' writers like Jevons and Marshall and many of Keynes's contemporaries. In doing this, Keynes is emphasising what he sees as common failings, notably an acceptance of the quantity theory of money and Say's Law. This characterisation of 'the classics' downplays other concerns of the earlier (pre)classical tradition, concerns with production, dynamic change and economic aggregates.

Keynes enjoyed his unconventional choices of whom to approve and disapprove and sometimes 'misrepresented his predecessors disgracefully' (Hollander 2011: 27). He was extremely erudite but inevitably his reading was partial. He read Smith within a couple of years of becoming an economics lecturer but remained 'allergic' to Marx. His understanding of marginalism derived overwhelmingly from Jevons and Marshall and he appears never to have paid more than cursory attention to Walras or Menger, marginalism's continental European co-founders. Knowledge is always incomplete; priorities and partialities, more or less acknowledged and defended, are inevitable. More remarkably, Keynes polemicised against authors he had not read and claimed innovation in ignorance of what had gone before or of was going on elsewhere. Myrdal criticises 'the attractive Anglo-Saxon kind of unnecessary originality, which has its roots in certain systematic gaps in the knowledge of the German language on the part of the majority of English economists' (cited in Patinkin 1987: 23). Keynes could read German but he seldom bothered with anything not in English. His particular reading in turn shapes his own theory, his seizing on earlier insights, notably those from Malthus, and his emphatic, sometimes over-emphatic, rejection of others, notably anything descended from Ricardo.

What follows is accordingly oriented to Keynes, not to a general history of economic thought to 1936. It concentrates narrowly on three themes. First, it discusses the classics as they are more conventionally understood by Marx, for whom it was a qualified term of approval. Marx distinguishes the likes of Sismondi, Smith and Ricardo from the 'vulgar' school of mere apologists. Amongst the latter, Say was a figure of Marx's withering contempt. This first section briefly identifies what was lost from this tradition in the later marginalist revolution, in terms of its treatment of economic aggregates and economic interrelation, which Keynes substantially recovers, and in terms of the classics' focus on production and growth, in which Keynes has little interest. This first section then discusses the beliefs which Keynes criticised, the adherence to the quantity theory of money and Say's Law. The second section introduces Jevons's and Marshall's marginalism, their vision of an exchange economy, the concepts of utility and disutility, and their attitude to money, production and labour. Keynes has a somewhat ambivalent relationship, both in and against this tradition. There is a sense in which he can point out its failings precisely through a more careful application of its principles. The third section discusses Keynes's own early work, particularly the *Tract on Monetary Reform* and the *Treatise on Money*. Keynes would retrospectively see himself as having been within the classical tradition when he wrote these earlier books (CWXIV: 24), but they anticipate important later themes and the *Treatise*, in particular, sometimes makes more radical departures, and attempts a more dynamic analysis, than would the *General Theory*.

The classics

Keynes's partial recovery of the insights of classical political economy

Keynes recognised Smith's greatness but, like most commentators, stressed Smith's support for the free market, rational self-interest and the 'invisible hand'. Smith said these things but much else besides, and Keynes's reading does some injustice to Smith and the broader classical tradition.

In particular, the classics emphasised questions of output, production and economic growth. Smith's (1997) starting point – literally book 1, chapter 1, page 1 – was with labour and the belief that through the division of labour the wealth of nations could be augmented. Production, of course, is a theme that Marx pushed much further in his depictions of capitalism's relentless accumulation. The point here is that while few economists would admit they are uninterested in growth, marginalism later came to redefine economics in terms of the distribution of scarce resources. This essentially takes these resources as given and sidelines questions of how they might be increased. Keynes blames the shift of economic focus on Ricardo's victory over Malthus. 'Ricardo is investigating the theory of the *distribution* of the product in conditions of equilibrium and Malthus is concerned with what determines the *volume* of output day by day in the real world' (CWX: 97).

Unfortunately, this loss of dynamism from economic theory is not something Keynes fully recovers. Keynes is concerned with the volume of output in terms of changing levels of employment but, in what he ignores, he drifts closer to the (neo)classical mainstream than the classics. He would later briefly acknowledge and regret that the *General Theory* 'neglects the process of capital formation' (CWXIV: 283). Where Marx and some of Keynes's contemporaries like Schumpeter and institutional economists attempt to integrate technological change into their theories, Keynes takes capital and technology as given (Dillard 1984). There are valid reasons for this neglect of dynamics in Keynes's avowedly short-run approach, but it implies that he is attempting something more limited than the classics.

Keynes does expresses sympathy with what he calls the 'pre-classical doctrine that everything is produced by labour' (1973: 213). He says this, however, particularly because he recognises that prices are inconstant, and he takes units of labour as a more stable accounting device, not as the epistemological foundation for his political economy. In a formal sense, Keynes's interpretation of the labour theory of value is close to that of Smith, taking profits as normal and counting them as part of costs, but, unlike for Smith, for Keynes there is little sense of adopting a labour theory of value as an explanatory concept.

Something similar can be said of Keynes's recovery of the importance of economic aggregates (CWX: 88). He identifies the interdependence of production and consumption and singles out Malthus for praise, particularly in reviving the concept of 'effective demand'. There is dispute about Malthus's real influence or whether Keynes just found Malthus's language a useful 'hook' on which to hang his new ideas (Hagemann 2019). But Keynes notices approvingly how Malthus is concerned with 'the balance of produce and consumption'. For Malthus the 'unproductive consumption' of the rich is a boon to progress, but he also encourages 'the employment of the poor in roads and public works' (Malthus, cited in Keynes CWX: 102). Keynes's emphasis on Malthus overlooks how, as Mattick writes, concerns with economic aggregates go back at least to the physiocrats and 'Quesnay's *Tableau Oeconomique*' (Mattick 1971: 20). Keynes's rediscovery of consumption is a recovery and development of themes already pervasive in classical political economy. But Keynes is right that 'regarded historically, the most extraordinary thing is the complete disappearance of the theory of demand and supply for output as a whole, i.e. the theory of employment, *after* it had been for a quarter of a century the most discussed thing in economics' (CWXIV: 85).

For the earlier tradition, the aggregates were also usually conceived in class terms. Consumption was typically straightforwardly associated with wages, saving with profits. The marginalists transform these into functions of individual behaviour (Caspari 2019). Here Keynes would remain closer to Marshall; the propensities to consume and save were related to income but understood as questions of degree and individual psychology.

Keynes also endorses Malthus over Ricardo in their attitudes to money. 'Malthus is dealing with the monetary economy in which we happen to live; Ricardo with the abstraction of a neutral money economy' (CWX: 97). Even before reading the Malthus correspondence, Keynes was rejecting standard interpretations of the quantity theory of money and Say's Law (Hollander 2019), and these rejections would be recurring themes, which will be discussed below.

Before doing so, it is worth a more general note on how Marx and the classical tradition sought underlying causes and to identify general historical trajectories of economic processes. This search, not only Marx's specific answers, were anathema to the neo-classical tradition. As so often, there are ambiguities and Keynes's endorsement of Malthus extended to the boldest, stupidest and most politically appalling grand theories of population. Elsewhere, too, Keynes clearly sees himself as able to unearth long-term trends, for example perceiving a decline in the marginal efficiency of capital. However, Keynes is usually wary of both long-term prediction and grand abstraction. Again, he contrasts Malthus favourably against Ricardo. 'In economic discussions Ricardo was the abstract and *a priori* theorist, Malthus the inductive and intuitive investigator who hated to stray too far from what he could test by reference to the facts and his own intuitions' (CWX: 95). Fitzgibbons argues that Keynes rejects precisely the search for science and underlying causes, epitomised in the labour theory of value. Economic analysis should remain superficial. There is only surface, no underlying reality. '[T]here is no long-run equilibrium (nor a Marxian dialectic propelled by hidden contradictions in the economy) ... the seething mind-boggling mass of surface fact is all there really is' (Fitzgibbons 1988: 129). This may exaggerate, but it resonates with Keynes's views on uncertainty, the greater epistemological security of the short run and of economics as a 'moral science'.

The quantity theory of money

Keynes's depiction and criticism of a single classical tradition hinges mainly on two related big ideas which Ricardo and the later neo-classical writers do indeed share: the quantity theory of money and Say's Law. The quantity theory goes back at least to the sixteenth century (Vilar 1984) but is best known in Fisher's twentieth-century formulation, according to which:

$$MV = PT$$

This equation maintains that the total quantity of money (M) multiplied by the velocity of circulation (V) is equal to the average price of the goods (P) multiplied by the number of transactions (T). Keynes himself was more familiar with, and his early work adopted, the 'Cambridge version', which used the symbol 'k' as a measure of the proportion of money people hold, rather than V, but k and V are simply reciprocals of each other and the equations amount to the same thing. Written as $M = kPT$, the Cambridge version can, however, be seen as emphasising, through the three variables on the right-hand side of the equation, the demand for money rather than its supply (Blaug 1997).

The quantity theory has been put to different uses. The mathematical identity becomes a theory by positing some of the variables as dependent or independent (Blaug 1997, Sheehan 2009). For the early mercantilists, inflows of money were welcome because they would increase the number of transactions, or the level of economic activity. Money (M) is proportional to transactions (T) if V and P are assumed constant. Smith mocked the mercantilists, claiming that they naively equated money and wealth, and insisted that 'wealth does not consist in money, or in gold and silver; but in what money purchases, and is valuable only for purchasing' (1999: 5–6, 14). Smith, as later Ricardo and Marx, was criticising those who sought 'monetary panaceas' (Blaug 1997: 22) rather than suggesting that money does not matter. But such arguments provide an important step towards the conclusion of money's insignificance, reached by many later interpretations of the quantity theory.

Now, increases in money simply increase prices. If the velocity of money and the volume of transactions are constant, M and P are proportional to each other. Fisher makes assumptions about banking technology to justify such a constant velocity of circulation (Sheehan 2009). Later, Friedman, honestly if more cynically, admits that the velocity and changes in the velocity 'have generally been calculated as the numbers having the property that they render the equation correct' (1987: 5). With more or less justification, money was assumed proportional to price, a proposition from which Keynes would long struggle to escape (Skidelsky 1983).

The quantity theory implies that changes in the quantity of money can distort price signals but that they do not have long-term effects on the economy. It does not matter if we call the price of something $1 or 100 cents, or we relabel cents as dollars and let $1 become $100. To believe otherwise is to suffer 'the money illusion' (Patinkin 1987). At most, there are temporary fluctuations and short-run redistributions because some prices are 'stickier', take longer to adjust, than others (Skidelsky 1983). Amongst other things, 'an increase in the quantity of money will temporarily depress interest rates but as soon as the new money has acted on prices, the interest rate will rise back to its "natural rate", the rate of profit on capital' (Blaug 1997: 126). Most economic analysis can then safely proceed, ignoring money, assuming that the economy operates as if by barter (Minsky 1986).

Keynes does not dispute that the mathematical identity can be written in such a way that it is tautologically true. What cannot be justified are the conventional interpretations which assume that money is purely a medium of exchange, making barter-like process more efficient. Once money can also store value, velocity becomes indeterminate. The propensity to hold money, liquidity preference, need not be reckoned proportional to income. This undermines any straightforward relation between money supply and price changes and allows that what happens with money can have real effects on the wider economy.

Say's Law

Amongst other things, the fact that money can be held rather than immediately spent invalidates Say's Law. It is worth briefly dwelling on this, despite what probably strikes many modern readers as its manifest silliness. According to Keynes, Say's Law maintains that supply creates its own demand. This can again be seen as saying that money does not matter, although in more sophisticated versions, Say's Law works its magic precisely through changes in money and the rate of interest.

Say extrapolates (Marx would say plagiarises) from Smith (1999) to insist that money is only the medium through which to obtain other products. Producers sell in order that they can buy, and 'the more we can produce the more we can purchase' and therefore 'a product is no sooner created, than it, from that instant, affords a market for other products to the full extent of its own value' (Say 1827: 78). Say is unambiguous here that this is an instantaneous process. Later, Say himself would acknowledge that his 'law of markets' might not hold in the short run (Hagemann 2019). More subtly, in Mill and subsequent formulations, interest rate adjustments produce equilibrium (Lekachman 1967). Any saving increases the supply of funds, putting downward pressure on the interest rate, increasing investment, diminishing savings and returning the world to equilibrium. So equality is achieved through the interest rate variation and need not be instantaneous. But Mill ends with the same conclusion that 'what constitutes the means of payment for commodities is simply commodities' (cited in Reddaway 1964: 99). Any short-run frictions or fluctuations need not cause analytical worries, with economic 'science' merely abstracting from these to assume long-run equilibrium.

Keynes accuses economists of tacitly accepting Say's Law, even when they did not really believe it literally, in their continued assumptions that the market works efficiently (CWXIV: 123). Amongst others, Keynes sees Marx as a follower of Ricardo and therefore of Say. Now Keynes senses a double victory. '[I]f Ricardian economics were to fall, an essential prop to the intellectual foundations of Marxism would fall with it' (CWXIII: 488). It is worth emphasising that Keynes's depictions of Marx's endorsement of Say are pure invention and that Marx (even by his own standards) had vitriolic contempt for Say and the 'absurdity' of his 'famous law' (Marx and Engels 2010, vol. 32: 124–5, 160). Of course, it is possible that Marx, as Keynes accuses his own contemporaries, tacitly, inadvertently, accepts Say's Law; but, as Chapter 7 will elaborate, although Marx's treatment is underdeveloped, he is aware that money is not neutral and nothing indicates that he thought capitalist economic relations were harmonious. Keynes's one-sided characterisation of the classics means, as Cottrell argues, that '[t]he General Theory does not repudiate the ideas which Marx actually took from Ricardo, and built upon, while the Ricardian ideas it does repudiate are ones Marx himself rejected' (2012: 160). Keynes also failed to acknowledge that several of his contemporaries also emphatically rejected Say's Law (Mattick 1971, Trautwein 2019). So Keynes exaggerates his own originality. But recognising 'the essential truth that Say's Law is a fraud and a delusion' (Sweezy 1964: 300) provided an important cutting edge for his attack on the economic mainstream.

The marginalist revolution

This section outlines key marginalist ideas as developed by Jevons and Marshall.[1] Marshall is the much more cautious writer, almost always qualifying any generalisation. As Keynes would later write, Jevons's book is 'simple, lucid, unfaltering, chiselled in stone where Marshall knits in wool' (CWX: 131). The marginalist revolution was begun simultaneously by Jevons, Walras in France and Menger in Austria, but it seems unlikely that Keynes read much more of Walras or Menger than he did of Marx (Fitzgibbons 1988). Therefore, it was Jevons who wrote '[t]he first modern book on economics (CWX: 131). Marshall was Keynes's teacher and mentor and in large part also his hero. 'As a scientist he was, within his own field, the greatest in the world for a hundred years' (CWX: 173). Even some of Keynes's more radical followers see him as Marshall's faithful disciple (Davidson 2009, Harcourt and Sardoni 1996). Keynes, despite his some-times radical language, would be a critic within the temple, a temple whose strange construction therefore needs some explanation for those unfamiliar. The fundamental claim of marginalism is that a theory of value should be subjective and (although Marshall qualifies this) based on exchange rather than production.

For Jevons, '*value depends entirely upon utility*. Prevailing opinions make labour rather than utility the origin of value; and there are even those who distinctly assert that labour is the cause of value' (1957: 1). Against this, '[t]he mere fact that there are many things, such as rare ancient books, coins, antiquities, etc., which have high values, and which are absolutely incapable of production now, disperses the notion that value depends on labour' (1957: 163). For Jevons, it follows that 'wages are clearly the effect not the cause of the value of the produce' (1957: l). We are in the world of Bentham and 'felicific calculus' (1957: 23). Individuals weigh their sub-jective pleasures and pains, and Jevons sees his task as 'tracing out of the mechanics of self-interest and utility' (1957: xvii–iii). 'Each person is to the other person a portion of the outside world ... Hence the weighing of motives must always be confined to the bosom of the individual' (1957: 14). These individual motives turn out to be easily described.

The fundamental idea is that the utility which individuals experience from any commodity declines 'at the margin'. In Marshall's phrase, '[t]he *total utility* of a thing to anyone ... increases with every increase in his stock of it, but not as fast as his stock increases' (2009: 78–9). The more we have of something, the more pleasure it brings but in diminishing amounts. The first pair of shoes, if we had none, brings more extra pleasure than the fourth, which in turn brings more than the fortieth. Qualifying this, it is worth reproducing Jevons's original depiction: see Figure 4.1. This indicates two features which conveniently disappear from later versions. First, the curve crosses the x-axis. As Jevons puts it, 'further quantities will have various degrees of utility; but ... beyond a certain quantity the utility sinks grad-ually to zero; it may even become negative, that is to say, further supplies of the same substance may become inconvenient and hurtful' (1957: 44). We can have too much of something and need to pay someone to take it away. Second, the curve does not cross the y-axis. As they become scarce, the first increment of some commodities, water to the thirsty, becomes almost infinite. Ever the rigorous mathematician, Jevons avoids either a radical discontinuity or suggesting that negative quantities have extremely high marginal utilities. Neither of these nuances, however, is allowed to interfere with the subsequent analysis, which largely assumes small positive changes in utility, agreement about what is good and bad, and disagreement only in terms of the relative worth attached by different people to different goods and different quantities.

The object of the exercise then becomes to determine how the myriad individual wants fit together, to distribute scarce resources. Different people have different preferences, and in sum this leads to goods having different 'schedules'. We all want, so the theory suggests, shoes, and beer, and books about political economy, but we do not all value them in the same way. People first satisfy their greatest desires, later lower ones: the second, third or twentieth increments of the goods people value highly or the first increments of something less satisfying. With scarce resources and a definite amount of money, we spend it on a bundle of goods so that the last shilling makes virtually no difference to our overall utility.

A free market then determines distribution. Money has reared its head but simply to facilitate barter-like exchanges. 'While demand is based on the desire to obtain commodities, supply depends on overcoming the unwillingness to undergo "discommodities"' (Marshall 2009: 116). This is precisely a calculus of pleasure and pain. We endure pain, make sacrifices, give up one pleasure in order to obtain another we value more. Even the meat-loving butcher can trade some steaks for the alcoholic brewer's beer, to their mutual advantage. For Jevons, '[b]y a market I shall mean two or more persons dealing in two or more commodities, whose stocks of those commodities and intentions of exchanging are known to all' (1957: 85). Jevons here

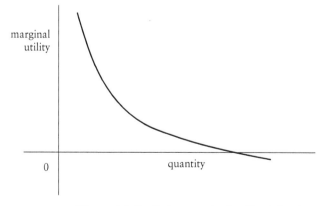

Figure 4.1 Declining marginal utility (after Jevons 1957)

builds perfect knowledge into the very meaning of the word 'market', and, of course, 'there must be perfectly free competition' (1957: 86).

Jevons likens the resulting equilibrium to that of 'a lever as determined by the principle of virtual velocities' (1957: vii). Marshall uses a slightly different physical analogy, maintaining that 'a stone hanging by a string is displaced from its equilibrium position, the force of gravity will at once tend to bring it back to its equilibrium position. The movement of the scale of production about its position of equilibrium will be of a somewhat similar kind' (2009: 288). This allows that equilibrium is not immediate but any 'frictions' can be taken as mere qualifications, anomalous 'inefficiencies' to be discussed later as special cases. The market efficiently joins supply and demand. It is possible for there to be overproduction in a particular industry and for there to be temporary gluts but never general ones, a proposition which Say's Law makes 'evidently absurd and self-contradictory' (Jevons 1957: 202).

The approach is essentially static, but time is important because people also value things' future utility. Evaluating utility over time potentially presents problems. For Jevons, there should, in principle, be an accurate weighing of probabilities, and '[t]he factor expressing the effect of remoteness should, in short, always be unity, so that time should have no influence. But no human mind is constituted in this perfect way: a future feeling is always less influential than a present one' (1957: 72). Therefore, future pleasure and pain are evaluated in the same way but at a discount.

This orderly discounting of future pleasure allows the marginalists a clever and politically pleasing trick. Deferred pleasure has less utility. Now, in forgoing their immediate pleasure, entrepreneurs can be reckoned to suffer a loss of utility for which they are entitled to an equivalent return, a 'reward for waiting'. For Marshall, costs include this 'rate of remuneration for waiting [which] … is an element of cost as truly as effort is' (2009: 291, 4). With this sleight of hand, the very real rabbit which is profit is pulled out of the theoretical hat of the marginalists' own fertile imagining.

Any idea of exploitation would be anathema, but Marshall does seek to integrate production and exchange, insisting on a symmetrical relation through a famous metaphor. 'We might as reasonably dispute whether it is the upper or the under blade of a pair of scissors that cuts a piece of paper' (2009: 290). In doing this, Marshall has been seen as reconciling marginalism with the earlier classical tradition (Kicillof 2018), but his primary objections are to classical political economy's 'disproportionate stress on the side of the cost of production' (Marshall 2009: 71). Nevertheless, 'the longer the period, the more important will be the influence of the cost of production on value' (Marshall 2009: 291). According to Keynes, '[t]he unnecessary controversy, caused by the obscurity of Ricardo and the rebound of Jevons, about the respective parts played by demand and by cost of production in the determination of value was finally cleared up. After Marshall's analysis there was nothing more to be said' (CWX: 205).

There is, however, a problem. Marshall is aware that production is carried out in firms, which cannot have subjective wants. But they do have costs, which for Marshall can be reckoned in the same way, by reintroducing money. Unfortunately, this also introduces some serious epistemological traumas. Money itself has utility. Already in Jevons, compared to a family earning 50,000 pounds a year, for one earning 'one thousand pounds a year, the utility of a penny may be measured in an exactly similar manner; but it will be much less' (1957: 140–1). For Marshall, similarly, '[a] shilling is the measure of less pleasure, or satisfaction of any kind, to a rich man than to a poor one' (2009: 16). As an aside, this has potentially egalitarian implications. 'Taking it for granted that a more equal distribution of wealth is to be desired, how far would this justify changes in the institutions of property, or limitation of free enterprise even when they would be likely to diminish the aggregate wealth?' (2009: 34). Marshall's answer is predictably conservative. We are reassured 'that economics deals mainly with events where things are in equal proportions (2009: 17) and that politically 'it is the part of responsible men to proceed cautiously and tentatively in abnegating or modifying even such rights as may seem inappropriate to the ideal conditions of social life' (2009: 40). Meanwhile Marshall hurtles over the conceptual precipice. His theory purports to explain prices in terms of subjective marginal utility but recognises that the money in which prices are measured itself varies in utility between individuals. Everything collapses into indeterminacy and circularity. Utility determines value and price, which can then be blithely assumed an adequate proxy for utility. Marshall simply affirms that any difficulties can be 'set aside during the first stages of an enquiry into existing economic conditions' (2009: 391). The explicit extension of marginalist thinking to money and interest rates by Fisher (1907), and what Keynes made of this, will be deferred until Chapter 8.

The extension of the same simple marginalist logic to labour and labour markets is also profoundly problematic. For marginalists, firms employ workers, just as they would capital equipment or raw materials, up to the point where it becomes unprofitable to do so. Similarly, workers work just so long as their pay accurately compensates their sacrifice. For Jevons, '[e]ach labourer must be regarded, like each landowner and each capitalist, as bringing into the common stock one part of the component elements, bargaining for the best share of the produce which the conditions of the market allow him to claim successfully' (1957: xliv). The disutility of work, and the sacrifice of the utility of leisure, are overcome by the utilities of the commodities bought with money wages.

Here it should be acknowledged that Jevons initially says something more complex than most subsequent marginalists. His original formulation assumes that wage increases bring declining marginal utility, as would be expected. But the (dis)utility of work is more complicated. Jevons suggests that the labour supply is unlike other commodities. 'A few hours' work per day may be considered agreeable rather than otherwise; but so soon as the overflowing energy of the body is drained off, it becomes irksome to remain at work' (1957: 171). So Jevons depicts a positive utility for a limited amount of work and negative utilities only above a certain level. He does not discuss the implications of this and later writes, 'I have expressed a feeling in more than one place that the whole theory might probably have been put in a more general form by treating labour as a negative utility, and thus bringing it under the ordinary equations of exchange' (1957: xiv). Perhaps not too much hangs on the peculiar shape of Jevons's depiction of the pleasures and pains of work or his nineteenth-century cod-psychology, but it provides an early warning not to expect people to behave like inanimate commodities. Conversely, as Polanyi writes, if it lives up to its responsibilities to behave like a commodity, labour 'will refuse to sell below the price which the buyer can still afford to pay. Consistently followed up, this means that the chief obligation of labor is to be almost continuously on strike' (2001: 239). In any case, and back to Jevons, the point where this negative utility equals the positive utility of the wage then determines the amount of work. 'As long as he gains, he labours, and when he ceases to gain, he ceases to labour' (1957: 177). We are reassured that '[e]very labourer ultimately receives the due value of his produce after paying a proper fraction to the capitalist for the remuneration of abstinence and risk' (1957: 273). Workers have a free choice whether and for how long to work, and Say's Law brings labour-market supply and demand into equilibrium. Voluntary unemployment becomes an impossibility.

Marshall's system is more cautious than Jevons' and almost always allows qualifications, to the extent it sometimes becomes hard to distinguish the qualifications from the core arguments. Two particularities are worth comment. First, in contrast to Walras and his followers, where in principle everything is evaluated and exchanged simultaneously, in general equilibrium, Marshall's approach was one of partial equilibrium, 'considering one class of society at a time' (2009: 87). This allows partial studies and the solution of 'problems too difficult to be grasped at one effort' (2009: 307). The first-order assumptions, Marshall insists, should not be taken too far, and forces neglected or assumed can then be reintroduced; 'released from the hypothetical slumber that had been imposed upon them' (2009: xiii). So, for example, economic problems are defined in terms of money (2009: 22, 27) but Marshall is aware that non-monetary, including domestic, work can be economically valuable (2009: 47, 61, 67). At least implicitly, Marshall acknowledges his theory's limited scope.

Second, Marshall (2009) also allows that the static, equilibrium approach is in principle only a first approximation. Growth is fostered particularly by saving, but 'progress may he hastened by thought and work; by the application of the principles of Eugenics to the replenishment of the race from its higher rather than its lower strains, and by the appropriate education of the faculties of either sex' (2009: 207). He acknowledges that time 'is a source of great difficulty in economics' (2009: 30). Not least, tastes and evaluations of utility change, potentially increasing rather than decreasing over time. Marshall insists that '[i]t is therefore no exception to the law that the more good music a man hears, the stronger his taste for it is likely to become' (2009: 79). As ever, Marshall pulls back from any deeper interrogation of such insights and insists '[t]he work to be done is so various that much of it must be left to be dealt with by trained common sense, which is the ultimate arbiter in every practical problem' (2009: 32). As Keynes puts it, '[u]nfortunately Marshall, in his anxiety to push economic theory on to the point where it regains contact with the real world, was a little disposed sometimes to camouflage the essentially static character of his equilibrium theory with many wise and penetrating *obiter dicta* on dynamical problems' (2011: volume 2, 406).

Keynes has a somewhat ambiguous relation to his marginalist forbears. Jevons and Marshall both at least implicitly accept Say's Law and the quantity theory, for Keynes the root of so much of the problem, and which questions of time and liquidity preference effectively undermine. He is withering in criticising the complacent satisfaction of assuming a long-run equilibrium, but, assuming a short-run analysis, Keynes avoids rather than addresses questions of dynamic growth. In terms of method, many scholars see Keynes as remaining substantially Marshallian, adopting a similar partial equilibrium approach (de Vroey 2011, Leijonhufvud 2006). Keynes usually thinks in terms of marginal utility as the basis of both consumers' and entrepreneurs' spending, and the *General Theory* will explicitly accept what Keynes calls the 'first classical postulate' that the 'wage is equal to the marginal product of labour' (1973: 5). But Keynes rejects a second postulate that in total, 'the utility of the wage when a given volume of labour is employed is equal to the marginal disutility of that amount of employment' (1973: 5). The labour market does not operate like others. Workers cannot choose their wages and hours of work. Here, as often, his critique is substantially an 'internal' one, showing that the economic mainstream fails even on its own terms (Chick 1983), but this orientation towards orthodoxy gives Keynes's own vision a particular marginalist skew.

Keynes's early work

The Tract on Monetary Reform and after

What follows concentrates on Keynes's two major books on money. The *Tract* was based on articles in the *Manchester Guardian* and, not being written exclusively for an academic audience, is a much easier book than either the *Treatise* or the *General Theory*, but it says some important things and makes some important anticipations of Keynes's later innovations. In many ways, Keynes's outlook in the *Tract* remains orthodox and there is little sense here that his recent work on probability impinges on his economics. Much of his understanding of what money is and of what money does remains conventional. Friedman would accordingly see this as Keynes's best book (Dimand 2019b). It is already possible, however, to see Keynes pushing against some orthodox assumptions and conclusions.

Keynes argues that mathematically the quantity theory identity 'is fundamental. Its correspondence with fact is not open to question' (1923: 61). He is insisting that logically it must be true but continues that this does not imply a straightforward relation between dependent and independent variables. A change in the quantity of money does not mechanically change prices. It is in this context that Keynes offers one of his best-known aphorisms:

> In the long run we are all dead. Economists set themselves too easy, too useless a task if in tempestuous seasons they can only tell us that when the storm is long past the ocean is flat again. (1923: 65)

The market economy works through changes in prices and this requires that prices can potentially have considerable economic impacts.

In particular, price changes redistribute income. Inflation even constitutes a form of progressive taxation. 'The burden of the tax is well spread, cannot be evaded, costs nothing to collect, and falls, in a rough sort of way, in proportion to the wealth of the victim' (1923: 39). The rich have more savings, the poor greater debts, which are reduced by inflation. This was the time of the German hyperinflation, and Keynes still feared inflation as a threat to capitalism's existence (Clarke, S. 1988). Deflation, however, represented a neglected danger. Falling prices, and fear of falling prices, 'injures the entrepreneurs' and 'a general fear of falling prices may inhibit the productive process altogether' (Keynes 1923: 34). As so often, Keynes advocates moderation.

> Of the two perhaps deflation is, if we rule out exaggerated inflations such as that of Germany, the worse; because it is worse, in an impoverished world, to provoke unemployment than to disappoint the rentier. But it is not necessary

that we should weigh one evil against the other. It is easier to agree that both are evils to be shunned. (1923: 36)

Already, states can and should intervene to good effect. Keynes discusses the need for stable monetary policy if 'we are to continue to draw the voluntary savings of the community into "investment"' (1923: 16). The need for price stability also implies the need for countercyclical government intervention. '[T]he time to deflate the supply of cash is when real balances are falling, i.e. when prices are rising out of proportion to the increase, if any, in the volume of cash, and that the time to inflate the supply of cash is when real balances are rising, and not, as seems to be our present practice, the other way round' (1923: 149). This need, Keynes concludes with his usual optimism, makes a managed currency 'inevitable', albeit he remains unwilling to entrust this management to a single authority and it becomes 'doubtful whether the bank rate by itself is always a powerful enough instrument' (1923: 68).

Keynes also identifies vested interests which might win policies against the national good. 'Small savers' and 'the entrepreneur class' together 'will generally bring it about that a country will prefer the inequitable and disastrous course of currency depreciation to the scientific deliberation of a [capital] levy' (1923: 55). Workers also have some agency; wages are not narrowly fixed, either at some subsistence minimum or by market forces. Amongst other things, it is possible for wages to rise, undermining profits (1923: 26).

Throughout the *Tract*, as in all his major works except the *General Theory*, Keynes is also concerned with the interplay of international and domestic relations (Flanders 2019). A key theme is the tension between exchange-rate stability and internal price stability. As usual, Keynes puts domestic priorities first. He even suggests that much-criticised fourteenth-century debasements of Edward III might be judged 'with a more tolerant eye if we regard them as a method of carrying into effect a preference for stability of internal prices over external exchanges' (1923: 131). The book appeared in the context of a post-WWI economy where Britain had not yet returned to gold but had followed policies keeping the pound close to the pre-war parity with the US dollar, which had remained on the gold standard. British competitiveness continued to decline, relative to the US, where productivity rose more quickly, and relative to other European countries, notably France, where governments encouraged currency values to fall. The *Tract* accordingly concentrated its fire on a 'frontal attack on one of the most deeply rooted and awe-inspiring pillars of the modern world – the gold standard' (Hansen 1953: 5).

Gold had appeared to provide stability in the late nineteenth century and might yet provide the 'best working compromise available', but this should not be mistaken for, or preferred to, 'a more scientific standard' (Keynes 1923: 132). Gold's nineteenth-century success was largely predicated on the wisdom of British legislators, while in the twentieth century the Federal Reserve was struggling to free itself from the 'barbarous relic' which gold had become and from 'the pressure of sectoral interest: but we are not yet certain it will wholly succeed' (1923: 138, 140). Keynes emphasises that there is nothing essentially stable about gold. New discoveries (and releases of gold from central banks) could reduce gold's price or produce a general inflation. Difficulties obtaining gold relative to increased general production and demand for money could now push its price upwards. It was not as if 'providence watched over gold, or [as] if Nature had provided us with a stable standard ready-made' (1923: 136). Instead, 'gold now stands at an "artificial" value, the future course of which depends almost exclusively on the policy of the Federal Reserve Board of the United States' (1923: 134). There is no 'invisible hand' proceeding to socially optimal outcomes.

The *Tract* was an insightful and polemical rather than a theoretical text. It consolidated Keynes's popular rather than academic reputation. At the same time, methodologically it remained substantially orthodox. By the middle of the decade, Keynes was embarked on a thoroughly and deliberately scholarly work, taking further steps away from convention.

A Treatise on Money

The *Treatise* is a huge and difficult book, leavened by some passages that are less abstractly theoretical than the *General Theory*. It does not yet directly take aim at Say's Law or rediscover Malthus as the basis for understanding effective demand (Brandis 1985). In at least two important related respects, however, it is a more radical departure from mainstream economics than the *General Theory*. First, Keynes takes a heretical position, which he will abandon, that savings and investment need not be equal. Second, the *Treatise* is based on an analysis of disequilibria rather than equilibrium.

To explain the heresy of the *Treatise* – that saving and investment need not be identical – it is worth beginning by saying why they might be thought equal. To get ahead of Keynes's own story, the *General Theory* provides a straightforward statement. A country's total income can be understood in terms of two components: that which is spent on investment and that which is consumed. Alternatively, income can be divided into two components: that which is saved and that which is consumed. So investment and saving are identical (Keynes 1973: 63).

In this, as Keynes would repeatedly insist, the *General Theory* reverted to orthodoxy, against his earlier view and those of several contemporaries. The *Treatise*'s argument is worth briefly sketching. Saving and investment decisions are 'taken by two different sets of people influenced by different sets of motives' (2011: volume 1, 279). Keynes professes an attachment to what he calls the common-sense wisdom, which seems sufficient to make a case that there can be saving without investment. 'That saving can occur without any corresponding investment is obvious, if we consider what happens when an individual refrains from spending his money-income on consumption' (2011: volume 1, 173). '[I]t should be obvious that mere abstinence is not enough by itself to build cities or drain fens' (2011: volume 2, 148). Nor can changes in any inclination to save explain patterns of investment, and 'the rate at which the world's wealth has accumulated has been far more variable than habits of thrift have been' (2011: volume 2, 149). Instead, the key is enterprise and profit. 'It is enterprise which builds and improves the world's possessions' (2011: volume 2, 148). 'If Enterprise is afoot, wealth accumulates whatever may be happening to Thrift' (2011: volume 2, 149). Warming to his theme, Keynes asks: '[w]ere the Seven Wonders of the World built by Thrift? I deem it doubtful' (2011: volume 2, 150). It appears entirely possible for there to be savings without these being directed towards investment, either today or tomorrow. 'Moreover, the evil is cumulative. For savings in excess of investment are wasted and do not materialise in any *net* increase to the wealth of the world' (2011: volume 2, 206). Saving can occur without investment. Conversely, it is entirely possible, at least in the short term, for there to be 'investment in excess of savings' (2011: volume 2, 164).

The vision becomes one of instability, highlighted by Keynes's famous 'illustration' of what he sees as the follies of thrift. Imagine a community only producing and eating bananas (2011: volume 1: 176–7). A thrift campaign leaves the same number of bananas with fewer buyers, causing the price to fall. Now all the bananas are sold but at a reduced price. The consumers buy the same number of bananas for less and the banana sellers experience losses. The banana entrepreneurs must now reduce employment or cut wages. Either way, the spending power of the public is reduced. But so long as that public continues to save in excess of (the now falling) investment, the process will be repeated and the growers continue to make losses. In this parable, the decline in output does not change the rate of excess of saving over investment, so there is no equilibrating force (Patinkin 1987: 26). Short of general starvation, the abandonment of the thrift campaign, or some alternative or exogenous stimulus, 'there will be no equilibrium position' (Keynes 2011 [1930]: volume 1, 178).

By insisting that saving and investment need not be equal, Keynes rejects the orthodox claim of adjustment by means of the interest rate. Say's Law had high interest rates stimulating saving and thence investment. A natural rate of interest achieved a stable equilibrium. Instead, for Keynes there is something closer to an inverse relationship and 'what stimulates one retards the other' (2011: volume 1, 264). This involves a key Keynesian claim. Money is not neutral.

Money is, of course, the book's central theme. Money and finance are reckoned analytically and economically primary. Profits (and losses) and the gap between savings and investment appear specifically as a result of monetary phenomena. Conventional wisdom sees money as primarily, if not only, a medium of exchange. 'But if this is all, we have scarcely emerged from the stage of Barter' (2011: volume 1, 3). Keynes instead begins the *Treatise* by insisting on the prime role of 'Money-of-Account; money as that in which Debts and Prices and General Purchasing Power are *expressed*' (2011: volume 1, 3). There are important variables in the supply of and demand for money, in 'the behaviour of the banking system … the cost of investment (so far as the purchasing power of money is concerned) and the value of investment … the emergence of profit and loss … the rate of remuneration offered by the entrepreneurs to the factors of production' (2011: volume 1, 182).

Money is itself a creature of the state rather than the market. With characteristic hyperbole, for at least the last 4000 years, money has been state money. 'To-day all civilised money is, beyond the possibility of dispute, chartalist' (2011: volume 1, 5). Keynes depicts four kinds of money: commodity, things like gold and silver coins; representative money, state money being backed by some 'objective' standard as when countries are on the 'gold standard'; pure fiat money without even a nominal commodity base; and bank money, which is merely an acknowledgement of debt, except in as far it is joined with state money (2011: volume 1, 9). Only the first three are 'money-proper' (2011: volume 1, 15) although the distinction proves hard to sustain and Keynes later recalls that banks issue cheque books and that an unused overdraft facility is a 'Cash Facility, in the fullest sense of the term' (2001: volume 2, 43). Keynes is well aware of, and had earlier expressed some sympathy towards, Innes's credit theory of money (CWXI: 465). The relation between credit and money and different monetary forms still generates controversy. Here, however, Keynes downplays any private money creation, and the slightly convoluted typography supports the simple conclusion that the state is central to monetary management.

States can intervene, controlling the supply of money, with this having profound effects but in complex relation with the market economy. It was not possible for monetary authorities to change prices merely by changing the amount of money. Although Keynes again accepts the Fisher quantity equation as a truism (2011: volume 1, 233, volume 2, 5), it is 'ill adapted' for treating 'the problem dynamically ... to exhibit the causal process by which the price-level is determined, and the method of transition from one position to another' (2011: volume 1, 133). Keynes argues that 'the price-level can be affected just as much by the decisions of the depositors to vary the amounts of real-balances which they ... keep, as by the decisions of the bankers to vary the amounts of money-balances which they ... create'. (2011: volume 1, 228). Money could be hoarded, implying that there is no single velocity of circulation. Keynes goes on to develop what he calls 'fundamental equations' purporting to explain complex sets of interactions between changes in money supply and demand for money from various sources. Amongst other things, cash in the hands of workers and income deposits in banks also have different effects to savings deposits. As in the *Tract*, 'a change in the available "counters", which does not affect everyone's holding equally (and in practice such changes never do), may have a fairly large lasting effect on relative price-levels' (2011: volume 1, 92). Price changes matter.

Similarly, while Keynes, following Wicksell, accepts the idea that there is a 'natural rate of interest', 'the rate which actually prevails [is] the *market-rate* of interest' (2011: volume 1, 154). The two may be very different, with changes unlikely to produce smooth aggregate adjustments as economic orthodoxy predicts. Effective interest rates are the resultant of complex interactions of multiple short- and long-term rates (de Carvalho 1996). There is no assumption of stability. Indeed, alternations in the terms of lending are at least usually the initiating variable in economic turbulence (2011: volume 1, 158). Slightly later, Keynes goes further to maintain that '[b]ooms and slumps are simply the expression of the results of an oscillation of the terms of credit about their equilibrium position' (2011: volume 1, 184). Such volatility, however, is not simply a 'bad thing'. Changing the monetary rate of interest also redistributes, with broader economic consequences. The difference between the market and natural rate can induce a 'Profit Inflation', which is the path to economic expansion:

> [S]o long as the money-rate of interest is held at such a level that the value of Investment exceeds Saving, there will be a rise in the price-level of output as a whole above its cost of production, which in turn will stimulate entrepreneurs to bid up the rates of earnings above their previous level. (2011: volume 1, 198)

Thus, '[a] fall in the rate of interest stimulates the production of capital goods not because it decreases their cost of production but because it increases their demand-price' (2011: volume 1, 211). Conversely, a rise in market rate of interest upsets the balance between investment and saving so that the price of capital goods falls (2011: volume 1, 201, 203). The rate of discount is the 'governor of the whole system'. Only this is 'subject to the will and *fiat* of the central authority', and only through this can it 'influence the rate of investment' (2011: volume 2, 211). A high bank rate will promote unemployment 'until the bank-rate is reversed or, by a chance, something happens to alter the natural-rate' (2011: volume 1, 206). Thus, 'on my theory, it is a large volume of saving which does not lead to a correspondingly large volume of investment (not one which does) which is the root of the trouble' (2011: volume 1, 179). Saving need not induce investment.

Fortunately, investments, not savings, are the economic drivers (2011: volume 1, 280). 'If entrepreneurs choose to spend a portion of their profits on consumption ... the effect is to increase the profit on the sale of liquid consumption goods by an amount exactly equal to the amount of profits which have been thus expended' (2011: volume 1, 139). Therefore, 'however much of their profits entrepreneurs spend on consumption, the increment of wealth belonging to entrepreneurs remains the same as before. Thus profits, as a source of capital increment for entrepreneurs, are a widow's cruse which remains undepleted however much of them may be devoted to riotous living' (2011: volume 1, 139). The 'cruse', or pot, refers to a biblical story in which God replenishes a poor widow's supplies of meal and oil. The parable here inverts the paradox of thrift but seems to assume full employment and something suspiciously like Say's Law.

Keynes later appears to qualify such conclusions, reintroducing the concept of unproductive consumption that he finds in Malthus. This is 'consumption which could be forgone by the consumer without reacting on the amount of his productive effort' (2011: volume 2, 125). A community then faces two sets of decisions: first, between investment and consumption; second, about what proportion should be consumed productively. Keynes argues that it is this second decision on which 'employment and unemployment depend', and that this requires a redistribution not a reduction of aggregate consumption (2011: volume 2, 126). Keynes does not provide much detail here but the implication is that a higher proportion of the income of the rich is likely to be wasted unproductively.

The depictions of investment as the economic driver, the re-emphasis on questions of distribution, and the distinction between the productive and unproductive can sound almost Marxist. But Keynes's understanding of profit is very different to that of Marx and to how it appears in a corporate balance sheets. This might not be immediately obvious from a definition as 'the difference between the cost of production of the current output and its actual sale-proceeds' (2011: volume 1, 123). But, as in Marshall, 'costs' are understood to include entrepreneurs' 'normal remuneration' (2011: volume 1, 125). Profits are zero 'in the usual condition in the actual economic world of to-day and for the equilibrium of the purchasing power of money' (2011: volume 1, 156). Profits only occur where there is a stimulus to increase production. With little sense of his earlier Burkean warnings about future uncertainties, Keynes then justifies increased profits in moral terms by a trickle-down effect, so that 'if we consider a long period of time, the working class may benefit far more in the long run from the forced abstinence which a Profit Inflation imposes on them than they lose in the first instance' (2011: volume 2, 162). Therefore, 'so long as wealth and its fruits are not consumed by the nominal owner but are accumulated, the evils of an unjust distribution may not be so great as they appear' (2011: volume 2, 163). As above, Keynes also makes clear that the remuneration of the factors of production comes last in the analytical story but that reducing wages to increase profits may be advisable.

The *Treatise*'s second volume also becomes more concrete, especially as it turns to international questions. The British authorities, in particular, had become adept at controlling the interest rate and the volume of cash in circulation (2011: volume 2, 225–31), but substantial difficulties potentially arise in managing national money in an international system. The *Treatise* was completed and published soon after the Wall Street crash and was able to articulate how international imbalances contributed to that debacle.

Keynes was again sceptical of claims that Britain's pre-war success was based on the gold standard and free trade rather than 'the transitory peculiarities of her position' (2011: volume 2, 307). The gold standard was itself a managed system, 'representative money', not an automatic self-equilibrating mechanism, and its use was double edged. It provided for uniformity and 'prevents individual follies and eccentricities' but 'hampers each Central Bank in tackling its own national problems, interferes with pioneer improvements in policy the wisdom of which is ahead of average wisdom' (2011: volume 2, 286). At the same time, 'by the complexity it introduces and its lack of central direction it multiplies disturbances of intermediate magnitude' (2011: volume 2, 287). Keynes now accepts that, pragmatically, a system based on gold is probably the best solution, but he doubts it will last for long (2011: volume 2, 389).

> This, then, is the dilemma of an international monetary system – to preserve the advantages of the stability of the local currencies of the various members of the system in terms of the international standard, and to preserve at the same time an adequate local autonomy for each member over its domestic rate of interest and its volume of foreign lending. (2011: volume 2, 304)

If money can flow freely between countries, the lower rates of interest necessary to maintain investment in an old country like Britain will see an increase in foreign lending, exacerbating the relative decline. Workers cannot benefit from 'capital accumulation, in the shape of higher wages, ahead of the workers in the rest of the world, except in so far as there is a drag on foreign lending' (2011: volume 2, 313). 'Credit is like water; – whilst it may be used for a multiplicity of purposes, it is in itself undifferentiated, can drip through crannies, and will remorselessly seek its own level over the whole field unless the parts of the field are rendered uncompromisingly water-tight' (2011: volume 2, 319). In practice, as money was likely to flow abroad, '[i]t may be a choice between employing labour to create capital wealth, which will yield less than the market-rate of interest, or not employing it at all. If this is the position, the national interest, both immediate and prospective, will be promoted by choosing the first alternative' (2011: volume 2, 376). Keynes accordingly advocates restrictions on capital movements and public works at home but also international cooperation and a supernational bank.

The *Treatise* said much more than it is possible to summarise here. It was wide ranging and ambitious, skirmishing against mainstream economics on many fronts. It failed to convince most critics and Keynes himself was unsatisfied with it, soon developing the different, and in many ways narrower, attack that would become the *General Theory*.

Conclusions

Keynes was trained by Marshall and understood economics in both its strengths and weaknesses in fundamentally Marshallian terms. By his own acknowledgement, prior to the *General Theory*, Keynes worked within the classical tradition as he redefined it. So although he mentions earlier work, both his criticisms and his innovations substantially develop from with the tradition of Marshallian marginalism. Chapter 2 described Keynes's worldview as substantially individualist and idealist, and his moderately conservative politics sought to reform not to overthrow the system which marginalism rationalised. Its 'internal' character nevertheless lends Keynes's critique particular power. Once time and money are taken seriously, in individualist, marginalist terms, the assumptions of the quantity theory and Say's Law collapse. Even accepting that individuals act in their own self-interest, it is a fallacy of composition to see this as automatically producing socially optimal outcomes. Keynes can reinforce this internal critique by drawing on earlier ideas, particularly of economic aggregates. Accepting a chartalist view of money, the state cannot be left out of economic analysis. At the same time, Keynes's critique is limited. He never engages systematically with the (pre)classical tradition, or with other unorthodox economic thinkers. Even as he attempts to develop a dynamic analysis in the *Treatise*, he ignores what his classical forebears, particularly Marx, or contemporaries like Myrdal had to say about power and production. As the next chapter will argue, many of the same themes recur in the *General Theory*, which also displays similar strengths and an even more powerful critique of the marginalist mainstream, but again an internal critique, undermining Keynes's claims to have developed a *general* theory.

Note

1   There is some anachronism in that my reading of Jevons is from the final fifth edition, from 1957, and of Marshall from the final eighth edition, from 1920, both of which long post-date Keynes's initial encounters.

5

Keynes's *General Theory*

Introduction

Keynes's *General Theory of Employment, Interest and Money* is a notoriously difficult book, which this chapter tries to explain as simply as possible. Keynes could be a great stylist and the *General Theory's* many quotable passages have enhanced its appeal. Elsewhere, however, Keynes's prose is dense and the arguments highly technical and convoluted. Sympathetic critics give a flavour of the difficulty. Heilbroner says the book has 'a forbidding title … and a still more forbidding interior' (1999: 269). De Vroey and Hoover see it as 'elegant, but not always transparent' (2004: 3). For Minsky it is 'a very clumsy statement' (2008: 12). Shackle bemoans its 'passages of tortuous complexity' (1972: 209). In contrast to other great works of political economy like Smith's *Wealth of Nations* or Marx's *Capital*, the *General Theory* was never meant to be understood by non-specialists. It assumes knowledge of the economic orthodoxy of the day, summarised in the previous chapter here but which had often become highly abstract and specialised, where not plain ridiculous. Keynes does avoid the mathematical formalism which pervades an account like that of Pigou (1933), one of his immediate adversaries, and which would come to dominate modern mainstream economics even more brutally. But Keynes professes little patience with other economists' difficulties, reminding Robertson that the *General Theory* was 'a purely theoretical work, *not* a collection of wisecracks' (CWXIII: 518).

The difficulties of comprehension appear to be confirmed in the way the *General Theory* has been subject to widely different interpretations. Keynes stresses his own revolutionary accomplishment (e.g. CWXIII. 192), and Davidson (2009) agrees that Keynes provides a fundamental rethinking of economics and perhaps of social theory in general. Similarly, for Varoufakis and his co-authors:

> Keynes went beyond even the most radical outsiders' criticisms. Keynes, unencumbered by the ideological baggage of radicals such as Friedrich

Engels, Lenin and Rosa Luxemburg ... was free as a bird to pick his own flight of fancy in search of insights into what on earth was going on. (Varoufakis et al. 2011: 204)

Others, including sympathetic followers, see the *General Theory*'s achievement as more modest. Lawlor (2006) sees it as formalising more adequately what might already have been derived from Marshall. For Dow, 'Keynes's approach was to demonstrate the minimum changes to orthodox assumptions which would generate a result of persistent unemployment which would not be eradicated by market forces' (Dow 1996: 63). Keynes accomplishes this demonstration of unemployment equilibrium, according to Dowd, by deviating from the neo-classicals 'with respect to only one assumption: that savings are a function of the rate of interest' (2004: 127–8).

In keeping with Keynes's own style for setting up his arguments as a middle path between unacceptable alternatives (O'Donnell 1989), what follows steers between the more radical and conservative interpretations. The *General Theory* provides a substantial critique of standard economics but it does this by engaging with mainstream economics on its own terms, and this qualifies claims of Keynes's radicalism. Subsequent chapters here go further in developing a constructive critique of what is useful and of the limits of Keynes's analysis. This chapter remains largely expositional, but it should already be clear that it offers only one of many interpretations. It cannot avoid simplifying some complex and contested arguments.

As if to highlight the simplification, the next section begins with a four-line summary of the *General Theory*'s argument, written by Harrod in 1935, and the chapter uses this as a framing device for the subsequent sections on savings and consumption, on money and the rate of interest, and on investment and employment. There follows a brief general discussion of how Keynes's vision leads to the prospect of 'unemployment equilibrium' and the possibility of state intervention to ameliorate this. A final substantive section discusses dynamic change, cycles and long-term tendencies, into which it suggests the *General Theory* provides important but subsidiary insights.

A very brief outline of the *General Theory*'s significant variables and relationships

Conflicting interpretations of the *General Theory* emerged even before the book was published. Keynes sent drafts to several friends and colleagues, with whom he becomes increasingly annoyed, amongst other things accusing Robertson and Hawtrey of not understanding what he was trying to do.

He made the same frustrated accusation to Harrod, who replies depicting Keynes's argument in terms of seven variables which together determine the level of employment. Figure 5.1 arranges this summary as a flow diagram in the style of what Sheehan (2009) labels a 'causal map'. Keynes replies to Harrod by saying: 'I absolve you completely of misunderstanding my theory. It could not be better stated' (CWXIII: 557). This is therefore accepted as a useful simplification. It is a huge simplification but, unlike so many subsequent readings, Harrod's summary is at least one which Keynes himself explicitly endorses.

The *General Theory* (Keynes 1973: 245) affirms the same independent and dependent variables, with just a slight change of phrasing. It emphasises consumption rather than saving (the two seen as simple alternatives, as will be discussed below) and finally it equates employment with national income. The following sections look at the independent variables in more detail, but it is worth a few preliminary comments on the overall schema and the interactions involved in this 'first approximation' (Coddington 1983: 20).

First, note that all arrows lead to employment and that it is on this which national income depends. The more people there are working, the more output, the more wealth. Employment and national income, for Keynes, are the 'dependent variables'. In saying this, Keynes is challenging the way mainstream economics is defined in terms of exchange relations and simply assumes 'a given value of employed resources' (Keynes 1973: 4).

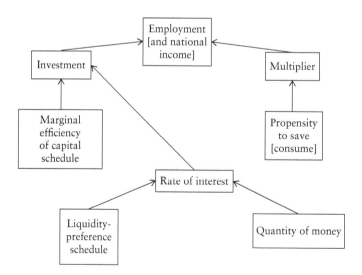

Figure 5.1 A schematic presentation of the *General Theory* argument (after Harrod, in Keynes CWXIII: 553, and Sheehan 2009).

For Keynes, classical theory is therefore really 'best regarded as a theory of distribution in conditions of full employment' (1973: 16). This is non-sense. Everyone knows that in practice employment and national income vary. Unemployment is a horrible persistent reality. 'It may well be that the classical theory represents the way in which we should like our economy to behave. But to assume that it actually does so is to assume our difficulties away' (1973: 34). Unemployment needs to be explained, not explained away as an unfortunate anomaly. Equally ridiculous, the mainstream theory assumes that the dependent variables are constant while allowing the factors which determine them to vary. For example, Keynes insists, we cannot 'assume at the same time that income is constant and that the propensity to save and the schedule of the marginal efficiency of capital are variable' (CWXIII: 559). Instead of assuming that everything is already in harmonious equilibrium at full employment, Keynes sets himself the task of investigating what determines the actual level of employment and output.

Second, all the arrows point only in this one direction. One thing causes another. Taken literally, the model has far more causal determinism than anything Marxists would dare. The ultimate determinants, the marginal efficiency of capital, the propensity to consume, liquidity preference and the money supply appear to be independent, at least of any other economic variables within the model. Keynes describes them as 'independent in the sense that their values cannot be inferred from one another' (1973: 184). He insists, for example, that 'one of my main points is precisely that changes in the propensity to spend are in themselves ... wholly and of logical necessity irrelevant to liquidity preference' (CWXIII: 515). Here Keynes seems to be saying that there is no link between the propensity to save and the interest rate, and this opens him to criticisms which will be discussed in Chapter 8. As will be discussed below, the marginal efficiency of capital is all about expectations of future returns, which themselves depend on the state of the market, so one might also wonder why there is no link between this and the propensity to consume (Alexander 1940). Later, Keynes does acknowledge complexity and a practical mutual independence. 'The division of the determinants of the economic system into the two groups of given factors and independent variables is, of course, quite arbitrary from any absolute standpoint. The division must be made entirely on the basis of experience' (Keynes 1973: 247). But Keynes rejects the standard practice (then and now) of bundling everything into simultaneous equations. It is more useful and more honest instead to declare conceptual priorities, even if only provisionally as a 'first-order' approximation, in line with common practice in 'ordinary discourse' where 'we keep "at the back of our heads" the necessary reserves and qualifications' (1973: 297, Kicillof 2018, Marshall 2009).

Of course, this leaves scope for endless controversy. How important are the reserves and qualifications? How well established are the priorities?

Third, an important element of Keynes's argument, which Figure 5.1 does not make clear, is that he insists that savings and investment are equal. By definition, they are the same. As mentioned in the previous chapter, his argument for this is simple. Total income can be understood as being divided into two parts: that which is invested and that which is consumed. But total income can also be divided into that which is saved and that which is consumed. So investment and saving are identical.

> I regard them as being merely different names for the same phenomenon looked at from different points of view. Saving is a name given to a certain quantity looked at as the excess of income over consumption. Investment is the name given to the same quantity regarded as the constituent of income other than consumption. (CWXIII: 551)

Any apparent discrepancy between saving and investment is the result of an 'optical illusion due to regarding an individual depositor's relation to his bank as being a one-sided transaction' (1973: 81). Of course, individuals may save or invest different amounts, but for the whole economy they must be identical. Keynes insists that in maintaining this identity he is being orthodox. What he regards as 'the classical school proper has accepted the view that they are equal' (1973: 177). 'All the classical economists, including in particular Marshall and Pigou, have always held precisely the view that I hold, that savings and investment are necessarily and at all times equal. There is no difference between us on this heading' (CWXIV: 15). The insistence on the identity of investment and savings contrasts with arguments of potential divergence made by some of Keynes's contemporaries like Robertson and that are crucial to Keynes's own arguments in the *Treatise on Money* and to several later readings of Keynesian economics (Mattick 1971, Heilbroner 1999, Harman 2009). The identity means that in Figure 5.1 it might be more accurate to bring together the boxes for investment and the propensity to save. They are at least unbreakably linked.

Fourth, Keynes's challenge to orthodoxy instead now involves a conceptual downgrading of savings and investment. Once again: 'Savings and investment are the determinates of the system, not the determinants. They are the twin results of the system's determinants, namely, the propensity to consume, the schedule of the marginal efficiency of capital and the rate of interest' (1973: 183). Notably, and in sharp contrast to conventional economic thinking, no arrows in Figure 5.1 run from consumption, savings or investment to the rate of interest. It is worth briefly reflecting on how this already means rejecting Say's Law, the suggestion that all markets, including labour markets, 'clear' perfectly and that unemployment is an impossibility.

As discussed in Chapter 4, even mainstream writers could be quite cautious and their acceptance of Say's Law could be implied rather than explicit. However, they continued to operate at least 'as if' unemployment was an impossibility, with savings and investment being brought into balance through changes in the interest rate. For Keynes, as above, savings and investment are already exactly equal. There is no such equilibrating mechanism. Amongst other things, the rate of interest does not have a straightforward relation with savings and consumption. 'It has long been recognised … that the total effect of changes in the rate of interest on the readiness to spend on present consumption is complex and uncertain, being dependent on conflicting tendencies' (1973: 93). Indeed 'the short-period influence of the rate of interest on individual spending out of a given income is secondary and relatively unimportant' (1973: 94). In particular, as discussed below, for Keynes the rate of interest and thence investment is determined not (or at least not simply) by decisions to consume or save but by liquidity preference and the supply of money from the central bank. This means that money is not 'neutral', in the jargon: it does not automatically bring supply and demand into line at an optimum level. What people do with money, notably in terms of valuing it for itself, has impacts on the wider economy. There may be equilibrium with full employment. Or there may not. Keynes stresses that his prefix 'general' is used to distinguish his theory from the classical assumption of market clearing and full employment, which is 'applicable to a special case only' (1973: 3). The greater generality means that what the 'classics' regarded as anomalies, particularly the persistence of unemployment, were things that had to be integrated into the theory.

Fifth, Keynes is concerned with aggregates. He is thinking in 'macro' terms. This provides a second sense in which his theory is general (1973: xxii). Aggregates matter in a way not (fully) appreciated by the economic orthodoxy. The invisible hand, channelling self-interested individualism into economic and social gain, should disappear from analysis as surely as it is absent from real life (O'Donnell 1989). Therefore, although in many respects Keynes remains the loyal student of Marshall, he cannot wholly accept a partial equilibrium approach because it requires implausible assumptions that particulars do not influence the whole (Chick 1983: 14). There is an ineliminable 'composite character of Keynes's argument' (Milgate 1987: 44). As discussed in Chapter 2, Keynes often stresses organic wholes and the need to recognise interdependence (1973: 297, CWXIV: 11–12). An important practical implication is that it is insufficient to sum the rational self-interest of each individual to obtain maximum social welfare. For example, Keynes argues:

> The rise in the rate of interest might induce us to save more, if our incomes
> were unchanged. But if the higher rate of interest retards investment, our
> incomes will not, and cannot, be unchanged. They must necessarily fall until
> the declining capacity to save has sufficiently offset the stimulus to save given
> by the higher rate of interest. The more virtuous we are, the more determinedly
> thrifty, the more obstinately orthodox in our national and personal finance,
> the more our incomes will have to fall when interest rises or long-term expect-
> ation continues adverse. (CWXIII: 449, see also 1973: 111)

Amongst other things, instead of supply creating its own demand, real
competition means 'producers want cheap labour but rich consumers. The
balance is struck at the point of effective demand' (Chick 1983: 109). Wage
cuts, good for any individual employer, might undermine consumption and
be bad for the system as a whole.

Sixth, most of the *General Theory* substantially shares with the mainstream a static or stationary approach, which depicts the economy in
equilibrium terms. There are a couple of chapters that suggest something
more dynamic, and questions of volatility and long-term change will be
discussed below. But most the *General Theory* provides a 'snap-shot' of
what Keynes is well aware is really a dynamic system. The first eighteen
chapters, according to Kregel, rely on a model of 'stationary equilibrium'. In
doing this, Keynes seeks to separate the slowly changing factors from those
with a more immediate impact on the particular questions he addresses. So
the variables that Keynes posits as 'givens' are not necessarily assumed to
be 'constant' (Kregel 1976: 218) and would not be constant if reconceived
over a longer period. But for the most part, Keynes does share conventional
assumptions of 'a given state of technique, resources and costs' (1973: 23).
These factors are therefore put beyond the scope of analysis. There is an
implicit time dimension, in that expectations of the future enter into present calculations, but there is little sense of how the future is predicated
on dynamic, technological change (Kregel 1976). Keynes's approach is
therefore more orthodox than that of other critics, like Marx of course,
but also contemporaries like Myrdal and Lindahl, who try to theorise the
economy in dynamic terms. Keynes insists: 'I'm far more *classical* than the
Swedes, for I am still discussing the conditions of short-period equilibrium'
(CWXIV: 183). Keynes himself later acknowledges the lack of dynamism
in the *General Theory* as a significant shortcoming (CWXIV: 283). When
Shove accuses him of being 'too kind to the "classical" analysis as applied
to the individual industry and firm', Keynes quickly concedes 'you are
probably right' (CWXIV: 1–2). Keynes's short-run equilibrium approach
does at least imply that his theory is somewhat less general than he would
have us believe. In some respects, however, this approach makes Keynes's
challenges to mainstream thinking more telling. He shows that there can be

unemployment equilibrium, even accepting important mainstream premises and a comparative static approach (Moggridge 1976). In particular, Keynes can show that claims that labour markets should 'clear' perfectly, that unemployment is an impossibility, are misplaced even on the mainstream's own terms. Unemployment is not the result of some unfortunate disturbance or cyclical disequilibrium: it is endemic, precisely an equilibrium phenomenon (Tabb 1999).

Finally, before examining Keynes's variables in more detail, it is also worth flagging that given what was just said about most of the analysis being one of equilibrium, Keynes's language can be confusing. Time and again he apparently discusses change, increases or decreases in one or other of his variables. This should be understood as compatible with the static analysis, as identifying (again with standard economic convention) tendencies of particular variables to change in one direction and how this tends to provoke corresponding changes in other variables. (We understand that the ball at the bottom of a well is in stable equilibrium because a 'movement' upwards provokes a counter-acting downward force.) Somewhat similarly, the analysis is simultaneously static but concerned with how what people know, or do not know, about the future impacts on their decisions in the present.

Consumption, saving and the multiplier

Of Keynes's independent variables, the marginal propensity to consume is probably the most straightforward. It is simply defined as 'the functional relationship between [income] ... and expenditure on consumption out of that income' (1973: 90). It is the proportion of income consumed.

For Keynes to posit consumption as an independent variable is itself something of an innovation (Sheehan 2009). There are precedents, notably in the work of the institutional economist Veblen, but as usual Keynes's analysis is shaped by his engagement with orthodoxy. According to neoclassical ideas of utility, people just happen to have particular wants, which they satisfy as best they can on the market, at most weighing present against future utility (Jevons 1957, Fisher 1907). In practice the economic mainstream simplified further, tending to take consumption as the residual of decisions to save (Sheehan 2009). For Keynes, consumption becomes something more complex and less arbitrary. He suggests 'thinking in terms of decisions to consume ... rather than of decisions to save' (1973: 65). Saving 'is no longer the dog but the tail' (Keynes, cited in Skidelsky 1992: 453).

Keynes initially stresses that the propensity to consume, like the attitude to liquidity and the marginal efficiency of capital, is a psychological phenomenon, which lies 'truly within the power of the individual' (1973: 65). He nevertheless begins with a quite lengthy discussion of a range of 'objective' and 'subjective' factors, with a chapter devoted to each of the two types (1973: 91–108).

To take these in order, Keynes begins by describing six 'objective factors' (1973: 89). The first of these refers to changes in workers' 'wage units'. The next three refer to entrepreneurs: to changes in income net of investment, to windfall changes in capital values and to changes in the rate of time discounting. The fifth objective factor is changes in fiscal policy and the sixth '[c]hanges in expectations of the relation between the present and the future level of income' (1973: 95). Exactly why this last is an 'objective' factor, is perhaps unclear, but it is anyway included, says Keynes, only for 'formal completeness'. Here, expectations are thought 'likely to average out for the community as a whole' and are 'a matter about which there is, as a rule, too much uncertainty for it to exert much influence' (1973: 95).

Keynes then elaborates eight subjective motivations 'which lead individuals to refrain from spending'. He summarises these as 'Precaution, Foresight, Calculation, Improvement, Independence, Enterprise, Pride and Avarice' (1973: 108). These are weighed against 'a corresponding list of motives to consume such as … Generosity, Miscalculation, Ostentation and Extravagance' (1973: 108). On top of these individual motivations we have four business motivations. These are '[t]he motive of enterprise … The motive of liquidity … The motive of improvement … [and] The motive of financial prudence and the anxiety to be "on the right side"' (1973: 108–9). This is one of the few places where the *General Theory* explicitly refers to 'corporations' rather than to individual 'entrepreneurs' and stresses institutional rather than private interests. It is also worth noting that 'liquidity' has quietly entered the story here, and as an institutional rather than individual preference, even if this plays little role in the subsequent theory. There would appear to be numerous influences on consumption.

Keynes decides, however, that the subjective factors, tastes and habits, as much as social structures, are 'unlikely to undergo a material change over a short period of time except in abnormal or revolutionary circumstances' (1973: 91). This allows them to be taken as given. The apparently complex consumption variable turns out to vary rather little. Most of the different factors are reckoned to have only trivial impacts, to cancel each other or to be stable in the short term (Lekachman 1967).

The major exception is changes in income and the concomitant changes in the propensity to consume. While still under the heading of 'objective factors', Keynes introduces:

> The fundamental psychological law, upon which we are entitled to depend with great confidence both *a priori* from our knowledge of human nature and from the detailed facts of experience ... that men are disposed, as a rule and on the average, to increase their consumption as their income increases, but not by as much as the increase in their income. (1973: 96)

This famous assertion has provoked much controversy around whether the changes are in absolute or relative terms. Keynes repeatedly insists that his main point, at least, is only that a greater absolute amount will be saved: 'when aggregate income increases, consumption expenditure will also increase but to a somewhat lesser extent. This is a very obvious conclusion' (CWXIV: 120).

At the risk of getting ahead of the descriptive narrative, this simple hypothesis has potentially profound implications for investment, underpinning the influential idea of the multiplier. The idea of cumulative spillovers had 'made sporadic appearances' in the economics of the nineteenth century and reappears in different versions in the 1930s (Laidler 2006: 48, Dimand 2019c). Keynes acknowledges Kahn's (1931) precedence (CWIX: 86–125). The idea is most easily grasped in the way investments in one area also benefit that sector's customers, workers and suppliers, from whom there are further knock-on effects. But if this seems intuitively plausible, it is also obvious that spillovers are not infinite, and Kahn's and Keynes's formalisation addresses this.

The idea can be 'telescoped' into a single moment, compatible with Keynes's static approach by simply recalling that investment is equal to saving and that the marginal propensity to save (or consume) is a definite fraction of income (CWVII: 122, Skidelsky 1992). Using some simple algebra, which can be safely ignored, from the above, the change in consumption (ΔC) can be written as a function (χ) of the change in income (ΔY). This function is less than one, because the point is precisely that not all of the extra income will be consumed.

$$\Delta C = \chi \cdot \Delta Y$$

It was also noted above that Keynes sees aggregate income (Y), as composed of consumption (C) and investment (I). Similarly, any change in aggregate income is composed of the change in consumption and investment.

$$Y = C + I \text{ and}$$
$$\Delta Y = \Delta C + \Delta I$$

We can then rephrase the above by saying that the change in income is equal to the change in income multiplied by the marginal propensity to consume plus the change in investment.

$$\Delta Y = \chi. \Delta Y + \Delta I$$

So now the change in investment is given by the change in income less the change in income multiplied by the propensity to consume.

$$\Delta I = \Delta Y - \chi. \Delta Y$$
$$\Delta I = \Delta Y (1 - \chi)$$

Or, conversely, the change in income is equal to the change in investment divided by the fraction not consumed.

$$\Delta Y = \Delta I / (1 - \chi)$$

This means that the change in income is a definite fraction of the change in investment, and this is greater than one. Therefore 'incomes will necessarily be increased at a rate which will normally *exceed* the rate of increased investment' (1973: 82). For example, if the propensity to consume is a half, income increases by twice the increase in investment. 'But there is always a formula, more or less of this kind, relating the output of consumption goods which it pays to produce to the output of investment goods; and I have given attention to it in my book under the name of the *multiplier*' (CWXIV: 121).

Keynes describes two extremes. If the marginal propensity to consume is near unity, 'small fluctuations in investment will lead to wide fluctuations in employment; but, at the same time, a comparatively small increment of investment will lead to full employment' (Keynes 1973: 118). If it is near zero, fluctuations will be small but large investments would be needed to produce full employment. 'In actual fact', Keynes suggests, 'the marginal propensity to consume seems to lie somewhere between these two extremes ... the worst of both worlds, fluctuations in employment being considerable and, at the same time, the increment in investment required to produce full employment being too great to be easily handled' (1973: 118). Nevertheless, if, somehow, it were possible to increase investment, it would become possible to achieve greater increases in income. The *General Theory* continues with Keynes's famous discussion of 'Pyramid-building, earthquakes, even wars ... digging holes in the ground known as gold mining' (1973: 129).

This immediately suggests that government intervention to stimulate investment can increase the size of the economy. Building 'houses and the like' would be better policy, but even burying bottles stuffed with banknotes 'would be better than nothing' (1973: 129). Keynes's examples come dripping with irony, always a dangerous mode, always liable to mis-interpretation. As Keynes explains to Beveridge, '[y]ou will not, of course, imagine that I am advocating digging holes in the ground. What I advocate is the application of labour to *productive* investment, and, if there were no productive investments left, then I should distribute incomes more equally so as to increase consumption' (CWXIV: 58). The multiplier does, how-ever, identify a logic of increased employment and income on whatever the expenditure is aimed at.

The multiplier undermines crude liberal arguments that government spending would 'crowd out' the private sector. These arguments (impli-citly) assume that full employment already exists. Conversely, the multi-plier assumes some level of unemployment (Mann 2017b), otherwise increased investment would not be able to employ more workers and raise aggregate income. 'Furthermore, if our assumption is correct that the mar-ginal propensity to consume falls off steadily as we approach full employ-ment, it follows that it will become more and more troublesome to secure a further given increase of employment by further increasing investment' (1973: 127). There are questions of degree and of the relative efficacy of any extra spending.

Lekachman (1967) identifies four reasons why there could be some 'crowding out'. First (going beyond Keynes's model discussed above) gov-ernment demand could raise interest rates, discouraging private investment, although as a feedback effect this is intrinsically less than the invest-ment being stimulated. Keynes says that 'governmental loan expenditure will divert resources which would otherwise have been employed by pri-vate enterprise – though only to a slight extent until full employment is being approached' (CWXIII: 460). Second, state investment producing excess supply might adversely affect confidence. As Keynes writes, '[t]wo pyramids, two masses for the dead, are twice as good as one; but not so two railways from London to York' (1973: 131). Third, again as Keynes makes clear, some of the stimulus would spill abroad in an open economy (1973: 120). Fourth, the marginal propensity to consume might be lower in a richer community (Lekachman 1967). This last qualification, in particular, requires some comment on the original hypothesis and the controversies it stimulated.

There are quite sharply different readings of Keynes's psychological law. A persistent interpretation suggests that Keynes thought people would spend relatively less of their income the richer they became (see e.g. Mann 2017b). Immediately after the passage cited above, Keynes himself writes that 'a *greater proportion* of income [will] ... be saved as real income increases' (1973: 97). He writes to Robertson: 'As wealth increases, undoubtedly the

marginal propensity to consume diminishes' (CWXIV: 92). Keynes, however, emphatically denies that this was part of his 'fundamental psychological law'. When it was pointed out to him (by his colleague and adversary
Pigou) that people were reading him in this way, Keynes responded quickly
and rather angrily. 'My assumption is that when incomes increase there is a
larger absolute amount of saving. As regards larger proportions, I make no
assumption' (CWXIV: 272).

At very low income, proportions surely change. At subsistence it is impossible to save at all, and a poor individual or community can save very little.
As wealth increases, so can savings. Fisher (1907), the arch-marginalist on
whom Keynes drew extensively, thought that the feckless poor were always
likely to value current consumption more highly. But, conversely, the moderately poor might experience a greater need to lay something by. If consumption really is a choice, it seems hard to generalise. Even the absolute
increases Keynes insists upon might want qualification. Keynes was an
admirer of Malthus, so he was aware of the possibility of disproportion-
ately large levels of consumption, and thence of any consumption gap, being
met, by the high-spending idle rich. Were saving to increase absolutely but
proportionately, then any significance as an economic variable in Keynes's
system purporting to explain employment and income would seem to disappear. It would still allow the multiplier as a more or less effective policy
tool, but neither redistribution nor growth would necessarily upset the economic apple cart.

Perhaps more importantly, for Keynes, there are processes of adjustment.
There is no reason to assume that income and consumption rise in tandem.
That alone is devastating for Say's Law and the mainstream (Chick 1983).
In particular, as income changes, people's consumption habits are likely to
adjust relatively slowly. So increasing wealth may, at least initially, tend to
lower the marginal propensity to consume. 'In the *short run* there is a good
deal of evidence to suggest that the *proportion* of income spent on consumption does change as income changes – because the *amount* spent on
consumption changes rather slowly' (Stewart 1972: 83). People then adjust
their behaviour but still with a higher level of saving than that with which
they began. Later in the *General Theory*, in discussing 'The Employment
Function', Keynes derives functions for elasticities of employment by
industry and considers the uneven effects of changes in aggregate expenditure (1973: 280–6). Here Keynes argues that spending will not rise proportionally across industries, 'partly because individuals will not, as their
incomes rise, increase the amount of the products of each separate industry,
which they purchase in the same proportion and partly because the prices
of different commodities will respond in different degrees to increases
in expenditure upon them' (1973: 286). This point about capitalism's

heterogeneity will be developed in Chapter 6. Keynes does not take it far but it allows that real consumption decisions, changes in quality as well as in quantity (whether absolute or relative), potentially matter (Hansen 1953).

Consumption is an important part of Keynes's story, neglected by the standard supply-side orientation. Consumer demand becomes a variable, subject to individual decisions and individual psychology. Keynes, however, while accepting that demand might be influenced by 'other factors such as taxation, confidence, the discount rate or even the long-term rate of interest' (1973: 91–5), fairly quickly shuts off most of the variability, and downplays the role of consumption decisions influencing, or being influenced by, either investment or the rate of interest, which are safely quartered in a different area of his scheme. Amongst other things, this relative de-emphasis calls into question interpretations which see consumption or demand management as the essence of Keynesianism. At the very least there is much more than this to the *General Theory* (Backhouse and Bateman 2006, Chick 1983).

Money and interest

In the *General Theory* Keynes is concerned with the consequences of a monetary economy. In contrast to his earlier *Treatise*, he says little about the origins of money, assuming it is supplied by the authorities. The preface insists that 'whilst it is found that money enters into the economic scheme in an essential and peculiar manner, technical monetary details fall into the background' (1973: xxii). Rather, the work 'is primarily a study of the forces which determine changes in the scale of output and employment as a whole' (1973: xxii). The argument is that the problems of investment and consumption arise in a specifically monetary economy, an economy where money matters, where money is not 'neutral'. Keynes argues that orthodoxy is fatally flawed, 'the flaw being largely due to the failure of the classical doctrine to develop a satisfactory theory of the rate of interest' (CWXIII: 489). He rejects the essentially magical idea that the rate of interest is a return to saving or waiting. 'For if a man hoards his savings in cash, he earns no interest, though he saves just as much as before' (1973: 167). Nor can rates of interest be understood as a straightforward product of the market's push and pull of demand for investment funds and supply of savings. Instead, the lines of determination run from interest to investment and savings, not in the other direction. Keynes later qualifies the 'not': there may be a reflux process. But the interest rate is understood to be fundamentally a monetary phenomenon, independent of the 'real', a product of the supply of money and the demand for liquidity.

As above, the supply of money is understood as determined by the monetary authorities: by the central bank. Keynes says little about this, broadly assuming the analysis of his earlier state-based or chartalist account of the *Treatise*, although that earlier work and many of Keynes's followers put much more emphasis on bank credit and its relation with state money. The *General Theory* does discuss how money needs to have certain properties, in particular a near-zero elasticity of production (private agents cannot manufacture it) and of substitution (other things cannot be used as money and money cannot be used for other things) (1973: 230–1). State fiat money and an adequately regulated banking system are understood to be able to achieve these objectives.

The idea of liquidity preference is more original and more slippery. For the classics, money merely facilitates otherwise barter-like exchanges. Nobody wants money itself: it is only a means to an end of buying useful goods. Time does not really matter and purchases, excepting a few unfortunate and theoretically uninteresting delays, occur instantaneously. Because the market is efficient, it would be irrational to save. Money could always be employed, either satisfying immediate wants or put to work earning more money. Against this, Keynes begins with what he describes as 'the ancient distinction' between money for transactions and money as a store of wealth. For the 'pre-classics', like Smith, Malthus and Marx, money was not only needed for transactions but could also store value. For Keynes, rather than physical hoards, liquidity is more typically simply equated with 'a bank balance' (1973: 168), but on several occasions after the publication of the *General Theory* he seems to equate liquidity preference with hoarding pure and simple (CWXIV: 70, 116, 117, 213). At the very least, Keynes's concept extends long-standing ideas and hoarding constitutes 'a first approximation' (1973: 174). The demand for money and monetary instruments cannot be conceived as simple miserliness.

Keynes's summary suggests three reasons for having a liquidity preference:

> (i) the transactions-motive, i.e. the need of cash for the current transaction of personal and business exchanges; (ii) the precautionary-motive, i.e., the desire for security as to the future cash equivalent of a certain proportion of total resources; and (iii) the speculative-motive, i.e. the object of securing profit from knowing better than the market what the future will bring forth. (1973: 170)

The transactions-motive includes both income and business aspects, while both these and the precautionary-motives can be seen as responses to the level of income or economic activity (Mann 2017b). Both could be assimilated without too much trauma into traditional accounts, although precautionary demand already raises issues of time and uncertainty. Where in the mainstream story there is no prospect of rainy days to come, uncertainty means that it often makes sense to hold money or other assets that could readily be converted into cash, rather than immediately spending income entirely on 'produced' goods. For Keynes, 'the importance of money essentially flows from its being a link between the present and the future' (1973: 293–4). '[O]ur desire to hold money as a store of wealth is a barometer of the degree of our distrust of our own calculation and conventions concerning the future ... The possession of actual money lulls our disquietude' (CWXIV: 116). Liquidity preference is a desire not for wealth for its own sake but for money that can be used when unforeseeable circumstances require (de Carvalho 1996).

Questions of time and uncertainty become central to the speculative motive, which brings more life into Keynes's system. Again this depends on 'the existence of *uncertainty*' (1973: 168), but if pessimism predominates in the precautionary motive, it is now a view that the future can bring better returns, which may increase liquidity preference. Here, the specific interests of financiers become central. Amongst other things, people are uncertain about the future rate of interest (1973: 169), different estimates of which lead to changes in liquidity preferences (1973: 169). Expected variations in the interest rate impact in turn on other financial assets offering a return, like shares (Panico 1987). Money will be spent, even borrowed and spent, if there is an expectation that stock prices will rise. Conversely, money will be held rather than spent if the 'bears' outnumber the 'bulls', if there are expectations of a decline in tomorrow's security prices (Lekachman 1967: 86). Changing expectations can become a self-fulfilling prophecy. There follow Keynes's famous examples; games of Snap and Old Maid and newspaper competitions in which success depends guessing others' opinions ... of others' opinions. 'We have reached the third degree where we devote our intelligence to anticipating what average opinion expects average opinion to be' (1973: 156). Buying shares 'for keeps' may be a bad strategy if the public value assets more lowly (1973: 155). Interest rates will themselves now rise and fall according to such changes in demand. Interest is the 'reward for parting with liquidity' or the '"price" which equilibrates the desire to hold wealth in the form of cash with the available quantity of cash' (1973: 167). Such desires for liquidity are at least substantially subjective and again emphasise expectations as an important economic variable.

For many subsequent Keynesians, particularly those identifying as 'post-Keynesians', the fact that the future is inherently unknowable becomes the essential element of their economics. According to Minsky, 'Keynes without uncertainty is something like *Hamlet* without the Prince' (2008: 55). Uncertainty and expectations matter to both liquidity preference and investment decisions (discussed below, but themselves also dependent on interest rates). Both liquidity preference and investment become potentially precarious, not mechanically determined by structural factors. However, as discussed in Chapter 2, it is not clear that Keynes himself gives quite such a leading role to uncertainty, and he also endorses some more mechanical reinterpretations of his theory (Backhouse and Bateman 2011). Keynes's philosophy need not send us into a world of radical indeterminism. In an apparent climb-down from some earlier hyperbole, Keynes continues that the rate of interest is a 'highly conventional, rather than a highly psychological phenomenon. For its actual value is largely governed by the prevailing view as to what its value is expected to be' (1973: 203). But at the very least there is a potentially volatile demand for liquidity and this, alongside the supply of money by the authorities, provides Keynes with an alternative to orthodox explanations of the rate of interest, which simply presuppose it as the rate which produces market-clearing equilibrium.

Priorities are reversed. The monetary is not determined by, but has serious implications for, savings and investment. For Keynes, '[t]he influence of changes in the rate of interest on the amount actually saved is of paramount importance, but it is *in the opposite direction* to that usually supposed' (1973: 110). High interest rates might provoke individuals to save proportionally more, but the first impact is to reduce total investment, so savings also fall. Therefore, in Keynes's alternative vision of the monetary economy, the demand for money as a store of value does not generate demand for investment or provide new funds for investors in the broader sense of the term (Chick 2019). 'Say's Law breaks down' (Brothwell 1988: 48–49). The classical position collapses.

There is some ambiguity about whether Keynes completely dismisses decisions in the real economy in interest rate determination or merely thinks them relatively unimportant. To Hawtrey, he wrote:

> I am unable to see that the changes in the schedule of the marginal efficiency of capital have any obvious or predictable effect on the liquidity function. I do not exclude the possibility, because in economics everything affects everything else, but I can discover no simple or direct relationship such as has been commonly supposed to relate the productivity of capital to the rate of interest. (CWXIV: 11–12)

Meanwhile, to Hicks he insists that 'my remark is to the effect that an increase in the inducement to invest *need* not raise the rate of interest. I should agree that, unless the monetary policy is appropriate, it is quite likely to' (CWXIV: 80). Later Keynes goes further still, writing that 'the increased demand for money resulting from an increase in activity has a backwash which tends to raise the rate of interest' (CWXIV: 110). Here, at least, it appears to become a question of priorities. Subsequently, Keynes would introduce a fourth source of liquidity preference; the finance-motive (CWXIV: 201–215), which explicitly acknowledges firms' investment demand. He even describes this as the 'coping-stone' of his theory (CWXIV: 220). However, it remains unclear exactly how far this modifies the substance of the *General Theory*'s analysis. Keynes later suggests not much (Dow 2019, Chick 2019). It seems reasonable to maintain that the fundamental claim remains that the rate of interest is not determined primarily by the propensities to consume and invest but by 'external' forces – by the monetary authorities and in the financial sphere – and that it hangs on psychology and convention. Not least, with an unmissable air of analytical circularity, interest rates hang on expectations of what interest rates themselves are expected to be (1973: 203, Fitzgibbons 1988, Kicillof 2018).

The other crucial determinant is policy and the supply of money by the authorities. Governments can intervene effectively. Through open-market operations, they can lower or raise interest rates by buying or selling securities (Lekachman 1967). Unfortunately, Keynes identifies an important asymmetry. 'For whilst a weakening of credit is sufficient to bring about a collapse, its strengthening, though a necessary condition of recovery, is not a sufficient condition' (1973: 158). So monetary policy is the first call, but it may prove insufficient.

Investment and employment

Investment and employment have been left to last, but as the full title makes clear, in *The General Theory of Employment, Interest and Money*, employment and unemployment are at the forefront of Keynes's analysis. Indeed, 'my doctrine of full [*sic*] employment is what the whole book is about! Everything else is a side issue to that' (CWXIV: 24). Keynes remains quite close to orthodoxy in his understanding of investment but is much more critical of the orthodox treatment of labour and labour markets.

To first consider investment, Keynes introduces his important concept of the marginal efficiency of capital, defined somewhat inelegantly 'as being equal to that rate of discount which would make the volume of the series of annuities given by the returns expected from the capital asset during its life just equal to its supply price' (1973: 135). It is essentially the expected rate of return on investment or rate of profit. Note again expectations as a significant qualifier. Keynes accepts what he calls the first classical postulate. Entrepreneurs are motivated by profit. They pay for capital and employ labour up to the point where they expect it will no longer pay to do so. Their costs to other firms are paid appropriately, and wages are similarly 'fair' in the sense of being equal to the marginal product of labour. Keynes assumes that firms are small, and usually describes them as individual entrepreneurs, so there is no monopolistic mark-up or distortion of the market. The demand for their products is not affected by their own output. Firms have 'horizontal demand curves', in the jargon (Chick 1983: 39). Firms sell output to consumers or other entrepreneurs, with profits simply the excess of the output over costs. As above, the approach is essentially static and Keynes sees entrepreneurs making decisions at moments when much can reasonably be taken as 'given': the skill and quantity of labour; the quality and quantity of equipment; technique; competition; consumer habits and tastes; disutilities of labour; supervision and organisation; and broader social structures.

The reference to the rate of discount in Keynes's definition of the marginal efficiency of capital emphasises that investment is related to borrowing costs and is something that Keynes believes will only occur if expected returns are at least equal to the rate of interest. Keynes argues that 'the inducement to invest depends partly on the investment demand-schedule and partly on the rate of interest' (1973: 137). The mere expectation of profits is not sufficient to motivate investment; expected returns need to be higher than the expected rate of interest (1973: 143–4). Otherwise, it would not pay to borrow in order to invest, or it would pay to put retained earnings in the bank rather than investing. Entrepreneurs evaluate the supply price of capital and the prospective yield.

\ Any difference with mainstream economics here is in the role Keynes affords to expectations (Marglin and Bhaduri 1990). It is expectations of future returns which will determine whether or not investments take place. Again, and as discussed in Chapter 2, it is not always clear how far Keynes's ideas of radical uncertainty inform the *General Theory* analysis. Minimally, various factors can affect confidence, in both the short and long term, so the marginal efficiency escapes precise determination. Entrepreneurs really do 'act' in the sense of making creative, transformative decisions (Davidson 2009: 113). '[S]hort-term expectations will largely depend on the long-term (or medium-term) expectations of other parties' (1973: 47), and given the impossibility of telepathy, decisions are made in situations where entrepreneurs cannot know what others will do (Varoufakis et al. 2011). Experiences will change expectations, but adjustments, including any increase or decrease in employment, take time (1973: 48). The analysis can seem to throw everything onto questions of psychology. 'If human nature felt no temptation to take a chance, no satisfaction (profit apart) in constructing a factory, a railway, a mine or a farm, there might not be much investment merely as a result of cold calculation' (1973: 150). Fortunately, however, Keynes sees 'a spontaneous urge to action rather than inaction' (1973: 161) as a characteristic of human nature. Ultimately, '[t]here is, however, not much to be said about the state of confidence *a priori*' (1973: 149). Estimates of prospective yield are precarious (Keynes 1973: 149–50) and the schedule of the marginal efficiency of capital can be unstable with investment the driving force of output and employment precisely in the sense that investment 'is most prone to sudden and wide fluctuations' (CWXIV: 121, Sheehan 2009: 130). It also seems reasonable to impute that the increasing scope of uncertainty into the more distant future means that the longer the capital asset can be applied, the less reliable profit forecasts are likely to be (Sheehan 2009). Elsewhere, the marginal efficiency of capital, and its gradual decline over time, seem predictable.

Keynes departs more radically from the mainstream in his depiction of labour markets. If the first classical postulate suggests that entrepreneurs treat labour 'fairly', according to free-market principles and from entrepreneurs' own perspective, Keynes questions what he calls the 'second classical postulate': that 'the utility of the wage when a given volume of labour is employed is equal to the marginal disutility of that amount of employment' (Keynes 1973: 5). The classics assume that labour markets work like other markets, settling at an equilibrium in which everything 'clears'. The implication is that any worker could increase (or decrease) their own employment. Involuntary unemployment, whatever the evidence to the contrary, cannot exist. Apparent unemployment is voluntary, merely reflecting workers' preference for leisure. Against this, Keynes argues that while firms can make rational decisions about how much labour to employ, workers are not in an equivalent position to match the utility of the wages being offered to the marginal disutility of the amount of employment (Brothwell 1988).

Keynes makes two arguments, the relation between which is not entirely clear (Shackle 1972). The first argument accepts, or at least appears to accept, a substantially orthodox claim that if there is unemployment, it is because wages are too high – but with Keynes adding the unorthodox rider that labour is in no position to reduce its own wages. In brief, Keynes does not dispute that 'with a given organisation, equipment and technique, real wages and the volume of output (and hence employment) are uniquely correlated, so that, in general, an increase in employment can only occur to the accompaniment of a decline in the rate of real wages' (1973: 17). Similarly, '*any* increase in employment involves some sacrifice of real income to those who were already employed' (1973: 81), and again, a 'reduction in money-wages is quite compatible in certain circumstances of affording a stimulus to output as the classical theory supposes' (1973: 257). With orthodoxy, the existence of unemployment therefore implies that wages are too high in terms of the product. Cuts in real wages are needed. But Keynes explains why they can be hard to achieve and socially disruptive. The experience of the British General Strike remained salutary. There are market 'imperfections', as Keynes's classical opponents would accept. But there is literally no 'market' for labour, on which supply and demand might be brought into line (Skidelsky 2019). Employed workers are unwilling to accept the necessary pay cuts. The unemployed would gladly work for less, but no employers are willing to engage them (Shackle 1972). Firms cannot simply start from scratch each day, dismissing their workforce and hiring the previously unemployed on lower wages.

Keynes sees a possible way out of the impasse through inflation. An important feature of Keynes's argument, ignored by the simplification of Figure 5.1, is the distinction between 'real' and 'money' prices, particularly between real and money wages. Because money is not neutral, it is necessary to factor in changes in prices. If utilities are subjective, workers might value the money wage rather than simply the real wage. More practically, unions resist cuts in money wages but are unlikely to strike against inflation. (Keynes wrote during deflationary times, and the preceding period of the gold standard had kept prices relatively stable; there was not yet the experience that became normal from the 1970s of persistent inflation, which unions and employers would factor into wage bargaining.) For Keynes, workers are twice foolish, not realising the economic benefits of wage cuts but easily duped by inflation, which can erode real income without a fight. This makes them 'though unconsciously … more reasonable economists than the classical school' (1973:14). Inflation would be less socially disruptive than direct attacks on wages, but 'a flexible wage policy and a flexible money policy come, analytically, to the same thing' (1973: 267). The argument has similarities to those of Keynes's mainstream opponents, identifying market imperfections or frictions and seeing unemployment as essentially a disequilibrium problem (Milgate 1987). More radical followers accordingly tend to repress this line of thinking in favour of a second argument in the *General Theory*.

Before moving on, this first argument does, however, allow a neat 'proof' of the involuntary nature of unemployment, by way of what Lekachman calls a 'mental experiment'. If prices rose, real incomes would fall. The 'rational' classical-world response to this would be for workers to work less. In fact, higher prices elevate profits and firms hire more workers. This shows that workers are willing to work at a lower real wage. Therefore, they must have been willing to work at the previously higher real wages and their previous unemployment cannot be considered 'voluntary' (Keynes 1973, 289–90, Lekachman 1967).

Keynes's second argument against the second classical postulate suggests that cuts in real wages might be ineffective because of their consequences for effective demand. Cutting wages might allow any one employer to recruit more workers, but there is a fallacy of composition in thinking that this necessarily leads to a general reduction of unemployment. 'A reduction in money-wages will somewhat reduce prices' (1973: 262), which in turn will have consequences for distribution and consumption. In an 'unclosed system' it will also lead to an improved balance of trade (1973: 262), which Keynes later maintains is a clear national good. In a closed system, however, the impact on the propensity to consume would, if anything, be negative, so that 'any hopes of favourable results to employment … [would be] due either to an increased marginal efficiency of capital … or a decreased rate of interest' (1973: 265). The fall in money wages might 'theoretically' allow a decline in interest rates but is unlikely to be adequate. First, there is a reaction to a fall in money wages on the marginal efficiency of capital, because falling wages are likely to lead to diminished expectations of final demand. Second, a current fall in money wages might lead to expectations of further falls. Third, and 'most fundamental', are 'the characteristics of money which satisfy liquidity-preference' (1973: 233). As above, investment and employment decisions are not the primary determinants of the interest rate. The effect may be in the 'right' direction, but 'a moderate reduction in money wages may prove inadequate, whilst an immoderate reduction might shatter confidence' (1973: 267). There are many unknowns in terms of expectations, but '[t]he essential character of the argument is precisely the same whether or not money-wages, etc., are liable to change' (1973: 27). Lower real wages mean reduced consumption.

This second argument is therefore a more fundamental challenge to the conventional account. Any role for labour-market imperfections is relegated conceptually, and restoring rates of profit by cutting wages is not necessarily sufficient to increase national income. Wage-cutting is hard to achieve and can potentially undermine effective demand.

The next chapter will discuss unemployment in more detail, but finally here it is worth reiterating that in all this, Keynes sees employment as the ultimate dependent variable and national income as hanging on this. Amongst other things, the analysis shifts the blame for unemployment away from workers and their too-high wages. It simultaneously has the effect of 'bracketing out' labour, in the sense that workers in Keynes's analysis possess little or no agency, little or no capacity to influence their own conditions (Chick 1983, de Angelis 2000). The decisions that matter are those of entrepreneurs and consumers and of those within financial markets, of financiers and the monetary authorities.

Effective demand and unemployment equilibrium

It is now possible to recap Keynes's overall schema and particularly to emphasise the centrality of the idea of effective demand. This is not simply total demand, with a crucial role again played by expectations. 'Effective demand is made up of the sum of two factors based respectively on the expectation of what is going to be consumed and on the expectation of what is going to be invested' (CWXIII: 439). As above, consumption is likely to be relatively stable, so changes in effective demand are most likely to be caused by fluctuations in investment spending, and these in turn generate changes in employment (Sheehan 2009). The classical position is reversed and investment drags saving along with it (Tily 2007).

There is no neat balancing of supply and demand. Decisions not to spend in one direction do not miraculously mean spending happens in another. Forgoing today's dinner 'is not a substitution of future consumption-demand for present consumption-demand – it is a net diminution of such demand' (Keynes 1973: 210). A rise in savings, which orthodoxy takes to provide a stimulus to investment, is likely to be accompanied by a falling propensity to consume. This would weaken entrepreneurial expectations and harm expected yields (Sheehan 2009). Conversely, it is perfectly possible for there to be situations where the propensity to save falls but, because this raises consumption, aggregate demand and income rise.

 Involuntary unemployment is not only possible but likely, and likely as a stable, equilibrium phenomenon, not just as a transitory dislocation (Chick 1983). Unemployment occurs not only when expectations are disappointed but when they are realised (O'Donnell 1989).

There is no self-regulating or 'natural rate of interest'. This idea, which Keynes had accepted in the *Treatise*, 'overlooked the fact that in any given society there is ... a *different* natural rate of interest for each hypothetical level of employment. And, similarly, for every rate of interest there is a level of employment for which that rate is the "natural" rate' (1973: 242). Now monetary forces enter fundamentally into the determination of investment demand and thence of the equilibrium position, but through a substantially independent role in establishing the interest rate (Skidelsky 1992). The rate of interest cannot be deduced from knowledge of prospective yield or the marginal efficiency, but instead arises within the financial sector (Keynes 1973: 137). Multiple equilibria become equally possible.

Finally, states can shift the equilibrium states. In the *General Theory*, policy aspects are also pushed further into the background than in Keynes's earlier works but the state plays an ineliminable economic role. In place of a natural rate of interest, Keynes now advocates a 'neutral' or 'optimum' rate as that which is consistent with full employment (1973: 243). Central banks' supply of money influences this, alongside a market-determined liquidity preference. No longer simply a passive residue of consumption, government spending can also stimulate investment through public works, where pessimistic private estimates of the marginal efficiency of capital prove a disincentive. Governments' use of monetary policy and public works to address unemployment would be both more socially acceptable and more economically sound than classical remedies based on cutting wages.

Dynamics, long-term tendencies and cyclical change

Most of the *General Theory*'s analysis is conducted in terms of static or stationary equilibrium (Kregel 1976, Sheehan 2009). In particular, it shows that unemployment is not a transitory, disequilibrium phenomenon. This addresses and refutes 'the classics' on their own terms. At the same time, this equilibrium analysis becomes vulnerable to familiar charges against the classics that they mischaracterise what is really a dynamic and volatile system. The *General Theory* also hints at, rather than providing, a more dynamic analysis, but three of its insights seem worth particular mention.

First, there is a suggestion of a dynamic equilibrium approach. The *General Theory* briefly moves to what Kregel calls a model of 'Shifting Equilibrium' (1976: 215). This is a vision in which the aggregate supply and demand positions shift as changing expectations of the future influence the present. Entrepreneurs' errors change their behaviour (Kregel 1976). This is still an equilibrium approach because it sees deviations in the form of disappointed expectations pulling the system back towards stable supply and demand relations. It anticipates what would later be called models of 'warranted growth'. Balanced growth can proceed if certain conditions are met. At least implicitly, however, this is always precarious.

Second, there is instability. Cycles and crises were always at least in the back of Keynes's mind. As Chick writes, '[t]he existence of unemployment equilibrium does not, after all, preclude the existence of unemployment *dis*equilibrium' (1983: 77). Each of Keynes's three prime independent variables are potentially unstable. The propensity to consume could change significantly, rendering the multiplier radically volatile. More likely, changes in expectations 'render the marginal efficiency of capital subject to somewhat violent fluctuations which are the explanation of the trade cycle' (1973: 143–4). The collapse of the marginal efficiency of capital is likely to coincide with increases in uncertainty, increasing liquidity preference, exacerbating the crisis, explaining sharp downturns and more gradual recoveries. Keynes does not say much about why entrepreneurial expectation should vary but is more expansive on financial volatility, the theme of the *General Theory's* famous chapter 12. There is little if any obvious equilibrium price for financial assets because there are not production costs like those in the commodity economy. Instead, speculators bet on the anticipations of other speculators. But with finance so fundamental to the productive economy, this leads to the possibility that 'enterprise becomes the bubble on a whirlpool of speculation' (1973: 159). The *General Theory's* depictions lead from finance to investment but, as mentioned above and discussed in Chapter 8, Keynes later equivocates, suggests at least a reciprocal reaction. Chick writes that 'it is not clear whether in Keynes's view it is the collapse of stock market prices or of entrepreneurs' long-term expectations of demand that really causes the trouble' (Chick 1983: 288). And while changing expectations might potentially produce collapse or exploding growth, Keynes believes the economic system exhibits a tendency towards stability. 'Fluctuations may start briskly but seem to wear themselves out before they have proceeded to great extremes, and an intermediate situation which is neither desperate nor satisfactory is our normal lot' (1973: 250). States can also intervene and, predictably in terms of the politics discussed in Chapter 3, Keynes suggests moderation. 'The right remedy for the trade cycle is not to be found in abolishing booms and thus keeping us permanently in a state of semi-slump; but in abolishing slumps and thus keeping us permanently in a quasi-boom' (1973: 322).

Third, there is some sense of progressive change over time. For Keynes, capitalist growth is itself a more or less natural process (Patinkin 1987). However, he also has a vision of a gradual decline in the rate of growth, with the need for intervention to sustain investment becoming more pressing. Despite the qualifications discussed above, Keynes believes that '[a]s wealth increases, undoubtedly the marginal propensity to consume diminishes' (CWXIV: 92). Shortfalls in consumer demand can potentially be overcome at the aggregate level by more investment, but this in turn becomes ever harder to achieve. In a sombre mood, Keynes contrasts the heroism of a former age with an increasing reluctance to take a chance. Now if 'optimism falters, leaving us to depend on nothing but a mathematical expectation, enterprise will fade and die' (1973: 162). Because it is based on expectations, the marginal efficiency of capital is reduced by fears that capital assets will be produced more cheaply in future, lowering today's prospective yield. Keynes argues that today's equipment competes with tomorrow's, which may well have lower costs and improved techniques, lowering its output price. 'In so far as such developments are foreseen as probable, or even as possible, the marginal efficiency of capital produced today is appropriately diminished' (1973: 141). If this provides profound insights into why entrepreneurs might limit their commitments, unless the *pace* of change is quickening it seems unobvious why this should herald a tendency towards decline. The reasonable pessimism of the 1930s seems to overcome Keynes's commitments to epistemological uncertainty. But at the very least, technological, economic and social change mean we cannot rely on depictions of a harmonious steady state.

The *General Theory* was forged during the Great Depression and has reasonably been associated with the unparalleled bleakness of conditions as well as with Keynes's advocacy of policies to change them. He continues to think it possible to return the economy to something approaching full employment, although the exact level remains undefined. There could be managed growth and the rate of interest driven down towards zero, euthanising the rentier and opening the possibility of a steadier prosperity.

Conclusions

There is a vast amount in the *General Theory* on which this chapter has not commented. Not least, Keynes ends with a provocative defence of mercantilism and trade restrictions. There is much else on which the chapter has touched only in passing, notably on price changes and their effects. As warned in the Introduction, the *General Theory* has also been subject to some quite radically different and more or less radical readings. Excellent book-length summaries are available (Sheehan 2009, Kicillof 2018).

This chapter emphasised Keynes's unorthodox choice of independent variables and how this enables his more realistic and more complex depictions of the economy. Crucially, the economy is not so governed from above as to produce socially optimal outcomes. Methodologically, Keynes stays close to the mainstream in the sense of depicting rational individual actions producing equilibrium situations. But Keynes shows that these equilibria can occur at different levels of income and employment. Decisions in consumption, but particularly by entrepreneurs and within finance, are subject to uncertainty, producing conditions in which expectations are met, so that there is no inducement to alter behaviour even in conditions of high unemployment. Individually rational strategies may exacerbate aggregate economic problems. The state is not outside the economy, an institution whose intervention can only cause harm, but capable through its control of the money supply and its capacity to stimulate investment of intervening to ameliorate the market's failings.

6

Unemployment: making Marxist use of Keynes

Introduction

The causes of unemployment remain under-theorised. It remains the case, as Keynes (1973) claimed in the 1930s, that economic orthodoxy assumes efficient market 'clearing' but is therefore obliged to explain unemployment using a theory that assumes the phenomenon does not exist. Unemployment has to be explained away in terms of market 'imperfections'. Elements of these orthodox accounts may be useful, and will be discussed below, but as stand-alone explanations they are unconvincing both theoretically and empirically (Sjöberg 2000). This chapter instead argues for a more adequate theory of unemployment by building on Marx and Keynes. Loyal followers of either scholar may construe as heresy any claim that a theory of unemployment remains to be constructed. Both already theorise unemployment. The suggestion here, however, is that they do so insufficiently and that a better theory can be developed through a critical, Marxist appropriation of Keynesian insights.

Marx and Engels already write extensively about unemployment. They are aware of unemployment, recognise its economic import-ance, and sympathise with the unemployed. Marx condemns a pol-itical economy that 'does not recognise the unemployed worker, the workingman, insofar as he happens to be outside this labour relation-ship' (Marx and Engels 2010, vol. 3: 284). He insists that capital needs unemployment, but it is less clear that he gave it analytical importance. He even writes of capital working on a 'population who happen to be unemployed' (Marx and Engels 2010, vol. 28: 453). The *Economic Manuscripts* that become *Capital*, and the copious correspondence concerning *Capital*, make only passing references to unemployment or the industrial reserve army (Marx and Engels 2010, vols 8, 29, 30, 31, Marx and Engels 1983). Passages towards the end of *Volume I* offer important bases for theorising unemployment, which will be discussed below, and Marx's method of working from the abstract to progressively more concrete analyses allows that a more genuinely adequate theory may well have been developed in the intended further volumes, but we are left with important insights rather than a satisfactory theory.

Similarly, as mentioned in the last chapter, Keynes (1973) provides at least two distinct theories: one of unemployment equilibrium and another of frictional unemployment. He adds important claims about what states can do to increase employment and, at least by implication, how what they otherwise (fail to) do contributes to unemployment. At the same time, Keynes's ideas often mirror the standard version he is criticising; his economic agents are typically asocialised individuals: entrepreneurs, financiers and consumers. His theory must at least be reckoned less general than he claims.

Meanwhile, as discussed in this book's Introduction, Marx and Keynes had very different social ontologies and any synthesis is potentially problematic. Their views on unemployment come close to being opposites. What is self-evidently pathological for Keynes is a normal, even healthy, part of capitalism for Marx. It is argued, however, that Keynes's insights can be appropriated and gain greater critical purchase when socialised and reworked into a Marxist framework, and that doing this can contribute to a more coherent overall understanding of unemployment.

The next section identifies two key Marxist claims about unemployment. First, created by processes of 'so called primitive accumulation', the 'reserve army' is a social and political achievement rather than an economic datum. Second, unemployment is functional for capitalism. It suggests that such functional arguments are useful but insufficient. The chapter accordingly continues by identifying important arguments in Marx and Keynes by which agents' motivations can be understood to reproduce unemployment. The second section briefly identifies Marx's depiction of imperatives to accumulate, which create alternative processes of labour recruitment and displacement. It warns against treating this as an equilibrium approach and suggests the need to examine concretely the dialectics of such processes. As the third section continues, Keynes's model of unemployment equilibrium contrasts with mainstream thinking to identify situations in which entrepreneurs rationally fail to increase employment. Keynes's model is static, and therefore limited, but it provides a potentially important 'snapshot' of what need to be reconceived as dynamic and changing processes. The fourth section accordingly develops claims made by both Marx and Keynes which identify how adjustment is also likely to be uneven and hence conducive to reproducing unemployment. In particular, Keynes's theorisations of labour-market imperfections can be generalised. The problems lie not, or not only, in the 'downward stickiness of wages', an idea found in Keynes and mainstream economics. There are multidimensional, sectoral, temporal and spatial processes of adjustment which mean there are at most only a series of moving equilibria. Any tendency to eliminate unemployment may be undermined before being realised. The fifth section turns to states and economic policy, reiterating that unemployment remains a contested political achievement. It suggests that Keynes is right that states can and do act and are able to pursue more or less effective employment policies. However, rather than Keynes's vision of benign state oversight eliminating unemployment, it may be through the actions of capitalist states that any functions of an industrial reserve army are realised, albeit only ever as an imperfect and contested social achievement.

Unemployment as a social and political attainment, not an economic datum

This section notes two central claims made by Marx and the Marxist tradition: the historical creation of a reserve army of labour and how this proves functional for capitalism. These provide useful underpinnings, but neither constitutes a sufficient explanation of unemployment.

Capitalism draws workers from elsewhere. It destroys pre-existing forms of labour and separates self-employed small farmers and artisans from their means of production. '[T]he social means of subsistence and production are turned into capital, and the immediate producers are turned into wage-labourers' (Marx 1976: 874–5). This 'so called primitive accumulation' creates the 'necessary supplies of free and rightless proletarians' (Marx 1976: 895). As Harvey (2005) reminds us, such primitive accumulation is not relegated to some ancient past. Indeed, for Marx 'the degeneration of the industrial population is retarded only by the constant absorption of primitive and natural elements from the countryside' (1976: 380). Small farmers still abandon the land to work, and often not to work, in the cities. Immigrants from poorer countries still supply cheap labour and disproportionate numbers of the unemployed for many richer countries. Other oversupplied workers languish in unemployment and the slums at home (Benanav 2015).

In a more fundamental sense, capitalism cannot create its own workforce. Of course, capital accumulation and labour's exploitation and resistance condition labour power's reproduction. Marx (1976) describes the destructive consequences for the working class of the brutality of early capitalism, while declining birth rates today also can be read, at least in part, as the product of falling wages and increasing work, and of resistance to this (Folbre 1982, Dunn 2011). But labour power cannot be (re)produced capitalistically (Polanyi 2001) and its reproduction and appropriation still occur substantially outside capital's direct control.

This immediately warns that any 'theory' of unemployment is inevitably inexact; unemployment is a contested social phenomenon, not an economic index capable of being precisely predicted. Amongst other things, economic theory risks obscuring the messy, often murderous, reality of capitalism for many of the world's poor (Benanav 2015). This also suggests it is no accident that Marx substantially defers a discussion of unemployment to a higher level of concreteness than in *Capital*. There may be long-run trends – for example underpinned by changing agricultural productivity, as Benanav (2015) suggests – but it also seems clear that associations between demographic changes, migration and levels of unemployment are weak. High levels of unemployment persist within rich-country economies, already thoroughly urbanised and with low levels of immigration. Without forgetting important relations of colonisation and resistance, or the political achievement of unemployment within countries, to which the last section returns, it is also worth examining processes intrinsic to capitalism as an economic system.

Here Marxists often identify how an industrial reserve army is functional. Capitalism 'needs an unemployed (relatively, at least) part of the population, i.e. a relative surplus population, in order to have the population necessary for its growth immediately available' (Marx and Engels 2010, vol. 28: 529). This allows both long-term and cyclical expansion (Marx and Engels 2010, vol. 4: 384). Unemployment also 'weighs down the active army of workers' (Marx 1976: 792), increasing competition between them and instilling the fear needed to limit wage demands and workplace insubordination (Marx and Engels 2010, vol. 32: 441, vol. 33: 386, de Angelis 2000). In places, Marx takes a very 'hard' line, seeing the industrial reserve army as 'a constant dead-weight upon the limbs of the working class in its struggle for existence with capital, a regulator for the keeping of wages down to the low level that suits the interests of capital' (Marx and Engels 2010, vol. 25: 261). Wages are 'determined not by the 950 who are employed but by the 50 who are unemployed' (Marx and Engels 2010, vol. 6: 419). Overwork and underwork are mutually conditioning. By lengthening the working day, 'One group of workers is … overworked, a corresponding group becomes unemployed, and the wages of the employed are forced down by the wage at which the unemployed work [*sic*]' (Marx and Engels 2010, vol. 30: 194). The worse the condition of the unemployed, the more salutary the effect (Marx and Engels 2010, vol. 8: 172).

Such claims retain considerable intuitive appeal. Were there to be a radical contradiction between unemployment and capitalism, their mutual persistence could hardly be so general. Conversely, it might be possible to

imagine mechanisms which preclude, or at least conflict with, the elimination of unemployment. Here it seems appropriate to note what some
economists label the Marx-Goodwin model. Goodwin's (2014) argument
suggests that as unemployment falls, labour demand increases, wages rise,
profits fall and workers are laid off, returning unemployment to its 'natural'
level. Any reduction of the 'normal' rate requires 'a decrease in the institutional strength of labor' (Shaikh 2016: 653). There is a certain Friedmanite
logic here, and Marx does at one point suggest something to this effect
(1978: 390). However, the idea of there being a 'normal' rate of unemployment seems ahistorical, divorced from the specific dynamics of capital accumulation and class struggle. Mainstream Keynesian ideas of there being
a systematic relation between wage growth and unemployment (Phillips
1958) will be discussed in Chapter 11, but the long-term and international
empirical evidence now looks weak.

Recognising the need for unemployment hardly explains its variability.
Even if we somehow impute 30 per cent unemployment as just what was
needed in 1930 and 3 per cent in 1950, we are left with regressed questions
of why exactly such different needs arose.

Meanwhile, all sorts of processes might be functional for capitalism but
exist at most imperfectly. Any need for unemployment also exists alongside and in tension with a prior and greater need for employed workers.
The latter need is more fundamental in the sense that only workers create
the value and surplus value on which capitalism depends. Capitalism is
unimaginable without exploited labour. It is at least possible to envisage
capitalism without *un*employment. Capital can find other ways to discipline labour. It can respond to the difficulties of extracting more absolute
surplus value concomitant with the removal of the threat of unemployment,
with more truly capitalistic methods of increasing relative surplus value.
Historically, at least at certain times and in certain places, capitalism has
prospered with very low levels of unemployment.

More broadly, this functional argument raises familiar but important conceptual problems. Indeed, it has been taken to epitomise Marxism's methodological shortcomings. Giddens sees arguments around unemployment as
the prime example of how 'Marx's analysis can be interpreted, and has often
been so interpreted, in a functionalist vein. Capitalism has its own "needs",
which the system functions to fulfil. Since capitalism needs a "reserve army",
one comes into being' (Giddens 1981: 18). Certain passages in Marx lend
themselves to such interpretations. However, as Giddens (1981) agrees, few
Marxists accept an unqualified functionalism, and functionalist claims need
to be treated cautiously. Capitalism does endure, but for most Marxists it
is also dynamic and changing and doomed. What capitalism needs is not
necessarily what it gets. Without reviewing these debates (see e.g. Cohen

1978, 1982, Elster 1982, 1985, Parijs 1982), as Callinicos (1989a) argues, functionalist argument may be an important explanatory step but it is also necessary to identify the agents and interests which reproduce phenomena, rather than (simply) explaining backwards from consequences.

Capital's contradictory dynamics

Marx sees capitalism as relentlessly dynamic. 'Accumulate, accumulate! That is Moses and the prophets!' (1976: 742). This accumulation also involves internal 'logics' which reproduce unemployment. From some of Engels's earliest writings, he and Marx stress how the introduction of labour-displacing machinery expels workers. 'Every improvement in machinery throws workers out of employment, and the greater the advance, the more numerous the unemployed' (Marx and Engels 2010, vol. 4: 429). 'Machinery always creates a relative SURPLUS POPULATION' (Marx and Engels 2010, vol. 32: 180). Meanwhile, as capital expands it also needs more workers, ultimately the only source of value and surplus value. 'Capital must therefore constantly posit necessary labour, in order to posit surplus labour; it has to multiply it (namely the *simultaneous* working days) in order to multiply the surplus; but at the same time it must suspend them as necessary, in order to posit them as surplus labour' (Marx 1973: 399). Capitalism can only destroy the jobs it has already created.

Marx's most systematic treatment of unemployment comes towards the end of the first volume of *Capital*.

> Capital acts on both sides at once. If its accumulation on the one hand increases the demand for labour, it increases on the other the supply of workers by 'setting them free', while at the same time the pressure of the unemployed compels those who are employed to furnish more labour, and therefore makes the supply of labour to a certain extent independent of the supply of workers. The movement of the law of supply and demand of labour on this basis completes the despotism of capital. (Marx 1976: 793)

There are simultaneous but opposing processes (Marx 1981: 359; see also Rosdolsky 1977, Callinicos 2014). The question arises of the nature of their relation. For Marx, capitalism is not an equilibrium process so there seems little reason why one might not 'win out'. Marx and Engels suggest that the labour-displacing effects of innovation predominate, at least in relative terms. Rosdolsky argues that in contrast to early capitalism, when the growth was proportional, as capital grows, for Marx 'the demand for labour power grows too, in the long run; but it grows in a "continually declining proportion"' (1977: 296). However, there seems little reason to insist on this theoretically. Conversely, nor does the insatiable demand for more exploitable workers appear to undermine unemployment, and there is little evidence of a tendency towards either systematically increasing or decreasing rates of unemployment.

This is not to suggest there is a cyclical or equilibrium path. Here it is worth flagging Sardoni's (1987) interpretation of both Marx and Keynes as precisely theorists of unemployment as a cyclical phenomenon. Sardoni concludes that neither Marx nor Keynes provides an adequate theory of cycles and that therefore neither provides an adequate theory of unemployment. He suggests turning instead to theories of monopoly capitalism and the work of Kalecki. This seems doubly misleading. First, whatever the effects of twentieth-century monopoly capitalism, unemployment long predates this. Second, whatever their shortcomings as theorists of cycles or crises – and this opens controversies that cannot be covered here – neither Marx nor Keynes (at least in the *General Theory*) understood unemployment primarily in cyclical terms. Capitalism's uneven and crisis-ridden character affects unemployment profoundly. Booms and slumps both highlight the need for a reserve army and help to constitute it (Marx 1976: 608, Marx and Engels 2010, vol. 4: 384, vol. 32: 206). But there is not much evidence of cyclical regularity, while capitalism's and unemployment's variability cannot explain the underlying processes, any more than Marx regarded explanations of price simply in terms of fluctuating supply and demand as sufficient. Capitalism is expansionary, while its crises are also 'turning points' taking the economy in new directions which never simply repeat the old, with implications for unemployment in terms of requiring analyses of volatility as part of broader processes of uneven development. As will be argued below, capitalism takes different trajectories at different times, and different 'mixes' of economic activities seem likely to be conducive to distinct patterns of unemployment.

Unemployment equilibrium

At this point it is useful to turn to Keynes's depictions of why the economy may get 'stuck' at a certain level of unemployment. Keynes's purpose was to show that with minimal alterations to conventional assumptions, there could be situations in which there is no inducement to move (even slowly and with friction, as the mainstream would allow) towards full employment (Dow 1996). Amongst other things, an important consequence of this approach is that most of Keynes's analysis in the *General Theory* is conducted in static or stationary terms (Meek 1967, Kregel 1976). The limits of this will be discussed below but, for Keynes, unemployment becomes a reality explained within the economic model rather than an anomaly to be explained away. The equilibrium approach means that Keynes's theory lacks the generality he claimed for it, but it illuminates important aspects of why particular levels of unemployment persist.

As seen in the previous chapters, Keynes argues that Say's Law applied to labour markets makes unemployment impossible (1973: 5). 'Say's law, that the aggregate demand price of output as a whole is equal to its aggregate supply price for all volumes of output, is equivalent to the proposition that there is no obstacle to full employment' (Keynes 1973: 26). In more sophisticated versions, adjustment occurs as investment demand and savings bring the interest rate to its 'natural' level. Instead, for Keynes, the interest rate is determined elsewhere by liquidity preference and the supply of money by the authorities. Entrepreneurs weigh expected returns from investment against the rate of interest and then make decisions on whether to increase employment.

As discussed in the previous chapter, there are problems with Keynes's 'model'. With the exception of the state, which itself appears providentially and is under-theorised (Balogh 1976), the variables are broadly conceived conventionally: individuals, whether consumers, entrepreneurs or financiers, make free choices. The consequences of these decisions might not produce the happy Benthamite imaginary, but the predicates are very similar. Keynes's positing of 'dependent' and 'independent' suggests an unusually determinist model, while there are also important 'missing' variables. Notably, Keynes substantially 'brackets out' labour. Doing this enables his rejection of the standard view of wage determination on competitive labour markets, but it also denies workers agency of their own. At the very least, Keynes's variables can be acknowledged as themselves dependent on complex social processes, other variables added and other lines of causation emphasised. However, there surely are lines of determination running between the factors Keynes identifies, specific moments of consumption and finance as well as of investment.

In relation to consumption, Keynes's claim that cutting wage shares of income might reduce effective demand with negative rather than positive implications for investment and unemployment seems entirely plausible. Of course, consumption is not 'wholly within the power of the individual' (Keynes 1973: 62). Capital's power impinges from top to bottom on how people consume or save: from the use of advertising to the state of pension provision, for example. But nor is consumption completely passive. Neither qualitatively nor quantitatively is it wholly determined. Real consumption decisions therefore affect investment and unemployment. At a simple empirical level, the relative reluctance, since the early 1990s, of Japanese consumers to spend or, alternatively, the acceleration of consumer spending and

\ debt in the US in the run-up to the sub-prime crash had significant impacts
on the economy and unemployment. In principle this is unchallenging, but
two issues seem to have militated against critical Marxist investigations of
demand. The first is an association of interest in consumption with an unsatisfactory under-consumptionist reading of capitalism's crises or its alleged
chronic stagnation. The second, more common, problem is a circular
understanding of the value of labour power as identically equal to whatever the wage might happen to be, effectively analytically shutting out the
vagaries of class struggle (Masterson 1998, Dunn 2011). Keynes reminds us
that effective demand for both investment and consumer goods are variables
which together at least contribute to the level of employment. Once consumption becomes a variable, there is, at least, no reason to believe that final
demand will rise in proportion to any increase in employment. Chick writes
that the propensity to consume will not rise proportionately with the ability
to consume and that this is sufficient to dispatch 'the Classics' (1983: 111).
How much, and what, people decide to consume can potentially 'lock in'
levels of unemployment.

There is also a distinct financial moment with potentially profound
impacts on investment and employment. As above, in the conventional
story, Say's Law works its magic through changes in the interest rate. An
increased propensity to save puts a downward pressure on interest rates,
provoking increased investment. Keynes instead sees the rate of interest as
determined within the financial sector, on the one hand mainly by financiers'
'liquidity preference', and on the other hand by the supply of money by
the authorities. The result is that '[t]he influence of changes in the rate of
interest on the amount actually saved is of paramount importance, but it
is *in the opposite direction* to that usually supposed' (Keynes 1973: 110).
Higher interest rates reduce investment, and therefore saving, even if savings
rise in relation to consumption. As will be discussed in Chapter 8, Keynes's
rejection of the 'classical' theory of interest is too emphatic, and he later
qualifies his claims that savings and investment have no influence. More fundamentally, for the earlier (pre)classical tradition, and for Marx, profit rates
underpin interest rates. Without this, the decisions within finance appear
essentially arbitrary, detached from those in the wider economy. Keynes's
individualism also prevents him examining the institutions within finance,
whether state or private, within which financial decisions are made. Again,
however, while the aggregate, long-term rate of interest may hang on profit
rates, individual firms face given levels of interest at least in part constructed
by financial decisions which then have at least some distinct influence on
investment and thence employment. Each firm confronts a financial system,
borrowing costs or financial opportunities which are 'given', not of their
own making or reducible to the making of aggregate productive capital.

Keynes also includes expectations in his understanding of the marginal efficiency of capital. Again, Keynes's vision is limited by his acceptance of what he calls the first classical postulate, that entrepreneurs rationally invest and recruit labour up to the point where declining marginal utility makes it unprofitable to do so. His own emphasis on uncertainty, however, points to the postulate's limits. He highlights that firms make 'real' decisions: real in the sense that they cannot be reduced to ideally rational responses to utility or to capital's imperatives. They act, not knowing how others will act. Firms' uncertainties might be better understood as conditioned by the particular volatile nature of capitalism, its competitive imperatives and economic dynamism, which mean that most investment is intrinsically speculative, aiming to throw more or new products onto the market in the hope that this will pay off in some more or less well-imagined future. Once uncertainty gets inside the firm it also raises questions, for example, in terms of how labour's struggles might condition investment decisions. There are also real choices, liquidity preferences, for non-financial firms. Keynes tends to see investment being funded by savings (in the sense of non-consumption elsewhere), but firms' own profits can be either used to fund investment or thrown onto financial markets, not least by buying firms' own shares. But, minimally, Keynes questions utility as something that could be 'quantified, measured, added and subtracted' (Dostaler 2007: 60). Firms then face real decisions about when and in what to invest, decisions which inevitably involve 'best guesses'. There is an inevitable element of groping in the dark for a way forward. Expectations are confirmed or refuted by experience, but the present and the past are necessarily unreliable guides.

For all its limits, Keynes's model thus provides at least a useful starting point for understanding why real decisions made about finance, consumption and investment can tend to leave the economy 'stuck' in positions where firms have little or no inducement to recruit more workers, and therefore for understanding why unemployment persists. Expectations are met, profits are made; why change course? Here Keynes's short-run, equilibrium approach seems to usefully identify that, at any given time, each firm does have a more or less given amount of capital and then makes real, discontinuous decisions about new investment. Circulating capital must be continuously replaced, but fixed capital investment can be postponed with little immediate damage. Skidelsky reasonably argues that in Keynes, there is no sense of movement through time, 'merely an album of snapshots' (1992: 600). Tarshis similarly describes the approach as providing a 'single reconnaissance photograph' rather than a 'motion picture' (1947: 11). We can, however, learn things from a snap-shot that are obscured by moving pictures, as, famously, from a still photograph of a running horse.

This begins to address what might be thought of as more of a puzzle for Marxists than is usually acknowledged. Firms seldom run at full capacity, seldom accumulate at anywhere close to their potential maximum (Baragar 2003). They accumulate cash reserves. They pay extravagant dividends, they buy back their own shares. Firms' decisions are inherently indeterminate, even speculative. For Keynes, if firms can 'earn' interest more safely, it may only be 'temptation to take a chance' that prompts investment (Keynes 1973: 150). Even allowing that uncertainty might produce expected returns above rather than below the rate of interest and for more dynamic and cut-throat competition than Keynes envisages, firms cannot anticipate the form this will take. In particular, other firms' behaviour is unpredictable (Varoufakis et al. 2011). There is no single, rational course of action. Doubts about the future mean that returns on investment are achieved only after some considerable time and are inherently risky. 'Wait and see' will often be an entirely rational strategy. If current expectations are met, there is little imperative to expand output, let alone for each firm, in each industry, to do so in just the 'right' proportions. At the very least, it becomes possible to predict an inertia within capitalism's relentless dynamism. The 'album of snapshots' might also help to reveal how the 'fit' between economic activities will vary in different conditions. At the same time, ideas of equilibrium become deeply misleading if taken as depictions of economic stability, and the next section will argue that they provide greater critical purchase when layered onto depictions of dynamic change and a dialectic of labour's displacement and recruitment.

Dynamic change and capitalism's global heterogeneity

The previous section suggested that Keynes's understanding of unemployment equilibria made sense as partial, incomplete moments but must be understood as providing 'snap-shots' of what are really broader processes of dynamic change. This section will argue that both Marx and Keynes also identify reasons why the process of change, the shift from any one putative equilibrium position to another, is likely to be uneven and disrupted, and that this also tends to reproduce unemployment. There are parallels with mainstream ideas about 'frictional unemployment', but here this cannot be seen as something anomalous, while the real heterogeneity of capitalism means that there are only ever likely to be a series of moving equilibria. Any imperatives towards clearing labour markets are likely to be self-undermining; even as we appear to move towards full employment, it disappears over the horizon.

Mainstream economists understand that in practice, unemployment exists. In the 'long run' unemployment (bizarrely) remains an impossibility, but more subtle versions of Say's Law allow temporary interruptions and the idea of frictional unemployment. There can be no permanent oversupply but rather, market efficiency is achieved only over time. Marshall's (2009) metaphor of a pendulum oscillating around an equilibrium position requires no great theoretical leap to allow movement through a more viscous medium and for deviations from the equilibrium to be prolonged. The standard trick is simply to add the phrase 'long-term'. With this, analyses proceed as if equilibrium were always already achieved. This introduces some substantial theoretical traumas. For example, Pigou (1933), a key target of Keynes's attack in the *General Theory*, simultaneously assumes equilibrium and periods sufficiently short that capital can be assumed constant. However, standard economics now admits 'frictional' unemployment. Workers lose jobs as particular firms fail, and it takes time for successful firms to find the right sort of workers to fill all their vacancies. In the mainstream, the argument nevertheless typically regresses to a convenient, not least politically convenient, explanation for the existence of unemployment and the failure of labour markets to operate freely in terms of the 'downward stickiness of wages', because of union (or perhaps government) interference (Friedman 1962). If wages could only be driven down to their 'true' level, unemployment would be eliminated.

The identification of 'imperfect competition' was important to some of Keynes's contemporaries, and 'friction' or 'stickiness' has become central to some subsequent Keynesian thinking. As above, Keynes's argument at least involves more than this, and Keynes at one point specifically defines involuntary unemployment in such a way that it excludes explanations 'due to a lack of homogeneity in the unit of labour' (CXXIV: 57). Elsewhere, however, he does insist on an inverse relation between real wages and unemployment and, despite many controversies (Skidelsky 2014, Wray 2014), this can reasonably be seen as a complementary or parallel argument (Keynes 1973: 17, 81; see also Hansen 1953). But where the mainstream invokes friction to explain away unemployment, Keynes attempts to explain it (Darrell 1937, Chick 1983, Davidson 2009).

It will be suggested here that there are important parallels between Marx and Keynes in terms of labour's non-homogeneity and that Marxists might make more of the idea. Keynes's criticisms of what he calls the second classical postulate, of wages accurately reflecting the marginal disutility of labour, mean rejecting the idea that labour markets operate as the mainstream imagines (1973: 34). Keynes argues that labour cannot fix its own wages. Rather, 'primarily it is certain other factors which determine the general level of real wages' (1973: 13). Changes to money wages will not follow through in terms of real changes, once the effect of wage changes on prices and demand are factored in. There are also fundamental asymmetries in the labour market. Most obviously, the level of employment 'cannot be *greater* than full employment' (Keynes 1973: 28). This immediately overthrows any orthodox oscillation around an equilibrium. Much more consistently than conventional economic thinking, Keynes also puts entrepreneurs at the centre of his story (Davidson 2009). Firms contract at a given wage and seldom, if ever, re-contract if once they have hired all the workers they want, there is still unemployment (Flaschel 2009). Often it is difficult to employ even new workers on lower wages than those already being paid and very costly to sack everybody to begin from scratch, even if labour laws and sufficiently supine unions allowed it (Chick 1983). Recent years have seen such strategies, but they are desperate and disruptive.

Keynes thus explains the downward stickiness of wages in terms of capital rather than labour. Workers are absolved of blame. At the same time, Keynes again leaves workers as isolated, individual utility maximisers, unable to struggle in (or against) their own interests, and provides little sense of changes over time (Chick 1983). Even treated in this narrow way, as utility-maximising individuals, labour's willingness to work at particular wages is complex. Once wages become high enough, for example, workers want less work and more leisure, not the reverse. They seldom have the choice. But workers actively struggle over their wages and the length and nature of their work. Liberal arguments see the self-serving interests and wage gains of the well organised, working to the detriment of the majority, increasing unemployment (Friedman 1962). However, even this highlights that organising makes a difference. The unionised can win higher wages. Wages and conditions vary across time and space. For Marx, capitalism is heterogeneous. Empirically, one section of workers can remain relatively well paid (Engels gives the example of German dye workers) while others are 'oppressed if not unemployed' (Marx and Engels 2010, vol. 24: 114). Certain trades may be more susceptible to seasonal fluctuations and unemployment – most obviously in agriculture (Marx and Engels 2010, vol. 49: 443), but London tailors could also suffer months of overwork, other months of 'chronic slackness and unemployment' (Marx and Engels 2010, vol. 33: 387). Marx was clear that unemployment varies between one part of the country and another and between countries (Marx and Engels 2010, vol. 32: 205, vol. 34: 39). Capitalism's inherently uneven dynamic means there are always 'spaces' and discontinuities, amongst other things, as workers more or less consciously refuse to behave like commodities.

This points to limits in the orientation of most of the Keynesian literature on the 'downward' stickiness of wages, with the presumption that it would be good to cut wages if only that were possible. However, arguments around wage inflexibility raise possibilities of going further. Keynes's own discussion of labour-market inflexibilities suggests a parallel set of problems of adjustment to those of wage-cutting, accentuated by the asymmetrical labour-market relations. Downward wage pressures, through their impact on demand, may be counterproductive. Conversely, we might hypothesise that upward pressures might increase employment. Upward stickiness, the persistence of relatively low wages, then also becomes a potential obstacle to economic growth and increased employment. If anything, this seems more typical. Labour's supply does not fall in the way that, say, iron nail production might be cut back if markets failed to clear. More broadly, labour's bargaining position is one of relative weakness. This becomes particularly apparent in the contemporary setting of union decline, 'flexible' labour markets and wage stagnation alongside persistent mass unemployment. As above, Keynes accepts the conventional marginalist arguments that with a rising marginal efficiency of capital, it would pay firms to raise existing employees' wages (up to the point of the newly raised marginal efficiency of capital). If wages were too low, firms could always hire more workers, so problems of unemployment do not arise. However, firms may struggle to pay only new recruits the appropriately higher rate and would resist paying all of their employees such a utility wage when they can get away with paying them less. At best, the inertia identified in the previous section suggests firms' expansion and recruitment is likely to lag behind increases in profits.

If wages and employment are most obviously irreducible to the perfect markets of the neo-classical imaginary, the mainstream also misrepresents how most other prices are established. The norm is to assume that firms are 'price-takers' because they are small in relation to the total market. The *General Theory* accepts this smallness, abstracting from the real conditions of monopoly. But even small firms are seldom price-takers in any literal sense. In some industries something close to this may occur, such as when a farmer takes her stock to auction. But it is atypical. Firms often decide on the selling price before goods leave the factory. Many consumer goods are literally manufactured with the price on the box. A mainstream or 'New Keynesian' literature simultaneously acknowledges and trivialises these processes as 'menu costs', but it is the free market which is the exception. Nobody bargains at the check-out over the price of their groceries. Major goods with expected long lives are often made to order. In general, inter-firm relations are characterised by a range of organisation and negotiation rather than just free markets (Chick 1983, Gereffi et al. 2005). The implication of stickiness, Keynes suggests, is that if firms' expectations are met at a given price and the commodities are sold, there may be little inducement to increase production and employment. If goods sell (too) well, the firm might as likely increase prices as increase production at the old price. Indeed this may be a better strategy, because increasing production involves costs (with Keynes and the mainstream assuming diminishing returns – but in any case real costs) with uncertain future sales. Firms' (perfectly rational) strategies may prove 'inefficient' from the point of view of job creation.

If this points us back towards ideas of equilibrium, in a dynamic and changing economy it also points to dislocation. Keynes describes how if the propensity to consume changes, for employment levels to be maintained, any concomitant changes in saving would need to be switched into investment (Keynes 1973: 98). This is possible but likely to become 'more and more troublesome' (1973: 127, 105). Here Keynes's macro-analysis, in particular his distinction between production for investment and for consumption, has many parallels with and (with some qualifications) might have been derived from Marx's *Capital II* (Fan-Hung 1939, Klein 1947, Tsuru 1994). The difficulties of balanced growth, already clear in Marx (1978) but only marginal to Keynes, could then also be derived from his insights (Harrod 1939).

A simple numerical example, following Marx (1978: 473ff), can illustrate this. Klein (1947) expresses a similar argument algebraically. Suppose, in a given turnover period, we have two departments of capital: one (I) producing means of production, the other (II) producing means of consumption. In Example 1 (I) is twice the size of (II) but they have the same organic composition of capital and rate of profit. This would allow simple reproduction if capitalists consumed all their profits (non-capitalistically); the output of Department I equals the constant capital of the two departments; the output of Department II equals the variable and surplus capital of the two departments. If, instead, say a half (in Example 2) or all (in Example 3) of the surplus value is spent capitalistically, this would require relatively larger capital goods sectors, as below. It is worth recalling here the discussion of the previous section about the real choices firms make about whether or to what extent to reinvest their surpluses and to anticipate problems of demand when they prefer liquidity to investment.

Example 1

I	$8000_c + 2000_v + 2000_s$	$\rightarrow 12000$	$[= 8000_c + 4000_c]$
II	$4000_c + 1000_v + 1000_s$	$\rightarrow 6000$	$[= 2000_v + 1000_v + 2000_s + 1000_s]$

Example 2

I	$9000_c +$ $2250_v +$ $(1125 +$ $1125)_s \rightarrow$ 13500	$[= 9000_c$ $+ 3000_c$ $+ 1125_s +$ $375_s]$		
II	$3000_c + 750_v$	$+ (375 +$ $375)_s$	$\rightarrow 4500$	$[= 2250_v$ $+ 1125_s$ $+750_v +$ $375_s]$

Example 3

I	$10000_c +$ $2500_v +$ 2500_s	$\rightarrow 15000$	$[= 10000_c$ $+ 2500_s +$ $2000_c +$ $500_s]$		
II	2000_c	$+ 500_v$	$+ 500_s$	$\rightarrow 3000$	$[= 2500_v$ $+ 500_v]$

However, extending the scenario in Example 3 in which firms do invest to the maximum, it is reasonable to anticipate this involving a degree of labour-displacing technological innovation, say in Department I. So the new capital is added, not, as previously, at a constant-to-variable ratio of 4:1 but at 9:1, so 2250:250. If, meanwhile, Department II continues to invest in expanded reproduction that would lead to numbers as below:

Example 3, continued

I	$12500_c +$ $2750_v +$ 2750_s	$\rightarrow 17000$		
II	2500_c	$+ 625_v$	$+ 625_s$	$\rightarrow 3750$

These (arbitrary) numbers suggest that the total social organic composition of capital has risen and the rate of profit has fallen: there is a *relative* displacement of labour. But more pertinent here, first, in value terms there is an overproduction (or insufficiency of demand for the products) in Department II ($3750 > 2750 + 625$), and second, there is a relatively greater mass of physical output in Department I; the point of innovation improving the technical composition of capital was to increase productivity.

The particular 'dislocations' are an artefact of the numerical examples, and in one sense they merely recapitulate the story of the difficulties of balanced growth or might be interpreted as the basis of a theory of crisis (Klein 1947, Clarke 1994). But even short of crisis, they suggest adjustments are required – a redistribution of value in price terms and a 'migration' of capital from I to II, less investment in I, and lay-offs, more or less easily achieved, over subsequent turnover periods. This example left the consumption sector as a 'passive' simple accumulator but it would be entirely possible to reconstruct the numbers. Different 'balances' between consumption and investment, and different periods of capitalist development, also seem likely to foster different dynamics in terms of levels of unemployment and difficulties of adjustment.

Here Goldstein (2009) makes a potentially useful distinction between 'offensive' and 'defensive' investments, which may predominate in different periods. The former involves capital widening, attempting to produce more, preferably without increasing costs proportionately. The latter involves capital deepening, 'focussing on new cost-cutting production methods to produce more cheaply, possibly without increasing output' (Goldstein 2009: 113). In practice, there is unlikely to be a neat distinction, but the potentially different effects seem revealing. Productivity-raising investment in consumer goods sectors is likely to reduce the value of labour power and increase the potential (relative) surplus value, while productivity-raising investment in capital goods sectors reduces the value composition of capital. Defensive, capital deepening strategies also seem likely to be exacerbated in times of crisis.

These broad sectoral relations can be seen as instances of a more general phenomenon. As seen in the last chapter, Keynes describes how changes in income will not translate into uniform changes in consumption and spending in every type of commodity (1973: 286). Nor do changes in the structure of investment occur immediately and frictionlessly and in just the right industries to produce the new mix of consumer and investment goods. Benanav identifies the unemployment-creating role of the grand global shifts, from agriculture to industry and services, and how these have implications for geographical unevenness, with many different activities more or less strongly tied to place (Benanav 2015, Benanav and Clegg 2010). However, in principle, the simplest change in spending from one good to another, from ice cream to iPhones, the production of which involves different capital compositions or turnover times implies potential dislocations of labour. There are numerous potential sources of inertia and dislocation, and market imperatives operate at best slowly and against resistance.

The argument here is therefore that friction, which began in the mainstream as a short-run anomaly, is something which Keynes usefully moves towards theorising. Economic life is a succession of short runs. Unfortunately, Keynes's (and many later Keynesians') narrow focus on the downward stickiness of wages truncates the potential of the insight, while ostensibly more radical post-Keynesians react by rejecting any micro explanation to insist that unemployment can only be explained as an aggregate, macro phenomenon (King 2015). Instead, inertia is pervasive but highly varied. Firms employ different strategies, which will depend on the characteristics of the industry, the time scale on which they operate, the nature of suppliers and customers, and so on. Stickiness therefore extends throughout the commodity economy and works both 'upwards' and 'downwards'. Placed in the context of capitalism's inherent heterogeneity and dynamic change, an analysis of 'friction' seems an important part of an explanation of why unemployment has remained an enduringly pervasive, if uneven, feature of capitalism over the whole run of its existence. 'Frictions' are better conceived as integral to the process rather than simply as resistances to a more fundamental free-market imperative.

Of course, Marx identifies a competitive imperative to expand, which often seems as invisible to Keynes as to mainstream economists. But investment is discontinuous, and a real inertia qualifies Marx's first-order abstractions. There will and must be new investment, but it need not be made today, nor even this month. Reconceived in the context of dynamic change, 'friction' implies that before any given firm increases its employment, the aggregate (or sectoral) macroeconomic conditions may have changed, undermining any positive effects on the whole. Because the economy is in a state of continual change, there is no reason to assume that any pressures towards the 'equilibrium' will be reached either smoothly or before the economy has moved on. There may be, in conventional terminology, an unreachable 'moving equilibrium' (Blaug 1997).

The importance and limits of state intervention

It is impossible here to delve far into grand debates about the relation between politics and economics or the nature of the state but, minimally, Keynes makes clear that it is unsafe to leave the state out of economic analysis. States act, and states' actions make an economic difference. As discussed in Chapter 3, interpretations of Keynes's political philosophy vary and, without recapitulating the controversies, it seems clear that Keynes sought to establish that states both should and could make effective economic interventions, which simple truth challenged important strands of economic orthodoxy.

States have real power over money. In a post-gold-standard world they can, within limits, simply create money. As above, in the *General Theory* the money supply works in conjunction with (private) liquidity preference to determine interest rates. Money is not 'neutral', and monetary policy may have positive (but in any case real) impacts on accumulation and thence on levels of unemployment. Keynes became increasingly convinced that monetary policy might be insufficient to combat unemployment. It may fail unless it changes sufficiently the expectations of firms or financiers. In such situations, Keynes favoured public works (and these rather than the later simple 'fiscal stimulus') as the means to achieve multiplier effects. States can invest when private actors are unwilling. Of course, the resources that states use are drawn from elsewhere in the economy, with real costs, but in conditions of unemployment, states do not simply 'crowd out' private spending. The 'crowding out' effects may increase with employment and, although he never makes it entirely clear, Keynes seems to favour unemployment rates of around 3 to 5 per cent rather than zero (Clarke, P. 1988, Skidelsky 2000). In general, however, there is no reason to believe that investment is a zero-sum game, and public works can raise the level of employment.

Keynes's depiction of states as able to provide rational social and economic direction in the national interest can seem embarrassingly naive. The state stands above social classes, staffed by gentlemanly intellectuals like Keynes himself.

Sidestepping the wider controversies in state theory, a Marxist critique of Keynes's view of the state cuts two ways. If, or to the extent that, unemployment is functional for capitalism, it should be understood not as a fortunate emergent property of capitalism's contradictory dynamism but as substantially achieved through policies enforced by capitalist states. Against Keynes, states have seldom if ever acted to eliminate unemployment, and some level of unemployment has almost always been a more or less explicit policy objective. The debates in the US at the end of WWII are salutary in this regard: employment but not 'full employment' was accepted as a policy goal, even at that high point of social conciliation.

At the same time, rather than capitalist states neatly fulfilling capitalism's needs, there can only ever be broad and vague limits to the acceptable levels of unemployment, which are socially constructed and contested. There is a danger of a straightforward Marxist reversal of Keynes's vision of benign states in favour of one of equally omnipotent malignity, where whatever states do becomes evidence of their character as capitalist instruments; unemployment disciplines labour, while reducing unemployment is conducive to national growth and social peace. States are themselves heterogeneous and complex rather than singular rational decision makers; they must obey capitalist imperatives but also respond to social struggles, and specific state institutions and individuals have interests of their own. States cannot be presumed to know, let alone have the capacity to do, what is just right for capitalism. Nor can levels of unemployment be read back as achievements of exactly whatever was needed.

Keynes's approach also raises a bigger methodological point, mentioned in previous chapters and which will be discussed in more detail in the chapters on money and finance, that Marx's conception of society is in principle global and states are themselves constituted within a global system of capitalist and inter-state competition. For Keynes, society and the economy are almost always conceived on a national basis. He is aware of the practical constraints on policy in an international context but, methodologically, societies and economies are discrete national entities. Keynes's aggregation, and all the subsequent 'macro' which he did so much to encourage, stops at the border – albeit that the border may then be porous. Instead, national economies need to be situated within a conditioning and constraining global context. Crucially here, national boundaries contain human movement (and to a lesser extent capital movement) and constitute a major 'friction' in labour markets.

More broadly, Keynes's identification of politics with state action only partially challenges the separation of politics and economics. Economic outcomes instead need to be understood as political achievements at a deeper level. Unemployment is a consequence, if often an unintended consequence, of open-ended social struggle.

Conclusion

This chapter has argued for a Marxist appropriation of Keynesian insights to better understand unemployment. Marx's general analysis of capitalism, of its need for an industrial reserve army and of the contradictory dynamics of accumulation provides an effective point of departure for understanding unemployment but needs to be augmented. Keynes's attack on conventional thinking shows how a simplistic supply-side model in which demand looks after itself is inadequate, and in doing so it provides a useful reminder to Marxists not to reduce finance and consumption to straightforward determinants of accumulation but to investigate their specific moments.

Keynes's principal argument is couched in substantially individual and static terms and so appears profoundly problematic, but the idea of 'unemployment equilibrium' can be a useful heuristic device. Decisions are made in real time, at moments when there are 'given' levels of capital and of unemployment, which can reasonably be depicted as a temporary balance from which there may be little internal imperative to move. Keynes insists that the future is uncertain. Amongst other things, this means that all social actors, including firms, are really making best guesses at what is likely to succeed. There is no reason to assume that these guesses sum around what Keynes's classical opponents might see as some ideally rational mean; indeed there is no reason to assume that any such mean is itself meaningful. Of course, such guesses are socially constructed rather than pulled out of thin air, and can be more or less well informed and confirmed or repudiated by experience, as Keynes accepted, but Marxist materialism provides firmer grounds for understanding why economic life makes particular things more or less likely. Capitalist imperatives provide the context for understanding the decisions that firms make and for why any temporary equilibrium is unstable. For firms, it often makes sense, however, to run at less than full capacity and to accumulate at less than any theoretical maximum, to invest and to recruit workers only slowly and reluctantly.

There may be pressures towards equilibrium, but they occur in the context of dynamic change. Marx wrote that 'consonance may be reached only by passing through the most extreme dissonance' (1973: 149). Decisions at the firm, industry and sectoral level potentially dislocate any movement towards balanced growth. In this context, the idea of frictional unemployment potentially regains critical purchase. Keynes moves beyond the mainstream apologia towards explanation. But the emphasis on markets and the downward stickiness of wages, which he shares with the mainstream, limits his critique. Once capital's inherent heterogeneity on both a spatial and a temporal basis is acknowledged, the idea of friction can be worked harder. 'Imperfections', power and institutional conservatism pervade capitalism, producing slow and partial adjustments, between sectors of capital and more broadly between firms and economic activities and across space.

Finally, the chapter returned to politics and state intervention. Unemployment is always political, never simply an economic phenomenon. States are capitalist states, existing in the context of class struggle and a global capitalist system, limiting attempts to manage capitalism in any one country. State intervention cannot adequately be understood in terms of the benign influence Keynes envisaged. Nor do states have privileged knowledge of an uncertain future. But state intervention has a distinct moment of its own, with real economic impacts. Therefore, as both Marx and Keynes would have accepted, theory should not be expected to achieve analytical precision, but this should not preclude attempts to understand better how economic dynamics produce and reproduce unemployment, in order also to better fight against it.

7

Money

Introduction

In a similar vein to the previous chapter on unemployment, this chapter and the next argue that there are problems and lacunae in Marx's understanding of money and finance which a critical engagement with Keynes can help to address.

This chapter again begins with Marx and assumes a degree of familiarity and sympathy with Marxist political economy in general and Marx's views on money in particular. Marx said profound things about money, some of which anticipate Keynes. But as de Brunhoff's (1976) sympathetic and honest account acknowledges, Marx's analysis of money in *Capital* remains sketchy. Amongst other things, Marx identifies money's different and often contradictory roles but leaves their interrelation under-investigated. There has subsequently been important Marxist scholarship which will be drawn upon in what follows. But it remains substantially the case, as Weeks argues, that '[o]bsession with Marx's theory of value and exploitation has resulted in little attention being directed to his analysis of capitalism as a money economy, even by Marxists' (1988: 202). Marx's own analysis also remained at a high level of abstraction which did not integrate an analysis of states' vital role in monetary affairs. Nor could Marx be expected to anticipate substantial subsequent changes in the global economy, not least the rise of powerful financial institutions and the general abandonment of commodity money. It remains impossible to prove an absence, and necessary to apologise for neglecting the accounts of which I am no doubt ignorant, but there are ostensible gaps and unresolved controversies in Marxist thinking about money.

Hodgson (1982: 17) also charges that Marxists have failed to integrate, or even to criticise seriously, important developments in Keynesian monetary economics. Keynes's treatment of money challenges the 'classics' as Keynes understood them, but it also challenges at least certain interpretations of Marxism in which just about everything becomes reducible to the imperatives of capital accumulation in the 'real' or 'productive' economy. This has potentially serious implications for broader Marxist analysis. Marxists agree with Keynes in insisting that money is not 'neutral'. There is a specific financial moment which can impact on investment. Therefore, if, or in as far as, a Marxist analysis of money remains incomplete, so too does any analysis of the broader political economy. Once again, the perspective in this book is that any Marx–Keynes synthesis needs to be made with care and Keynesian insights criticised and socialised, but there are potential gains to be made from a serious critical engagement. This chapter accordingly identifies three related areas where such a constructive dialogue can potentially enrich monetary analysis.

The first involves thinking about money's social relations and its material properties. The long first section begins with three central propositions from Marx. First, money is a social relation not a thing (CW vol. 6: 145). Second, money is primarily a measure of value as socially necessary labour time. Third, and more controversially for Marxists, precisely because it is a social relation, that measure is inherently imperfect. Amongst other things, money has different functions which potentially come into conflict with each other, potentially qualifying each other. It is then argued that the 'not a thing' part of Marx's formulation should also be qualified. Historical materialism recognises that money has specific material properties, which both reflect and reflect on capitalist social relations, potentially taking them in new directions. The section then draws on and extends Keynes's thinking about money's essential properties, which can be more or less adequately met by different material forms. It sees the choice of particular forms as the outcome of contested social conflicts. The shift between different monetary systems – bimetal, gold, gold exchange, pure fiat money, electronic money and so on – are neither simply policy choices nor the requirements of some abstract capitalist teleology, and they can have substantive economic repercussions.

Following from this, the second section argues that money matters. This should be an uncontroversial truism, but the fact that money is not neutral has important, under-investigated implications, obscured by thinking about money's 'functions'. Money cannot simply be 'read off' from developments in the wider economy, and it has at least some real influence on that economy, which needs to be reintegrated analytically. Keynes mistakenly accuses Marx of being a follower of the quantity theory and Say's Law, but Marx's dismissal of these is somewhat summary and the details of Keynes's critique of the mainstream view that money does not matter, that money is neutral, usefully highlight the ineliminable importance of money, the specific financial and state monetary moments, and how these impact on the real economy.

The third section continues that an engagement with Keynes's concept of liquidity preference, extended and understood as a social and institutional phenomenon, can enrich Marxist monetary analysis. While Marx recognises the importance of hoarding, his analysis remained unfinished and at times suggests that hoarding is simply functional for capital accumulation, leaving under-investigated its potentially disruptive effects. Marxists can better understand these as second-order effects of capital accumulation and its contradictions and as predicated on institutional structures, not individual preferences, but the specific financial moment needs to be reincorporated into any adequate analysis of contemporary capitalism.

This discussion then informs that of Chapter 8, which considers credit and interest. There it will be argued that Marx (and the classics) are right to identify the basis of interest in profit but that this can only be the analytical starting point. Again, there is a real financial moment, the product of both state and private financial agency, which needs to be critically investigated and incorporated into an understanding of the determination of interest rates but thence also of profit rates. There are contested relations of class, intra-capitalist and state power, which shape finance and thence also the wider economy. Chapter 9 accordingly considers the state and institutional financial power in greater historical specificity.

Money is a social relation but its material properties matter

Marx insists that '[m]oney is not a thing, it is a social relation' (CW vol. 6: 145). This remains an important insight, subsequently rediscovered by any number of sociologists of money, albeit too often grafted onto an otherwise mainstream monetary theory (Soderberg 2014: 6). That money is at least primarily a social relation allows different ways of doing money and warns against fetishising any particular form. We do not need to suffer an epistemological breakdown when, having said that money is gold, we discover that what we call money is manifestly no longer gold. But this can only be the starting point. First, it is necessary to interrogate the nature of the social relation. Marx begins by stressing money as a measure of value, and this will be defended very briefly below. But there are immediately reasons to qualify this, to see the value relation as only a first approximation, even if a vital one. Second, the 'not a thing' part of the phrase also needs qualification. Historical materialists can weary of rebutting accusations of crude determinism. But materiality, here including the material characteristics of money, can matter profoundly. Alternative forms work differently, can perform money's different functions more or less well and win the support of different social interests. So it is accepted here that Marx's analysis does not require commodity money (Davis 2010, Williams 2000), but the move away

from commodity forms presents analytical challenges and means that capitalism works differently.

Marx begins his critique of political economy with money as a measure
of value. *Capital* describes how commodity money can become the universal equivalent, embodying socially necessary labour time, against which
other commodities can be compared. Marx posits the equality of apparently different goods, 20 yards of linen and one coat (1976: 140), and then
introduces the equivalence of a certain amount of commodity money, two
ounces of gold (1976: 157). 'The simple commodity form is therefore the
germ of the money-form' (1976: 163). Money's own value is determined,
like that of any other commodity, by the amount of socially necessary labour
required for its production. For Marx:

> The first main function of gold is to supply commodities with the material
> for the expression of their values, or to represent their values as magnitudes
> of the same denomination, qualitatively equal and quantitatively comparable.
> It thus acts as a universal measure of value, and only through performing
> this function does gold, the specific equivalent commodity, become money.
> (1976: 188)

Marx's theory of value has been almost incessantly attacked since he first
articulated it, but Marx was dismissive of challenges that he needed to prove
the idea (Marx and Engels 1983: 148). For Marx, value is a social theory.
It is valid at the level of the social totality, helping to explain particularity,
rather than something directly manifest in every instance: in the price of
every ice cream or dodgy derivative. Value and surplus value underlie prices
and profits but are not immediately, identically, equal. Indeed, the need for
science hangs on the non-immediacy of the correspondence between theory
and experience.

This gap between theory and concrete reality should, however, warn
against jumping too quickly between value and money. Even with commodity money, and at the analytical level of *Capital*, money necessarily
provides an imperfect measure. There is an inherent problem with a measure
that is also a variable. Money as commodity money itself has value, and as
such it becomes an unstable measure of the value of other things and of
alterations of value over time and across space (Murray 2005: 56). This was
already noted by Smith, and Marx makes the same point in his discussion of
Steuart (Vilar 1984). The problem is a bit like trying to measure the expansion of a solid in an oven by placing it alongside a metal ruler. Subjective
utility theories of money accordingly rapidly descend into incoherence. For
marginalism, utility is purely subjective: it is measured by money, towards
which money people will have different subjective utilities. The system
disappears into radical circularity. For Marx, the prejudice of a basic human

equality provides a theoretical anchor to the concept of value as socially necessary labour time. Nevertheless, gold values can still drift quite a long way from this stable anchorage. If gold is commodity money, then as productivity in the gold-producing sector changes, it is only possible to know the relative changes in the value of other commodities. Marx makes this clear in relation to bimetallism:

> If therefore two different commodities, such as gold and silver, serve simultaneously as measures of value, all commodities will have two separate price-expressions, the price in gold and the price in silver, which will quietly co-exist as long as the ratio of the value of silver to that of gold remains unchanged, say at 15 to 1. However, every alteration in this ratio disturbs the ratio between the gold-prices and the silver-prices of commodities, and thus proves in fact that a duplication of the measure of value contradicts the function of that measure. (1976: 188)

For Marx, it is only by social custom that gold becomes money in the first place (1976: 162). Money is, to repeat, 'a social not a material category' (Williams 2000: 439). Marx insists that '[i]n its form of existence as coin, gold becomes completely divorced from the substance of its value. Relatively valueless objects, therefore, such as paper notes, can serve as coins in place of gold' (Marx 1976: 223–4). In advanced capitalist nations, already in Marx's day, credit and credit money replaced specie (Marx 1981: 648, Williams 2000), and Marx discusses the possibility of departing from metal altogether (Marx 1973, Williams 2000), although the problems that paper money introduces into the analysis remain, as de Brunhoff accepts, 'not entirely clear' (1976: 35).

Marx's depiction of money as primarily a measure of value has parallels with Keynes's (2011) starting point in money as a unit of account and professed sympathy with the labour theory of value (Keynes 2011: volume 1, 1973). But Keynes does not link the two ideas. Indeed, Keynes's sympathy with the labour theory of value is really saying that labour – but not money – is reasonably constant and therefore a better measure. What matters here is that value, in the Marxist sense, becomes something which money can only ever measure approximately. The use of non-commodity money, lacking any intrinsic value, underscores the problem. It can only 'stand in' for commodity money (Arthur 2005) more or less reliably and on the more or less fragile trust in the issuing authority. This becomes strikingly apparent in inflationary times and in an international system of many currencies and volatile currency exchange.

Marx goes on to describe how money has further functions (Marx 1976, Itoh and Lapavitsas 1999). Putting value first amongst these relegates what in liberal accounts is money's primary, if not only, function as medium of exchange. For Marx, money as a social relation cannot be understood as something 'already there', as if 'commodities enter into the process of circulation without a price, and money enters without a value, and that, once they have entered circulation, an aliquot part of the medley of commodities is exchanged for an aliquot part of the heap of precious metals' (Marx 1976: 219–20). Money is also a store of value. This allows that it can overcome apparent obstacles to capital's reproduction. There is an inherent lag between the production and realisation of value. This also involves all sorts of unevenness. 'One sort of commodity requires a longer, another a shorter time for its production. The production of different commodities depends on different seasons of the year. One commodity may be born in the market place, another must travel to a distant market' (Marx 1976: 232). The hoarding and release of money can ease the process.

Credit money goes further. Marx describes how using mere tokens, it becomes possible that '[t]he seller sells an existing commodity, the buyer buys as the mere representative of money, or rather as the representative of future money. The seller becomes a creditor, the buyer becomes a debtor' (1976: 233). Promissory notes and bills of exchange extend commercial credit from capitals where there are already surpluses to those where production and exploitation have not yet occurred. These bills of exchange can circulate like money: indeed they become the 'actual commercial money' (Marx 1981: 525). 'By and large, money now functions only as a means of payment, i.e. commodities are not sold for money but for a written promise to pay' (Marx 1981: 525). Unlike commodity money, there is no physical substance and these bills of exchange can expire and disappear in returning to their issuer. So long as payments balance, such 'money functions only nominally, as money of account' (Marx 1976: 235).

In moving away from a commodity base, such a credit money system becomes inherently fragile. Individual defaults ruin particular businesses. A 'general disturbance' now means that 'money suddenly and immediately changes over from its merely nominal shape, money of account, into hard cash' (Marx 1976: 236). The development of banking systems can concentrate money capital into large masses and allay individual default risk but also potentially amplifies and generalises the problems. Marx describes the growth of what he calls money-dealing capital, for which the 'borrowing and lending of money becomes their special business. They appear as middlemen between the real lender of money capital and its borrower' (1981: 528). Now the banks themselves issue bills, banknotes, which become acceptable as money. Raising themes to which the next two chapters will return, 'in most countries the major banks that issue notes are a peculiar mishmash between national banks and private banks and actually have the government's credit behind them, their notes being more or less legal tender' (1981: 529). This idea of a 'mishmash' usefully contrasts with some (post)Keynesian binaries which either insist that money is a creature of the state or market, or insist on monetary theories of credit or credit theories of money.

Marx's identification of different functions of money and their conceptual ordering provides an enduringly powerful contrast with mainstream vulgarity. It nevertheless leaves ambiguities, and the language of 'functions' is potentially misleading. As mentioned in the previous chapter, Marxist analysis cannot be functionalist in a strong sense, where the causes of phenomena are simply explained backwards from their effects. An element of functionalism may be defended as a 'first-cut' explanation of why and how certain features of capitalism persist, but capitalism is dynamic and changing and riddled with contradictions.

It is no surprise, therefore, that Marx insists that money's functions can also come into conflict, notably for example its functions as a measure of value and as a medium of circulation (Marx 1970: 121). These potential conflicts between money's functions are well established in the Marxist literature. They becomes particularly stark once non-commodity tokens come to stand in for commodity money. These function effectively as media of circulation but are fragile as measures and stores of value (Campbell 2005: 154). In Marx's time, paper could be acceptable in domestic markets but not in the international arena. As above, the store and release of hoards can be functional, moving money to where it is needed, mediating relations between its measure of value and medium of circulation functions (de Brunhoff 1976; Marx 1970: 126). But, as will be discussed in more detail below, it becomes at least implicit that hoarding can be dysfunctional.

The fact that money has different and potentially conflicting roles means that each function becomes 'compromised'. Because money has different functions, they modify each other; so money as a medium of circulation and as a store of value upset its ability to measure value. The hoarding and release of gold by central banks, for example, could have substantial effects on prices. Given that there are conflicts, money as a measure of value cannot be presumed always to win comprehensively, or there would be no conflict. So when Itoh and Lapavitsas, for example, insist analytically on 'a strict ordering' (1999: 40), this needs to be understood cautiously, in a specific sense whereby earlier concepts are applied and revised – that is, in the sense of sublation and return, rather than as a steady ascent. The other functions must be capable of 'getting at', of modifying, what we knew, or what we thought we knew, about money as a measure of value.

This becomes particularly clear in considering national monies in a global context. Marx's method abstracts from nation-states, it is not an analysis of national economies which then 'spill over' into an international economy (Pradella 2014: 142). The level of society in Marx's 'socially necessary labour time' ultimately only makes sense at the level of the totality. It is, in principle, global rather than national. Accordingly, the society within which money is the measure of value is in principle global. At the same time, this is a highly differentiated or variegated society. For Marx, gold worked as world money, even as national systems allowed deviations from its discipline. Today, money is substantially state-backed. Without gold, we have only competing fiat monies and it becomes more precarious to assume that national currencies somehow accurately measure values. Marx proposed to introduce state and inter-state relations at more concrete analytical levels, but the profundity of his existing insights should not obscure the unfinished nature of his work.

What is also clear is that although Marx says money is a social relation not a thing, the material properties of money can matter profoundly. Different forms of money may perform money's different functions more or less well. Gold stores value but may be a poor medium of circulation, fiat monies the reverse. Different social interests may then favour different resolutions to the conflicts over monetary forms. This can be seen again and again: in the nineteenth-century debates and struggles around the 1844 British Bank Act, around bimetallism in the US in the late nineteenth century, around the gold standard in the twentieth century and recent debates about the Euro. Capital lacks the teleology to select some abstractly ideal functionality, and if the forms of money do work, it is only ever as the resultant of competing social interests. Of course, there can be a process of capitalist trial and error and change, but monetary forms can 'lock-in' particular relations which can then only be transformed more or less traumatically.

By the time Keynes was writing, the nineteenth-century monetary certainties had dissolved. It was clear that money need not be based on precious metals, and Keynes describes gold as a 'barbarous relic' (1923: 138). He also identifies how the apparent stability of the nineteenth-century gold standard had itself been more the product of good fortune and careful management than of an automatic market mechanism. For Keynes, however, dethroning gold did not mean that anything could rule as money. The *General Theory* discusses how money's functions require certain properties, which help to explain how particular monetary forms may function differently.

First, for Keynes, money needs to be an object whose carrying costs are low and the power of disposal of which is high; it must be liquid (1973: 225–6). Things which rot, physically or socially, and things which other people may be unwilling to accept, make for poor money. Gresham's Law (that bad money drives out good) and the distinction between different qualities of money suggests that the 'power of disposal' becomes hard to pin down. Gold coins may be the 'best' money, but in practice people only offer bad tokens. It is apparent, however, that some things work more or less well.

The carrying and storing costs of different forms of money can vary considerably: gold versus silver and either form of metal versus paper, for example. Already by the time of the French Revolution, the sheer weight of gold had become cumbersome for Parisian porters having to carry it (Mandel 1969). By the twentieth century, the relative dearth of metallic gold limited its use as a medium of circulation. The risk of bank failures can make 'carrying costs' hard to calculate, and 'power of disposal' may lie along a continuum rather than being absolute. So the different requirements or dimensions of liquidity may make any straightforward ordering impossible (Chick 2019) and may vary across monetary forms.

Keynes goes on to identify particular, necessary characteristics of money – first, 'a zero, or at any rate a very small, elasticity of production, so far as the power of private enterprise is concerned' (1973: 230). Money, for Keynes, 'cannot readily be produced' (1973: 230). It cannot be something into the production of which firms could simply divert resources if profits elsewhere fell. Money cannot grow on trees. However, even ignoring the long history of tobacco as legal tender in the US (Galbraith 1995), in a world of commodity money there clearly is at least some 'elasticity of production'. In the long term, the bullion famine of the fifteenth century and corresponding high 'prices' of specie played a major role in stimulating the European Navigations and the plunder of the sixteenth century. To degrees that remain disputed, inflows of specie to Europe then promoted inflation, the early versions of the quantity theory, and economic growth (Vilar 1984, Arestis and Howells 2001). The point here is that the causal relations can run from prices to supply rather than the reverse. There is at least an association, and, for gold, some crude relation between prices and production levels could still be discerned in the twentieth century (calculated from USGS 2018). Paper and electronic fiat money obviate this problem of elastic supply 'so far as the private sector is concerned'. For Keynes, British authorities (and as seen in previous chapters, Keynes's focus usually remained firmly on Britain and the US) could be trusted not to allow the hyperinflationary catastrophes experienced in continental Europe, so there was little to fear in gold's abandonment. The use of 'credit money' and questions of money's endogeneity or exogeneity, discussed in Chapter 9, might call this into question. The distinction between 'private enterprise' in credit creation and elsewhere becomes significant. The production of different forms of non-state money may also be more or less elastic, even as this makes their ability to work as money more or less precarious. Money at least needs to have characteristics that allow some form of institutional monopoly over its production (Dillard 1980). For Keynes, moreover, such a low elasticity of production is not a sufficient condition.

Second, money must also have a zero, or near-zero, 'elasticity of substitution' (Keynes 1973: 231). Other things cannot be substituted for it, or it for those other things. Other factors like land have a near-zero elasticity of production but have other uses. So whatever is money is used (more or less) exclusively as money. A little gold jewellery might cause few difficulties, but tobacco is again inherently more problematic (Melitz 1976). State-backed fiat money would again appear to work best. As discussed in Chapter 4, most emphatically in the *Treatise* (2011: volume 1), Keynes articulated trenchant support for chartalist views that all money proper was state money. But states could also allow 'free coinage', the conversion of gold and (for example in the US until 1873) silver into legal tender. Strictly private and foreign money can and does substitute for state money to varying degrees in different countries. Again it is a question of degree but, as Dillard puts it, what is crucial to the argument is that 'the utility of money to individuals falls less rapidly than the utility of any specific form of wealth' (1980: 258). People, with Keynes as ever making little distinction between individuals and firms, rationally hold money rather than spending it on other things. Kicillof argues that in a positive sense, Keynes's reasoning around liquidity appears to become circular. '[A]n asset becomes money because it is liquid, but its liquidity rests precisely on the fact that it is money' (Kicillof 2018: 387, see also Chick 1983). If something is money it is acceptable as money. But Keynes does provide criteria for evaluating how different forms of money might work only more or less effectively.

The social conflicts around gold and sound money are worth a brief further comment. Despite opponents' caricatures, Keynes remained an opponent of high inflation, amongst other things proposing anti-inflationary measures in the late 1930s while British unemployment rates remained very high. Keynes also invented what became a famous warning that Lenin favoured debauching the currency as a means to revolution (CWII: 148). This was a complete fiction (see Fetter 1977), but it helps to emphasise that monetary questions are class questions. Monetary questions were class questions for Marx too in his opposition to the Currency School and to the 1844 Bank Act. Defence of 'sound money' is typically an anti-working-class austerity position. But, as in 1844, there is seldom a single, agreed capitalist monetary orientation. Capitalism changes and so do monetary forms. Of course, powerful vested interests fought to retain a gold-exchange standard. As above, Keynes had touched on broader social conflicts in the earlier *Tract*. These largely disappear from the *General Theory*, but he remains clear that moneyed interests and national interests need not coincide. Again, in the post-WWII period a system which had appeared to work well for capital ceased to do so and became the focus of sharp conflicts. Minsky writes that '[a]s banking innovation accelerated in the 1960s and 1970s, it became apparent that there are a number of different types of money, and that the nature of the relevant money changes as institutions evolve' (Minsky 1986: 252). A language of evolution can be misleading, and if Keynes is right and there is little substitution between money and other commodities, there is a lock in effect. Alternative monies can develop, but the shift from one dominant form of money to another typically involves crises and social conflict rather than gradual change. A class analysis is needed to understand these monetary turns, why one monetary thing, one form of money, supersedes another.

Money is therefore a social relation, but it has different functions which may come into conflict and different forms which can have different economic consequences. Different social interests are likely to favour particular 'solutions' to functional conflicts and particular monetary forms. This also has theoretical implications. Marx expresses analytical priorities but they cannot be more than that, so money as a measure of value cannot be fixed and absolute. Money's other functions come into conflict with the measure of value function, modifying it. Keynes's identification of money's functions can become abstractly ideal, but this need not diminish the importance of the variables he identifies. The next two sections will develop this critique of Keynes, looking at the non-neutrality of money and liquidity preference.

Money matters

Money is not neutral. Money matters, potentially modifying what occurs in the productive economy. Although this was something on which Keynesians put more emphasis, few Marxists would disagree. Money becomes the essence of capitalism; M-C-M'. Amongst other things, it is the anarchic nature of the specifically monetary economy that makes capitalism intrinsically crisis-prone. However, thinking in terms of money's functions can obscure the active role of money, and Marxists have seldom explicitly investigated how the non-neutrality of money involves reshaping accumulation. Of course, many scholars with Marxist backgrounds have recently depicted a new era of finance-led capitalism (Bryan and Rafferty 2005, Dumenil and Levy 2004, Lazonick 2012). The point here is a broader one, less about the emergence of a new paradigm than about the need to always investigate the relation between money and the 'real' economy. This does not then require money's analytic priority, but it suggests that the world of money and finance needs to be taken seriously as at least a second-order effect which reacts back onto the productive economy, reshaping it in non-trivial ways.

Non-neutrality is fundamental to Keynes's critique. He insists that 'neutral money' is 'a nonsense notion' (CWXIV: 93). In rejecting this, Keynes exaggerates his own originality. Mattick maintains that he 'shared honours with Hawtrey, Harrod, Cassel, Wicksell, Fisher and a host of long-forgotten "money-cranks", particularly Proudhon and Silvio Gesell' (1971: 5). Keynes sees Marx as one of the classics, in the sense of accepting money neutrality. Marx does occasionally use a language of money as a veil. But this is in the sense of money masking exploitation and capitals' productive interconnections (Marx and Engels 2010, vol. 29: 27, 156). Marx's ire was directed at those who saw the solutions to capitalism's ills in a monetary fix. Money makes everything appear to occur in a realm of free exchange rather than a world of exploitative production. Apparently unbeknownst to Keynes, Marx was equally emphatic in his rejection of Say and the quantity theory. Quite apart from Marx's fine line in personal vitriol, he wastes little time with Say's 'famous law' (Marx CW vol. 32: 124–5), stressing that it is invalidated by production on an enlarged scale, when applied to the international scene (CW vol. 32: 160), and that, even amongst its followers, 'Say's rigmarole' could now only be invoked in times of prosperity and had to be 'thrown to the winds in times of crisis' (CW vol. 32: 131). Marx is equally brusque with Ricardo's acceptance of the quantity theory, which stems from his regard for 'the fluid form of money in isolation' (cited in de Brunhoff 1976: 35). Marx is suggesting that money is mystifying, that its social power cannot be grasped by beginning with exchange (Soderberg 2014), not endorsing the mainstream view that money is unimportant.

Keynes nevertheless develops an original critique of the classics, who he insists held two incompatible theories of money. The first is really one of 'non-monetary money' (Kicillof 2018: 148). According to Keynes, '[m]ost treatises on the principles of economics are concerned mainly, if not entirely, with a real-exchange economy; and – which is more peculiar – the same thing is also largely true of most treatises on the theory of money' (CWXIII: 409). From Hume to Samuelson, mainstream writers assert that money simply allows an efficient exchange economy (Ingham 2004, Hoover 2012). Analysis usually begins with commodity money but quickly parks money's specificity by depicting money itself as invariable. Formal acknowledgements that the marginal utility of money itself depends upon wealth (Jevons 1957, Marshall 2009) are dropped for the sake of convenience, and it is assumed that '[m]oney with constant purchasing power represents a constant marginal utility' (Kicillof 2018: 152). Money does not matter. For this first classical view, money is simply a veil, which needs to be drawn aside to uncover the real economy beneath (Schumpeter 1954a).

By contrast, what Kicillof calls the 'second classical treatise' allows that money might itself be subject to economic laws. 'The demand for the commodity "money" in its capacity as commodity [i]s nothing particular, as it depends, ultimately, on consumers' preferences and needs based on utility' (Kicillof 2018: 158). The ancient quantity theory now becomes, in standard interpretations of the Fisher equation, an imperative that the state supply of money should manage prices (Friedman 1987). From a theoretical point of view, money's production is separated from that of the wider economy, and for Friedman it might as well be assumed to be dropped from the skies. Money does now matter, and any distortion of price signals has serious consequences, but 'neither demand nor supply grants it intrinsic value … instead of its price being what governs quantity, it is now the arbitrary quantity put into circulation that governs the value of money' (Kicillof 2018: 160).

With these two alternative mainstream approaches to money, Keynes writes, '[w]e have all of us become used to finding ourselves sometimes on one side of the moon and sometimes on the other, without knowing what route or journey connects them' (1973: 292). Keynes accordingly attempts to develop a unified theory of money. If, as the neo-classical view insists, price signals are paramount, what happens to money should affect the wider economy.

This is true of price changes and expectations of price changes. As above, Keynes's earlier work made clear, for example, how inflation redistributes income, how 'a change in the available "counters", which does not affect everyone's holding equally (and in practice such changes never do), may have a fairly large lasting effect on relative price-levels' (2011: volume 1, 92). Inflation's redistributive effects, for example, potentially have contradictory implications for profits and effective demand (Keynes 1923, 2011: vol. 1). Cuts in money wages might set in motion a deflationary spiral (Rivot 2019). Expectations of price changes also become vital in relation to expectations of interest and profit, making it rational to spend or to hold money. These forces may pull in different directions, but they require that the monetary has real economic consequences.

Money also matters decisively in terms of interest rates, which do not settle at some natural rate but are determined (at least substantially) independently of savings and investment demand. As discussed in Chapter 5, taken literally, Keynes's model becomes highly determinist. He posits the supply of money (itself taken as set by the authorities, or 'exogenous') and liquidity preference (discussed below) as (something close to) autonomous variables, which help to explain the 'real' economy but which themselves remain inadequately explained. Both finance and state authority are constrained by the wider economy, but they are not reducible to it, and financial actions have substantial and often unpredictable consequences.

Keynes agrees that the money supply matters but in more complex ways than suggested by the quantity theory or later monetarists. In conditions of less than full employment, more money may lead not to increased prices but to more economic activity, more employment. In common with the existing Cambridge approach, Keynes put more emphasis on the demand for money than on its supply. More fundamentally, for Keynes, the velocity of circulation was inconstant and unpredictable. In the *Treatise*, 'the price-level can be affected just as much by the decisions of the depositors to vary the amounts of real-balances which they ... keep, as by the decisions of the bankers to vary the amounts of money-balances which they ... create' (2011: volume 1, 228). The *General Theory* abandons 'real-balances' and introduces liquidity preference to express this willingness to hold money. As Minsky puts it, '[t]he argument shows that we cannot understand how our economy works by first solving allocation problems and then adding financing relations; in a capitalist economy resource allocation and price determination are integrated with the financing of outputs, positions in capital assets, and the validating liabilities' (Minsky 1986: 159–60). Money cannot be safely ignored and the economy treated as if it were based on barter. Indeed, liquidity preference and the supply of money affect the interest rate, which becomes a crucial causal variable, determining the level of investment and employment.

Keynes is therefore articulating a 'monetary theory of production' (CWXIII: 408ff). He has reasonably been depicted as being primarily a monetary economist and as suggesting money is analytically primary (Patinkin 1987, Skidelsky 1992, Davidson 2007, 2009, Minsky 2008). Keynes's monetary priorities also mean that he is not simply throwing extra variables into an otherwise orthodox simultaneous-equations model. He has dependent and independent variables, determinates and determinants (1973: 245, 183). As above, there are later qualifications and acknowledgements of interdependence (Keynes 1973: 247, CWXIV: 11–12) but, amongst other things, Keynes's one-sidedness leaves him vulnerable to the criticisms of Hicks (1937) and Hansen (1953), discussed in Chapter 11, which would reintegrate Keynes with the classical mainstream.

Even if contestable as a substantive theoretical system, much of what Keynes says about the impact of money and credit on production is enduringly powerful. Of course, it is possible to go further, both to socialise the variables and to interrogate the ordering. Keynes's stress on the monetary variables leaves what he says about production largely orthodox. Regarding money as first a measure of value and interest as ultimately derived from profit (as will be discussed in Chapter 8) allows a more convincing anchoring of monetary relations than could be achieved by looking at the world the other way round and trying to explain value relations by beginning with money. Nevertheless, the specific demand for money, whether from productive capital or from within finance, and states' monetary policy cannot be reduced to passive reflections of the productive economy. The implication, which Marxists need to keep in sight, is that there is a financial realm within which there are real economic decisions – 'real' in the sense that they have non-trivial impacts on the wider economy.

The point becomes stark in the way major economic crises have often been accompanied by changes in monetary arrangements, with real social struggles over these shifts. Marx wrote extensively about the 1844 Act, particularly in opposition to the Currency School, and its insistence on maintaining strict links between banknote issue and gold. Few subsequent Marxists have been as interested in what have sometimes seemed technical intra-capitalist monetary squabbles. But what happens to money and, not least, what states do to money can have serious implications for the wider economy. Polanyi's (2001) famous account sees the 1844 Act as a vital moment in establishing modern capitalism. If this puts too much emphasis on political determination, the passage of the Act made a substantial economic and political difference. Similarly, the post-WWI decisions to return to gold standard mattered, as did those in France to return but at a devalued rate. It is not fantastic to imagine that the British General Strike might not have occurred if Keynes's advice to stay off gold had been heeded in 1925. The arrangements at Bretton Woods and the post-WWII system's subsequent abandonment had at least some impact on the wider economy, and considerably different impacts on different national economies. The use of inflation in the 1970s and the turn to monetarism at the end of that decade have been the subject of important Marxist studies (e.g. Krippner 2011), and most Marxists had little difficulty opposing the high interest rate policies of the 1970s and 1980s, with their deliberately recessionary and avowedly anti-labour motivations. Conversely, by the 2000s low interest rates and bank lending substantially provided the basis for the housing boom and the sub-prime crisis. The point here is simply that policy could clearly make an economic difference. Of course, neither the authorities nor financiers make decisions in conditions of their own choosing, but real financial decisions and changing monetary forms influenced accumulation and class relations.

Hoarding or liquidity preference as an important socio-institutional phenomenon

Marx largely sees hoarding as functional for capital, with the store and release of value potentially smoothing accumulation (1976: 231–2). He is also aware of potential dysfunctionalities and why, as a consequence, Say's Law is nonsense. At the same time, Marx's analysis remains underdeveloped and the potential causes and consequences of hoarding remain worth further investigation. This can potentially be enriched by building on Keynes's idea of liquidity preference. This reintroduces what he acknowledges as the 'ancient distinction between the use of money for the transaction of

current business and its use as a store of value' (1973: 168). In his subsequent defence, Keynes often reverts to a language of hoarding pure and
simple (CWXIV: 70, 116, 117, 213). There are very different emphases in
terms of causation. At least in the first instance, where for Keynes liquidity
is preferred, for Marx investment is declined (Lederer 1936). Conceptual
priorities matter to both Marx and Keynes, but there is a two-way process
and the specific financial demand has real, potentially disruptive, impacts.

    This section unavoidably trespasses on the discussion of credit and
interest in the next chapter, but for Keynes in the *General Theory*, rather
than there being a natural rate of interest efficiently matching savings and
investment, interest rates are determined through the interaction of the
supply of money by the authorities and liquidity preference. Liquidity preference in turn has three determinants: transactions and precautionary and
speculative demand. The last constitutes the most dynamic element and
is Keynes's most original contribution. Transactions and precautionary
demands, and Keynes's subsequent addition of a finance demand, all seem
reasonably commensurate with mainstream views that reduce finance to a
function of the real economy. With speculative demand, the financial system
develops a separate logic in which speculation can become a self-fulfilling
prophecy. Assessments of returns, not least of returns in relation to the rate
of interest, become the determinants of the rate of interest.

    To a degree still disputed, Keynes's *General Theory* views are predicated
on his original understanding of uncertainty. Quite typically, the 'central
idea' of the *General Theory* is 'that the role of money derives from the existence of ignorance and uncertainty from which the classical system abstracted'
(Clarke, S. 1988: 236). Practically, future rates of return on investment and
interest are unknowable and in an important sense themselves speculative.
Money can then provide a bridge between the present and an uncertain
future. It is not irrational to hold money idle when better rates of return may
become available at some unknowable future time. Speculation is Keynes's
'*reductio ad absurdum* of the doctrine that the benefits of all are best met
through the free play of individual desires' (Fitzgibbons 1988: 90). It is not
irrational to buy financial assets whose price depends not on any underlying
cost but on other people's estimation of their likely return. We soon enter
the world of Keynes's famous second- and third-order games, 'where we
devote our intelligence to anticipating what average opinion expects average
opinion to be' (1973: 156). In short, as Tily writes, '[t]he liquidity preference schedule is derived as a cumulative distribution function of individual
speculators' expectations of the rate of interest and the funds they have set
aside for speculation' (2007: 189). We can end with the situation of financial
dominance where 'enterprise becomes the bubble on a whirlpool of speculation' (Keynes 1973: 159). For Keynes, the conventional understanding is

reversed: 'interest has been usually regarded as the reward for not-spending, whereas in fact it is the reward for not-hoarding' (1973: 174).

There is much that is problematic. Again, Keynes's analysis appears to hang on the interaction of independent asocialised individuals. For Keynes 'the fact that each individual investor flatters himself that his commitment is "liquid" … calms his nerves and makes him much more willing to run a risk' (Keynes 1973: 160). Keynes's own earlier criticisms of economists' neglect of institutional power have largely disappeared (CWIX: 284–5). Liquidity preference seems either indeterminate or to hang between 'conventional judgement' and 'animal spirits' (Dow 2019), suspended on some rather flimsy psychology (Skidelsky 1992). Persuading individuals to lessen their attachment to liquidity and towards long-term investment then becomes at least an important part of Keynes's solution (Davis 1992).

However, there are important qualifications to Keynes's individualism. As discussed in Chapter 2, there are reasons to think his individualism does not run particularly deep, and he provides hints at a more social theory (O'Donnell 1989, Davis 1994). People behave conventionally and predictably (1973: 199, 203). Both Sheehan (2009) and Kicillof (2018) see the changed, corporate nature of capitalism as still essential to Keynes's *General Theory* argument. 'Instability is amplified by the separation of ownership and control, stock market valuations determined with inadequate information, casino-led stock markets and the fluctuating character of both speculator confidence and the state of credit' (Sheehan 2009: 119). Keynes's chapter 15 on 'the Psychological and Business Incentives to Liquidity' is notable for saying much less on individual psychology than elsewhere, and much less than is often imputed.

A reworking of Keynes's ostensibly individual determinants as social constructions might not, therefore, do much damage to his system but, at best, the nature of the social construction, the relation between individual agents and social structures, warrants further elaboration. Many authors from within the Keynesian tradition have accordingly identified the limits of depictions of liquidity preference as an individual, psychological phenomenon and tried to go beyond them. For Minsky, 'questions need to be answered in the context of the institutions and financial usages that actually exist, not in terms of an abstract economy' (Minsky 1986: 112). Liquidity preference only makes sense if financial institutions are able to 'hold up' money rather than acting as frictionless intermediaries. There need to be, in Hahn's 'terminology "resting places" in the demand for nonproducibles' (Davidson 2010: 256). The fiction of financial institutions as simple intermediaries between savers and investors becomes less plausible as the range of purely financial and intra-institutional financial activity expands. The explosion of financial derivatives, traded and held primarily within the financial sector, takes liquidity preference to new levels.

The acknowledgement of the need for a more thoroughly socialised analysis is therefore not necessarily a specifically Marxist one, but a Marxist epistemology provides bases for interpreting the context of individual beliefs and actions. As Lapavitsas argues, '[m]oney certainly functions as means of dealing with uncertainty in a capitalist economy, but this is primarily due to the economy's capitalist character' (2006: 145). It is a simple Marxist truism that capitalism's competitive dynamism imposes imperatives and constraints, but it is impossible to anticipate the future in detail and, in a deep epistemological sense, it is indeed unknowable. More particularly, people and firms cannot know how others will react and must form expectations about the future, and thence second- and third-order problems of the type Keynes identifies (Itoh and Lapavitsas 1999), but this does not require a descent into radical indeterminism. People act within broad parameters of understanding of likely outcomes imposed not least by capital's dynamic imperatives and confirmed or refuted by experience. Nor is liquidity preference purely a financial imperative which reacts on the real. Keynes's later reintroduction of a finance motive for liquidity also explicitly incorporates this as a business imperative (CWXIV: 201–15). As Shackle writes, for real economy firms 'a long life will depend upon survival through the many vicissitudes and the freedom to take audacious gambles without final catastrophe, and that survival and freedom will depend at many a crisis on liquidity' (1972: 216). Liquidity preference then becomes an (imperfect, distorted) reflection of accumulation and class struggle not an arbitrary product of speculators' psychology. Finance is not a world unto itself but is constrained and conditioned by the wider political economy. Not least, and again as Keynesians like Minsky (1986) acknowledge, even if finance comes to resemble a casino, the funds available to the speculators ultimately come from elsewhere.

Minimally, the individuals, at least those making the decisions that really count at an aggregate economic level, in finance as in the real economy, typically act within large institutions which condition their behaviour. Of course, some rich individuals control more money than medium-sized states. But most financial assets are held by huge institutions of one sort or another. Chapter 9 will sketch some historical examples, but the contrast between the nineteenth and twenty-first centuries is quite stark. Although he already discerns a centralisation, banking in Marx's day was largely small-scale, with limited liability protections only introduced in England in 1862 (Davies 1996). Today there are still vast numbers of small financial businesses, but the giants dominate. In 2016, the world's ten largest banks alone controlled assets amounting to $25 trillion (a third of world GDP) and made profits of \$317 billion (*The Banker* July 2016, World Bank 2018). Vast physical hoards still exist. The central banks of Germany, France, Italy and China alone hold \$500 billion's worth of gold between them, a small fraction of their total reserves (IMF 2020). Large institutions are directly responsible for most of the cash in circulation and for the outstanding loans.

There are clear commensurabilities between Marx and Keynes, with real-economy demand reducing hoards (Robinson 1966). Conversely, as Heilbroner asks, why 'would businessmen expand their facilities when they look to the future with trepidation' (1999: 266)? Recent decades have seen leaps in the level of corporate retained earnings, and these have also been thrown onto financial markets. Real-economy corporations not only saved rather than borrowing or reinvesting profits but instituted new financial practices, notably through share buy-backs, which drove up prices, further encouraging the diversion of money away from investment (Milberg and Winkler 2010). 'Hoarding has increased and has been difficult to mobilize with much intensified liquidity preference due to worries about the future and lack of promising opportunities for industrial investment' (Itoh 2005: 190). The financialisation of real-economy corporations makes little sense as a passive response to interest rates, as Keynes's *General Theory* first-order approximations would have it, because these rates have been at historic lows. Nor do interest rates and liquidity preferences make sense in abstraction from the returns available for real-economy investment.

There are dynamic feedback mechanisms, however, and the analytical point is that hoarding is potentially dysfunctional for capital conceived as a whole. Liquidity preference, considered as an institutional phenomenon, helps to explain this potentially contradictory relation with money's functions as a measure of value and medium of exchange. The concentrations of capital and of power within finance continued to vary across countries but increased dramatically in the last decades of the twentieth century. Marxists have not been immune from exaggerated depictions of recent transformations as a misguided or malevolent change of heart by policy-makers or as predicated on financial capitalists' new-found greed, but they can also find the bases of these in underlying reorientations of capital. Marx's conceptions of the changing dynamics of accumulation provide a necessary first-order basis in profits and their allocation, however much financial decisions then influence accumulation.

Conclusion

This chapter can be concluded very simply and briefly: money is a social relation and social relations establish what material forms of money are adopted. Money, to be money, must have certain properties and fulfil certain functions, but it has different and potentially conflicting functions, meaning that it is only ever an imperfect measure of value, medium of exchange or store of value. There can be no ideal money, and forms and functions 'work' better or worse for different social interests. They also work for any putative collective capitalist interest only imperfectly and as the outcome of open-ended struggle. Where Keynes almost always began with money, a Marxist approach instead begins from the side of production and class relations. But there needs to be a pincer movement, as it were, and at least also a supporting approach from the side of money. The monetary forms impact on accumulation in non-trivial ways: in particular, hoarding or liquidity preference, understood as an institutional phenomenon, holds up money in finance in ways that do not simply reflect but also contribute to the dynamics and to the inertia of the productive economy. Similarly, as the next chapter will discuss, interest rates and financial profits may ultimately derive from, but are not reducible to, capital's profitability.

8

Profit and interest

Introduction

This chapter turns to questions of interest and interest rates, and it is perhaps here that Keynes's 'solecism', positing the followers of Ricardo, the likes of Mill, Marshall, Edgeworth and Pigou, as the 'classics' (1973: 3), is most seriously misleading. There is little continuity between the tradition of Smith, Ricardo and Marx and the mainstream understanding of interest against which Keynes sets himself. It will be argued that starting within, and directing his critique towards, the will-o'-the-wisp which is conventional theory, Keynes provides an insufficient basis for an effective alternative. He can demonstrate the fallacies of his opponents' priorities but cannot secure his own. The concessions he is forced to make to his critics then effectively neutralise his critique, allowing it to be reincorporated into an only moderately reformed mainstream. It will be argued that the classics, as Marx understood them, can provide an anchor for Keynes's insights and guard against such an appropriation. At the same time, Keynes's insights should provoke a constructive reform of the classics, as analysis moves from an abstract generality to concrete investigations of profit and interest and their relation.

The next section therefore goes back to the classics, understood in the more conventional sense, and to Marx, and why they see profits in the wider economy as providing the basis for any adequate theory of interest. It will be argued that this remains an essential starting point against standard economic depictions of free-floating forces of supply and demand or an apparently autonomous determination by financial variables. The financial sector can ultimately only appropriate a share of value created elsewhere. It is, however, necessary to go beyond this simple fact, and a critical engagement with Keynes can add valuable nuance.

The second section therefore revisits Keynes's critique of orthodoxy and his alternative depiction of interest rate determination. There are two alternative mainstream views, one positing interest rates as simply

167

tending to a natural rate that brings aggregate supply and demand into line, the second treating money itself in marginalist terms and seeing interest rates as determined by time preferences for money based on income, wealth and subjective evaluations of utility. Keynes points out the insufficiency of both mainstream views and, as seen in previous chapters, instead sees interest rates as determined through the interaction of liquidity preference and the money supply. Initially, Keynes posits these as wholly independent of what happens in the wider economy. This proves unsustainable and Keynes later retreats. But acknowledging more complex interdependence undermines his claims to provide a coherent alternative theory and lends itself to the reincorporation of Keynes's insights.

The third section argues, following the discussion of the previous chapter, that Keynes's insights into liquidity preference and state power can be better reinterpreted as second-order effects, grounded in a classical/Marxist view of profits as the basis of interest but acknowledging questions of institutional power within finance, in the state and inter-state relations, from which both Marx and Keynes abstract. So reinterpreted, Keynes's insight allows progress beyond the classics' generalisations particularly in terms of understanding interest rate variability. Arguments about institutional specificity, particularly in relation to the state, and the impact of money and finance on capital accumulation are developed more concretely in the next chapter.

Marx and the classics

This section briefly sketches and defends Marx's views of interest, even as it argues for going further. As often, Marx builds on classical foundations, on Smith and Ricardo, and the essential point here – that interest is derived from profit – is also reaffirmed by Schumpeter and (at least occasionally and more obliquely) by modern mainstream economists.

The 'classics', as Marx understood them, already linked interest and profit. For Smith, the rate of interest is roughly half the rate of profit (1997: 200). He never really explains this but sees market imperatives as the driver. Different statutes 'seem rather to have followed and not to have gone before the market rate of interest' (1997: 192). For example, Smith describes how laws passed by Edward VI (1537–53) prohibiting all interest are 'said to have produced no effect, and probably rather increased than diminished the extent of usury' (1997: 191). Attempts to restrict interest rates severely, outright proscriptions (by Smith's time long since abandoned in Britain) or setting low legal maxima would drive lending underground and have the perverse effect of increasing the rates charged, with a premium for illegality because loans become high-risk from the lenders' point of view (1997: 454). As often, Smith is not simply advocating laissez-faire and he thinks there should be a legal limit which 'ought always to be somewhat above the lowest market price' (1997: 457). Too low a rate and lending is driven into illegality, too high and the irresponsible might be encouraged. For Smith, Britain's then legal rate of 5 per cent where the government borrows at 3 per cent and private rates are 4 or 4.5 'is perhaps as proper as any' (1997: 457).

Ricardo sees '[t]he rate of interest … ultimately and permanently governed by the rate of profit (1951: 297). He says little more, and Schumpeter accuses 'Ricardo and his epigoni' of seeing profit and interest as 'plainly synonymous' (cited in Conrad 1963: 11). However, Ricardo's 'governed by' makes his views distinct from those of later mainstream thinkers, most conspicuously Knight, in whose writings the identity of profit and interest conflates the categories, effectively saying that all money-making could be understood as earning interest and considered under the same rubric (Conrad 1963). The classics distinguished between the concepts. Ricardo also immediately adds that interest is 'subject to temporary variations from other causes' (1951: 297). There could be all sorts of reasons for fluctuations in supply and demand, with conditions of war and peace (very much still at the front of Ricardo's mind in 1817) making a major difference, particularly through demand for government loans (Ricardo 1951). Ultimately, however, interest is derived from profits.

Marx stood within the classical tradition in this sense. Profit rates set the maximum of the rate of interest, at least under normal circumstances. Profits themselves are derived from, are the monetary form of, surplus value generated by the exploitation of productive labour. The distinction between productive and unproductive labour needs a brief comment; it is controversial, even amongst Marxists, and at best hard to operationalise (Laibman 1992). But the conceptual point is clear enough. Not every economic activity produces new value. Marx includes popes, priests, police and moneylenders amongst the unproductive. For Marx (e.g. 1973: 328), this is not about material production, as it was for Smith. School teachers, opera singers and clowns can all be perfectly productive. In Marx's examples, from the standpoint of the capitalist, an education factory is conceptually little different to a sausage factory (Marx 1976: 644, 1044). But some firms live off the profits generated elsewhere. This would be obvious in the case of outright robbery – which example seems sufficient to establish the principle. But other work may be socially useful, keeping the peace, caring for the elderly, without contributing to the production of new value. It was noted in Chapter 4 that Keynes introduces a category of 'unproductive consumption', which adds nothing to productive effort (2011: volume 1, 125), and this allows much the same point. Although there are many disputes and many grey areas, Marx and most Marxists see finance in this light. Financial capitalists are a 'class of parasites', or at best 'honourable bandits' (Marx 1981: 678, 679).

This is not saying that finance is simply a 'bad thing' or even necessarily a 'drag' on the real economy. The financial system may enable capitalist growth. But even then it does so through redistributing not creating wealth. To borrow Keynesian examples, burying bottles stuffed with banknotes, or redistributing income from the rich to the poor, may be conducive to growth but these are not themselves productive activities. Any positive role is a second-order effect, distinct from production. Finance may enhance capitalist production but its profits are derivative. Ultimately the productive economy is the only source from which financial profits derive. Finance's apparently parasitic existence is possible, however, because interest-bearing capital has a unique use value, giving the borrower the ability to generate profit. The unique and derivative character of interest becomes apparent in the contrast with the commodity economy where the goods exist prior to the redistribution of value on the market. Financial profits are only made retrospectively, when and if the loan is repaid. For Marx, interest must therefore be conceived as merely a 'part of average profit'.

As unfashionable as it has become to remember Marx, this view of interest as a distinctive form of profit never disappeared entirely. Schumpeter (1954b) has an unusual view of profit based on monopoly, highlighting how profit is incompatible with the perfectly competitive, circular-flow models of orthodoxy. These also imply that money is pure medium of circulation, with no need for borrowing and lending. It is only in a dynamic, growing economy, with real profits, that borrowing also becomes worthwhile. Again, it is corporate profits that produce interest. Modern textbooks can implicitly endorse this basic proposition. Hoover (2012) argues that in the long term, corporate profitability leads to yields from stocks. But stocks and bonds are substitutes and move together, albeit imperfectly. So profit is the driver. Standard interpretations also now depict financial firms as 'intermediaries', with financial wealth not to be confused with 'real wealth' (Hoover 2012: 175). Even Friedman (1987) rewrites the quantity theory of money in income terms to exclude financial transactions, because these add no value. Whatever its derivation, this argument recalls the centrality of corporate profits, emphasised by Marx and the classics, which the neo-classical tradition would reject.

For Marx and most later Marxists, the implication is that in normal times the rate of interest must be greater than zero but less than the rate of profit. Keynes will be discussed below, but he confirms this in a 'backwards' sense: were rates of interest to be higher than expected returns on investment, productive capital would not invest. There is an important area of agreement, albeit reached from different angles.

Beyond this, Marx (1981) insisted that interest rates cannot be determined by any law. There cannot be a 'natural' rate of interest. In this he was anticipating Keynes in rejecting Say's Law. Instead, there is a cruder fight for profit shares. The third section below will suggest that it is possible to say more about these through a critical appropriation of Keynes, but attempts have also been made from within the Marxist tradition to extend Marx's insights. As Shaikh (2016) argues, there seems no reason to stop at Marx's negative, with profits merely setting the maximum.

First, time matters. The most casual acquaintance with the data suggests that any relation between profit rates and interest rates is loose. For about a decade and a half from the mid-1970s, the US bank prime rate was consistently above the business profit rate (Shaikh 2016). Of course, such profit rates (measured in money terms and after value has been redistributed) are different from those usually understood by Marxists. It is clear, however, that interest rate variations do not follow profit variations very closely and the limits set on the rate of interest by the rate of profit are, at most, rough and long term. This is a very obvious point, which Marx makes. Times of crisis, which are times of low profits, can also be precisely times when it becomes possible for interest-bearing capital to make a killing. The fact that interest is only sustainable in the long term as a share of profit does not prevent more or less short-term variation and redistributions to financiers.

Second, according to Marx's broader analysis, the redistribution of value between capitals is achieved according to their costs rather than according to the value produced by any particular firms' own workers. It seems entirely possible to include financial capital under the same rubric. Money-dealing capitalists would expect to achieve economy-wide average rates of profit. In as far as their profits are produced through lending (rather than through, say, the various other modern methods of financial extortion), these too set the rate of interest. Meanwhile, financial firms' costs become a constitutive part of the social whole, even if they are not themselves producing surplus value (Shaikh 2016). The size of the unproductive economy in general, and of finance in particular, influences the general rate of profit (Rotta 2018). The recent expansion of finance has been widely depicted as at least contributing to low aggregate growth (Harvey 2005, Foster and McChesney 2012, Lapavitsas 2013). Even if financial expansion is more symptom than original cause, the backwash effects may be important.

Third, it is necessary to look concretely at the institutional dynamics of financial and other firms, of states and of class relations. It is evident that there are multiple interest rates rather than just one. As Keynes highlights, finance does not involve only a straightforward lending from finance to 'productive' capital, and there are other sources of demand, other sources of liquidity preference, not least demand from within finance itself.

Keynes's critique of the mainstream and its limits

Keynes's view of interest rate determination was outlined in Chapter 5. As usual, there are two parts to Keynes's story: what is wrong with the classics, and his alternative model.

Without recapitulating Keynes's overall argument, interest rate determination is central to his critique. Indeed, he sees conventional economics as fatally flawed, 'the flaw being largely due to the failure of the classical doctrine to develop a satisfactory theory of the rate of interest' (CWXIII: 489). Again, there are two orthodox views: one that interest can be safely ignored, the other that it obeys marginalist laws.

The first view Keynes criticised, descended from Mill, was that of a natural rate of interest, which brings savings and investment into equality. Keynes's criticisms of this in the *Treatise* were outlined in the second part of Chapter 4. Keynes argues that it is entirely possible that achieved money rates might vary from any such natural rate. Chapter 5 introduced Keynes's more radical departure in the *General Theory*. Now Keynes rejects the idea of there being any such natural rate of interest. Although, for Keynes, savings and investment are necessarily equal, it is illegitimate to assume automatic adjustments from savings, via the interest rate, to investment. There is an important difference between goods markets, where particular *ceteris paribus* claims can be justified to allow such depictions of supply and demand, and interest rates, where they cannot, because interest rates themselves will affect output and the prices of other goods (Conrad 1963). For Keynes, higher interest rates induce proportionally more saving but retard investment (CWXIII: 449). An increase in the propensity to save may do 'little or nothing to reduce the rate of interest' (Skidelsky 1992: 553). It becomes entirely possible to reach situations where the limits of effective demand produce disincentives to invest in wealth-producing, employment-producing activities and for there to be an unemployment equilibrium. Instead of being achieved by interest rate adjustments, 'the equality between the stock of capital goods offered and the stock demanded will be brought about by the prices of capital goods' (Keynes 1973: 186). Consequently, '[t]he influence of changes in the rate of interest on the amount actually saved is of paramount importance, but it is *in the opposite direction* to that usually supposed' (1973: 110). So much for the first classical view.

The second, contrasting strand of orthodox thinking applies ideas of marginalist, subjective utility to money. In particular, Fisher insists that interest is at least 'not wholly an affair of goods, but is partly one of money' (1907: 78). It is worth briefly dwelling on this account, to which Keynes acknowledged debts.

For Fisher, the theory of interest should bear a strong resemblance to the theory of prices. There is no absolute standard of value, and 'any absolute standard is absolute only to the particular individual' (Fisher 1907: 84). To establish an equilibrium in the market, we need differences of supply and demand. But interest is distinguished from commodity markets by time, because it involves the 'exchange between present and future goods' and people make different evaluations of 'present enjoyable income over future enjoyable income' (Fisher 1907: 86). The rate of interest is therefore 'an index of the preference ... for a dollar of present over a dollar of future income' (1907: 3). There are 'errors', or what modern economists might term 'imperfections', under-estimates of the future, but for Fisher there are also intrinsic processes because of the relative scarcity of the present in relation to the future. If a person is growing richer, a dollar one year hence will be worth slightly less, for Fisher by say 1 per cent (Fisher 1907: 84). But individual's wealth, their expectation of future income and their personal attributes will all affect their preferences (Fisher 1907: 98).

As Marshall and others had emphasised, a dollar has a different utility to the millionaire and the poor labourer (Fisher 1907: 84). This leads to different preferences for present and future dollars, and 'the smaller the income the higher is the preference for present over future income' (Fisher 1907: 94). Of course for the poor, both the present and future utility of a given dollar is relatively greater, but of the two, the present utility increases more. 'Any one who values his life would prefer to rob the future for the benefit of the present, so far, at least, as to keep life going' (Fisher 1907: 94). Fisher also argues that in general, '[t]he effect of poverty is often to relax foresight and self-control and tempt one to "trust to luck" for the future' (Fisher 1907: 95). People will also have more obviously subjective time preferences. People evaluate risk and 'lay up for a rainy day' (Fisher 1907: 100). This might, but need not, involve lowering time preferences. Different individuals make judgements based on foresight, self-control, habit, life expectancy and their interest in the lives of other people (Fisher 1907: 103). Having children particularly decreases the time preference, and 'an increase in population, therefore, will, other things being equal, reduce the rate of interest' (Fisher 1907: 108). Not denying other factors, and 'perverse individuals' who act counter-intuitively, Fisher locates the crucial determinants in income: its size, time-shape, composition and probability (Fisher 1907: 102–3).

For each individual, there is a price at which it seems worthwhile to lend or borrow. A person will borrow up to the rate of their marginal term preference. For example, if, initially, they have a term preference of 10 per cent and the prevailing interest rate is 5 per cent, they borrow, say, $100. This borrowed money increases their current income and reduces their time preference, perhaps to 8 per cent. They borrow another $100 and further increments until their time preference meets the 5 per cent interest rate (Fisher 1907: 119). From the other side, an individual with a time preference of 2 per cent would be willing to lend at (anything over) 2 per cent but is able to get 5 per cent. Lending $100 reduces their present income and increases their time preference, but they continue to lend until this has reached the market rate (Fisher 1907: 120). Individual preferences provide the push and pull. So where for individuals the interest rate appears fixed, '[f]or society as a whole, the order of cause and effect is reversed' (Fisher 1907: 130). The picture of a market-determined interest rate emerges. The market is not fundamentally different from that for commodities like sugar. 'The rate of interest is simply the rate of preference, upon which the whole community may concur in order that the market of loans may be exactly cleared' (Fisher 1907: 131).

Fisher's second approximation discusses how a greater range of income streams will lead to steadier rates and how capital has options in term of the size and time-shape of its preferences. This market is not isolated from others, and buying and selling property, for example, has the same results (Fisher 1907: 125). Fisher also, finally, acknowledges investment income, assumes that savings and investment are equalised by the rate of interest, and so in a formal sense ends up back with Mill. Conrad (1963) accordingly categorises him as having a 'non-monetary' theory of interest. The point of this detour, however, is to emphasise that there was already an alternative tradition that emphasised specifically monetary determinants of the rate of interest. Many of Keynes's contemporaries, notably Robertson in the theory of loanable funds, already acknowledged there was a push and pull coming from both monetary and non-monetary factors.

Keynes agrees that because the rate of interest is essentially the price of borrowing money, it is determined, like other prices, by the interplay of demand and supply (Stewart 1972). But he tries to identify priorities, seeing the supply and demand for money as being achieved substantially independently of investment. So this is closer to Fisher and critical of the first strand of orthodoxy. Keynes argues that proponents of the orthodoxy accept that:

> the marginal efficiency of capital is equal to the rate of interest. But they tell us nothing as to the forces which determine what this common level of marginal efficiency will tend to be. It is when we proceed to this further discussion that my argument diverges from the orthodox argument ... [The first strand of orthodoxy maintains that] the marginal efficiency of various assets are independent of money, which has, so to speak, no autonomous influence, and that prices move until the marginal efficiency of money, i.e. the rate of interest, falls

into line with the common value of the marginal efficiency of other assets as determined by other forces ... My theory, on the other hand, maintains that this is a special case and that over a wide range of possible cases almost the opposite is true, namely, that the marginal efficiency of money is determined by forces partly appropriate to itself. (CWXIV: 103)

The 'almost' and 'partly' in the last line represent something of a retreat from the *General Theory* view, but the message is essentially the same. Keynes sees interest rates as established independently of profits and of investment demand, but unlike Fisher and the monetary theories of interest he posits two much more specific independent variables – the supply of money by the authorities and the demand for money from within finance: liquidity preference. After a brief note on how Keynes defines the interest rate, these supply and demand factors will be considered in turn.

Keynes offers a slightly convoluted definition of the rate of interest as 'nothing more than the inverse proportion between a sum of money and what can be obtained for parting with control over the sum of money in exchange for a debt for a stated period of time' (1973: 167). It is the 'reward for parting with liquidity' or the '"price" which equilibrates the desire to hold wealth in the form of cash with the available quantity of cash' (1973: 167). In principle, as for Fisher, other commodities can attract a rate of interest but the particular properties of money ensure that it is 'the money-rate of interest which is often the greatest' (1973: 223). Three things impinge. First, some assets produce a yield in terms of themselves through involvement in the production process. Wheat is a common example. As seen in the last chapter, money, unlike other commodities, is used solely (with relatively minor exceptions, such as when gold is used to make jewellery) as money and 'its utility is solely derived from its exchange value' (1973: 231). When demand increases, this does not 'slop over into a demand for other things' (1973: 231). Second, there is a 'carrying cost': '[m]ost assets, except money, suffer some wastage or involve some cost through the passage of time' (1973: 225). Third, there is liquidity: 'the power of disposal over an asset during a period may offer a potential convenience of security, which is not equal for assets of different kinds' (1973: 226). The expected return is then equal to its 'yield *minus* its carrying cost *plus* its liquidity-premium' (1973: 226). The liquidity premium becomes key to determining both what counts as money and the rate of interest.

On the supply side, as discussed in Chapters 4, 5 and 7, Keynes sees the authorities as providing money. There can be derivative forms in credit and bank money, but these ultimately hang on 'money-proper', issued by the state. Money supply influences interest rates over which (sidestepping many controversies for the moment) states therefore exert vital influence.

Given the vagaries of liquidity preference, however, this does not provide a mechanical lever. At anything other than full employment, 'the long-term market-rate of interest will depend, not only on the current policy of the monetary authority, but also on market expectations concerning its future policy' (1973: 202). There is also a crucial asymmetry. In the short run, monetary authorities can set high rates. The post-Keynes world would provide powerful examples. Major states like the US remained the most trustworthy borrowers and, as in the early 1980s, could effectively establish very high, economy-wide norms. Even if these were inherently unsustainable in the long term, they could be relied upon to apply economic brakes, with corporations facing higher borrowing costs and new investment likely to occur only if expected returns were higher than the rate of interest. Conversely, 'whilst a weakening of credit is sufficient to bring about a collapse, its strengthening, though a necessary condition of recovery, is not a sufficient condition' (1973: 158). Keynes saw cuts in interest rates as an appropriate first, stimulating, response to economic contraction. But they might be insufficient. In the Great Depression and again in recent years, such has been the liquidity preference, in relation to low expected returns in the real economy, that very low, even negative, real interest rates have little stimulating effect.

Fortunately, where monetary policy fails, states could intervene by provoking investment and, through multiplier effects, stimulate further employment. As Keynes's own advocacy of public works and his refutation of simplistic arguments against 'crowding out' make clear, state and private activity is not zero sum. As discussed in Chapter 3, and again in the next section and the next chapter, there are problems with Keynes's understanding of the constraints and motives of state actions. But, minimally, it is clear both that states act, for example printing money and setting base rates, in ways that would at least normally be expected to affect the private economy and investment.

On the other side of Keynes's formula, rather than the time preferences of savers and investors, liquidity preference involves complex motives for holding money rather than less liquid assets. Keynes stresses the motives, particularly the speculative motives, within the financial sector. There are transactions and precautionary demands for liquidity, but these are relatively stable and the dynamic element comes from speculative demand. Economic uncertainty makes it entirely rational to hold money, and financial sector actors in particular do so, with varying subjective liquidity preferences, not least according to their expectations of what the future interest rate is likely to be, cumulatively influencing the rate of interest. Uncertainties are magnified by stock market speculation. Money will be spent, even borrowed and spent, if there is an expectation that stock prices will rise. This becomes a self-fulfilling prophecy if the 'bulls' outnumber the 'bears' and stock prices rise 'and yields accordingly do drop' (Lekachman 1967: 85). Lenders find it correspondingly harder to attract investors, and interest rates fall. Conversely, expectations of a decline in tomorrow's security prices leads to selling and to rises in the interest rate (Lekachman 1967). Keynes was also ahead of his time in distinguishing between 'real' and 'nominal' interest rates. A world of unpredictable inflation adds an extra dimension of guesswork to any evaluation of expected returns.

Keynes thus highlights that there is a distinct demand for money from within finance, but he ultimately has no theory of why this and *not* – or why this *more than* – the demand from investors influences the rate of interest. He initially depicts his financial variables as determining but apparently not themselves determined in any way by investment. 'My whole point is that *no* theory of interest can be derived from marginal efficiency. My theory is that, given the marginal efficiency of capital, then the rate of interest, whatever it is, derived from quite different sources, tells us on what scale investment will take place' (CWXXIX: 631). For Keynes, as Coddington criticises, it appears that 'wealth-holding decisions are given analytical autonomy, and … the rate of interest is thereby cut loose from economic "circumstances"' (Coddington 1983: 53). Keynes himself was clearly uncomfortable with the apparent mono-directionality and, as seen in Chapter 5, he later retreats, acknowledging an interaction and subsequently introducing a fourth 'finance motive' derived from entrepreneurial investors' liquidity preference. He even describes this as the 'coping-stone' of his interest rate theory (CWXIV: 220), although its analytical relation to the broader argument remains unclear.

Without some theory of profit, Keynes cannot turn his critique into a convincing alternative explanation of the ultimate derivation of interest. As above, he professes sympathy with the labour theory of value but treats it as an accounting device rather than a theory of profits, which, for the most part, simply remain 'normal'. Profits are even regarded as a component of costs, following the standard practice since Smith (1997). Keynes had proposed a theory of 'abnormal' profits in the *Treatise* (Keynes 2011), with entrepreneurs able to take advantage of price changes to receive more than they paid in wages or to other firms. Such profit inflations could therefore be realised through a redistribution at the expense of labour and rentiers. Kicillof (2018) extends this to attribute to the *General Theory* a more broadly mercantilist theory of profit, concluding that it relies on relative scarcity and abundance, which of course might explain how individuals increase their wealth but cannot explain how a society as a whole makes profits and grows. Whether or not this mercantilist reinterpretation is accurate, the general point remains that Keynes no more has a satisfactory general theory of profit than do his 'classical' opponents.

Without this, we regress to an essentially magical understanding which Keynes finds in the mainstream. As seen in Chapter 4, Keynes is particularly emphatic in his rejection of the idea, found in Mill for example, of profit and interest being a reward for waiting, a 'return for abstinence'. Such claims could gain some theoretical foundation in the early marginal utility theorists' understanding that future utility is discounted against the present (see e.g. Fisher 1907). To save is to forgo current utility and reap its equivalent reward. But, amongst other things, Keynes's views on uncertainty undermine any such calculus. The future is unknown and unknowable, and the more distant the future, the more uncertain it becomes. Most fundamentally, waiting cannot be generative. Interest cannot be a reward for waiting without ascending to a miraculous realm where nothing produces something. 'For if a man hoards his savings in cash, he earns no interest, though he saves just as much as before' (1973: 167). Other liberal apologetics fail in much the same way; interest cannot be a reward for risk taking, for if a woman lends without interest to her feckless sister, she risks as much as if she bought junk bonds. Economists who see waiting and risk as the source of profits might be invited to contemplate enriching themselves by standing in the middle of a busy motorway. Knight's annotations of Fisher's text make essentially the same point. 'Well and good, – except for the facts, Take away productivity of capital & there would be a rate of interest so established. But it would be as likely to be negative as positive & could but be extremely small either way' (in Fisher 1907: 133). Without a basis in profits, Keynes's analysis of interest similarly becomes indeterminate, vulnerable to the accusation that other variables matter more than those he prioritises.

As Kicillof writes, just as there was a circularity in Keynes's understanding of money and liquidity, so now 'the rate of interest turns out to be, essentially a synonym for the liquidity premium that individuals are willing to pay due to the fact, precisely, that money is liquid' (2018: 388, see also Robertson in Keynes CWXIV: 98, Chick 1983). Keynes's later concession that there are alternative sources of demand implicitly acknowledges the problems but leaves the relationships indeterminate. As Robertson writes rather acerbically of Keynes's qualifications, 'I understood, of course, that your "liquidity preference" is a hotch-potch' (CWXIV: 226). Robertson's comment serves to assert the similarities with his own ideas of loanable funds, which tend to throw the many variables together, allowing that there can be the sources of demand and supply which Keynes identifies but also any number of others. Many would now accept the importance of the variables Keynes's pinpoints, but few would agree on the overwhelming importance that he initially claimed for them.

The apparently arbitrary one-sidedness of the *General Theory* is something which supporters of the IS/LM (investment savings/liquidity money) approach would identify and address (Hicks 1937, Hansen 1953), albeit at the cost of a reintegration of 'Keynesianism' with the simultaneous-equations mainstream. The IS/LM approach will be discussed in Chapter 11, but it proposes independent schedules of the supply and demand of money and liquidity (LM) and for investment and savings (IS). Both these schedules reflect how the relationships change according to national income and the rate of interest, with their intersection neatly establishing the actual rate of interest. Hicks and Hanson are also suggesting that this intersection might occur where changes in the rate of interest have little impact on the levels of investment or where they cause large changes. In the first case it would be necessary to adopt 'Keynesian' policies to stimulate investment (to shift the IS curve), whereas in the second case the classical argument holds and interest rate adjustment (shifts in the LM curve) would suffice. Financial and investment demand are incorporated on an equal footing. Economists have what looks like a conventional supply-and-demand diagram and policy-makers a simple tool, without any hint of radical uncertainty or Keynes's more critical conclusions. What IS/LM does successfully highlight is that the supply and demand for money cannot be adequately conceived in isolation from the real economy.

Returning to the view of Marx and the classics discussed in the first section, and seeing interest as ultimately derived from profits, provides an anchorage from which to reconceive Keynes's insights. As Lederer (1936) argued from the beginning, it is more useful to begin with investment refused than with liquidity preferred. Financial speculators are ultimately speculating on real-economy outcomes which are eventually confirmed or rejected by experience (Burczak 2013). Except in times of direst need, firms would expect to pay less than their expected returns. But financial firms are no respecters of such hierarchy, and what is paid depends on power relations, including the credit ratings firms can buy and the state support upon which they can rely.

Profit, interest and financial power

Finally, this section makes the simple point that lending and borrowing always involve relations of power. For Marx, the fundamental power relation is that of capital over labour and this provides the basis for the theory of value, his understanding of exploitation, profit and thence interest rates. These relations inform, but do not determine, the power of financial capital and of states, to which Keynes points. These and other relations in turn condition value and exploitation. Their relative importance may be hard to specify theoretically but they are not beyond quantitative evaluation.

Claiming an analytical priority for profits involves making deductions about the logic of capital, not asserting an absolute, transhistorical law. The historical record makes clear that lending at interest pre-dates modern capitalism – according to some accounts, by several millennia (Aglietta 2018). Interest-bearing capital, for Marx, became bound up with its 'twin-brother' merchant capital, long preceding capital's dominance and existing 'in the most diverse socio-economic formations' (1981: 728). However, older ancient and feudal uses of credit were relatively peripheral to the overall economic system, and the rise of specifically capitalist borrowing represented a qualitative as well as a quantitative shift.

The most conspicuous transformations are the sheer dynamism, growth and thence size of the capitalist economy, inconceivable as the product of finance and without which the growth and size of modern finance would itself be inconceivable. Within this, Keynes's ideas add vital critical purchase to what can be very abstract and negative first-order classical claims about the priority of profit.

Money can be hoarded, or liquidity preferred, as Keynes suggests. There is a specific demand from within finance. But to understand this, as mentioned in the previous chapter, it seems necessary to add that money fails to 'move on' from savings to investment, that it gets held up. Keynes himself largely overlooks questions of institutional power. He elegantly rejects the fallacies of composition which bedevil mainstream economics but seems to perpetuate a similar fallacy in relation to liquidity preference. For Keynes, 'people just as truly save when they add to their idle cash as when they lend it out at interest' (Chick 1983: 183). But in the second case, if one person saves, another borrows. So what is straightforward for each individual leads to 'severe, perhaps insuperable, difficulties in defining aggregate savings' (Chick 1983: 182). It is, however, possible to identify 'churning' and the growing share of national and global incomes it consumes and also relatively straightforward to identify patterns of distribution and redistribution.

The data in Table 8.1, taken from Dumenil and Levy (2011), prompt some schematic comments. The institutional power of finance has risen. Rather than being competed away, as visions of efficient markets but also Marx's first-order approximations would predict, finance has been able to extract profits and to corner an increasing share of the corporate total (Fine 2010). As above, this has been widely depicted as having significant negative implications for overall economic growth. The essentially parasitic nature of finance means that it cannot indefinitely devour its host. But there are all sorts of feedback mechanisms between the monetary and the real in dynamic and shifting relations, rather than an automatic self-limiting adjustment.

Corporate borrowing has also increased, but rising financial profits in turn prove attractive to real-economy firms, which themselves become increasingly financialised, with increased retained earnings and share buy-backs inflating their financial value, even as they divert resources away from productive investment.

A second crucial transformation brought by the rise of capitalism is the apparent separation it achieves between economics and politics. Mainstream economists before Keynes tended to simply ignore the state. But if he brings back the state, for Keynes and most of his followers the state and market remain methodologically separate. We have a (non-state) economy, reckoned 'endogenous', and state agency, reckoned 'exogenous', with different roles assigned to each. Keynes tended to treat the money supply as 'exogenous' and to see this as interacting with the endogenous liquidity preference. Several modern followers come close to reversing this, depicting bank credit as constituting an endogenous money supply, while the state determines interest rates exogenously. This will be discussed in slightly more detail in the next chapter; here it is sufficient to note that states' institutional power makes them crucial not only as suppliers of money but also as borrowers.

State credit instruments constitute a large share of the demand. Historically, vast sums were lent to feudal rulers, and states were fundamental as borrowers from the beginning of modern finance. It was state debts which created the Banks of Amsterdam and England. Government bonds have long been key financial assets. Until the mid-nineteenth century, state securities, like the British consuls, dominated the market (Homer and Sylla 2005). In contrast to feudal times, modern states' credit tends to be relatively good, allowing them to set high, national economy-wide-determining rates of interest in the short run. But this ultimately depends on confidence that they can continue to raise revenues from a profitable productive base (at home or abroad). Low interest rates are more easily sustained, but even

Table 8.1 Net debt of US sectors (per cent of GDP) (Dumenil and Levy 2011: 104–5)

	1952	1980	2008
Non-financial sectors	79	102	192
Households	–3	30	68
Business	19	40	67
Government	60	25	48
Financial sector	–82	–103	–152
Rest of world	3	1	–40

large, powerful states need buyers for their bills. US Treasury paper is now sold at auction (Stigum and Crescenzi 2007) so there need to be buyers at the designated price: so low rates are only achievable because buyers find Treasury paper an acceptable low-risk asset. But tame central banks can circumvent this, at least to some extent, themselves buying Treasury paper, as in practices of quantitative easing. Minimally, '[p]ublic authority, after all, prints both money and the government securities' (Lekachman 1967: 86).

There is no guarantee that states' monetary intervention will produce predictable effects on broader interest rates. As Robinson writes, 'Keynes perhaps exaggerates the ease with which the authorities can control the complex of interest rates' (1966: 71). Nor, as of course Keynes insisted, is there any guarantee that those interest rates will produce predictable effects on investment. It may be state spending, rather than its printing money, which has the greater impact (Skidelsky 2019). So Keynes is right to insist that states are a vital, ineliminable factor in financial affairs and, as the next chapter elaborates, state practices and policy matter crucially, in ways irreducible to the imperatives of capital but never 'autonomously' of those imperatives.

Dumenil and Levy's (2011) figures also show that the US is borrowing from the rest of the world. This reiterates the importance of international power relations. Even large, powerful states are constrained: in an international context, limited for example in terms of their ability to issue money without this undermining their purchasing power. The situation, of course, becomes more acute for weaker states, particularly those needing to borrow in currencies which they do not themselves control. The extraction of spectacular interest rates on Greek government debt in the aftermath of the 2007–09 financial crisis proved a stark example but, in general, poorer and weaker states must pay more. State debt and central government debt securities, not least US Treasury paper (amounting to more than half of the $23 trillion world total at the end of 2017; BIS 2019), remain vital to the operations of modern finance across the globe. States' power and inter-state power relations matter, sometimes decisively. They shape rather than merely responding to class and intra-capitalist dynamics within borders and in international relations.

Finally, the sharp rise in household borrowing has been widely reported. It makes a nonsense of depictions of households as savers/lenders to firms as investors/borrowers, by way of neutral financial intermediaries. It also suggests that this household borrowing has grown in economic significance. It is obvious but worth repeating that workers, peasants and the poor in general pay more to borrow than capitalists, while the small capitalists pay more than the big. Marx already describes this, with the peasant enmeshed 'ever deeper in the webs of usury' (Marx 1981: 130) and extortionate rates of interest paid to pawnbrokers (1981: 729, 736). He reports 100 per cent interest reckoned usurious in Charlemagne's time but local burghers taking as much as 216 per cent in mid-fourteenth-century Germany (1981: 732). Underlying modern finance is the ancient principle that those with money can enrich themselves at the expense of those without, and modern finance remains a class question in this immediate sense. Extractions from workers have become increasingly important. Soderberg's (2014) work on the 'Debtfare State' outlines the range of contemporary extractions, through credit cards, student loans, payday loans, microfinance and housing. Microfinance, widely held out as a means of poverty alleviation and economic development, has also managed to incorporate millions of the world's poorest into long-term, high-interest debt dependency (see also Chowdhury 2009, Bateman and Chang 2012). The overall rise of household indebtedness is particularly marked within the US. Table 8.1 shows the changing position of households, from net savers in the 1950s to the main source of lending in the 2000s. Alternative sources suggest some very different numbers, and those here should therefore be treated cautiously, but the direction of change is unambiguous. Unsustainable housing finance was, of course, the catalyst of the crisis of 2007–09.

Conclusion

Financial sector profits derive from those in the productive economy, which set limits to interest rates which can be sustained in the long term. It is possible to go beyond this simple but important truth, which Marx develops from the classical tradition. Shaikh (2016) adds that financial firms would expect their share of profits on a similar basis to other capitalists according to their costs. It is also possible to incorporate elements of Keynes's critique. Re-anchored on the classical basis of profit generation in the wider economy, Keynes's two key variables, liquidity preference and the money supply, can be worked harder. The bases for changing liquidity preferences become, in the first instance, reasonable predictions of future returns in the productive economy, not autonomous changes of heart. For example, money is held and churned within the financial sector because of low returns on productive investment. But there is an internal dynamic to finance whereby high returns suck an increasing share of profits, as has occurred in recent decades. At least in the short term, power relations between lenders and borrowers determine what has to be paid. Similarly, states' power does not allow them to conjure resources from nothing, but capital's trust in leading states allows them to borrow cheaply and to set low interest rates which resonate throughout the economy, or to set high rates which choke off investment. In both cases there are, at least, demonstrable feedback effects from finance to the real economy. This will be illustrated more concretely in the next chapter.

9

Money and states in capitalism's uneven development

Introduction

This chapter builds on the basic arguments of the two previous chapters. Money is an inherently imperfect and shifting measure of value. It is endogenous to capitalism but this is not equivalent to seeing it as 'non-state', because the state itself needs to be conceived as within, not without, the capitalist system as a whole. Institutional forms change how money works, and the actions of these institutions, particularly of states, matter in the sense of making a real difference not only to monetary forms but to accumulation.

The next section comments generally on debates around exogeneity, endogeneity, and the role of the state and other institutions in managing money. The second section illustrates this, drawing on important historical examples of the essential role of states and other financial institutions in monetary affairs and hence in capital accumulation. It is impossible to tell the history of money within the scope of a single short chapter, but six important examples emphasise the conceptual points. Making fewer direct references to the work of Marx or Keynes, this section develops the earlier discussions about money and interest, particularly about the non-neutrality of money and the need to take this seriously in terms of its impacts on capital accumulation and to move from the relatively abstract accounts to concrete depictions of institutional relations.

Endogenising the state

The previous chapters suggested that the level of abstraction at which Marx was working in *Capital* leaves an insufficiency in his analysis of money. This follows from his avowed method of moving from the abstract and general to the concrete and specific. It need not, therefore, be seen as a mistake or aberration, but it does require those subsequent concrete investigations of particular monetary forms and the 'second-order' reflections-back of how these in turn influence accumulation.

As discussed in Chapter 7, Marx recognised the possibility of moving away from commodity money. In such situations, the state becomes vital. For money to have 'universal validity, it is in the end regulated by law' (Marx 1976: 194, Davis 2010). However, if Marx recognised states' role in sanctioning or even creating money, that role at least leaves challenging problems. The real power of states, amongst other things, qualifies or compromises money's ability to measure value, requiring a careful situating of the state in relation to money and value and an integration of the state into a global economic analysis.

States, as Keynes insisted, have a substantial monetary power. They act, and what they do matters whether in terms of the money supply or the interest rate policy. Again, it is a great strength of Keynes's critique of orthodox thinking that he brings in the state as an economic agent. There is, however, an important sense in which he reproduces the misleading orthodox state–market binary, which then recurs in subsequent depictions of exogeneity and endogeneity according to which the state is an exogenous actor, capable of standing outside or above the economy. The idea of exogeneity can be invoked in different ways; for example, it can be used to put relatively slow-moving variables out of short-term analysis. Keynes took levels of technology as given, which seems appropriate for his short-term analysis of unemployment equilibrium. It seems harder to justify excluding money on this basis. Keynes clearly thought the quantity of money could be altered, and to good effect, within the time-frame he envisaged. But he saw this coming from the monetary authorities, from outside the market economy, and this is the sense in which many of Keynes's followers identify money as exogenous.

To briefly recap Keynes's argument, money is supplied by the state. He is particularly emphatic in the *Treatise*, insisting that for at least 4000 years, money has been state money. 'To-day all civilised money is, beyond the possibility of dispute, chartalist' (2011: volume 1, 5). The *General Theory* says less but broadly accepts the same perspective, simply seeing 'the quantity of money as determined by the action of the central bank' (1973: 247). Money is money through state authority. Money is money because states accept it in payment of taxes and other debts (Keynes 2011). At times, state authority in a post-gold world can appear unlimited. Keynes's definition of money, in terms of a low elasticity of production, appears to define out private credit money. By definition, only state money counts as money and (a little counterfeiting aside) the private sector elasticity of production is zero. Keynes does implicitly qualify this view, describing banks issuing money and supplying credit. His understanding, however, is at least primarily one in which money is created by public authorities. For much of the previous millennia (the first coins were minted about 2600 years ago) the world economy used commodity money, so Keynes is insisting that even this becomes money through state authority: it does not automatically work through some invisible hand, as the classics since Hume had insisted.

There would, however, appear to be an uncomfortable convergence between Keynes and the monetarist mainstream, at least in as far as both accept that states control the money supply. Putatively more radical 'post-Keynesian' theories reject this to insist instead on endogenous money, inverting Keynes's own positions. Instead, money comes from the market, not the state (Moore 1988, King 2015). Private financial institutions respond to firms' demands. Historically, private banks issued their own notes and continue to issue credit, which amounts to money. Even where lending is limited by reserve requirements, banks can borrow from other banks and invent new vehicles to circumvent regulation. The very notion of a 'money supply' becomes questionable (Weeks 1988). States are powerless to limit this, although they may be able to influence, even determine, the 'price' of money, the rate of interest (Moore 1988, Niggle 1991).

Claims that states do not create money seem hard to maintain. The notes that roll off the printing presses are money, 'high-powered money', even if they are not the only money. The examples of hyperinflation seem sufficient to make the point. If the Zimbabwean government had been unwilling to create money, to print ever-higher denomination notes, there could hardly have been the extraordinary hyperinflation of the 2000s. It seems unlikely that the demand for extra money was coming from an exuberant private sector. In many countries, the banking system is itself state owned or state controlled. This is the case of many of the world's largest banks, in China and many other poorer countries. But historically, many rich-country banks have also been state owned. A few still are. At the very least, there are all sorts of things that states can do and, pragmatically, most post-Keynesian endogenous money theorists accept that states have some influence on both the quantity of money and the rate of interest (Niggle 1991, Wray 1992).

This is not to suggest the opposite – that money is necessarily state money. This is recognised by at least some contemporary chartalists (Rochon and Rossi 2013). It seems a necessary conclusion for Marxists. Marx saw gold as money. It was a commodity essentially like anything else: twenty yards of linen, to one coat, to two ounces of gold (1976: 157). Money as gold, as commodity money, had value because like other commodities it embodied socially necessary labour time (1976: 188–98). It was produced like other commodities and was introduced into Marx's economic system prior to state intervention. For Marxists, however, money cannot be taken as 'endogenous' in a conventional economic sense to mean 'non-state'. Apart from anything else, states are perfectly capable of controlling gold production and have often done so. Conversely, private banks have historically issued banknotes and modern bank credit can serve as money (Galbraith 1995, Davies 1996). Today, cryptocurrencies and local trading schemes have at least some of the properties of money. States may have more power than other institutions but they are not a conceptual world apart. Just as commercial banks can be state owned, central banks (the Bank of England from 1694 until 1946, others like South Africa's Reserve Bank today) can be private.

The broader point is that states' power is itself not 'exogenous'. State power is inseparable from capitalist power, while recognising that states exist within an inter-state and essentially global capitalist system also undermines any crude exogenous/endogenous distinction. The standard discussion of endogeneity or exogeneity hangs on a 'states or markets' dichotomy beloved by mainstream economists and political scientists. The distinction is profoundly misleading in general and particularly in relation to modern money. Marx saw the split between politics and economics as a capitalist 'reification'. It was unimaginable in feudalism; wealth begat power, power begat wealth. Capitalism appears to separate the two. Power is the job of government (and now the subject of political scientists). The economy was a separate benign world of 'freedom, property, equality and Bentham' (Marx 1976: 280). Economics (losing the previous designation as 'political economy' around the turn of the twentieth century) could proceed as if it were unconcerned with politics, as if capitalism did not depend on the prior dispossession of workers and as if wealth was no longer connected to power.

Capitalism creates a degree of separation unimaginable in feudalism. Not every billionaire is a political ruler nor every political ruler fabulously rich. But the state does not exist outside capitalism conceived as a whole. Politics and economics are not separable. In a world of commodity money, gold could be compared to linen and coats and be exchanged privately. But the world of modern money depends on trust. For the time being, there is trust in states to provide money more than there is trust in private businesses. But it is a question of degree, and people can lose trust in states. In practice the actions of both private and public banks influence money and the interest rate. As several post-Keynesians acknowledge, 'money is neither purely exogenous nor purely endogenous' (Chick 1983: 236). Indeed, both Marxists (de Brunhoff 1976, Lipietz 1985) and Keynesians (Mehrling 2012, Smithin 2016) have posited a hierarchy of money, allowing conceptual and practical priorities but also for changing forms and an integration of state and private credit money. The broader point is that it is necessary to 'endogenise' the state (Dow 1996).

The idea of exogeneity therefore points to the fundamental strengths and weaknesses of much of Keynesian economics. Keynes's simple acknowledgement that states are important economic actors immediately presents a problem because Keynes lacks a theory of the state. While at one pole, Keynes's vision appears to be one of asocialised individuals, at the other he injects a similarly asocialised state. Even sympathetic accounts have accused Keynes of flipping between methodological individualism and methodological nationalism, with little analytical sense of institutional differentiation within or beyond state boundaries (Galbraith 1995). As discussed in Chapter 3, Keynes exaggerates the potential for states to overcome conflict within civil society and prioritises the national as the singularly appropriate level of economic aggregation. States are substantially conceived as exogenous to the system being described. Keynes's challenge to the faith in the invisible hand accordingly installed an equally unsubstantiated faith in the benign hand of the state (Balogh 1976). Recently, Mann (2016, 2017a) has argued that 'Keynes is our Hegel', capturing something of the sense of how Keynes sees states as effective arbiters of contests and dislocations within civil society while leaving the state itself unexamined as a social institution. Therefore, if the importance of the state in monetary affairs again points towards the potential utility of critically appropriating Keynesian insights, Marxists can socialise the state, recognising states as constituted within an intrinsically global capitalist and inter-state system, in ways substantially foreign to the Keynesian worldview.

Three aspects are worth particular emphasis in relation to money and finance. First, states are shaped by institutional power within their borders. Modern states are capitalist states in relation to their domestic economies. Marx and Engels's famous formulation of the state as the executive of the whole bourgeoisie needs to be handled with care; it can be conducive to determinist and teleological interpretations in which everything states do turns out to be for the capitalist best in the best of all capitalist worlds. State policy is contested, with different social interests fighting for different monetary practices, but that states' objectives are dominated, albeit incompletely, by capital's imperatives needs little elaboration. As de Brunhoff writes, 'the monetary power of the state is necessarily limited by the social power which money gives to the private individuals who hoard it' (de Brunhoff 1976: 47). For example, states set interest rates through their borrowing but this implies willing lenders. The state is more capitalist state than benign social overseer.

Second, states are hybrid institutions with power and interests of their own. This has been stressed by the Weberian tradition, both in general and in relation to money, as if it were devastating to Marxism (Skocpol 1979, Ingham 2004). Of course, this very point was central to the young

Marx's (1975) criticisms of Hegel. States' own distinct interests mean they cannot stand above or apart from society. This depiction of self-interested states became a secondary aspect of Marx's mature thought but it never disappeared, as his writing about Bonarpartism, for example, makes clear (Miliband 1983). As his repeated polemics make clear, Marx was hardly neutral about state policy in general or monetary policy in particular. It follows that states cannot be adequately conceived as simply derived from capital: the need for stability begets gold, the need for easy money begets a fiat system and so on. At the same time, nor do states make free choices. Volcker decides one thing, Greenspan another and so on. Keynes's analysis has parallels with the second of these alternatives, tending to underestimate the political and economic constraints and imperatives which states face. But there is an opposite danger of neglecting the reality of alternative choices and states' own interests in making them. The growth of state budgets and bureaucracies, if anything, makes states' own interests a more relevant dimension of financial power, notwithstanding claims of neo-liberalism and state retreat, discussed in Chapter 12. Recent policies of quantitative easing would appear to provide examples, failing miserably in terms of their declared objectives of providing economic stimulus but successfully buying back government debt. Other institutions, including other financial institutions from the Medici and Fuggers to Soros's Quantum Group, compete and cooperate with states, lend to them, speculate on them or against them. States, however, make real monetary decisions: real in the sense of choosing between alternatives and in that these decisions impact on the conditions of capital accumulation.

Third, states exist within a constraining and conditioning global and interstate capitalist system. Amongst other things, this underscores the difficulties involved in conceiving money as exogenous. Money is ultimately only comprehensible at a global level. In practice, from his earliest writing, Keynes acknowledges potential international constraints on state policy (Patinkin 1987). As his personal biography confirms, Keynes was the ultimate insider looking out; and there is then a consistency in his understanding of the state 'from within', as an institution, capable of enlightened redirection through the power of persuasion, not least his own. This pragmatism also meant that Keynes recognises the limits of state power in practice, most obviously in his discussions of the effectiveness or otherwise of monetary policy, and his experiences, for example on the Macmillan Committee and in his wartime negotiations around Bretton Woods, show that he recognises problems and constraints on policy in the international context. Keynes's vision, however, remains essentially national, and his understanding of the state as exogenous puts these issues at the boundary rather than seeing them as integral to the system being analysed. Despite ostensible similarities between the *General*

Theory and *Capital* in their abstraction from the particularity that is the nation-state, what is for Marx, in principle from the start, an analysis of the (capitalist) world economy (into which it becomes necessary to integrate an analysis of states and international dimensions) is for Keynes an analysis of the national economy, with more or less permeable boundaries.

The adequacy of nation-centric views has been challenged from many quarters in recent debates around globalisation. In discussion of finance, this has seen some exaggerated depictions of state retreat, even the death of geography (Strange 1998, O'Brien 1992). Historical narratives of money highlight that the global dimensions are ancient. Cohen (1998) points out that the idea of one country, one currency, is a myth. As will be seen below, credit becomes possible in an international context, where foreign exchange could disguise interest rates proscribed by usury laws. Marx saw state fiat money as able to stand in for money at the national level but with gold remaining necessary as world money and the ultimate measure of value. In a world which has long since abandoned the gold standard, we only have various, often rapidly fluctuating national fiat currencies. Currency competition provides a degree of discipline through which value reasserts itself, but only in rough and ready sort of way, with state intervention, through both open-market and interest rate manipulations, a still permanent feature of the global economy. There are currency hierarchies, in which some become acceptable beyond domestic boundaries while others struggle to gain acceptance even amongst locals. The role of leading currencies, particularly the US dollar, allows their home states to borrow more cheaply on global markets than they could do if relying on national capital. In short, the international dimensions of money and finance underline the social and conditional construction of nation-states and national boundaries and the inadequacies of nation-centric epistemologies.

States, money and the changing dynamics of capitalism

Some important historical examples illustrate how states and other institutions matter, in terms of monetary arrangements but also in terms of how these monetary arrangements influence the overall trajectory of capitalism. As above, *Capital* substantially abstracts from the state and Marx never wrote the promised further volumes. This leaves room for interminable Marxist controversialising on the state in general and on the state in relation to monetary affairs in particular. This section uses the historical examples primarily to identify the essential role of states and inter-state relations in monetary relations and thence in economic development more generally. The examples are focused on Europe but it is implicit from the start that money should be understood 'globally'; if Europe took the lead some time in the first half of the last millennium, it drew on the rest of the world. As above, value is conceived globally and states develop within an inter-state system (Barker 1978, Rosenberg 2006). Money does not generally emerge first as something purely national which only later extends to relations with outsiders. Such developments are entirely possible, and there are historical examples, but it is equally possible for money to be first and foremost important in international relations. Whatever the historical bases, state and inter-state relations fundamentally condition monetary relations, which then profoundly influence wider economic development.

It is impossible to tell the history adequately, and of course there is no historical counterfactual of how different things might have been. What follows merely identifies six historical moments to illustrate how the institutions of finance, particularly the state, inter-state and monetary relations, 'get at', impact upon, accumulation and broader economic development in more than incidental ways.

Italian city-states, credit and Forex trading

Claims for the timing of the origins of capitalism vary by several centuries. An influential proponent of an early start, Braudel locates 'the whole panoply of forms of capitalism – commercial, industrial, banking' (1985: 621) – as already developed in northern Italy in the thirteenth century. There were at least important innovations in money and finance and thence continuities from the Italian experiences of these to modern capitalism.

The wealth of the Italian city-states was tied to their role in trade. Particularly in Florence, extensive manufacturing also developed (Braudel 1985) and the city-states' wealth in turn enabled the maintenance of their unusual political form, their ability to resist incorporation into the feudal, absolutist states dominating most of Europe (Anderson 1979). The city-state form in turn underpinned key monetary innovations.

Arrighi argues that '[h]igh finance in its modern, capitalist form is a Florentine invention. Its foundations were laid during the trade expansion of the late thirteenth and early fourteenth centuries' (1994: 96). Italian city-states issued distinct and reliable coins which circulated far beyond their borders: florins, Venetian ducato, Genoan *lira di buona moneta*. The effective coordination in the city-states was double edged. 'Although coinage was a jealously guarded instrument of the state, it inevitably enabled economic power to escape from state control' (Ingham 2004: 100). The smallness of city-states also made currency exchange between them an essential part of economic life. Money changers, operating from benches (or *banca*), proliferated and many of these grew into deposit banks (Kindleberger 1984).

The Florentine Medici epitomise how successful bankers could themselves take over the state, but the money could also be taken elsewhere, a process encouraged by the inherent small scale of the city-state economies, which may have been an important basis of, but became also an important limit to, their success.

Trading relations, including long-distance relations, typically came to be conducted using bills of exchange rather than specie. The bills of exchange could not be 'discounted' because of prohibitions against usury, but money changing provided a way of circumventing the restrictions. 'The equivalent of interest was realised, and credit provided, by the buyer of the bill paying as a rule at an exchange rate below that at which the drawee ultimately paid the bearer' (Kindleberger 1984: 39). In short, lending could be disguised in the prices of the exchange contracts and payments by bills of exchange, within Italy and beyond (Ditchburn and MacKay 2007). By the fifteenth century, delays in payment would allow interest to be officially sanctioned and usury could conveniently be redefined as 'excessive' interest (Davies 1996).

The Italians did not invent credit, which has an ancient history and was found elsewhere in the Middle Ages (Woolley 1963, Kindleberger 1984, Davies 1996). Indeed, the Italians themselves were lending to foreign feudal rulers who excused themselves from the usury prohibitions, to popes and to the monarchs of Spain, France and England, before the legal objections were relaxed (Jones 1997). There were some spectacular defaults and since monarchs could not be sued, they typically paid higher interest rates than private borrowers (Homer and Sylla 2005). In turn, sovereign debts often came to be secured by cities, the City of London or the Hotel de Ville of Paris, reflecting but in turn contributing to the growth of alternative sources of economic power within the feudal system. But if Italians did not discover credit, the particular forms of banking practice they introduced became pervasive.

From bullion famine to great inflation

After the demographic collapse of the fourteenth century, Europe's population and economy grew substantially in the fifteenth. But the growing relative scarcity of commodity money, particularly gold, became an impediment. The 'price' of gold and the incentives for discovering new supplies increased accordingly. This spurred the famous European Navigations: profit-seeking ventures sponsored by the feudal Portuguese and Spanish states. As the Portuguese Navigations went south then east they brought back gold, while, following Columbus, the Spanish went westwards. Initially, this too brought back gold. The 'Great Bullion famine' of fourteenth and fifteenth centuries was ended with the Caribbean gold cycle of 1494–1525, achieved first through stealing largely ornamental gold, then through forced labour panning alluvial deposits. But gold was soon overtaken by silver. American silver bought goods, not least from China, where there was little market for European products but where silver was much more highly valued than gold, with ratios closer to 6:1 compared with 15:1 (Davies 1996).

By the late sixteenth century, vast quantities of silver flowed to Seville and Spain and thence to the rest of Europe. Spanish 'pieces of eight' 'invaded the whole world' (Vilar 1984: 138). This influx has widely been seen as stimulating the 'great inflation', in turn stimulating economic activity (Keynes CWIX: 323–4). Amongst other things, inflation could increase profits through the employment of forms of less-than-free labour where wages were still mainly set by custom. Inflation also eroded stored value and encouraged dishoarding and further economic activity (and further inflation). The more or less forced extraction of specie from the Americas has been seen as at least an important element in Europe's subsequent ascendency.

Such claims that the influx of specie was key to European capitalism have been widely contested (Banaji 2010). Not least, economic growth did not occur primarily where the inflows or the inflation were greatest: not in Spain or Seville (nor for that matter closest to Potosi in Peru). Within Spain, colonial demand encouraged commercialisation but turned agriculture away from cereal production, with devastating consequences for the local population and economy (Anderson 1979). Arestis and Howells's (2001) post-Keynesian account insists money is endogenous, with inflation following rather than causing growth. They are keen to refute quantity theory understandings, which the specie inflows did so much to initiate. However, money is not neutral, and while there was no doubt a highly mediated relation between the influx of specie and the beginnings of capitalist development, it seems reasonable to admit silver inflows, hanging on Spanish imperial power, having inflationary effects, with redistributive and stimulating consequences.

Central banking in the United Provinces

The most rapid sixteenth-century expansion occurred in Spain's northern colony. As with the Italian city-states, the Dutch Republic owed much of its wealth to international trade. In the first instance, this was primarily intra-European, particularly from the Baltic, but by the seventeenth century the activities of the Dutch East India Company became increasingly important, largely and more brutally displacing the Portuguese in the exploitation of the Indies. It was a 'chartered company', private and more clearly organised on capitalist lines than the Iberian traders, but it was supported by the government, which protected its exclusive rights over overseas commercial spaces. The company issued shares which would be the mainstay of the Amsterdam bourse, itself not without precedent but providing new levels of share volume, fluidity and speculative freedom (Arrighi 1994). If to a lesser extent than in its Italian predecessors, Dutch production was largely export oriented, further accentuating the Republic as the focal point of European trade and thence of the disparate currencies produced within the context of wider European growth (Galbraith 1995, Vilar 1984).

Crucial to overcoming the ensuing monetary chaos was the establishment in 1609 of the state-owned Amsterdam central bank, the Wisselbank, which successfully centralised money. Most of the disparate coins were reminted 'as an internationally viable currency, the *negotie-penningen* (trade coins)' which became the dominant global currency (Vilar 1984: 204). Again, the Dutch did not invent the central bank and the Wisselbank was explicitly modelled on that of Venice. But its success led to imitations, greatly spreading the ambit of central banking. Trust in the control of commodity money simultaneously allowed specie's partial abandonment at home and, through fractional reserve banking, the expansion of the effective money supply (Chown 1994, Galbraith 1995).

Britain and the age of the gold standard

The term 'financial revolution' has been widely if controversially applied to important changes in England in the late seventeenth and early eighteenth centuries, following the 1688 'Glorious Revolution' (Fratianni and Spinelli 2006). These established the 'Treasury' as a national rather than monarchical institution, the adoption of the gold standard, and the Bank of England, in 1694 as a private bank but originating in loans to the state and controlled by parliament (Homer and Sylla 2005). Over the next two hundred years, Britain became the centre of the industrial revolution and the world's dominant imperial power. That does not allow a simple association between the financial changes and the subsequent economic success, but they did at least prove compatible.

Two things seem particularly notable. First, fractional reserve banking proliferated, more or less controlled by the authorities and the Bank of England. There were many earlier examples of banknotes '[b]ut the innovation of the Bank of England was that it added to the functions of deposit and clearing banks those of a deliberately organised issuing bank, capable of offering ample credit in notes' (Braudel 1974: 360). Internally, Britain operated on a gold-exchange standard. The link with gold was mediated, allowing the money supply to greatly exceed the monetary base. Amongst other things, country banks issued their own notes, which were formally redeemable against either Bank of England notes or gold. The remove from central bank control allowed an extra degree of freedom and monetary expansion. The qualified victory of the Currency School in the Bank Act of 1844, reprioritised 'sound' money, restricted the activities of the country banks and limited central bank lending via a 'rigid quantitative relationship between its gold hoard and its banknote liabilities' (Itoh and Lapavitsas 1999: 155). Its notes could equal two-thirds of the lapsed issue of other banks, but the remainder of its notes and any further increases had to be covered by gold and equivalent increases in its reserves. The Act became a centrepiece of Polanyi's (2001) claim that 'the free market was planned'. However, existing private banks were allowed to continue and private bank-note issue in England (the Scottish banking system remained distinct) would last until 1921 (Davies 1996). The Act was repeatedly suspended when it proved inconvenient. Meanwhile the use of cheques and other money market instruments proliferated. With no English laws against interest, only legal maxima, it was also possible from an early stage to create undisguised loans in the form of 'inland bills of exchange' (Homer and Sylla 2005: 146). Both public and, by the second half of the nineteenth century, private bond markets expanded rapidly. The point here is that institutional forms change and need to be studied historically. Chick (1992) acknowledges this in her elegant schematic depiction of a shift from exogenous to endogenous money with the evolution of the British banking system. She makes clear that this depiction is highly stylised but, in repeating the exogenous–endogenous binary, risks exaggerating both sides of the determination: the extent to which money was ever purely a creature of the state and to which it has become purely private. States and other institutions continued a long history of what Marx called a 'mishmash', of complex interaction shaping money and interest.

Second, the gold standard was never the automatic system Hume envisaged. From the beginning, the English state paid heavily to restore the value of the pound and subsequently the mechanism required British authorities to set a higher gold:silver ratio of 15.93:1 compared with 15:1 on the continent, and latterly to offer higher interest rates, in order to attract gold (Vilar 1984, Davies 1996). By the second half of the nineteenth century, Britain ran persistent deficits. Gold continued to serve powerful vested interests; financial capital and important import-dependent indus-tries like cotton benefitted from both stability and an overvalued currency, as did imperial investors into overseas markets. Systematic overvaluation, however, implied that gold had long ceased to serve any putative 'national interest', and it contributed to Britain's relative decline. By the inter-war period, gold had become Keynes's 'barbarous relic', finally abandoned igno-miniously in 1931. As states engaged in competitive devaluation and as they increased trade barriers, they could more easily impose fiat monies within their borders.

The US: *from monetary plurality to dollar dominance*

If British regulation and the authority of the Bank of England at least allowed the impression of a coordinated, centralised monetary system, the early history of the US looked very different. The Federal Reserve System and the New Deal banking regulations, which would finally prove enduring, were only completed long after the US had achieved economic pre-eminence. The country had risen with an apparently diffuse monetary regime, even what Davies (1996) calls a 'free-for-all' in private and state banking.

A wide variety of state and private money proliferated from the colonial period well into the nineteenth century. Tobacco remained legal tender in Virginia for over two hundred years (Galbraith 1995). North Carolina had seventeen different forms of legal tender in 1775 and even with independence, foreign coins circulated widely in the US, particularly Spanish piastres, or pieces of eight, which ceased to be legal tender only in 1857 (Davies 1996). Fights over public and private paper money, and for the retention of silver, continued: social contests often couched as contests against the vested interests in gold. At a federal level, a system of bimetallism was adopted in 1794, at a 15:1 silver:gold ratio. This formally lasted over a hundred years, but in practice gold rather than silver became the standard by the 1870s, with the debasement of silver coins. The Civil War had already seen the authorisation of paper currency in 1862 and 'greenbacks' lasted until 1879. Private banks proliferated, their number rising from four in 1790 to 1562 by 1860 (Davies 1996). Banks issued their own notes, of equal nominal value but of varying degrees of trustworthiness. Amongst other things, the number of notes in circulation and the relatively simple printing techniques available also proved conducive to widespread counterfeiting (Carruthers and Ariovich 2010). The unreliability of banknotes also prompted innovations in credit, with the extensive use of trade credit, supplied by sellers rather than banks. This was particularly important in the rural economy but extended widely, 'so virtually all firms were embedded in a web of debtor–creditor relationships ... and this meant that credit shocks starting in one location could soon be felt everywhere' (Carruthers and Ariovich 2010: 29). Amongst other things, it was in this environment, that credit ratings agencies grew rapidly, already rating over a million individual firms by 1900 (Carruthers and Ariovich 2010). Banks also enjoyed very different levels of supervision in different states. New York had reserve requirements of 12.5 per cent but other states had little or no such provision. Two attempts were made to establish a central bank, one in 1791, the second in 1817, but both failed (Davies 1996).

There was, however, structure behind the apparently chaotic system. After 1862, private banknote issues were taxed and therefore declined while the different state regulations encouraged a pyramidal system, in which local banks held reserves at large banks in larger towns, with the New York banks at the apex. The interlinked financial system was predictably conducive to contagion, with substantial echoes of Marx's warnings. There were 1748 bank failures in the twenty years to 1913 (Galbraith 1995). Largely as a response, the Federal Reserve System was finally established that year. But the new regulations proved insufficient to prevent another dramatic round of 8812 bank failures between 1930 and 1933 (Davies 1996). Tougher New Deal legislation finally created a clearer division of state and private financial responsibilities and 'fire-walls' between different activities. The situation prior to this nevertheless underlines how different state and non-state institutions could interact to underpin the financial system in what had already become the world's leading economy. A straightforward state/non-state, exogenous/endogenous distinction looks out of place. As Shaikh asks of those who see interest rates as determined by the central bank, 'what determines the rate of interest when the central bank rate follows the market rate, or when central banks have not yet come into existence?' (2016: 482–3). Treasuries and central banks became the core of modern financial systems but first amongst a range of powerful institutions, not as an alternative to free-market individualism.

Once on gold, the US economy's dynamic growth relative to others meant that stable currency values increased US competitiveness. Gold flowed inwards. Such surpluses, as Keynes insisted, were conducive to growth via low interest rates, which the Federal Reserve also maintained. By the inter-war period these were fuelling the bubble the bursting of which in 1929 soon witnessed the abandonment of gold and the descent into international currency competition.

Bretton Woods and its demise

The next chapter will discuss the story of Bretton Woods and its demise in slightly more detail. The simple analytical point here is that the Bretton Woods monetary system of the post-WWII boom was organised. The practice was ambiguous; it was a US-led system, albeit with important class support also in the UK (Helleiner 1994), while the regime only worked in a way close to that envisaged at the initial conference for a few years from the late 1950s (Mandel 1978, Parboni 1981). It was an organised system in the sense of being chosen from alternatives, like those put forward by

Keynes (CWXXV). The resulting regime, including the formal structures of the IMF, clearly impinged on the wider post-WWII economy, including anti-Keynesian asymmetries in its respective attitudes to surplus and deficit countries. The system allowed currency stability for a protracted period, despite changing rates of productivity growth, or that national monies could co-exist without simultaneously being accurate measures of value. Tensions emerged within the system as value, only concealed or suspended, asserted itself, undermining the fixed-exchange-rate regime. The subsequent fluctuations suggest that there was still no unambiguous global measure of value. Speculation by wealthy private institutions could throw currencies onto a switchback ride on a daily basis, but the new 'floating' system also retained many elements of the previous regime, including the deep entanglement of states in monetary affairs both within and across borders and a US currency central to the global economy, now achieved without even formal commitments to gold.

The crisis of the 1970s and its resolution also had a vital political dimension in that breaking the gold link (and for other countries the link with the dollar) allowed governments to pursue inflationary policy, devaluing real wages and both state and corporate debts, all of which had been rising in the late 1960s (Krippner 2011). The inflationary experiences were unplanned in the sense that governments repeatedly failed to achieve particular targets; workers could factor inflation into wage demands, contributing to an upward spiral. But policy was at least permissive of inflation. At the same time, inflation also devalued capital and financial assets and could only be a short-term instrument. The turn to monetarism in the late 1970s, in the form of radically high interests, moved to restore trust in money and coincided with a shift to open battles with labour. High interest rates provoked a steep economic downturn and would have been unsustainable over a longer period. But with labour's subsequent retreat, falling labour shares of income around the world, and concomitant disincentives to consume and invest, there was little need to persevere with high interest rates as either an anti-inflationary or an anti-labour device. By the 2000s, it became clear that even very low interest rates and aggressive policies of quantitative easing might not restore either inflation or investment. While the overall economic slowdown was nothing like that of the 1930s, Keynes's warnings appeared to be confirmed and states' monetary arsenal appeared to be greatly diminished.

The switch to high interest rates in the late 1970s also precipitated the Latin American debt crisis, the resolution of which brought the 'Washington consensus' restructuring. It established the open, liberalising environment, the associated trade-surplus strategies of many poorer countries, and thence the accumulation of vast foreign reserves, primarily of US dollars. This use of the dollar, and often more specifically US Treasury paper, as a store of value, helped to maintain US seigniorage, allowing it to run persistent deficits. US consumers enjoyed cheap imports and US corporations cheap foreign investment opportunities. At the same time, the US as a territorial economic space was undermined and with it the basis for the perpetuation of the dollar's hegemony. The existence of powerful vested interests warn against over-hasty obituaries, but the current system again sits on deep structural contradictions.

From history back to theory

Briefly recalling these stories of money and finance and their changing form underlines two simple points. First, states make decisions, but not in conditions of their own choosing. To begin with the conditions, capital imposes limits on all states, but to varying degrees. State choices are conditioned by economic and social relations, both global and local. This is an obvious Marxist truism but one worth repeating against more optimistic Keynesian injunctions to reform monetary policy on either a national or a global level. Financial institutions and interests can, in the extreme, take over existing states as a going concern (the Medici method), but more usually they exert a less direct but profound influence. States' decisions are also conditioned by inter-state relations, again something which nobody familiar with either history or the contemporary global economy is likely to dispute but something underplayed by the methodological nationalism of standard textbooks or by a rigid reading of Marx's schema in which the domain of the international only follows that of the state.

Keynes was concerned mainly with Britain, and his evidence was overwhelmingly either British or American. Even then, national policy was constrained, particularly with the use of gold as an international standard. But there are shifting dynamics of state and private capital's power, while claims of state authority over money and the idea of specifically national money come closer to the truth for leading economies than for weaker ones. Up to the early modern period, few states established exclusive state money, while rulers paid more to borrow than private capitalists, a priority reversed at least until very recently and for weaker states. Leading states retain enormous power, for example intervening as vast buyers and sellers of currency and through interest rate manipulation. But the economy is global and the law of value ultimately asserts itself at a global level. Non-commodity money needs the economic containers of states but simultaneously needs to escape them. So while dollar seigniorage, much as Keynes thought of Britain and the gold standard in the 1920s, has plausibly been seen as continuing to confer national economic advantages, it also contributes to the decline of industry and (in relative terms) the US as an economic space.

The global dynamics highlight the limits of the endogenous/exogenous distinction which runs through both mainstream and Keynesian thinking. The state is never 'outside' the economy. The problem with the distinction becomes particularly stark when weaker currencies are considered. A fully dollarised economy, giving up its national currency as in modern Ecuador or Zimbabwe, could hardly be said to have an 'endogenous' money supply, while the experiences of hyperinflations in weak economies suggest that even such states remain the driving force rather than 'endogenous' demand for bank loans. Hayek's (1976) proposals to deny states exclusive rights to issue money remain an outlier, even amongst liberal economists. The global economy constrains what states can do but, contrary to influential narratives of globalisation and free-floating, de-territorialised finance, state choices and inter-state relations continue to impact profoundly on money and finance.

Second, these choices therefore also make a substantive difference to subsequent economic development. As above, there are no historical counterfactuals, but the world surely would have looked very different had not the Italian city-states circumvented proscriptions on credit, had Europeans not extracted and imported vast quantities of South American silver, had the Dutch Republic not introduced effective central banking, had the British not maintained a gold standard, had the Bretton Woods system not had its systematic anti-Keynesian biases, or had the inflationary and anti-inflationary turns of the 1970s and 1980s not reshaped capital–labour and international relations. In each case, the forms of accumulation were transformed by the monetary transformations.

Conclusions

The previous two chapters covered enormous ground and were accordingly unable to do justice to the depth of either Marx's or Keynes's thinking about money and only occasionally engaged with the vast secondary literatures. This chapter's historical narrative similarly made no claim to completeness. However, it began to concretise what the previous chapters suggested: that the critical appropriation of Keynesian insights enrich a Marxist monetary analysis.

First, Marxists can legitimately defend the analytical priority of social relations of production and of exploitation and accumulation in the real economy, but taking the non-neutrality of money seriously means that what happens in the world of money and finance is not reducible or narrowly determined by this. Money has a moment of its own, which influences that exploitation and accumulation. At least at certain times, money and monetary decisions appear to have made a major economic difference.

Second, money is a social relation, not simply a thing, and rival social interests benefit from the adoption of different monetary forms, which can potentially have profound economic consequences. It matters economically but also politically whether there is gold or fiat money, whether authorities can produce inflation or financial corporations transmit electronic money around the world.

Third, Keynes reintroduces the state into economic analysis, and while he treats state intervention as an asocial and benign force, the fact of this intervention, in general but particularly in monetary affairs, is also a challenge to any Marxist analyses which want to stop at the analytical level of *Capital*. This was an analytical level beyond which Marx promised to go, and beyond which it is necessary to go to understand the importance of the state in monetary affairs. Any appropriation of Keynes also needs to be sensitive to changing historical forms. The chapter's very brief historical notes confirm what to anyone not too firmly entrenched in conventional economic thinking (or in more dogmatic versions of post-Keynesian monetary theory) would be rather obvious: that states and other financial institutions played vital, active but changing roles in capitalist organisation and reorganisation.

10

Keynesianism in practice?

Introduction

Blaug writes, '[t]here were two Keynesian revolutions: the revolution in economic policy and the revolution in theoretical opinion within the economics profession' (1994: 1212). This chapter focusses on the policy and practice, the remarkable post-WWII boom and its unravelling in the 1970s. The next chapter looks at the theory. It is in the sense of policy reorientation that the quarter-century from the end of WWII until the 1970s is most often understood as a Keynesian age. Indeed, for many accounts, it is this period of managed capitalism and sustained growth and stability which gives meaning to the term 'Keynesianism'.

There are difficult questions about the connections between the theory and the practice. Keynes's followers have been keen to claim the economic success of the theory. For Davidson, the unprecedented economic growth was as a direct consequence of following Keynes's policy prescriptions (2009; see also Stewart 1972). Other writers find little of Keynes in the practice of leading countries or in the workings of the international system (Matthews 1968, Clarke, S. 1988).

Of course, practice never matches theory exactly, so asking whether the history justifies the label might seem uselessly speculative. The answer cannot be categorical. But it is worth considering whether or to what extent the long boom followed Keynes's ideas, not least in a period where policies are widely perceived as having been reversed and in which many people opposed to austerity in the twenty-first century do so in the name of a 'return to Keynes' (Skidelsky 2009), questions which will be revisited in Chapter 12.

The first section here, concentrating on the experiences within leading rich-country economies, argues that much of the economic history and policy is hard to square with anything in Keynes. A version of Keynesianism became economic orthodoxy and Keynes's followers at times sat in high places, but there was a specifically Keynesian revolution only if the term is interpreted broadly or loosely. The second section considers the international system in this period, identifying elements of which Keynes clearly would have approved, particularly in the implementation of controls on cross-border capital movements. However, the post-WWII Bretton Woods system also had strongly anti-Keynesian elements, particularly in the way it disciplined trade-deficit but not trade-surplus countries. The greatest national economic success stories of the period, Japan and West Germany, had anti-Keynesian domestic policies imposed upon them after the war but prospered, not least through export orientations. The third section considers the crisis of the 1970s and the abandonment of the Bretton Woods system. Keynes's followers are understandably less keen to accept responsibility. Now, for Davidson, the boom hit problems because 'Keynes's analytical vision of how to improve the operation of a market-oriented entrepreneurial system had been lost' (2009: 95). It is unobvious that there was such discontinuity; if the boom owed relatively little to Keynes, so did its demise. Come the crisis, however, policies that at least appeared to draw on Keynes were implemented without conspicuous success. Lacking the historical counterfactuals, it is hard to judge whether alternative policies – whether anti-Keynesian or more determinedly Keynesian – might have worked better. Nor did the 1970s involve anything like the depression of the 1930s, at least in leading rich-country economies. The crisis, however, was widely perceived as a crisis of Keynesianism and the section reconsiders its implications for Keynesian policy prescriptions and the meaning of Keynesianism.

Was the long post-war boom Keynesian?

There are different meanings of the term 'Keynesianism'. Indeed, the association with the experiences of the long boom has created a distinct sense according to which the question becomes tautological. Even understood more strictly, as meaning 'of or derived from Keynes', there are ambiguities. Most narrowly, it might mean 'taken from the *General Theory*'. But as discussed in Chapter 5, the book is seldom read, difficult and contested, with no single accepted meaning. Elsewhere, Keynes said different things. As Bateman argues, 'Keynes's own ideas about economic policy were famously fluid' (2006: 275). More broadly still, Keynesianism might refer to an encouragement of government intervention, particularly through monetary and fiscal policy. Going beyond this, but going back to the principles discussed in Chapters 2 and 3, Keynesianism might be understood as a general economic and political philosophy steering between state socialism and the free market (Backhouse 2006, Mann 2017a). The argument here substantially supports only the broader interpretations; it is possible to point to continuities between Keynes's ideas and the practices of the post-WWII period, but there are too many divergences for an association to be easily accepted.

The story of the coming of social and economic reorientation is well known and can be discussed briefly. The Keynesian age began as the product of a particular conjuncture of economic conditions, intense social struggles and transformed inter-state relations in the period around WWII. Keynes advocated a reform strategy but so too did others to his political left and right, many of them better organised, in socialist or Christian democratic parties. Weir argues that what became 'Keynesianism emerged as the moderate alternative to planning' (1989: 85). National and nationalist solutions became pervasive in the 1930s, superseding earlier international commitments to laissez-faire. This was epitomised by the rise of fascism, but intensified international competition also characterised the democratic allies, for example with the implementation of competitive currency devaluations and increased barriers to trade. Economic revival in the late 1930s had more to do with the drive to the war than deliberately stimulating economic policy. By the end of WWII, the US dominated the Western capitalist world to an unprecedented extent. Now, US anti-communism and Cold War politics became crucial to policy at home and abroad. Keynes was influential within Britain and in the wartime negotiations with the US leading to, and at, Bretton Woods. Some of his followers already held important positions within the US administration. So there were direct Keynesian influences but these ran alongside and sometimes in competition with US geopolitical interests.

This reading, of course, contrasts with the great importance Keynes attached to economic ideas, not least his own. As he famously put it, 'sooner or later, it is ideas not vested interests, which are dangerous for good or evil' (1973: 383–4). But at least in the US, the New Deal reorientation, in both its domestic and international dimensions, preceded the *General Theory*, and Hall (1989b) suggests that the *General Theory* had little direct influence during Keynes's own lifetime. In the academy, something that came to be understood as Keynesian economics became generally accepted but the *General Theory* itself was never widely understood. Even the Keynesian neo-classical synthesis remains impenetrable to most non-specialists and 'had little immediate political impact' (Clarke, S. 1988: 241). Any diffusion of Keynesian ideas was necessarily highly qualified and highly mediated.

Particular state forms could be important to this mediation. Weir argues that the nature of different states made them more or less susceptible to Keynesian influence (Weir 1989, Weir and Skocpol 1985). The British political system was hierarchical, making it both hard for Keynesians to win influence and also then hard to remove them. Having fended off Keynesian

ideas until 1941, once captured, the British Treasury could become a vehicle
for their propagation. Winch argues that '[i]n the case of Britain one could
argue that the required changes in the state's capacity to adopt and imple-
ment Keynesian polices were in fact minimal' (1989: 111). By contrast, the
more open character of the US state allowed the earlier appointment of
Keynesians to positions of influence, and several economists influenced by
Keynes already played a key role by the late 1930s (Hall 1989a, Harrod
1951, Salant 1989). Compared with the UK, the US system also allowed
the Keynesians' easier subsequent removal, particularly with the onset of
the Cold War. This was most dramatically illustrated in the accusations
of spying levelled against White but also reflected in the rejection of full
employment as a policy objective (Hansen 1953) and the passage of the
Taft-Hartley anti-union laws. By a similar token, Kennedy could later bring
leading Keynesians back into government (Backhouse and Bateman 2011).
But if different institutional arrangements facilitated or obstructed the ascent
of what came to be known as Keynesianism, this too has implications for
the meaning of the term. As Minsky argues, 'regardless of the view of what
Keynes is all about, it must be agreed that, to the extent that our institutional arrangements were, in the main, set prior to 1936, our basic institutional arrangements were not enlightened by perceptions drawn from the
Keynesian revolution in economic analysis' (1986: 8).

Of course, already by 1941 Keynes himself was firmly ensconced in the
British Treasury and influencing policy. The old 'Treasury View', insisting
on balanced budgets, was decisively broken. More than this, Keynes had
helped to establish that the Treasury and the budget should be economic
tools, not merely a set of government accounts (Skidelsky 1992). As
mentioned in Chapter 1, however, wartime conditions meant that the sort
of policies which have come to be associated with Keynesianism were no
longer needed and Keynes himself no longer advocated them. Even before
the war, Keynes had stressed that in the changed conditions of rearmament,
policy should change accordingly. During the war his views became firmly
anti-inflationary, and more radical friends discerned regress and reconciliation with the establishment (Clarke, S. 1988, Skidelsky 2000). Keynes
remained a Liberal Party member but favoured coalition, apparently particularly comfortable as an advisor to the Conservative-led wartime coalition. Keynes did support the Beveridge proposals for the post-war welfare
state in Britain but contributed to their moderation, including postponing
rights to higher old-age pensions (Harrod 1951, Moggridge 1976).

Keynes had more serious misgivings about the post-war Labour government and its more ambitious reforms. The *General Theory* famously
concluded with a call to control or 'socialise' investment. On the one
hand, this was explicitly couched as an alternative to the nationalisation

of production. The major nationalisations of mines and railways were completed after Keynes's death, but the chronically shambolic state of these industries meant he had been little opposed. He was apparently furious with the Labour government's nationalisation of road hauliers, although even here he added '[y]ou must not count on my opposition as a settled policy' (cited in Harrod 1951: 641). On the other hand, Keynes did advocate socialising investment through state control of finance, and here the Labour programme did little, giving the private sector a relatively free hand. The state was 'enabling, rather than directive [it] ... had no mechanism by which to directly control the rate of allocation of investment' (Clarke, S. 1988: 297). The Bank of England was nationalised but it never became a vehicle for directed investment policy, as would be the case, for example, in Japan. So, on this count too, reorientation was hardly Keynesian.

Weir's comparison of Britain and the US suggests that 'political factors mediated the meaning of Keynesianism in each country' (Weir 1989: 85). The depression was experienced in distinct ways and already met with different responses. Hall (1989a) suggests that in the US, even pre-dating the Keynesian appointments, specifically Keynesian policies were implemented as a response to the 1937–38 recession. This Keynesianism without Keynesians would seem to confirm the point made in Chapter 1 that Keynes's own ideas developed as one strand amongst a broader response to the failures of laissez-faire. Weir (1989) also argues, however, that whereas in Britain Keynesian ideas met little opposition from financial interests, in the US, by the end of WWII, the Chamber of Commerce, the National Association of Manufacturers and the Farm Bureau joined forces to effectively oppose the 1945 Full Employment Bill.

Beyond the US, Britain and Canada, it is still harder to trace direct connections from Keynes to economic practice. Ideas of demand management, which themselves pre-dated Keynes, were influential but existed alongside and to some extent in competition with alternatives like direct economic planning and nationalisation. By the late 1940s, more radical plans and explicitly socialist influences were largely defeated, particularly with the influence on European countries of the US and of Marshall Aid. A broad policy consensus in Europe could emerge, however, shared by 'the political moderate Left and the conservative Right ... British Labour politicians, as well as French Gaullists and Christian Democrats in Germany and Italy' (Berend 2006: 213). Many sympathetic commentators accordingly accept it as misleading to associate with Keynes the resultant general widening of the role of state intervention. The welfare state and a general encroachment of the government into economic life, let alone systematic wage rises, were not part of the programme (Bateman 2006, Dostaler 2007, Hansen 1953, Peden 2006, Tobin 1986). In France, bank nationalisation afforded the state financial control, and Boyer argues that this facilitated a radical reforming Keynesianism rather than the 'bastard' approaches elsewhere (1986: 82). But it becomes harder still than in the anglophone countries to attribute this to a direct influence from Keynes's ideas rather than older dirigiste traditions. The *General Theory* was translated into French in 1939 but not widely disseminated (Skidelsky 1992). Beyond bank nationalisation, policy-makers 'worked within a framework that was clearly more anti-liberal that that within which Keynesianism was situated' (Rosanvallon 1989: 189). The rather different and more conspicuously anti-Keynesian situation in the defeated countries, Japan and Germany, will be discussed below, but across most of the Western capitalist world, investment decisions remained overwhelmingly in the hands of the private sector, and private finance, rather than being squeezed as Keynes advocated, would subsequently grow at least as fast as the overall economy (Krippner 2011, Papadimitriou and Wray 2008).

The subsequent long boom was unforeseen and was essentially unplanned, in the sense that it was the unintended consequence of the post-war social settlements. As discussed in previous chapters, Keynes had rela-tively little interest in production, and why what he called the marginal efficiency of capital might change. He did believe that the marginal effi-ciency of capital and thence rates of investment would tend to fall, and this would not be borne out. Blaug argues that 'the full employment and overall employment conditions of the 1950s and 1960s were everywhere attributed to the deliberate pursuit by governments of Keynesian policies, although it was in fact private investment that filled the postwar gap in effective demand' (1997: 649). Of course, private investment itself involved high levels of planning within firms that Keynes's *General Theory* orien-tation on individual entrepreneurs tended to overlook, and this too might therefore be understood to go beyond its compass. But private investment now drove remarkable sustained gains in productivity. Blaug continues that the boom therefore falsified Keynes's prediction of chronic deficiency of effective demand because 'private investment was bound to fall behind full-employment savings' (1997: 650). It becomes quite a stretch to asso-ciate the causes of the boom with the adoption of any specifically Keynesian orientation.

Issues of employment and unemployment could also run counter to Keynes's prescriptions. Papadimitriou and Wray comment that '[r]ather than achieving full employment through job creation, policy offered welfare and Social Security to remove people from the labour force' (2008: xiii). 'True enough, both the British and US governments "targeted" unemploy-ment. But the targets were repeatedly revised downwards as actual results exceeded the targets. Low unemployment, it seemed, was not caused by the pursuit of low unemployment targets; the low unemployment targets were caused by low unemployment' (Skidelsky 2000: 500). Again, unanticipated economic success seemed to be the driver. Keynes, of course, had also argued that in conditions of full employment, the classical theory would come into its own. US unemployment levels, in particular, were never actually close to zero but, by Keynes's own reasoning, low unemployment meant conditions close to those where the old economic orthodoxy he had challenged became adequate.

The boom also demonstrated that it was entirely possible for real wages to rise and for unemployment to fall simultaneously. This was a possibility Keynes, in agreement with the classics, if for different reasons, had rejected. Now, rising productivity was accompanied by real wage rises, which allowed the unique 'Fordist' arrangements of sustained rises in consumption and economies of scale. Amongst other things, in many countries the war had also left the position of organised labour much stronger. Depictions of 'tripartism' between the state, capital and labour exaggerate this strength – labour was at most a junior partner in the post-war settlements – but workers and their organisations won real concessions (Armstrong et al. 1984, Gourevich 1989). Government and employer strategies for dealing with labour's rise are widely interpreted as providing the context for the domestic Fordist settlements in the post-war period (Rupert 1995, de Angelis 2000, Eichengreen 2007). Of course, Keynes already objected to unions' tyrannical self-interest and sectional strength in the inter-war period, when they had been much weaker than after WWII.

It is nevertheless possible to argue that policies could be 'consistent with Keynes's thought although not derived from it' (Dillard 1986: 122). For example, labour's relative strength may have contributed to greater income equality and thence to maintaining stability and effective demand in ways broadly compatible with Keynes's ideas. He would also presumably have approved the negotiated rather than more overtly conflictual class settlements.

In general, even with the return of peace and prosperity, states remained more economically interventionist than previously. Liberal myths about the free-market economy contrasted more sharply than ever, at this time of unprecedented growth and prosperity, with a high level of planning. In the US, direct federal government spending spiked with the war but showed no sign of returning to the levels of the pre-New Deal era. The state's increased direct economic importance involved, amongst other things, underwriting welfare and thence consumption norms in ways that would have been quite foreign to the earlier liberal settlements but to which Keynes seems likely to have been sympathetic. It was suggested in Chapter 3, however, that Keynes's supported increased state intervention on essentially liberal grounds, merely raising the level of what he believed to be the necessary minimum. It is unobvious that he would have supported the sustained rises in state spending which the period witnessed. Nor is it clear how the very different levels of state spending in leading countries can be similarly Keynesian.

Monetary policy did appear to be able to control a trade-off between unemployment and inflation; the Phillips Curve identifying this relation post-dates Keynes and will be discussed in the next chapter but has, at least retrospectively, been widely perceived as providing a specifically Keynesian policy tool (Forder 2019). The role of confidence, so important to Keynes, also reasonably allows that the expectation that states would intervene when necessary also helped to sustain growth in a specifically Keynesian way, even without practical resort to such intervention (O'Donnell 1989, Brenner 1998). Conversely, there is some irony, given the importance of unpredictability to Keynes's analysis, that it was precisely the predictability of the boom that allowed supposedly Keynesian policies to be practised. There was little evidence of the uncertainty and the volatility of liquidity preference that Keynes had described and which warranted state intervention.

But Keynes believed that states could and should reduce the uncertainties and volatility of a market economy. He supported a more equal distribution on both positive and normative grounds, and in most rich-country economies this was achieved through redistributive taxation and social spending. The many social and welfare programmes too, while clearly not specifically Keynesian (Tobin 1986, Hall 1989c), can plausibly be included under the rubric of reform capitalism which he advocated. Hall argues that while Keynes cannot claim direct responsibility for the growth of the welfare state, his attack on the idea of the need for a balanced budget loosened fiscal constraints that allowed more generous social programmes (Hall 1989a). Keynes explicitly identified himself with a middle way between laissez-faire and communism, and in this sense 'Keynesianism' could reasonably designate an ideology of social consensus, which urged national interests and 'responsible' behaviour on both capital and labour (Rosanvallon 1989, de Angelis 2000). What became Keynesianism as a broad ideology and practice of the social consensus involved a more or less coherent mixture of specifically Keynesian ideas and visions for wider reform.

One important if sometimes neglected area where Keynes's influence can reasonably be claimed is in the development of the statistical apparatus and bureaucracies associated with national accounting and the more detailed management they allowed. Eatwell suggests that in the period to 1951, 'the major influence of Keynesian ideas was on the presentation of budgetary policy and the construction of the statistical apparatus that made that presentation possible' (1986: 68). In France, it was even claimed that

'Keynesianism is national accounting' (Rosanvallon 1989: 185). Again, this work had begun before Keynes, particularly in the US (Salant 1989), and received a great boost from the imperatives of the war economy, but the rise of national accounting went along with an increasingly interventionist policy and seems clearly something of which Keynes would have approved. A prerequisite for effective state intervention was being able to measure the economy, and state activity and the statistical work stimulated and legitimised each other (Negri 1988). This also reinforced a specifically national vision of the economy, a vision substantially aligned with Keynes's.

Finally, an influential interpretation of Keynes sees governments as providing fiscal stimulus to counteract recessions, with states therefore developing budget deficits. By this criterion the period was clearly not Keynesian. Most governments ran consistent surpluses, recovering huge post-war debts remarkably quickly (Eatwell 1986, Harman 1984, Matthews 1968). It was the expansion of private credit money rather than state spending that tended to accompany increasing aggregate demand (Davidson 2009). In a sense, however, this criticism is illegitimate. The active and effective use of monetary policy, to both stimulate and restrict, may not be specifically Keynesian but Keynes always envisaged states' primary response as being through monetary policy, and only where this proved insufficient did he call for public works, and this rather than fiscal deficits. Keynes was also concerned with damping both sides of capitalism's volatility. Although stimulus measures were the thrust of his policy prescriptions in the 1930s, Keynes later made it clear that he also favoured a parallel set of policies restricting overinvestment (Harris 1953, Pilling 1986, Davidson 2009). There was some countercyclical demand management (Hall 1989a) but it also seems clear that demand management, whether stimulating or restricting, played relatively little part in the boom. Hall's (1989c) remarkable collection, having set out to show their influence, concluded by identifying instead the high 'the degree to which Keynes' ideas about demand management were resisted or ignored in many countries' (Hall 1989b: 367).

The overall state spending increases included huge military budgets. These have been described as producing a process of 'military Keynesianism'. Cold War competition provided an ongoing stimulus, amongst other things with military spending acceptable to capital in a way that Keynes's reforming ideas were not (Baran and Sweezy 1968). International comparisons suggest caution. The countries with the highest levels of military spending, the US and Britain (and of course the USSR), grew more slowly than Japan and West Germany, countries debarred from similar spending. And while an argument can be made that it was the systemic stimulus provided by US spending which was crucial, allowing the lower spenders to 'free ride', France presents an intermediate case, with high levels of military spending and very strong growth. In any case, the unplanned character of military competition allows this as 'Keynesianism' in at best a very weak sense.

What came to be understood as Keynesian ideas emerged in the context of heightened class struggles and were institutionalised in the social compromises at the end of WWII. Keynes's ideas themselves can be seen as contributing to that class compromise (Hall 1989b). They contributed, however, alongside others, with Keynes's ideas proving amenable to selective appropriation, 'often used to *justify* a range of practices associated with the "mixed economy"' (Hall 1989b: 367). For example, rising real wages, hardly part of Keynes' original vision, could be assimilated to accounts emphasising the importance of effective demand. Social peace, which Keynes had largely assumed, could underpin popular support for Keynesian ideas (Salant 1989). The meaning of 'socialisation of investment' could be stretched to include nationalisation. Finance grew rather than being repressed but it appeared to do so in a controlled way, resembling Keynes's bubbles on a stream of enterprise. Everything could be claimed as Keynesian. Famously, by 1965 Milton Friedman announced that 'we are all Keynesian now' (cited in Dostaler 2007: 257) while Marxist political economists articulated theories of under-consumption bearing a close family resemblance (see Baran and Sweezy 1968). Opponents, both Marxist and liberal, were confined to the fringes or now revised their perspectives.

Bretton Woods and the international system

A second crucial dimension of the long boom was the unique international settlement. Some elements of this might reasonably be described as Keynesian, and Keynes himself voted for the basic structure both at the Bretton Woods conference and subsequently as its champion in the British House of Lords. Important elements of this system, however, were either anti-Keynesian or Keynesian in at most a conditional and qualified sense. More broadly, the fact that the international system remained essentially competitive undermined the Keynesian desire to achieve a more managed capitalism. Starting from a low base, the post-WWII regime facilitated a return to a more open, liberal order.

Before looking at the post-WWII system, it is worth briefly sketching a few key elements of the earlier system and its demise, and of Keynes's attitude to this. The world economy prior to WWI was generally understood to operate on laissez-faire principles. Levels of trade, foreign investment, capital movement and human migration were high. As ever, ideology was one thing, practice another. Amongst leading states, only Britain had practised anything approximating textbook openness for any substantial time. Keynes (2011) pointed out some considerable discrepancies between theory and practice even in Britain, particularly in the conscious management of the gold standard. Outside Britain, the supposed basics of an open economy – the gold standard and free trade – were accepted only for short periods (Broz 2000). Germany and the US had caught up with and overtaken Britain while adopting protectionist and interventionist practices. Many parts of the world lacked even formal national sovereignty, remaining part of colonial empires.

Attempts to reconstitute the liberal world order after 1918 were undermined, particularly by the asymmetries of the Versailles settlement. They collapsed with the onset of the Great Depression. Even as formal cross-border transactions declined, the rapid spread of the depression in the 1930s itself demonstrated an interdependent global economy. Even the US, the richest and most powerful country, for example, responded to gold outflows in 1932 in similar ways to those now deemed necessary to prevent capital flight, with sharply deflationary policies (Kenwood and Lougheed 1992). What happened in one national economy had repercussions and required action by governments elsewhere. By 1931, even Britain had abandoned trade openness and the gold standard. By 1937 gold was universally abandoned. The attempt to shift the burden of unemployment onto other countries produced a predictable competitive inward spiral. Not least, economic competition increased military competition, which finally pressed budgets towards deficits and the adoption of what might be seen as more Keynesian policy in many countries (Lee 1989).

It was suggested in Chapter 3 and elsewhere that Keynes exaggerates the power of states within their domestic economy but that he was well aware of international constraints on state power. He made his name through his denunciation of the Versailles Treaty, amongst other things arguing that the success of laissez-faire depended on maintaining a balance of international forces and that demands for reparations from Germany would prove unsustainable (CWII, Davidson 2009). He opposed the 'despotic control' of the gold standard almost from the beginning (Lekachman 1986). At times, at least, he opposed free trade, not least because conventional Ricardian trade theory was invalidated by its assumptions of full employment. His views changed, but as early as 1933, Keynes had argued that he sympathised 'with those who would minimise, rather than with those who would maximise, economic entanglement between nations … let goods be home-spun whenever it is reasonably and conveniently possible … It should not be a matter of tearing up roots, but of slowly training a plant to grow in a different direction' (CWXXIII: 236). Free capital mobility allowed damaging outflows from Britain (Keynes 1973: 21). Keynes's arguments put him at odds with the then dominant laissez-faire ideology of unrestricted free markets. His opposition, however, was a pragmatic, and pragmatically British, one. If the international system could be better organised, and preferably organised by the British, it could allow mutual gains.

International trade and financial imbalances between the US, Britain, France and Germany contributed to the debacle of 1929, while intensified competition contributed to the depth of the depression and the drive to war (Kindleberger 1973). As early as 1940, Keynes (CWXXV) was working on plans for an alternative post-war order involving international coordination. As at the domestic level, Keynes advocated a more thoroughly organised system. His proposals and his personal interventions would be a major feature of the Bretton Woods conference of 1944. Keynes' visions, however, were at best partially realised (Williamson 1985). White and the US were largely able to persuade their allies to adopt their plans for the post-war world. Reorganisation could only happen under US direction. Two world wars, a depression of unparalleled depth and breadth, and the presence of an apparently viable communist alternative left the US in a uniquely strong position within the Western world-system. Balogh only exaggerates when he says that Bretton Woods was imposed on Britain by diktat, because 'Britain was bankrupt' (Balogh 1976: 74).

US attitudes themselves had shifted from those of the inter-war period. Perhaps above all, the relative and absolute wealth of the US and the productivity of US capital were unparalleled. The failures (particularly the failure to prevent war) and the outcome of the war had also refashioned post-war responses and the meaning of liberal world order. On the one hand, fascism was discredited. On the other, any 'communist threat' was transformed. Previously, notwithstanding the efforts of the Comintern and any number of red scare stories, in geopolitical and economic terms the USSR was isolated and contained. By the end of the war, its influence stretched to the Elbe, while radical, sometimes communist-led, social movements emerged within several leading countries. The communist threat was more plausible. This too appears to have been conducive to a greater consensus between leading capitalist powers. The Cold War also increased the relative strength of the US amongst its allies and the preparedness of America to assume the leading role it had previously been 'unwilling' to assume (Kindleberger 1973). In some tension with his claims for the boom as Keynesian cited above, Davidson sees 'a strange confluence of forces occurring after World War II', involving mathematisation and anti-communist politics, which overturned Keynes (2009: 169). The point, once again, is that the outcomes were Keynesian in at most a qualified sense.

The Keynesian elements to the post-war agreements included a general acceptance of national states' responsibilities for managing their economies within the international system. Bretton Woods allowed capital controls between countries permitting governments to set interest rates primarily according to domestic policy requirements without this producing hot-money flows and rapid swings in foreign exchange values. It therefore afforded more scope for domestic policy autonomy than either the gold standard or the era of financial mobility which would develop from the 1970s. There were restrictions on finance, even if these hardly threatened the euthanasia of the rentier (Konings 2010). The US, however, did not apply capital controls and by the 1960s, large volumes of dollars circulated beyond US borders. By the 1960s the UK and US governments were at least tacitly accepting the growth of these Eurodollar markets and the restoration of the City of London as a global centre of deregulated finance (Helleiner 1994, Strange 1986, 1998). Dissent at the proliferation of dollars, essentially unpaid US debts, grew, notably from France. But at least until the late 1960s, US leadership would be more or less readily accepted by its allies.

Similarly, in relation to other issues, there were at most compromised or semi-Keynesian practices. Keynes had proposed to overcome the restrictions of gold through an international currency, which he called '*bancor*', which could be bought but not sold for gold. 'Keynes's main object was to enable exchange-rate adjustments to be made in an orderly way, and to help countries with balance of payments troubles' (Kahn 1976: 15). Instead, the system centred on the US dollar, itself fixed against gold at $35 an ounce and with other currencies then pegged against the dollar. The dollar potentially provided more liquidity than a strict gold standard, but in common with the gold standard, it prioritised exchange-rate stability. In practice, America's 'benign neglect' of the value of the dollar meant that the IMF did allow other countries to adjust their pegged values downward, to devalue their currencies. But, as discussed below, the gold-dollar focus militated against unilateral dollar adjustments and involved an anti-Keynesian asymmetry that would become important to the system's unravelling.

Keynes also advocated an international bank or what he called a 'Clearing Union'. The Bretton Woods institutions, the IMF and World Bank, looked rather different. The IMF and World Bank did typically push a qualified or 'embedded liberalism' (Keohane 2005). For example, during this period, World Bank lending encouraged state-led development projects in poorer countries. Their institutional power, wealth and bureaucracies meant that the institutions developed discrete organisations and dynamics, which were not reducible to the interests of leading states. Nevertheless, there was an unmistakable US dominance. Keynes wrote to Kahn on 13 March 1946 that '[t]he Americans have no idea how to make these institutions into operating international concerns, and in almost every direction their ideas are bad. Yet they plainly intend to force their own conception through regardless of the rest of us' (cited in Kahn 1976: 25). Ultimately, the US controlled most of the International Financial Institutions' votes because it controlled most of the funding, although the overall level of funding was also much lower than Keynes had wanted.

When the US did fund post-war reconstruction in Europe it did so dir-ectly through Marshall Aid, which came with anti-communist strings attached. De Angelis writes that it was 'not a coincidence that the Marshall Plan was announced in the same month as the [anti-union] Taft-Hartley Act' (2000: 73). The role of Marshall Aid in European recovery has been much disputed (Eichengreen 2007) but amongst other things, it provided dollars with which Europeans could buy US goods, and as European econ-omies recovered they bought more. US trade surpluses grew throughout the 1950s, only partially offset by increased foreign investment.

One aspect of the post-war regime was strongly anti-Keynesian. The Bretton Woods and IMF arrangements punished only countries running trade deficits, forcing their deflation, without comparable constraints on the surplus countries. This contrasted with Keynes's proposals for a series of punishments of creditor countries, including the confiscation of surpluses beyond a certain level (CWXXV, Thirlwall 1976). Such a plan would have required adjustments of both deficit and surplus countries, the surplus increasing domestic consumption, rather than deficit ones merely consuming less. The alternative, one-sided emphasis on deficit countries' adjustment also contained the seeds of the system's downfall.

Prolonged prosperity changed the priorities of Western capitalist econ-omies. As international economic entanglements grew and prosperity continued, they fostered complacency about the dangers of this. The story of the inflexibility and eventual unravelling of the post-war Bretton Woods regime is well rehearsed. A crucial anti-Keynesian element of the story is the rise of Japan and Germany. Of course, in both countries there was organisa-tion rather than individualism and the free market. In Germany the 'social-market' economy has been seen as pre-empting Keynesian ideas and policies (Allen 1989: 264), although Hall (1989a: 23) argues that association with similar policies under the Nazis had discredited more obviously Keynesian policies. In Japan, state policy direction became a vital feature of a distinctive 'model' of capitalism alongside the close collaboration between major firms and state agencies (Coates 2005, Johnson 1982). One institution, the Economic Planning Agency, responsible for national income statistics and for developing economic plans, was avowedly Keynesian (Hadley 1989). Finance could be directed towards strategic industries by the Ministry of Finance, the Bank of Japan and the Ministry of International Trade and Industry. But these semi-Keynesian aspects sat alongside restrictive fiscal policy. The victorious powers, principally the US, imposed strongly anti-Keynesian budgetary constraints with a tight money/anti-inflationary bias on the defeated countries. The separation of the German central bank from political control and the constitutional requirements of sound 'ordo-liberal' (Blyth 2013) monetary policy were firmly established. Only in the late 1960s and early 1970s under the 'Grand Coalition' and Brandt's SPD government were explicitly Keynesian ideas briefly popular (Allen 1989: 263). Even then, they were much constrained by the constitutional settlement. In Japan, Ishibashi, the finance minister in 1946, favoured Keynesian policies but was purged by MacArthur's headquarters (Hadley 1989), and legislation requiring balanced budgets would only be amended in 1966 (Hall 1989a).

Both Japan and Germany initially had significantly lower wages and relative levels of domestic consumption, justifying low currency values. Also, with lower levels of military spending, again imposed by the victorious powers, a higher proportion of their surpluses could be retained in civilian investment and put into research and development. This is only part of the complex story of catch-up but, for whatever reasons, productivity growth was more rapid than in the US, and this gradually undermined the fixed-exchange-rate regime. Low levels of domestic consumption and restrictions on expansionary policy meant that export markets were correspondingly more important. The asymmetries of the system, which initially allowed US surpluses to go unpunished, by the 1960s allowed German and Japanese surpluses to grow. US trade surpluses declined. There was little imperative for Germany or Japan to revalue their currencies and no mechanism for the US to devalue; the dollar was fixed against gold. Along with rising costs, particularly associated with the war in Vietnam, the overall US balance-of-payments position became strongly negative and its gold reserves diminished. The overall levels of imbalances that developed by the 1970s seem slight by recent standards but they contributed to the accumulation of dollars outside the US and to undermining the fixed-exchange-rate system.

It is reasonable to maintain that the boom owed something to more interventionist policy and economic coordination at both national and international level. The unique dynamics of capital accumulation and class relations, however, were not reducible to this. Arms spending may have produced Keynesian effects but for un-Keynesian reasons. The forms of organisation, accumulation and class struggle and the ideas invoked by policy-makers varied hugely even across leading Western capitalist countries. The incorporation of all of this hotchpotch of social relations, restructuring and policy reorientation as 'Keynesian' dilutes the term's meaning to something close to 'not laissez-faire'. The post-war practice was at most Keynesianism conceived very broadly and very moderately.

The crisis, and the crisis of Keynesianism

By 1974, the global economy had entered its first major recession since the immediate post-WWII years. After years of boom, where Keynes's remedies from the 1930s appeared unnecessary, now the Keynesian moment appeared to have returned. A period of severe crisis (interrupted by brief spurts of growth) continued for something like eight years. Nor would there be any return to the growth and stability of the long boom. As might be expected, interpretations of why the boom ended and of the adequacy of the policy responses vary considerably.

Mainstream, liberal accounts, which had been marginalised during the boom, could now rediscover that government interference in the market was the root of at least most of the evil. For anti-Keynesians, any credit for the boom is ceded to interventionist policy at most partially and grudgingly. Increases in international trade or in productivity, generated or spread essentially exogenously, are more important. Conversely, the collapse of the boom is readily attributed to bad policy. The Bretton Woods currency regime built rigidity into the system, while the 'stagflationary' spiral now demonstrated the fallacies of the Keynesian reflationary strategy. Little of this narrative is plausible. Ideas that too much government intervention within national economies was directly responsible for the crisis seem hard to sustain except in the most catch-all sense that government intervention, and especially state-run enterprise, is inherently inefficient and that those inefficiencies are bound to reveal themselves eventually. As above, until the crisis bit, governments were running modest fiscal surpluses, so conventional arguments against 'crowding out' hardly seem germane. Levels of government spending were high, but in the US they declined significantly in the years immediately preceding the crisis, from 18.1 per cent of GDP in 1970 to 16.9 per cent in 1973 (World Bank 2018). The monetary system's inflexibility many have ended in sharp dislocations but, at least in principle, the system had also already been abandoned prior to the economic crisis. The nominally market-based system would not prove conducive to a more stable international currency regime in the years that followed. The crisis itself would discredit suggestions of a Phillips Curve trade-off between unemployment and inflation, widely perceived as an effective Keynesian policy tool, but, to paraphrase Keynes, a properly brought-up classical economist can hardly admit this failure as a cause of the crisis because money is supposed to be neutral, so inflation cannot cause real economic problems.

The response from the Keynesian side is more interesting, if also somewhat contradictory. Keynesians who had claimed credit for the boom now distanced themselves from the downturn, which could be attributed to a misapplication or an insufficient application of Keynes's ideas. For example, Davidson writes of the downturn that post-war 'economists failed to adopt the logically consistent innovative theoretical framework laid down by Keynes' (2009: 19). According to Bateman, Keynes himself had not argued for many of the things that the right were attacking, and so the attacks against 'Keynes himself were misplaced and aimed at a straw man' (2006: 287). Keynes, for example, had never advocated the widespread nationalisation of industry, as had occurred in much of Europe. He had advocated a repression of finance, which had not occurred. For the more radical, perhaps more consistent, followers, this involves an important admission that Keynes's ideas had not been applied, as suggested in the first section of this chapter. One implication, however, would be that any claims to economic superiority remain theoretical. Keynesianism retreats from the corridors of power to a narrow academic heterodoxy. At the very least, the crisis raised important questions about the relation between the original theory and what had become conventional Keynesian economics and about the adequacy of ideas, developed in the Great Depression, which had gained acceptance in times of prosperity.

With the crisis, it looked as if something closer to Keynesian policy prescriptions were attempted. Again, it is possible to claim that these responses involved a misapplication of Keynes. Papadimitriou and Wray, for example, agree with the liberal critics that by the 1970s, neo-classical/Keynesian synthesis policies 'made matters worse' (2008: xiv). It is always possible to contest the details, but real interest rates turned very low, often negative. There were substantial increases in state spending, if seldom the 'public works' Keynes advocated. Direct intervention in the form of price and wage controls were implemented. By many measures, the responses were found wanting. Growth remained sluggish and unemployment increased. Instead of a trade-off between the two, both unemployment and inflation jumped. It is, of course, also impossible to know either what would have happened without the stimulus measures that were pursued or what would have happened had they been pursued more determinedly.

In this context it is important to stress that the failures should not be exaggerated. At least in rich-country economies, there was no return to the horrors of the Great Depression. Table 10.1 contrasts the changes in per capita wealth for the G7 countries between 1929 and 1933 and between 1973 and 1977. The 1970s was a period of recession but there was still overall growth. Unemployment rose but, amongst these G7 countries, to rates above 7 per cent only in Canada and Italy, nothing like the 20 and 30 per cent levels of the 1930s or the double-digit levels that would again become normal in much of Europe in the twenty-first century.

Table 10.1 Changes in GDP per capita in the 1930s and 1970s (calculated from Maddison 2003, World Bank 2018)

	1929–33	1973–77
Canada	-31	+7
France	-10	+9
Germany	-12	+10
Italy	-6	+11
Japan	+5	+5
UK	-4	+1
US	-31	+5

One important aspect of the crisis of the 1970s which made it very different from the 1930s was that where that earlier crisis had been deflationary, now prices continued to rise, despite recessionary conditions and high levels of unemployment. Questions of inflation raise particularly important issues for Keynesian thinking. Rising prices could most easily, most conveniently, be explained in terms of the 'oil shock', through which the exporting countries in the Organization of Petroleum Supporting Countries (OPEC) restricted output and achieved price rises. The argument goes that these were then passed on to the wider Western economies. A less deliberate rise in oil prices followed the 1979 Iranian revolution. However, while oil and oil prices had become very important to the Western economy, there are reasons to doubt this as an adequate explanation. First, prices had begun rising prior to the oil shock. Second, rising oil prices actually moved money out of the Western financial system, to the exporting countries, even if much of this was then recycled as 'petrodollars' to the Western banks (Galbraith 1995). Third, the ability of firms to pass on rising costs in any straightforward way involves some heroic assumptions about monopoly pricing and raises questions why firms did so only now in response to oil prices, when they might presumably have done so before. The oil price rises seem to be better understood as at most 'triggers' rather than 'causes' of either the crisis or its inflationary nature (Jayawardena 1990: vi).

States, after 1971 freed from the gold-dollar constraints of the Bretton Woods period, at least facilitated rising prices through easy-money policy. Krippner (2011) argues that inflation was a strategy. As seen in Chapter 4, for monetarist interpretations of the quantity theory, which Keynes confronted, there is a straightforward relation between the money supply and the price level, hence rising prices must be the product of a rising money supply. Keynes questioned this relationship, agreeing that the authorities could control the money supply but seeing any effects of this on prices as indirect, achieved via changes in the interest rate, with increases in employment likely to absorb (at least much of) any extra money. However, if liquidity preference were to remain unchanged, increases in money would lower the interest rate, with stimulating effects, increasing demand and thence prices. So states could influence prices and deliberately stimulate inflation, but by means of highly mediated and uncertain relations.

As will be discussed in the next chapter, many of Keynes's followers, unwilling to accept state profligacy as responsible, took a more radically anti-monetarist position, and instead attributed rising prices to rising wages. Dean argues that Samuelson and Hicks as well as the 'revolutionaries' like Kaldor and Robinson all shared the 'emphasis on wage-sourced inflation' (1980: 21). 'As inflation persisted while unemployment and overcapacity rose, it became clear to the Keynesian mind that inflation could not simply be the result of "overfull" employment, but could only be the result of the ability of militant trade unions to enforce inflationary pay rises on employers' (Clarke, S. 1988: 302). Wage rises could also now be held responsible for falling profits and the wider crisis. As often, it was possible to find some textual support although 'Keynes' allusions to it were sporadic and tentative' (Dean 1980: 33). Keynes had also argued than nominal wage rises would be more than cancelled by price rises as they increased demand. Any such demand-pull was clearly not occurring in the conditions of 'stagflation' in the 1970s, when rising wages and prices coincided with high levels of unemployment. The new wage-push theories raise awkward questions about why workers suddenly demanded and won much higher nominal wages rises in the early 1970s, where they had not done so previously. The situation in France in 1968 was exceptional; for capital, wage rises became a price worth paying to buy off the apparently revolutionary threat. Elsewhere, until the mid-1970s, wage demands ate into profits without having major inflationary consequences. In the US, the labour share of income peaked in 1969. The peaks occurred somewhat later in most European countries but wage shares were falling even as prices rose in the late 1970s. It seems clear that by then, unions were largely playing 'catch-up', factoring existing price rises into wage claims but doing so with increasing difficulty and decreasing success. Figure 10.1 shows this take-off of inflation in the early 1970s, particularly from 1973 and 1974 – that is, after the high point of labour militancy in most countries. Of course, unions had not yet begun their headlong retreat of later decades and rising nominal wages no doubt contributed to spiralling inflation, but the depiction of labour as prime mover seems empirically wrong, theoretically ill founded and deeply politically loaded.

As Krippner's (2011) work on the US shows, the state was able to deflate its own debt but real-economy corporations also gained from inflation as debts were reduced and as real wages fell. Keynes had advocated deflating real wages in the 1920s and 1930s, but the levels and details of the 1970s inflationary experience are hard to square with his proposals. States were unable to achieve particular desired rates of inflation and avowed targets were repeatedly missed. However, states were broadly tolerant of high levels. Predictably, opposition developed from financial interests, which saw their assets devalued. As real-economy corporations, given recessionary conditions, became less willing to invest, they too had less interest in borrowing even at very low real interest rates and they also became savers, increasingly financialised and accordingly less tolerant of inflation.

The negative proof of this change in corporate attitudes comes in their (sometimes grudging) acceptance of the effective (if equally ad hoc and imprecise) monetarist reaction. The official abandonment of Keynesianism in the UK came in 1976 with acquiescence to IMF loan conditions and Labour prime minister Callaghan's notorious pronouncement: 'We used to think you could spend your way out of a recession but I have to tell you in all sincerity that this is no longer the case' (cited in Ormerod 1994: 123). Two things are notable here. First, the IMF was essentially following its standard practice, even if this had not previously been required of major rich-country economies. Second, '[f]ar from imposing deflationary policies on a reluctant government, the [1976] IMF loan provided an alibi with which to head off mounting political opposition' (Clarke, S. 1988: 314–5). Powerful domestic

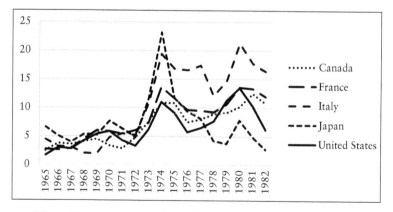

Figure 10.1 Consumer price inflation, 1965–82, selected countries (World Bank 2017)

class interests welcomed austerity. The period of heightened class struggle from 1968 revealed the 'social consensus' to be very thin.

In the US, the decisive deflationary turn came a little later, with the 'Volcker shock' officially signalling the introduction of monetarism if in practice using very high interest rate rather than monetary adjustments to induce recession. French attempts at stimulus continued into the early years of the Mitterrand government but were then reversed. By the mid-1980s, 'neo-liberalism' became the norm in most rich countries, although this too varied to such an extent that it is again questionable whether the single term can adequately capture the diverse practice. Fine and Harris argue that:

> Keynesianism ignores the fact that the capitalist state, responsible for the reproduction of capitalist relations, is forced to permit and even at times precipitate crises. For crises are not only disastrous for sections of the bourgeoisie and, of course, the working class; they are also the preconditions for renewed capitalist accumulation. (1979: 133)

The crisis and its resolution severely damaged the core Keynesian idea that states were wise, impartial managers (Skidelsky 1992).

Conclusion

The boom involved a mix of practices; it was much less laissez-faire than the pre-WWI era and some of the transformation can reasonably be characterised as Keynesian. There were, in general, higher levels of government intervention and oversight and there was income redistribution. Of course, no government followed the letter of Keynes's prescriptions. Perhaps if we compare the numerous regimes that have been labelled 'Marxist', either by themselves or by others, the discrepancy between theory and practice may not seem too great. Avowedly 'liberal' and 'democratic' regimes similarly stretch the meanings of these terms to breaking point. It does seem likely that Keynes would have been comfortable with much of post-war policy in many rich countries, not least Macmillan's 'Middle Way' in Britain. None of which is to suggest that the policies were 'caused' by Keynes, while the great international variety, for example in the levels of state spending and commitments to combating unemployment and fiscal responsibility, suggests that it cannot all have been equally Keynesian.

It is correspondingly hard to attribute the boom to the adoption of Keynesian policies in any straightforward way. Higher levels of state involvement may have contributed, especially to uncertainty-reduction and stability. The fundamental transformation of the period, however – levels of capital accumulation and productivity increases that allowed both profits and real wages to increase simultaneously – runs not so much counter to Keynes as outside the scope of his system.

Similarly, Keynes may have lost important battles at Bretton Woods but the international system had Keynesian elements, in allowing states to impose capital controls and more broadly in its managed nature. However, it also contained strongly anti-Keynesian characteristics, in its general encouragement of increasing economic entanglements and its specific deflationary biases. These two characteristics contributed to imbalances of the sort against which Keynes warned and which contributed to the breakdown of the system. In short, it is possible to attribute both the successes and the failures to Keynes or to not following Keynes (Boyer 1986) but it is implausible to claim all the evidence on one side.

The responses to the crisis were at best partially Keynesian and at best partially successful. Again, it is impossible to determine definitively the correspondence between the parts. As with the boom, the period was Keynesian only in a rather broad or general sense. Some of the practices match Keynes's prescriptions quite closely, some can be read as following the spirit if not the letter, some operate outside Keynes's system and some run counter to it.

All of this suggests caution in advocating a return to Keynes. These are themes to which Chapter 12 returns, but the conditions which created the long boom no longer exist. This is not to discount the possibility of some kind of reformed capitalism emerging, but this would surely be of a different stripe from the original Keynesian practices, if just as much an unintended consequence of contested social struggles.

11

Keynesian theory after Keynes

Introduction

Keynesian scholarship is enormous and diverse. It is impossible to know, much less to present, this contradictory richness in a single chapter. Rather than feigning an overview of the literature, the chapter sketches three broad trajectories to make an argument that each of these strands of the Keynesian critique remain limited by an ambiguous and unsatisfactory break with neo-classical economics. The problem can perhaps be couched in terms of the analogy with physics mentioned in the Introduction. Keynes saw his theory as general in the same sense as Einstein's general theory of relativity. This incorporated not only special relativity but also the earlier Newtonian physics as a special case. Newtonian physics is imperfect but still useful, from civil engineering to rocket science. This is not true of neo-classical economics but much of the Keynesian theory behaves as if it were. A better physics analogy might be pre-Copernican astronomy, which accepted the basic Ptolemaic system of orbit around the earth, even as it better explained the observed discrepancies by adding ever more epicycles to the theory. Again and again, for Keynes himself and for his followers, the neo-classical world of rational individualism and free markets remains the centre of the analytical universe, even as more epicycles are added to explain how the real world deviates from this, often quite drastically.

The chapter first considers neo-classical synthesis Keynesianism, associated with Samuelson's textbook introduction to economics, the IS/LM models of Hicks (1937) and Hansen (1953), and the Phillips Curve interpretation of inflation. As Hicks's (1937) title, 'Mr. Keynes and the "Classics"', would have it, here the attempted reconciliation with the mainstream is overt and Keynes's criticisms become a special case of the system he was criticising.

Second, the chapter looks at market imperfections, considering alternative New Keynesian and 'post-Keynesian' accounts, with briefer notes on money and financial instability. Despite declarations of mutual hostility, the relatively moderate New Keynesians and the putatively more radical post-Keynesians have much in common. As Shaikh (2016) has argued, the emphasis for both remains on imperfections, implying that the unreal neo-classical world of perfect competition remains central to the vision, even if as a focus of antagonism. There is often common ground too in hopes that states can reduce the imperfections or ameliorate their consequences.

Third, the chapter considers another strand of post-Keynesians, which, with more emphasis on time and uncertainty, can accuse the other currents of misappropriating Keynes and losing sight of his more radical criticisms. Once again, there are profound insights but their analytical power tends to be reined in as they are marshalled for an in-house squabble with mainstream economists aiming to provide better advice to existing rulers. Even as a more fundamental critique, the identification of radical uncertainty shows the follies of much of the existing economic formalism without providing the basis for an alternative political economy.

In making this critical argument, I am aware that I am committing horrible crimes of omission and commission. Even if the general criticisms are valid, there is, of course, a vast scholarship saying much that is eminently useful, and containing counter-examples to the case made here. If I cannot do justice to the literature as a whole, I hope at least to fairly characterise some important problems.

The Keynesian mainstream

Keynesian economics quickly became orthodoxy in the years after WWII, at least in the Anglo-American world. There are many powerful criticisms of this new orthodoxy and important claims that it misrepresents Keynes. It is worth emphasising, however, that during the boom years, few seemed to notice the discrepancies (Skidelsky 1992) and, as suggested in the previous chapter, if the post-Keynesian critique is correct, policy was never Keynesian and his supporters can no more claim credit for the boom than they can accept blame for its breakdown. In as far as Keynesian ideas did influence policy, it was this moderate version. Throughout the period of the Keynesian boom, the neo-classical Keynesian synthesis *was* Keynesian economics, an economics which purported to reincorporate Keynes's *General Theory* as a special case of classics.

Samuelson coined the term 'neoclassical synthesis Keynesianism' (Davidson 2007: 208) and provided the textbook version. Republished in multiple editions, the textbook became the standard introduction to economics in most English-speaking universities, while also being widely translated. It is impossible to go into detail. Linder (1977) provides an almost line by line dissection. The focus here will instead be on two key ideas, IS/LM and the Phillips Curve. The IS/LM framework ostensibly transcends the binaries: of orthodox quantity theory, for which money has no influence on the real economy, and of a Keynesianism for which the real economy has no influence on the monetary. But it does so at the cost of suggesting a neat equivalence and potentially stable equilibrium. The Phillips Curve recognises the reality of unemployment but recasts it in terms of mechanical balance with inflation.

The idea of IS/LM begins with Hicks's (1937) elegant paper 'Mr. Keynes and the "Classics": a suggested reinterpretation'. Keynes apparently read the paper and approved (see e.g. Backhouse 2006). Against the elevated status it would later assume, Hicks was quite modest in his claims for his 'little apparatus' (1937: 156), describing it as a 'rough and ready sort of affair' (1937: 158) and one which, ignoring questions of distribution, price changes and timing, was intended like Keynes's book before it as 'neither the beginning nor the end of Dynamic Economics' (Hicks 1937: 157). He acknowledged that '[t]here is indeed much more in the *General Theory* of Keynes than this formal model, and very much more in some of Keynes's other writings, which can quite properly be used to elucidate his work' (cited in Tily 2007: 285). So criticisms may be better directed at what IS/LM became than at its original purpose, but Hicks is explicit that the *General Theory* argument should be seen as offering only a 'special theory' and that 'The General Theory is something appreciably more orthodox' (1937: 152).

Keynes in the *General Theory* provides a powerful critique of the classical views which see money as neutral. Economists had seen interest as determined by supply and demand within the real economy, bringing consumption and production into equilibrium, and leaving monetary variables little or no independent role in determining production and consumption. Sympathetic critics like Hicks (1937) and Hansen (1953) were quick to point out that Keynes appeared equally one-sided. He had monetary variables, and particularly expectations of the rate of interest, determining investment. But these monetary variables were themselves independent of those in the 'real' economy. As discussed in Chapters 5 and 8, Keynes equivocates and at times admits a reflux, some mutual determination, but he would broadly continue to maintain that there was no clear line of causation between levels of profitability and levels of interest (CWXIV: 11–12).

Hicks frames his famous IS/LM model as overcoming both forms of one-sidedness, as an integration of Keynes and the classics. '[Classical] theory descends from Ricardo, though it is not actually Ricardian; it is probably more or less the theory that was held by Marshall. But with Marshall it was already beginning to be qualified in important ways; his successors have qualified it still further. What Mr Keynes has done is to lay enormous emphasis on the qualifications, so they almost blot out the original theory' (Hicks 1937: 150). Hicks's claim is that Keynes's theory is in fact not general but specific.

Hicks referred to the monetary side of his diagram as LL. What follows sticks fairly closely to Hicks's formulations but uses the now standard 'LM' (liquidity money) terminology adopted by Hansen (1953). According to the quantity theory, money (M) is proportionate to income (Y). For a given income, there is a given amount of money. The rate of interest is the means of bringing savings and investment into line and is not itself affected by income. This simple classical relation can be represented graphically by a vertical line in an 'interest/income' space. Keynes, by contrast, describes a more mediated set of relations. He agrees that money is supplied by the authorities but sees demand for money as determined by the interest rate, and this is at most indirectly related to income. Fundamentally (neglecting many equivocations) for Keynes, this is determined by liquidity preference and not by income. So the demand for money could be depicted as a horizontal line in a similar interest/income space.

For Hicks, the demand for money depends on *both* transactions and speculative motives, on income and on the rate of interest. He draws a curve LM, such that the demand for money increases with both interest and income; see Figure 11.1. So instead of horizontal or vertical lines we have an upward-sloping curve. But rather than there being a smooth upward slope, and therefore contrary to modern textbook presentations (e.g. Sloman and Norris 1999), there are clear minima and maxima. There is a minimum rate of interest, absolutely at zero and in practice at some margin above that, which makes it worthwhile to lend. There is also a maximum level of income which can be financed by a given quantity of money. Even if the quantity theory is rejected as an absolute (because not all the money is used to increase income) money is limited to the level of income. So the LM 'curve' has two relatively straight sections. At lower levels of interest and income it resembles Keynes's depictions, at higher ones it converges with the standard quantity theory view. This curve a is a 'schedule' or what Colander (2013) describes as a 'money market equilibrium curve', depicting the points where there is an equality of the demand for liquidity and the supply of money.

The second step in Hicks's argument is to insist that this monetary economy interacts with the 'real'. The LM curve interacts with a goods market equilibrium curve (IS or investment = savings), which incorporates the effects of changes in the rate of interest on rates of investment (Colander 2013). For the classics, rising income just makes everybody richer, with no effect on other variables like the rate of interest, while the rate of interest

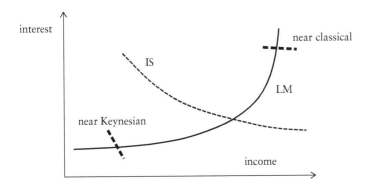

Figure 11.1 IS/LM (after Hicks 1937)

needed to bring saving and investment into equilibrium does not change with income. Hick outlines how this is likely to play out in terms of the proportional demand for employment in the investment and consumption goods sectors so that the IS curve is horizontal in the same interest/income space. For Keynes, by contrast, there is a tendency for the propensity to save to increase with income. As income increases, lower rates of interest are needed to sustain investment. Hicks accepts that particularly if there are high levels of unemployment, 'IS can be relied on to slope downwards' (1937: 158).

This second curve can then be drawn in the same space as the LM curve; see Figure 11.1. The point where the LM and IS curves cross now gives a determinate level of interest and income. Hansen (1953) puts some numbers on his axes but these are purely illustrative and, as with Hicks's original formulation, the schematic presentation does not yet establish the values or where the curves intersect, and it is the diversity of possibilities that gives IS/LM much of its attractiveness. If the intersection lies 'upon that part of the (L-M) curve that is decidedly upward-sloping, 'the classical theory will be a good approximation'. If it lies to the 'left', 'Mr. Keynes' theory becomes valid' (1937: 154).

IS/LM purports to add to the generality of the *General Theory*. For mainstream economists, it also has a reassuringly familiar shape. It allows 'macro' to look like 'micro' and to be analysed in the same basic way. It provides a simple device for simultaneously analysing the real and the monetary economy, for establishing the equilibrium income and rate of interest for every level of money. It also provides the basis of a straightforward policy instrument. Monetary policy can shift the LM curve or fiscal policy can shift the IS curve. Assuming in both cases that the object is to increase income, this can be seen as moving the curves to the 'right' in the interest/

income space in Figure 11.1. Where LM becomes vertical, no shift in IS can increase GDP, for the income velocity of money has reached its limit (Samuelson et al. 1973). Where LM is horizontal, if IS is nearly vertical (very Keynesian, for example with high levels of unemployment), changes in LM will make little or no difference but changes in IS will make major additions to income, and it becomes time for Keynesian intervention. Whatever its limits, the IS/LM posits mutual determination rather than seeing interest rates as set purely either by the requirements of real-economy equilibrium or by liquidity preference, and then impacting on the other variables in a mono-directional process (Coddington 1983).

But if IS/LM became Keynesianism, more radical interpreters could point out sins of both omission and commission. The IS/LM formulation substantially leaves out uncertainty, or at least safely quarantines it as an apparently stable influence on liquidity preference. IS/LM also omits any mention of the institutional specificity of money in terms of the relation between private banking and the monetary authorities. Money remains 'exogenous'. The discussion in Chapter 8, above, suggests that this does little violence to Keynes, but without either uncertainty or these institutional specificities the device lends itself to a view of stable equilibrium. IS/LM provides no sense of financial volatility, which for many Keynesians remains central. Keynes's finance motive had already incorporated investment demand, if somewhat vaguely. The implication is that the IS and LM relationships cannot be understood separately and then combined but should be seen as interdependent, implying that there need be no unique equilibrium position (Minsky 1986, Arestis 1996). Hicks himself would later become critical, particularly of the mechanical ways in which IS/LM was interpreted (Davidson 1978).

Alongside IS/LM, the Phillips Curve provided a second Keynesian device, now for managing inflation and unemployment. It reports, or proposes, a simple, non-linear inverse relation. Less unemployment means more inflation, and vice versa. This has antecedents in Keynes, who had at least hinted at such an inverse relationship. As discussed in Chapters 5 and 6, a part of Keynes's understanding of unemployment involves frictions in the labour market. In the jargon, wages are sticky-downwards and inflation can unstick them. Reducing real wages can increase employment (1973: 267). The discussion of stickiness in the *General Theory* suggests possible, provisional relations and that these alone are insufficient to account for unemployment, but later Keynesians would turn the relation into a much more mechanical affair.

Phillips (1958) initially presented his curve as an empirical observation of wages and unemployment in Britain, but it suggested a policy trade-off (Weeks 2011: 18). He detected a reasonably stable relationship between the level of unemployment and the change in money wages over time, first between 1861 and 1913 then extended to 1957. Phillips's data for 1861 to 1913 produced only six points, all sitting very close to his proposed curve. Later data fitted less well (Leeson 2013a). Phillips admitted his results were tentative and in need of further investigation (1958: 299). He nevertheless concluded that unemployment of about 5.5 per cent was associated with money wage changes of about zero. Unemployment rates about 2.5 per cent were associated with money wage changes of about 2 per cent. That 2 per cent rate was roughly equal to the growth of productivity, so the 2.5 per cent unemployment rate was compatible with price stability (Vane 2013). As in the quantity theory, if income or the number of transactions is increasing, people should be becoming richer in real terms. There is a need for more money and for increasing real wages simply to maintain price stability. But wages should only increase in line with productivity. Much like Keynes, Phillips himself wrote that 'I would question whether it is really in the interests of workers that the average level of hourly earnings should increase more rapidly than the average rate of productivity, say about 2 per cent per year' (cited in Leeson 2013b: 538).

Other studies soon produced similar results, including for other countries such as the US. Particularly by the post-war period, the relationship also occurred over a relatively narrow range of values, although levels varied a bit between countries (Ormerod 1994). For example, Shaikh (2016) shows quite a close fit in the US between 1955 and 1970 but with higher unemployment than in the UK, in the range of 3 to 7 per cent and inflation between 1 and 6 per cent.

Other economists soon formalised the Phillips Curve as a causal economic relation rather than just an empirical association. An excess demand for labour, the result of frictions in the labour market, led to increased money wages. The wage rises were translated into a general inflation through assumptions that prices are tied to marginal or average costs, of which wages were the major component (Shaikh 2016). Both of these assumptions, of labour-market frictions and mark-up pricing, imply imperfect markets, discussed in the next section. Here, however, increased income is seen as leading to excess demand for labour, which increased demand causes unemployment to fall. But the relationship is non-linear; unemployment cannot be less than zero so the decreases in unemployment occur by increasingly small amounts (Vane 2013). The theories, notably by Lipsey in 1960 and Hansen in 1970, had the effect that the curve could be lifted out of the empirical evidence and employed quite independently of (and indeed sometimes in frank contradiction to) it (Shaikh 2016). Versions of the Phillips Curve became widely accepted.

In one sense, the conclusion was pessimistic. 'Macro-economic policies, monetary and fiscal, are incapable of realizing society's unemployment and inflation goals simultaneously' (Tobin 1972: 252). Policies to reduce unemployment brought higher inflation, and vice versa. On the other hand, the Phillips Curve provided policy-makers with a useful tool. Indeed, 'much of the subtlety of Phillips' analysis was replaced by wishful thinking about the potency of macroeconomic manipulation' (Leeson 2013b: 533). Assuming a stable relationship provided a choice between unemployment and inflation. Although it had Keynesian origins, some monetarists could accept the trade-off. They shared the view that states could control the money supply and therefore, at least indirectly, prices and the level of unemployment. Government control over the quantity of money becomes a justifiable exception to laissez-faire (Cagan 1987).

Any empirical relationship between unemployment and inflation appeared to break down in the 1970s, prompting criticisms and Keynesian responses, which will be considered below. 'The fact that the monetarists could be shown to be wrong or cheating in their arguments represented no solace. Both the monetarists and the Keynesians have been proven completely wrong by recent events' (Balogh 1976: 85). The Phillips Curve nevertheless continues to be invoked by both Keynesian economists and mainstream institutions (Palley 2015, BIS 2017, 2019). It is more subtle than a simple dogma that unemployment cannot exist, and it justifies pro-unemployment policies in the name of fighting inflation. Even where Phillips fell into disfavour, the economic mainstream had to recalibrate, away from assumptions that unemployment did not exist, to assumptions that it had a natural or a 'non-inflationary' level.

Finally, it is notable that Phillips Curve interpretations treated inflation and unemployment as unambiguous economic and social evils. There was some evidence that governments of the right preferred unemployment, those of the left preferred inflation. As discussed in Chapter 6, Keynes is clear that unemployment is an evil, if less clear about what exactly constituted full employment. He was much more ambivalent about inflation, sometimes favouring moderate inflation and always thinking this better than equivalent deflation. The Keynesians who accept the Phillips Curve may see unemployment as the greater evil than inflation but do nothing to dispel the general mainstream view that inflation was also an unqualified evil. This is a hugely conservative assumption, unsupported by evidence either of national growth rates (Pollin and Zhu 2006) or effects on equality, but, as will be discussed below, it is an assumption that several of the putatively more radical Keynesians would accept. As inflation took off in most rich-country economies in the 1970s, many Keynesians became vehement opponents of inflation and supporters of anti-labour policies to combat it.

Mainstream Keynesianism was therefore more subtle and more useful to policy-makers than pre-Keynesian orthodoxy. But this subtlety and utility were substantially conservative. Most broadly, this version of Keynesianism established macroeconomics as a world apart from the micro-world of the marginalists. In a sense this was a great advance. Policy-makers no longer had to work on the basis of theories that assumed either that policies made no difference or that the differences they made were bound to be deleterious (Minsky 1986). But the split involved conceiving the state as extra-economic or able to influence the economy 'exogenously', to turn on a monetary tap at will. National income could now be conceived as the sum of consumption, investment and government spending, as if governments themselves were doing something else entirely, obeying a separate rationale while consumption and investment continued to be understood as determined by the actions of utility-maximising individuals. The separation allowed the incoherent, individualist micro, which Keynes had done so much to contest, to continue substantially unchanged, only later to challenge the separation on its own terms, to recolonise the macro with claims that it needed to be given micro foundations.

Imperfect competition

This section considers the ideas of three sets of scholars – new-Keynesians, theorists of monetary instability and post-Keynesians – most of whom would be unhappy to be lumped together. Despite many antagonisms, they share an emphasis on market imperfections and see the state as the vehicle for overcoming these.

New Keynesianism emerged in the 1970s, accepting much of the neo-classical critique of IS/LM and the Phillips Curve. In as far as New Keynesians remain distinctively Keynesian, it is in their stress on market 'failures', 'frictions' and 'imperfections'. Of course, such things had always been an important trope of the economists Keynes was criticising, quite explicitly in Marshall and Pigou. However, the insistence that markets are imperfect has a textual basis in Keynes and again helps to bring essentially conventional economic thinking closer to the real world. For the New Keynesians there are therefore conventionally understood pressures towards equilibrium but pervasive imperfections mean that any movement can be sluggish, and that markets may not achieve abstractly optimal outcomes. Labour-market imperfections are often a key concern (Gerrard 1988). These were discussed at some length in Chapter 6, where it was also argued that a language of 'imperfections' can be misleading because unemployment can be profoundly functional to capitalism but that frictions of various kinds and various degrees do indeed pervade capitalism.

The emphasis on where the frictions and market failures lie varies considerably in different accounts. Frictions can be conceived in different terms and can refer to differences between individuals, goods, access to credit, the nature of transactions and the availability of information (Bludnik 2009, Mott 1989). Lavoie (2009) depicts three distinct strands. With some overlap, the first strand emphasises market imperfections, or 'stickiness', and how these can amplify economic fluctuation. The second strand stresses that this is true not only of nominal but also of real variables. The third strand identifies problems of coordination, here accepting a general equilibrium analysis but, with more radical post-Keynesians, 'questioning the existence of a natural rate of unemployment' (Lavoie 2009: 22). Here, the focus will be limited to questions of money, inflation and the critique of the Phillips Curve.

At this point it is useful to have a brief Friedmanite diversion. At monetarism's core was the enduring faith in the quantity theory. Assuming a constant velocity of circulation, for Friedman, 'inflation is determined by, and equal to, the rate of growth of the money supply minus the rate of growth of output' (Vane 2013: 271). This too was thought reasonably stable. In the long run, money neutrality would assert itself. However, in the short run, it was possible to have a Phillips-like relationship. Where Keynes's 'classics' posited full employment, Friedman instead depicts a 'natural' rate of unemployment. It is then only profitable for firms to employ more than this 'natural rate' if real wages fall. For this to happen and additional workers to become available, they must believe that their real wages will rise. In true 'classic' style, unemployment is assumed to reflect the subjective preference for leisure or disutility of labour.

So, if prices rise (for some reason – but governments rather than unions are seen as prime mover) this also has the potential to increase profits, as price rises precede and exceed those in wages. Reductions of real wages occur as the prices of commodities are bid up to make production worthwhile for firms. Now, as Glyn writes, 'price increases due to excess demand tend to feed on themselves ... supplemented by speculation' (1977: 150). Constant money wages mean falling real wages, rising employment and falling unemployment. Workers now demand higher money wages simply to 'catch up' and return the labour market to its 'true' equilibrium position. Such wage rises push unemployment back to its natural rate and a new short-run Phillips Curve at higher prices.

For Phelps and Friedman, the Phillips relation thus only holds in the short run and what had originally been an empirically observed long-run phenomenon becomes a short-run theory. In the long run, there is instead a vertical 'natural' or 'non-accelerating inflation' rate. Attempts to increase employment beyond this mean accelerating inflation financed by inflationary monetary growth (Vane 2013). Monetary changes initiate inflation, which leads to rises in money wages and a vicious cycle if the monetary authorities try to accommodate. 'Since the higher employment associated with price increases could not be sustained, a corollary was that zero inflation was the appropriate target for policy' (Perry 2008: 413). Commitments to full employment meant governments' responses to recessions produced rapid monetary growth with only ever temporary relief from unemployment and accelerating inflation. The response for Friedman was monetarism and a return to the need to restrict the money supply.

There are some conspicuous problems with the idea of a natural or non-accelerating inflation rate of unemployment (NAIRU), which new-Keynesians identified. First, unemployment below its natural rate requires that firms are irrationally hiring more workers than they can profitably employ and/or that workers are irrationally accepting jobs where they would be better off unemployed (Tobin 1972). Second, Friedman and the subsequent literature largely stress the perils of accelerating inflation but logic requires a parallel deflationary spiral. The triumph of Friedman and the monetarists 'was also not consistent with flexible price accelerationist models which predict that prices and wages will fall when the economy is operating below its natural rate' (Perry 2008: 413–4). 'By symmetrical argument, unemployment above the natural rate signifies excess supply in the labour market and ever-accelerating deflation' (Tobin 1972: 237). Needless to say, we have not witnessed this. In practice, nor was there accelerating inflation. History has seen a few devastating hyperinflations but these were associated with wars and revolutions, not wage rises (Tobin 1972: 251). Third, there is huge variation over time and across countries. In particular, since the 1980s, converging low inflation has been achieved with diverging unemployment levels. Since inflation rates have held reasonably steady over the past 30 years, with no hint of ever-accelerating inflation or deflation, presumably this period has seen unemployment close to its 'natural' rate. We are therefore forced to conclude that this 'natural' rate varies hugely across time and place. Greenspan acknowledges that the NAIRU 'has always proved elusive when estimated in real time' (2008: 170).

Much New Keynesian thinking seeks to explain this empirical variation. Where Friedman sees the money supply as in the gift of the monetary authorities, and sees causation running from money to prices (Glyn 1977), New Keynesians suggest that the NAIRU was affected: by institutional specificities, which of course are infinitely varied; by the actual rate, so there are hysteresis effects; and by aggregate demand, so a recession can pull the Phillips Curve 'to the right' (Stockhammer 2008, Vane 2013). The path is opened to multiple 'non-inflationary' rates.

Many New Keynesian (and post-Keynesians) also reject monetarist claims of money's source. Instead they accept the so-called 'new monetary consensus' adopted by most central bankers, in Britain from as early as the 1959 Radcliffe commission, that the money supply is endogenous, provided by bank credit in response to firms' demands (Lavoie 2009). Central bankers can only control money's price, the interest rate. New Keynesian theory could also incorporate government agency into a macroeconomics that augmented or could replace the neo-classical Keynesian synthesis. Now assuming a natural or non-inflationary rate of unemployment, the Phillips Curve is replaced by a formula in which inflation hangs on the central bank and its credibility, which while acting on imperfect information, is signalling its intention to achieve low inflation. Meanwhile, IS/LM is superseded. The LM curve is replaced by a monetary policy operating rule, which, following Taylor, raises interest rates when inflation is above target and lowers them when it is below (Arestis and Sawyer 2002), narrowing the scope for intervention to rule-based, monetary measures. The IS curve is replaced by an aggregate demand equation derived from the equality between output and demand (Say's Law returns) but incorporating both forward and backward adjustments accounting for sticky prices. In this scenario, there was not much that states could do but, like the monetarists, much of what states could do revolved around securing sound money.

Others saw a much bigger role for the state. For example, Stiglitz (2002) challenges the crude Washington Consensus measures imposed by the IMF on poorer countries, and Stiglitz (2010) and Krugman (2012) oppose post-GFC austerity and advocate more aggressive stimulus measures. Even here, it is worth emphasising that intervention is conceived as making markets work rather than as an alternative mode of economic organising. This, of course, seems quite consistent with Keynes's own liberalism, but as Fine and Milonakis write of Stiglitz, his approach shares much with the mainstream and 'relies on the standard methodology and tools of the trade. He appears radical by comparison with neoliberalism but not relative to the Keynesianism of the postwar period, let alone interwar institutionalism' (2009: 139). Arestis and Sawyer (2002) simply identify New Keynesianism with the 'Third Way' politics of Blair and Schroder.

In terms of theory, Lavoie (2009) depicts both the synthesis Keynesians and the different varieties of New Keynesians as now safely ensconced within the neo-classical canon. They broaden the scope and plausibility of economists' claims but in doing so, as Fine and Milonakis (2009: 66) write, the non-market and non-rational are explained as a consequence of 'market imperfections', and the ideal of perfect markets is reinforced as the analytical bedrock against which economics can increase its analytical compass. New Keynesians become particularly effective 'economics imperialists', able to assert economic methods, an asocialised methodological individualism, onto other social sciences. Amongst other things, this vision of economics largely excises, or simply ignores, key Keynesian concerns with liquidity preference and financial volatility.

Alternative currents of Keynesian thinking have indeed applied imperfectionist insights specifically to financial markets. With Keynes, financial markets have a peculiar dynamic of their own which means there is no reason to expect them to obey laws of supply and demand. Probably the best-known ideas here are associated with Minsky's financial instability hypothesis and Soros's theory of reflexivity. Minsky is usually seen as a post-Keynesian while Soros (2013) sees himself as a philosopher, drawing on Knight as well as Keynes. Both sets of ideas, however, can be seen as important versions of 'imperfectionist' thinking.

Minsky builds on the logic Keynes described, according to which it becomes entirely rational in financial markets to make decisions on the basis of other people's decisions. Rising asset prices are often an incentive to buy rather than to sell. Money and financial assets do not obey laws of supply and demand. As discussed in Chapter 7, money is not 'produced' by the private sector. Minsky (1986) depicts a scenario whereby stability breeds instability as past bubbles fade from the memory and rising asset prices encourage more precarious forms of borrowing, provoking bubbles which eventually collapse as crisis quickly turns euphoria into an opposite revulsion. Stringent financial regulation is needed to at least dampen financial volatility.

Echoing Keynes's descriptions of economics as a moral science, in which people's actions cannot reasonably be likened to those of falling apples, Soros (2013) insists that 'participants' thinking is part of the reality they have to think about, which makes the relationship circular'. Again with Keynes, people are fallible. There is no guarantee that experience brings perceptions and reality into some objective alignment. Instead, feedback loops can pull them further apart. As Shaikh describes, Soros's theory of reflexivity involves the mutual interaction of expectations, actual prices and 'fundamentals'. 'The end result is a process in which actual prices oscillate turbulently around their gravitational values. Expectations can induce extended disequilibrium cycles in which a boom eventually gives way to a bust' (Shaikh 2016: 446).

The ideas of both Minsky and Soros represent a considerable departure from mainstream economic thinking, predicting cyclicity and volatility rather than a stable equilibrium. Nor is money neutral, so these disequilibrating processes have real and sometimes profound impacts on the wider economy. The break, however, remains a limited one. Notions of cyclicity and volatility continue to be conceived in relation to an underlying equilibrium position, around which the economy oscillates but to which it finally, if painfully, returns.

The conventional identification of market imperfections involves an insistence that the world should shape up to the theory, that the imperfections should be ironed out by breaking labour organisations and eliminating state interference. As Piore puts it, orthodoxy explains 'the behaviour of imperfections only in their absence. And, in their presence, it prescribes their elimination' (cited in Hillard 1988: 10). Conversely, for Keynes, the recognition that the economy does not work as mainstream thinking insists can legitimise non-market practices, particularly state intervention, as needed to achieve socially useful objectives. But there is a similarity in that, as Coddington writes, for many Keynesians, 'any discussion of market failure goes hand in hand with a parallel discussion of its correction by government action' (1983: 35). Finance, in particular, should be thoroughly regulated (Minsky 1986). So this contrasts with a crude libertarianism, pervasive in the economic mainstream, but does not require an in-principle difference with more subtle thinkers like Hayek.

A somewhat different line of imperfectionist thinking is important to a post-Keynesian tradition. The term 'post-Keynesianism' is contested and many scholars would be hard to pigeonhole. The next section looks at what Lavoie (2009) calls 'fundamentalist' post-Keynesianism, associated with Davidson, which puts particular stress on uncertainty or non-ergodicity. Here, the ideas of imperfect competition in the tradition of Kalecki and Robinson will be briefly discussed. Most post-Keynesians see themselves as more radical, and as more Keynesian than their mainstream and New Keynesian counterparts. Mann, while also sympathetic to New Keynesian accounts, accepts that '[a]t an interpretive level, those who take the approach of attempting to align Keynesianism with Keynes's own ideas – generally known as "post-Keynesians" – win any match decided by historical or theoretical accuracy' (2013: 2). Robinson, in particular, is highly critical of the misappropriation of Keynes's thought by those she labels 'bastard' Keynesians (1978: 256).

Robinson's work on imperfect competition pre-dates Keynes's *General Theory*. In some respects it represents a more profound departure. As noted in Chapter 5, there are ambiguities in Keynes and different readings, some of which suggest that he too was looking specifically at an economy dominated by large corporations (Kicillof 2018). My reading, following Dow (1996) and Dowd (2004), suggested instead that (for the most part) Keynes accepts the mainstream's individualism, if only to enable him to engage with orthodoxy on its own terms. Robinson's and later post-Keynesians' recognition that competition is not atomistic involves an important step away from the mainstream. Where Keynes almost always depicts individuals, the

Robinsonian tradition is more willing to look at structures, to go through Smith, Ricardo and Marx to identify market mechanisms 'activated not by the wills of individuals, but independently of them' (Milgate 1987: 45). Individual rational choices, even allowing that these may produce sub-optimal economic outcomes, cannot be the basis of a realistic economic theory (Backhouse 2006).

More prosaically, emphasis is usually placed on 'oligopolistic markets, where a few large firms, the megacorps, dominate a series of smaller firms' (Lavoie 2009: 32). Neither the invisible hand of market forces nor a ficti-tious Walrasian auctioneer set prices.

> Prices are *set* by firms. If they are price takers, they will simply imitate the pri-cing policies of the leading firms in the industry. The latter then are the price leaders. These dominant or barometric firms must decide on the price that they will charge, and this price becomes the benchmark for the rest of the market. (Lavoie 2009: 35)

The different price and production possibilities faced by firms, presented for example in the initial Keynesian economic textbook by Tarshis (1947), pro-vide a more realistic starting point. Keynes himself acknowledged that taking the degree of competition as 'given' had been a mistake (Dos Santos Ferreira 2019). More or less complex models are then developed to describe the distributions of power between firms and consumers (e.g. Reynolds 1987).

Robinson also recognised that capitalism was an inherently dynamic system and therefore, at least implicitly, criticised a Keynesianism which remained tied to a static, equilibrium approach (Baragar 2003). Kalecki, whose claims to have anticipated the *General Theory* are often accepted, explicitly uses Marxist terminology and had earlier described Keynes as a leading 'bourgeois economist' (Sawyer 2019: 369). Kalecki's insights, particularly into the operations of corporate power, monopoly pricing and intra-class distribution, have been embraced by important strands of Marxist thought (Baran and Sweezy 1968, Foster and McChesney 2012).

Again, even this strand of post-Keynesianism is itself diverse (Lavoie 2009), precluding any systematic review, and the critical comments that follow no doubt do injustice to particular accounts. There are, however, at least five respects in which this tradition remains limited and in which it shares much with its New Keynesian counterpart.

First, as Shaikh argues, despite the antagonism between New and post-Keynesians, '[t]he irony is that both sides end up viewing reality through an "imperfectionist" lens' (2016: 4). The stress on imperfect competition again at least implicitly posits the perfection of the free market as the ideal from which everything else is a distortion. A perfectly competitive capit-alism is imputed, either in some bygone age or as the standard according to which organised capitalism must be judged. As above, Marx insisted that monopoly (at least as it is being understood here) and competition are not alternatives but the capitalist norm. Questions of corporate power, of its degree and its impacts, remain worth investigating, but positing these as primary explanatory variables only makes sense against the neo-classical ideal of free markets and perfect competition. The Kaleckian identification of monopoly as a problem can be interpreted in an anti-capitalist (or at least anti-corporate) sense but it implicitly celebrates the entrepreneur and small business. This is consistent with Keynes and an important strand of his analysis of how dynamic pressures towards equilibrium are realised at most slowly and unevenly. The *General Theory*, however, in largely accepting the degree of competition as a 'given' (1973: 245), allows Keynes's analysis to achieve much more than this.

Second, the Kaleckians also tend to adopt an equilibrium approach, albeit sometimes one of dynamic equilibrium. Kalecki himself referred to 'quasi equilibria', to describe short periods in which there was a given stock of capital (Lopez and Assous 2010: 23), a similar manoeuvre to Keynes in the *General Theory*, if similarly limiting the analytical scope. The more dynamic approaches may recognise that it can be hard to sustain the necessary conditions for balanced economic growth (Harrod 1939, Halevi and Kriesler 1992), and there are parallels in this work with Volume II of Marx's *Capital* (Marx 1978, Fan-Hung 1939). The underlying assumption, however, remains that such equilibrium growth is usual. Even cyclical deviations from equilibrium, which were the essence of Kalecki's (1971) original contribution, implicitly pose equilibrium as the healthy norm to which capitalism should and could return if only it were suitably managed.

Third, and largely congruent with this stress on equilibrium, money plays little independent role in most of the discussion of imperfect competition. Sawyer (1996) suggests that Kalecki's model becomes essentially similar to those of the mainstream and New Keynesians (see also Davidson 2007). Money 'is assumed to be credit-driven fiat money, so that the money supply responds to the needs of circulation' (Shaikh 2016: 191). 'From a theoretical perspective, many post-Keynesians rejected the theory of liquidity preference. In doing so they denied the central component of Keynes's theory as well as losing the route to interest rate manipulation through debt-management policy' (Tily 2007: 286). The absence of money, at least as an active ingredient, is particularly apparent in a 'neo-Ricardian' or 'Sraffian' approach, in which everything is conceived in 'real' terms. Lavoie argues that this Sraffian critique is effectively 'an internal critique of neoclassical theory' (Lavoie 2009: 21), although one might add a critique too of a particular interpretation of Marxist value theory (Steedman 1977). Ricardo was, of course, a major point of attack for Keynes for precisely these reasons. It was by association with Ricardo that Keynes also damned Marx. As such, although often accepted as post-Keynesian, these approaches have little to do with Keynes and probably go beyond the remit of this book. Perhaps as a consequence of accepting equilibrium and a neglect of the vagaries of a specifically money economy, there is also often a penchant amongst modern followers for highly formalised and mathematised approaches, contrary to Keynes's and Kalecki's own warnings (Lopez and Assous 2010).

Fourth, Kaleckians recognise the existence of classes but conceive them in distributional terms rather than in relation to production, with labour's interference in the market often seen as reprehensible. Robinson's (1964) summary dismissal of the labour theory of value was noted in the Introduction and, as Weeks writes, '[a] major empty box in mark-up models is the theory of total profit, for while the degree of monopoly might be a plausible explanation of differential mark-ups, it cannot explain the average mark-up for the economy as a whole' (Weeks 1988: 200–1). Some post-Keynesians profess a political radicalism, notably Robinson in her Maoist phase. The bulk of the economic literature, however, seems to assume an abstractly rational capitalist system. Particularly in the 1970s, at a time of labour's combativeness, post-Keynesian interpretations of inflation put the responsibility on labour and called for disciplinary action. In this there is a parallel with moderate New Keynesians like Tobin, as ostensible radicals like Kahn and Kaldor explicitly endorsed wage repression. Having rejected the quantity theory and said that governments cannot influence inflation, they had to put the blame elsewhere (Dean 1980). 'Inflation is primarily the result of unresolved conflicts over income shares. It is not a monetary phenomenon' (Goldstein and Hillard 2009: 9). Galbraith similarly sees unions as prime movers but adds the normally implicit need for corporate power to pass on the wage rises (Galbraith 1995). The policy implication was (negotiated) wage repression, to the extent that 'Post Keynesian economics was associated in the public mind with support for incomes policy and little else' (King, cited in Davidson 2007: 233). One might object that the most fundamental market imperfections are those of wealth inequality, which compel most people to work for capital on conditions of capital's choosing (Mott 1989). Ignoring these in theory, and opposing labour's attempts to address them in practice, many post-Keynesians joined the ranks of capital's apologists.

Fifth, for most post-Keynesians, the state may not be as 'benevolent and class-neutral' as it was for Keynes (King 2015: 59). There is often acknowledgement that corporate size involves power, which potentially undermines the authority of national government (Bhardwaj 1986: 79). For Kalecki (1943), specifically capitalist states could not tolerate full employment and were pressured by specifically pro-capitalist rather than just neutral market forces. But states largely continued to be seen as capable of providing informed direction. Typically, the state remains at least relatively benign and able to reconcile social conflict: a vision of state capacities very similar to that of Keynes, the more orthodox Keynesians considered above and at least some of the more fundamentalist post-Keynesians discussed below.

As above, dealing with a rich tradition of post-Keynesian thought inevitably does it considerable injustice. The critical comments are not intended as summary dismissal, and would be disputed by many who subscribe to the label. The discussion is intended instead as a warning of ostensible problems and to caution against thinking that a Keynes–Marx synthesis is something the Kaleckians have already accomplished.

Post-Keynesians mark II: money, time, uncertainty and analytical nihilism

This section briefly discusses post-Keynesianism as Davidson understands it, adopting a 'small tent' definition. The tradition is particularly concerned with questions of uncertainty and non-ergodicity. The section first discusses Davidson's rather strict entry criteria: negatives whose critical content many heterodox economists, including Marxists, might accept, and positives which quickly shut out the radicals and bring Davidson's approach back into close connection with mainstream economics. The section then discusses time and uncertainty more broadly, particularly in relation to Shackle's interpretation, suggesting that this anticipates a broader socio-philosophical tradition of postmodernism, in both its strengths and weaknesses.

For Davidson, to be a post-Keynesian requires adopting what Davidson sees as Keynes's fundamental premises. In the first instance, this involves embracing negatives, the rejection of 'the classical axioms that Keynes threw out ... (1) *the neutrality of money axiom* (2) *the gross substitution axiom*, and (3) *the axiom of an ergodic economic world*' (2007: 217). In terms of faithfulness to Keynes, Davidson's first two criteria seem straightforward. These are Keynes's long-standing criticisms of the quantity theory and Say's Law. As others have done, Davidson sees Keynes as 'primarily a monetary theorist' (2007: 216), even if, as seen above, money falls into the background in the *General Theory*, it remains essential to the argument that money is not neutral. Say's Law is invalid and, empirically, 'substitution effects between subgroups are virtually nil. In fact, substitution effects, which are so central to neoclassical theory, are confirmed only when goods are similar to one another (fruit juices and sodas, for instance)' (Lavoie 2009: 28). Non-ergodicity will be discussed below. It was not a term used by Keynes himself but relates to the importance of uncertainty in a more than probabilistic sense, so that the future cannot be induced from the past. Again, as discussed in Chapter 2, it is not clear how far this insight is to be pushed, and much hangs on how far it is pushed, but it is clearly an important element of Keynes's thought. As usual with Keynes there is room for disagreement, but the interpretation here accepts each of these as important elements of Keynes's critique.

Davidson's negative list imposes more restrictive entry criteria than most other post-Keynesians adopt (see e.g. Lavoie 2009: 12–15). It deliberately excludes those Davidson considers neo-Ricardians and Kaleckians, for whom money and uncertainty play little or no part (Davidson 2007). Depending on how strictly the third point is interpreted, the list would not be sufficient to exclude many other heterodox economists, either institutionalists or most Marxists. (Davidson is happy to repeat Keynes's and Robinson's claim that Marx was a believer in Say's Law, which would involve accepting gross substitution. As above, and despite its repetition, this is nonsense.) This negative list would allow that it remains possible, as King (2002) says, to generalise the *General Theory*. King is referring to attempts by Harrod and others to develop more dynamic growth models (see also Kregel 1976). But it potentially becomes possible to interrogate much else that Keynes assumes, or assumes constant: for example his assumptions about psychology, capital, the national economy and so on. It becomes possible to argue, as in the preceding chapters here, that even where Keynes is substantially correct about these things, we need more – on class, on power, on the global economy and so on – in terms of capitalism's historical concreteness. The arguments here are avowedly Marxist rather than Keynesian but would seem compatible with Davidson's exclusions.

Perhaps sensing the difficulties, Davidson also introduces positive entry requirements. To be admitted to the post-Keynesian canon it is also necessary to accept '(1) Marshall's and Keynes's concepts as equilibrium analysis and their approach to supply and demand function analysis, and (2) the need for an axiomatic formal logical approach to developing a theoretical framework' (2007: 257). With this, Davidson yanks us rather abruptly back towards orthodoxy. The depiction of Keynes himself as a Marshallian has some plausibility. Keynes had enormous respect for his old teacher and often used partial equilibrium methods. But there was clearly much in Marshall against which Keynes rebelled. He names Marshall as a key representative of the classics which the *General Theory* repudiated. Davidson's second condition seems aimed particularly at winning the ear of more acceptable Keynesians like Tobin and Solow (Davidson 2007: 257). He insists it is 'possible to beat the classical mainstream on their own playing field, if we can engage them in a debate' (Davidson 2007: 247). Whatever the motivations, such a post-Keynesianism seems doomed to a shadow life as a critique of orthodoxy, safely inoculated against engagement with anything more radical. As Davidson can now insist, 'there is not much in Marx that is applicable to Keynes's analytical framework' (2007: 243). This resonates with Keynes's own horrors at an eclectic institutional approach and contempt for Marxism, but it simultaneously ignores Keynes's repeated warnings against the limits of formal, mathematical approaches (1973: 162, CWXIV: 301).

Davidson's insistence on formal supply-and-demand analysis also appears vulnerable to the challenges raised by uncertainty and non-ergodicity. These are open to a range of interpretations, but for Davidson (2009) non-ergodicity means that we cannot extrapolate from past evidence; the vast bulk of economic statistics become useless as a guide to the future, if not completely worthless. Attempts to reduce the economy to sets of simultaneous equations become unsustainable.

Perhaps more remarkable in this context is that the state appears exempt from these epistemological problems, still able to leap in as saviour. Davidson writes that:

> The endemic problem is ... the impossibility of reliably foreseeing the future in a nonergodic world ... Keynes and the Post Keynesians believe that the business cycle is not endemic to a capitalist system but rather the result of bad monetary (and fiscal) policies. (Davidson 2007: 234)

Policy-makers appear to live in an ergodic world apart, able to advise wisely and to make good policy, free of capitalist imperatives and of Keynesian epistemology.

Shackle (1972) takes ideas of uncertainty further. From Keynes's (1921) earliest writings on probability, he is clear that there is much that we cannot know. Economic life is fundamentally uncertain, particularly as we look further into the future (1973: 147–64; CWXIV: 109–23). For Shackle, uncertainty underpins liquidity preference (1972: 216), but its remit now extends much further. For example, 'investment is a law to itself, dependent (if at all) on too elusive and involved a skein of subtle influences ... to be ever captured in any intelligible, let alone determinable, equation' (1972: 218). The whole system of conventional economic thinking collapses. In particular, Shackle recalls Keynes's comment that 'Equilibrium is blather' (Shackle 1972: 233). There can be no search for underlying causes. Surface appearances are all there is (Fitzgibbons 1988). Shackle suggests a way forward, which he again attributes to Keynes.

> Keynes solved this problem by a bold (if somewhat accidental) resort to what I have elsewhere ventured to label a kaleidic method. Situations are portrayed by curves (or their equivalent) in two dimensions, connecting at most three variables ... But the meaning of these situations is that of momentary, ephemeral glimpses at selected and rare points of a mainly un-adjusted, groping and

speculative process, involving vast numbers of variables subject in many cases to an inherent restlessness and precariousness. (1972: 72)

These momentary, ephemeral glimpses might be accepted as partial equilibria, and Shackle saw the system as one which spontaneously 'reconfigures and re-equilibriates' (cited in Littleboy 2019: 445). But such partial equilibria clearly operate in a much more restricted sense than Marshall envisaged.

There are some striking anticipations here of postmodern philosophy: of Lyotard's (1984) rejection of grand narratives, of laws of history, while accepting small-scale, particularist insights. Too much has undoubtedly been predicted too confidently by too many. On the other side of the coin, just as postmodernism could spin out into a vacuous nihilism (Callinicos 1989b) the Shacklian strand of post-Keynesianism seems to suggest that all attempts at big-picture economic theory are unconscionable. Shackle embraced Coddington's (1983) characterisation of this perspective as 'analytical nihilism' (Bateman 1987).

Such pervasive radical uncertainty seems hard to square with claims of faithfulness to Keynes, as discussed in Chapter 2. Bateman argues that it 'explains neither the years he put into producing *The General Theory*, nor the time he [Keynes] spent after its publication attempting to clarify its meaning and importance' (1987: 117). Keynes confidently made both theoretical claims and policy recommendations (Coddington 1983: 98). More importantly, this view of radical uncertainty under-estimates the real, knowable compulsions of the capitalist economy.

Interpreting what Lavoie calls 'dynamic historical time' in a less destructive sense can usefully recognise that decisions taken at any one point have real implications; there is what Myrdal (1957) had earlier called a path-dependency or circular and cumulative causation. The short term affects the long term and it becomes necessary to map the path from one to the other. Lavoie gives an example of 'historical time as applied to consumer choice theory: past choices will influence future choices. It is a kind of hysteresis effect: the current situation depends on the path taken in the past. The initial choice of, say, an X-Box, will eliminate the need to purchase a DVD player in the future' (2009: 31). In a similar vein, Krugman's (1990, 1993) New Economic Geography identifies how past decisions, not an abstract current economic rationale, determine economic locations and trade patterns. The effects of particular actions become hard to predict, for example in terms of the contradictory effects on profits and aggregate demand of changes in wages. All this raises genuine epistemological puzzles, which cannot be addressed here. Minimally, as Keynes warned, it undermines any crude mathematical approach.

Economic processes remain indeterminate, capable of being shaped and reshaped by human decisions and social struggles. But this need not leave us in a state of radical incomprehension. The histories, geographies, different economic forces, need not be put off-limits to scientific investigation. It is necessary to be cautious in our claims to knowledge and to know that it is always imperfect, but it is unnecessary to capitulate to an admission of complete ignorance of long-term, big-picture, structural processes and less still to expect unique reservoirs of wisdom within a benign state.

Conclusion

The different strands of after-Keynes thought discussed in this chapter all make plausible claims to be based on Keynes's own ideas, even as they take them in different directions. In a sense, it is testament to the creative importance of Keynes's innovations that they should lead to a flowering of such different offshoots. The IS/LM Keynesians and New Keynesians most clearly attempted a reconciliation with the economic mainstream. Even after 40 years of anti-Keynesianism in politics and academic economics, many avowed Keynesians sit in high places and many of their ideas remain policy common sense. With the crisis of the 1970s, however, many apparently Keynesian assumptions were challenged by a newly confident liberal orthodoxy. New Keynesians accepted that macroeconomics needed a micro foundation, reinstating individuals as the epistemological foundation of economics. Market imperfections, particularly informational asymmetries and frictions, continued to provide grounds for thinking that the invisible hand might not guide those individuals to socially or economically optimal outcomes, but the distance between many Keynesians and the neo-classical tradition diminished. Post-Keynesians discovered that much of what other Keynesians had been saying and which had been taken for Keynesian policy, after all, owed little to Keynes. A more radical economic rethinking was required. In particular, different post-Keynesians stress imperfect competition, the role of money and questions of economic uncertainty. This chapter has suggested, however, that the radicalism can be exaggerated.

Consistently with Keynes's own worldview, most Keynesians continue to see economics as capable of providing advice to rulers. Where in Keynes this is occasionally recognised as an avowedly bourgeois activity, most of his followers write in more naively non-class terms, as if states could provide some abstractly better policy. For both New and post-Keynesians, visions of market imperfections remain central – imperfections, that is, conceived according to the imagination of neo-classical theory. For the more conservative, the real world should better conform to the theory; for the more critical, the state should redress the attendant market failures. At the very least, the neo-classical theory is reinstated as the pattern according to which the real economy is assessed. On a different track, more radical reinterpretations of uncertainty unsettle the conventional reference points but, in failing to provide an alternative epistemological basis, tend either to spiral out into a knowing acceptance of economic ignorance or to be reined back, once again, into an unsubstantiated faith in the supervening competence of states.

12

The decline of Keynesianism and the prospects for return

Introduction

Because there are many interpretations of Keynes it is impossible to adjudicate definitely on the prospects for a return. Indeed, the first section of this chapter argues that there are grounds for saying that Keynes never went away. There have been major policy reorientations, and some of these, particularly more inegalitarian and pro-finance policies, run against both the spirit and the letter of Keynes. But for all the liberalising achievements in major rich-country economies, much of the economic practice of the post-WWII boom period endures. Active monetary policy and low interest rates have become the norm, while budget deficits have reached new heights. The situation in many poorer countries is different but again ambiguous. The Washington Consensus policies imposed since the 1980s debt crisis provoked restructuring and some sharp policy turns but with great variation. Many large, poorer-country states remain big and interventionist. So there are continuities, while some of the changes, in privatisations and restrictions on labour organisation, can only cautiously and with qualification be depicted as anti-Keynesian.

The second section argues, however, that structural shifts have weakened national bases of economic organisation, potentially limiting the scope and efficacy, and crucially also the institutional supports, of Keynesian intervention. The growth of finance and of financial power alongside industrial 'globalisation' pull in an anti-Keynesian direction. There is a vast, if contested, literature which suggests this restructuring also means that any future return towards Keynes becomes more difficult. There are, at least, powerful vested interests in maintaining an open economy.

The third section then briefly reflects on the experience of the global financial crisis of 2007–09. The crisis confirmed that leading states retained the capacity to intervene effectively, although hopes of a more radical, long-term reorientation were soon disappointed in policy

248

reversals which brought severe austerity, particularly in Europe. The preceding argument suggests there was an economic rationale for such a turn: it was bad, but not mad, as some of Keynes's followers saw it.

The fourth section considers arguments that the growing environmental crisis requires an interventionist Keynesian response. There have been influential calls for a Green New Deal or simply green Keynesianism. There is a constituency for change in economic interests and a powerful social movement, but there are also dangers in a lowest-common-denominator approach which 'greenwashes' insufficiently radical reform, which can be undone by the dynamics of capitalist and inter-state rivalry.

The final section argues that reining in capital in more consistently Keynesian ways would require a leap of political faith which probably goes beyond anything that Keynes's own political philosophy would allow. Keynes's vision of states providing stability to an unstable capitalist economy remains distant. This is not to discount the possibility of reform but suggests that its achievement requires going beyond Keynes.

The persistence of Keynesianism

The crisis of the 1970s has been widely perceived as achieving a sharply anti-Keynesian turn. This section qualifies that view. Many changes were indeed anti-Keynesian. An ideology of market efficiency and an antipathy to the state in general and to budget deficits in particular became pervasive. Policies encouraged financialisation and greater inequality. In practice, however, states remained interventionist, notably in both monetary and fiscal policy, often in ways that seem distinctly Keynesian. Many of the Keynesian structures established in the earlier period remained intact. Other liberalising changes were only very broadly or loosely anti-Keynesianism.

A pervasive ideological shift has been widely acknowledged. According to Lucarelli:

> The revival of pre-Keynesian economic doctrines witnessed the revival of Say's law of the market in its modern guise as the 'efficient market hypothesis'. The ideology of these laissez-faire doctrines was embellished with the dogma of budget surpluses, the abandonment of full employment policies and the winding back of the state. (2011: 5)

He continues:

> In the absence of countervailing modes of state regulation and governance, market fundamentalism inevitably destroyed the post-war Keynesian institutions and modes of regulation. (Lucarelli 2011: 5)

Many others, including many Marxists, have similarly described such an ideas-led, liberalising transformation (Harvey 2005, Lapavitsas 2013). Within the economics profession, the anti-Keynesian reorientation seems well established. Under different guises, neo-classical economics was reasserted. Keynesianism and particularly more radical post-Keynesian approaches were exorcised. Macro approaches had to be built on micro foundations. In political discourse, the celebration of business and business imperatives came to dominate.

Helleiner's (1994) influential account of the re-emergence of global finance suggests that, at least initially, reorientation was a policy choice. As more countries took that choice, however, 'competitive deregulation' increased the pressures on others to follow. Once the genie is out of the bottle, as it were, it cannot easily be returned. With the collapse of communism after 1989 and the apparent onward march of economic globalisation, free markets were widely perceived as having triumphed, finally so in Fukuyama's (1992) famous formulation. Attacks on organised labour undermined the previous period's gains, with Reagan's defeat of US air traffic controllers and Thatcher's defeat of British coal miners providing signal moments. By the 1990s, many former social-democratic parties distanced themselves from Keynesian ideas and embraced privatisation and deregulation.

The process, however, can be exaggerated. Even as ideology, the situation is ambiguous. Powerful liberal ideas, in Thatcher's phrase that 'there is no alternative' to the free market, worked alongside other conservative invocations of nationalism and tradition, the 'Victorian values' which Thatcher was also keen to claim (Pilbeam 2003). Much of Keynes's intellectual influence endured, with nothing comparable to the marginalisation of the 'cranks and radicals' who had propagated proto-Keynesian ideas between the wars. Keynesians of various stripes continued to publish hundreds of learned articles. Perhaps more fundamentally, the mainstream arguments of rational expectations and market efficiency are literally useless, except as ideology. As Backhouse argues, they imply that '[u]nless the government took private agents by surprise, the private sector would neutralize the effects of policy changes' (2006: 30). Except where governments have special access to information, there is no possibility of policy activism (Dean 1980). Such doctrinaire academic versions of economic liberalism could never inform the decisions of those who actually ran state machines. More fundamentally, Keynes's vision of ideas-led change was always problematic, and neo-liberal ideology now fitted at best poorly with the achieved restructuring or policy reorientation (Cahill 2014).

In terms of substance, any retreat from Keynes was highly uneven. As discussed in Chapter 10, the earlier period should be judged Keynesian only with caution and qualification; many aspects of the system had little to do with Keynes and there were other aspects of which he would surely have disapproved. That said, there was a signal rejection of Keynes in the 1970s, with the British Labour government's declarations against fiscal stimulus in 1976 and the US 'Volcker Shock' of 1979. Again, it is debatable whether the policy practice ever followed the monetarist theory, which projected itself as the alternative to Keynesianism, but Volcker did succeed in producing a sharp economic downturn and, after a considerable lag, an era of much lower inflation. Other countries followed suit, more or less enthusiastically. Volcker's interest rate rises also pushed many indebted countries, especially in Latin America, towards default and thence eventually to the IMF and structural adjustment. There were also important anticipations of this liberalising turn in the 'Chicago Boys' experiments in Pinochet's Chile, but this now became more general as 'Washington Consensus' policies were imposed in many poorer countries. Chapter 10 suggested that this too highlights continuities. The IMF agenda had long been liberalising. Meanwhile in Europe, it was the existing German 'ordo-liberalism' (Blyth 2013), emphasising central bank independence, sound money and fiscal restraint, which became the dominant model informing moves to European union and which became locked into the institutions of Europe after 1992, particularly with the adoption of the Euro.

There were also continuities in the opposite sense of large states intervening effectively in broadly Keynesian ways. Glyn's (2006) account of the preceding period does much to dispel the hyperbole around transformation. Figures for overall levels of spending and taxation by leading states show little evidence of retreat. At most, there was a levelling off of the rises which had characterised the previous period. Table 12.1 shows levels of government spending of the G5 largest rich-country economies as a percentage of GDP from 1925 to 2005. In each case, levels in 2005 were much higher than those of the pre-Keynesian 1920s. In each country they were also higher than those of 1965 and at least comparable to those of the 1970s. Far from an absolute decline, even relative levels of social spending on average increased significantly across the OECD after 1980 (Glyn 2006). Poorer countries' experiences were more uneven, but many upper-middle-income countries also saw consistent rises in taxation and spending (Ortiz-Ospina and Roser 2018).

Much state intervention could also still look remarkably Keynesian. The Volcker Shock, lifting interest rates to induce recession, can indeed be seen as radically anti-Keynesian (although Keynes continued to defend similar measures taken in the early 1920s). Some Keynesians then interpret the subsequent period as one long Volcker Shock. Tily writes of '25 years of dear money', that '[i]n the early 1980s, long-term rates of interest rose rapidly and have remained at a high level ever since' (2007: 8). But under Greenspan,

Table 12.1 G5 government spending as a proportion of GDP, 1925–2005 (Ortiz-Ospina and Roser 2018)

	1925	1935	1945	1955	1965	1975	1985	1995	2005
France	15.9	24.8	23.3*	21.0	21.8	22.9	54.4	57.8	56.3
Germany	12.3	13.6**	n.a.	30.3	29.4	51.8	49.6	58.4	49.8
Japan	2.2	3.7	12.3*	19.9	20.8	29.6	35.4	37.5	36.6
UK	26.5	26.0	71.7	32.5	37.6	53.1	53.8	47.5	46.2
US	4.2	10.0	45.7	18.0	30.0	36.6	39.9	40.6	39.0

*1946
**1934

Volcker's successor at the Federal Reserve from 1987 to 2006, US interest rates turned downwards, with a policy of responding to economic downturn with quick and decisive cuts, the 'Greenspan put'. Rates continued to fall, until even radicals were crying foul (Brenner 2003). The arguments above in Chapters 8 and 9 suggested that states' ability to determine interest rates is limited and, in the medium to long term, low rates should be seen as a consequence of low rates of profit. The evidence, however, confirms that across rich-country economies, low not high interest rates became the norm.

In terms of fiscal spending, while the rhetoric turned against Keynesian strategies and the rules of the EU proscribed large deficits, the practice suggested little diminution. Indeed, while Volcker still had his foot on the economic brake, the 1980s soon saw this combined with the economic accelerator of reflationary budgets, the classic contradiction of 'Reaganomics'. Reagan's deficits were initially dominated by rather un-Keynesian tax cuts for the rich and arms spending but, even with the end of the Cold War, budget deficits continued to rise in the US and many other rich-country economies, at least until the retrenchment after the GFC. The US figures, shown in Figure 12.1, are broadly typical for those countries for which data are available, showing consistent but countercyclical deficits: rising in the crises of 1990, 2000 and 2008 but falling with booms and even achieving surpluses in the 1990s. Many 'automatic stabilisers' associated with large welfare states remained in place. Several Eurozone countries broke their own spending rules, even prior to the GFC. Meanwhile, from the 1990s Japan implemented massive state-led spending policies: Keynesian stimulus to the point of 'concreting over the archipelago' (McCormack 2002, OECD 2018). Across the OECD, budget deficits were, on average, higher as a proportion of GDP in 2001–04 than they had been in 1974–79 (Glyn 2006).

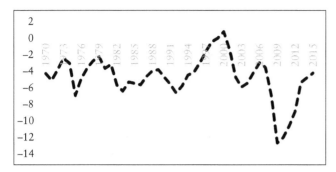

Figure 12.1 US government balances as a percentage of GDP, 1970–2015
(OECD 2018)

Many states did introduce more regressive policies, whittling away at welfare and statutory pensions and introducing means tests while reducing taxes on corporations and the rich. The US cut the top rate of income tax from 70 per cent in 1979 to 37 per cent in 2018. The UK figures are 83 and 45 per cent (Ortiz-Ospina and Roser 2018). Inequality increased in most rich countries. It seems fair to assume that rising inequality represents an anti-Keynesian achievement (Piketty 2014) and Keynes's arguments against regressive redistribution can reasonably be invoked. Keynes, however, had never opposed inequality as such, only the levels he encountered in the inter-war period. There was a moral element to this; like his teacher Marshall, he recognised that the utility of money was greater for the poor than for the rich. But Keynes was disdainful of Benthamite utilitarianism, so care is needed in translating this into an argument for the greater happiness in any straightforward way. Keynes's arguments for redistribution were primarily economic. Reducing the consumption of the poor, who saved less, could have deleterious consequences on effective demand. Recent changes again make this a real concern. But at the same time, Keynes posed his arguments against what he saw as a one-sided under-consumptionism of New Liberals like Hobson, and it is unobvious that he would have opposed some tax cuts from the levels achieved in the boom period. Keynes also wanted to maintain profits. The income-tax rises he supported in the 1930s were far below those achieved by the 1960s and early 1970s. Data on inequality are sparse for the pre-Keynesian years, but it also seems likely that much of continental Europe and Japan remain considerably more equal than at that time and more equal than perhaps Keynes would have thought possible. Again the experiences of poorer countries in recent decades are more mixed, with some evidence of a tendency of rising inequality but with many more exceptions (Solt 2020).

Of course, the causes of within-country inequality are disputed. A 'strong' version of the globalisation thesis sees states as forced to adopt inegalitarian policies (Frieden 1991). There is evidence, however, that across the OECD, redistributive tax policies were still reducing inequality in 2008 by, on average, 33.8 percentage points on the GINI index. Nor did large welfare states or significant deficits prove debilitating to national growth, as liberal discourses suggest (Garrett 2000), and more equal countries tended to grow more quickly in GDP per capita terms. The US was an outlier, in that taxation effected only a 16.6 percentage reduction in inequality, but as the largest and most powerful state, presumably through policy choices and not economic compulsion (Ortiz-Ospina and Roser 2018).

Financialisation and globalisation are discussed below. Briefly here, the increasing size and wealth of the financial sector seems unambiguous, with sharp rises too in the level of international financial transactions. This seems straightforwardly anti-Keynesian; Keynes saw rentier profits as a brake on the productive economy and he thought that finance, above all, should be primarily national. It should be emphasised, however, that it can be misleading to depict finance as having been repressed in the earlier post-WWII period; the size and wealth of the sector grew, if not as fast as it would subsequently (Konings 2010, Krippner 2011). As the next section suggests, it is unobvious that finance now escapes control.

Of course, large, rich states, particularly the US, have more financial power than poorer, weaker ones, and this touches on the broader point that the Washington Consensus policies imposed liberalisation on poorer countries, which had often previously adopted state-led development strategies (Backhouse and Bateman 2011). It brought a brutal austerity in which many countries suffered severe economic contraction and rising inequality. The subsequent picture, however, has typically seen a return to growth and been more mixed in terms of inequality. And while few developing-country governments now espouse state socialism, the largest and most successful, like the famous BRICs – Brazil, Russia, India and China – clearly succeeded with, and arguably because of, strong, interventionist states.

Two other liberalising reorientations seem interesting in terms of Keynes because it is hard to suggest that they directly contradict his ideas. First, states privatised swathes of previously nationalised industry and public sector provision. Keynes probably would have been appalled at things like the privatisation of prisons and public utilities and the extent to which British governments were willing to 'sell off the family silver', to quote his friend Macmillan. In general, however, Keynes opposed state ownership of industry. Finance was another matter but, again, here little was nationalised to begin with, at least in the Anglo-American world. There is an important sense in which all this becomes 'extra-Keynesian'. Keynes said little about it, while the levels of state ownership in the supposedly Keynesian period varied widely across countries often considered similarly Keynesian.

Second, states also passed anti-union laws. Keynes thought unions had too much power in the 1930s and would presumably have thought something similar in the 1960s and 1970s. To oppose this power he preferred policy manoeuvre and negotiation to confrontation, so the (failed) British 'Social Contract' and (successful) Australian 'Accord' better fit his prescriptions than the approaches of Thatcher and Reagan, but it is hard to call anti-union policy anti-Keynesian unless Keynesianism broadens to become a vacuous synonym for anti-liberal.

Accordingly, the rhetorical negation of Keynesianism should be treated cautiously. What passed as Keynesianism – high levels of state intervention and of countercyclical intervention – persists across rich-country economies. It remains substantially true, as Hall wrote 30 years ago, that '[n]o government has yet been able to shed the responsibility for economic management that the Keynesian era bequeathed to it' (1989b: 391). 'Embedded liberalism' still involves facilitating international transactions but simultaneously accepting the existence of domestic welfare states (Keohane 2005: 187).

Economic reorganisation

Economic reorganisation since the 1970s has been substantial. Categorical depictions of novelty always risk understating continuity (Lawson 1997, Vilar 1984) and claims of neo-liberalism, globalisation, the new economy, financialisation are all potentially problematic (Gordon 2000, Henwood 2003, Dunn 2009, 2017, Toporowski 2015, Venugopal 2015). But the world has changed. Two elements of the post-1970s restructuring – the growth of finance and deepening international economic integration – seem particularly relevant to the question of the persistence of Keynesianism and the possibilities of return.

First, the size and power of finance has grown. New financial instruments and institutions have proliferated. And while financialisation has sometimes been characterised in terms of 'disintermediation', involving a decline in the role of bank lending, the burgeoning size and wealth of major banks was one of the period's outstanding features. The power of finance can be direct. Depictions of 'regulatory capture' suggest that bodies like the US Securities and Exchange Commission became dominated by the interests of the industry they oversee. But, in terms of novelty, the more important claims are those of an economic, even technological, shift in which the power of finance to move money around the world instantly and in almost unlimited quantities gives it power over people and institutions that are territorially bound, particularly over nation-states (Strange 1986, 1998, Frieden 1991). In the extreme, states simply transmit the dictates of global capital. Attempts to develop Keynesian policies, especially to run budget deficits, become deeply damaging (Cerny 1996, 2000, Cox 1996). The abolition of capital controls between countries has been amongst the more conspicuously anti-Keynesian changes of recent decades. The possibility of adopting policies, particularly interest-rate policies, to meet domestic needs diminishes as finance can arbitrage over the slightest differences, can flee to wherever it can secure the best return. State practices are apparently forced to converge.

There is a powerful logic to this argument of financial power, but more Keynesian-minded scholars identify reasons to be cautious. Not only was it policy decisions that allowed finance to move money across borders in the first place, but there also remains little technical reason why more restrictive policies could not be reintroduced, at least by the more powerful states, should they so choose (Henwood 1998). States too have access to the new technologies, while finance, in practice, remains highly geographically concentrated: tied to place and tied to other sources of wealth and power within major centres, particularly within rich-country economies. It is also potentially misleading to see contemporary finance as 'deregulated'. As argued in Chapter 7, money always hangs on questions of trust and authority, but more than ever, in a world of virtual, non-commodity money, finance is embedded in rules and institutions and, where necessary, bankrolled by supportive states (Moran 1991, Aglietta 2018). Bank oversight and state lender-of-last-resort functions still underpin new financialised forms of capitalism. The crisis of the 1970s affirmed Keynesianism rather than ending it, in the sense that central banks proved effective lenders of last resort (Boyer 1986), a role reconfirmed and extended in 2008. The contrast with the cascade of bank failures after 1929 is stark. Many poorer countries still impose controls on capital flows without conspicuously debilitating consequences. The need to rein in finance was, of course, already a major theme in Keynes's thinking about Britain in the 1920s and 1930s and in his proposals for the post-war system. This may remain economically advisable and technically possible, even if the growth in the size, wealth, power and mobility of finance do present substantial challenges.

The growth of finance is also inextricably connected to the decline of investment, particularly of industrial investment, in rich countries and to economic 'globalisation'. The scare quotes stress that the spatial reorientation is hardly global. Amongst other things, contrary to depictions of a race to the base, corporate relocation largely continues to ignore the poorest countries. There has been much hyperbole and there are reasons to be sceptical particularly about politically loaded narratives of state powerlessness, which tell workers and others that it is pointless to seek reform. Capital's mobility is neither intrinsically novel nor unlimited. However, if Keynes thought it best, where possible, to let goods be home-spun, the world has moved far from that vision. The social and geographical distances between production and consumption have grown. Global integration produces powerful vested interests in preserving an open, liberal order. As exports increased, sustaining domestic markets became less important for capital, undercutting an important institutional support. Capital's backing of the liberalisation of international economic relations, of its right to move goods, services and money across borders, becomes increasingly locked in the further the process proceeds.

There are precedents for high levels of economic interdependence then being reversed, but contemporary globalisation reached new heights. Levels of gross capital formation (roughly equivalent to 'investment' in Keynes's sense) across high-income countries fell consistently from an average of 27.2 per cent of GDP in the 1970s to just 21.4 per cent in the 2010s (World Bank 2019). This potentially presents economic problems for states seeking independent policy. Keynes's arguments for restrictions to trade and financial movement in the 1930s, if explicitly always couched in terms of 'national interest', could implicitly also speak to, and for, a powerful bloc of domestically oriented capital, which in most countries is now much weaker.

The global financial crisis and its aftermath

There is now a huge literature on the GFC: on how the anti-Keynesian or neo-liberal turn of preceding decades led to the crisis, and on the subsequent policy twists, from financial rescues and apparently Keynesian fiscal responses to austerity as a means of recovering the resulting debt.

Without reviewing the literature, there are powerful reasons for seeing the liberalising policy and economic restructuring as the cause of the crisis (Dumenil and Levy 2011). In particular, growing inequality within the US fed the growth of finance, fed both borrowing and lending. Trade imbalances reflected changing economic structures but also fed into the dollar recycling and the American financial explosion. Policy reform encouraged mutually reinforcing processes at domestic and global levels, while global integration also meant that countries without domestic financial bubbles of their own were caught in the backwash, either directly, because financial institutions had jumped onto the US bandwagon, or indirectly as the financial crisis turned into a global slump (McNally 2011). Capitalism is essentially an international, or perhaps better an a-national, system. 'Planning' at a national level is undermined by capital's global character and by inter-state competition. Dumenil and Levy (2011) also argue that the neo-liberalism of which this was a crisis can itself be seen as the outcome of the crisis of the earlier, regulated system, and that the crisis this time opened the possibility of another reorientation, returning us to a less liberal, more Keynesian world.

The responses to the crisis gave the lie to notions of state powerlessness. Initially, huge financial institutions went bust or teetered on the brink. Many real-economy corporations went under. By 2009, there was a sharp economic contraction. States soon intervened effectively, throwing money at finance but then also introducing substantial fiscal stimulus measures. Globally, by the following year, recovery was well underway. This is not to make light of the appalling hardships that many people continued to suffer; there could be aggregate growth which left millions behind. Levels of unemployment remained high much longer after this contraction than most previous ones. For capital, however, what matters most is restoring profitability and growth, and here government intervention appeared to work. Moreover, this appeared to be recovery without a crisis, in the sense of economic downturn becoming a fundamental turning point. The substance of the previous period seemed intact. Investment, particularly in manufacturing, continued to contract in rich countries while it rose in poorer countries. Trade and global finance stuttered a bit, but there was no generalised retreat. Stimulus policies gave way to austerity. States' intervention sustained rather than changed the old trajectory.

For Keynesian critics this was at best a missed opportunity. The turn to austerity was 'madness' (Arestis and Pelagidis 2010, Krugman 2012), prolonging the misery, postponing recovery and leaving the world vulnerable to a repeat experience. It is true enough that policy often appeared to follow the crudest neo-classical schemas. To see this as 'madness', however, repeats the Keynesian fallacy of conceiving the economy and economic interests in abstractly general and national terms. A persistent and concerted global stimulus might indeed have been more effective in restoring growth. More equitable distribution and, as even the IMF (2011) acknowledged, the elimination of global imbalances would build a more sustainable trajectory. What this overlooks, of course, is that powerful vested interests supported austerity. Cutting wages and benefits could restore profits. And if that potentially exacerbated demand problems, any one country could hope to increase competitiveness and sell abroad. The difficulties this competition introduced were felt particularly starkly in the Eurozone, without the cushion provided by currency adjustments. This is not to defend austerity policies, and at a global level, cutting aggregate demand is indeed counterproductive. But there were real imperatives in inter-state and inter-capitalist competition which made it rational (Dunn 2014). As the previous section suggested, the extent of global integration today may not invalidate Keynes's proposals of the 1930s, but the economic interests in maintaining openness and the economic difficulties in changing course have become commensurately greater.

Environmental Keynesianism and the Green New Deal?

The growing ecological crisis and a growing acknowledgement of this crisis have also raised demands for Keynesian responses. The climate catastrophe is the most acute of the environmental challenges, but there is a crisis of many other things, including water shortages, pollution, biodiversity loss and the destruction of marine environments. An awareness of environmental destruction is not new. Marx, for example, already described how capitalist urbanisation created a 'metabolic rift' between people and nature (Marx 1975, Foster 2000). There has subsequently been a long and rich tradition of ecological economics, seeking to understand and redress the problems. It is impossible here to review this literature but there are diverse currents of green economics thinking. Some of this runs in considerable tension with Keynesian economics as it is usually understood. 'Traditional Keynesianism is growth-oriented, while ecological economics stresses limits to growth' (Harris 2013: 1). However, the crisis gives ecological issues a new urgency and many proposals at both national and international level have a distinctly Keynesian flavour.

Demands for a synthesis of environmental and Keynesian ideas gained currency in the wake of the GFC and the stimulus responses. Several national packages included commitments to environmental projects. Some calls to go further reference other proximate traditions; notably, those advocating a Green New Deal invoke Roosevelt and the US experience, but several explicitly advocate 'green Keynesianism' (Cato 2013, Harris 2013, Goldstein and Tyfield 2018). Initial calls for a Green New Deal came from oppositionists within Britain but were embraced by global institutions including the UN Environment Program (Barbier 2010, Aşici and Bünül 2012, Cato 2013, Bauhardt 2014). The G20 pledged itself to 'sustainable green growth' (Barbier 2011). For their advocates, such policy responses were necessary to reverse environmental destruction but could also provide a vital economic stimulus. There could be an alignment of green and economic objectives, the latter reconceived as sustainable development of a new type based on technological innovation, green public infrastructure and recycling (Aşici and Bünül 2012).

There was a convergence too in the recognition, from both environmental and economic perspectives, of institutional and market failures which showed that faith in free markets and conventional economic thinking are inadequate (Barbier 2011, Harris 2013). Keynes provides an attractive alternative. Perhaps most broadly, Keynes foresaw a future of satiable material needs and short working weeks, while his views of the good life involved aesthetic principles rather than simply the pursuit of ever more material gains (CWIX: 321–2, Cato 2013). More immediately, government intervention is needed both to regulate and as a driver of technological innovation. States can make the long-term investment decisions to which private, risk-averse firms cannot commit (Goldstein and Tyfield 2018). But reform proposals also often assume a distinctly Keynesian flavour in being couched as enabling rather than opposing private enterprise, as providing the right conditions in which private innovation is 'crowded in' (Aşici and Bünül 2012, Goldstein and Tyfield 2018). They champion a Keynesian middle way, between the destructiveness of business as usual and the difficulties of achieving radical overhaul. States can represent, or can be nudged towards representing, a general interest.

There were grounds for optimism, with reform proposals having potentially powerful backers. Business interests declared for the green agenda. This extended beyond the obvious construction projects in wind farms and the manufacture and installation of solar panels. High-tech industries, infrastructure providers and major Silicon Valley firms portrayed themselves as part of the solution (Goldstein and Tyfield 2018). Corporations, even including major oil companies, acknowledged the need to shift to investments into renewable energy. Of course, this should not be exaggerated and there was often a 'greenwashing' of environmentally destructive practices. For example, the use of biofuels could be included in the lists of clean energy sources (Aşici and Bünül 2012) and electric cars celebrated as less damaging than petrol-fuelled ones while still leaving a huge environmental footprint. But there is at least a potential capitalist constituency for change. Beyond corporate capital, many smaller firms committed to producing in sustainable ways, with several authors identifying the rise of a grass-roots, alternative or 'solidarity' economy, amongst other things concentrating on local economies to reduce the environmental costs of long-distance trade (Bauhardt 2014). Crucially, a remarkable rise in environmental activism demanded action. Again there is a long history, with ebbs as well as flows, but the renewed activism, centred on school students and the example of Greta Thunberg, has put environmental demands at the centre of political agenda in many countries. This book is being completed in the midst of the coronavirus crisis, the lockdown associated with which has put the street protests on hold, and it is hard to anticipate how or in what ways they will resume. But, from the political fringes, the idea that environmental destruction could not be tolerated became mainstream.

There was a pressing need for state and inter-state action. Again, recent experiences provide some grounds for optimism. As above, stimulus measures in response to the financial crisis showed that despite many pronouncements of ineffectiveness, states remained capable of acting, and of acting quickly and effectively. The coronavirus crisis raises similar issues of the need for, and the possibilities of, effective intervention. It is far too early to pronounce on the causes, let alone the consequences, of the pandemic. But the economic interconnectedness at least contributed to the rapidity of the spread, most obviously in countries like the UK where no attempt was made to test or track people arriving from high-incidence locations, while privatised infrastructure and health care made remedial action more difficult. Again, however, governments (with different strategies and degrees of competence) were able to act, both negatively in imposing restrictions and positively in increasing health and supply provisions and to mobilise resources in ways that had been deemed impossible in the previous decade of austerity. As lockdowns sent economies into recession, the alternative strategies for recovery, of austerity or of stimulus and redistribution, were again being articulated. For many people, the crisis also confirmed that a return to business as normal was insufficient, that what had become the business norms may both have contributed to the pandemic and created the conditions where the poorest and ethnic minorities were most vulnerable. But even the immediate responses showed the possibility of action and alternative futures.

The economic, ecological and health crises also demonstrate the need for international cooperation, if largely through their absence. For decades, international competition has bedevilled attempts to enforce environmental standards. There have been some successes, most obviously in the Montreal protocols limiting chlorofluorocarbons. But there have been more failures, whether on whaling, nuclear non-proliferation or international trade (Barbier 2011). The World Trade Organization notoriously disallowed environmental concerns from impinging on national trade policies (Dunkley 2004, Gallagher 2008, Harris 2013). International agreements on climate change were notoriously weak, even before the US rejection of the modest ambitions of Paris. There were some possibilities that competition could spur countries to adopt cleaner, 'leapfrogging' technologies and suggestions that this motivated the relatively high proportion of post-financial-crisis stimulus directed towards green projects in Korea and China (Barbier 2010). Nevertheless, the need for international agreement if there is to be meaningful reorientation has been widely recognised.

Sadly, an enormous gap remained between the political urgency and effective action. Despite some robust declarations, environmental destruction escalated. The planet got hotter. Deforestation continued. Atmospheric carbon dioxide levels reached new peaks. The World Bank's estimate of the economic cost of carbon dioxide damage had it rising from 0.64 per cent in

1970 to 1.48 in 2010 and further to 1.83 in 2018 (World Bank 2020). Crude oil production rose from 3.4 trillion tonnes in 2000 to almost 4.0 by 2018 (OECD 2020). Motor vehicle production rose to a peak of 97.3 million in 2017, up from 61.8 million just eight years earlier (oica.net 2020).

Car production perhaps best exemplifies the fundamental problem of attempting to reconcile ecological and capitalist ends. Capital needs to accumulate. Regulations to make individual cars less polluting, however important, are quickly negated by increased vehicle numbers (Tienhaara 2014). And if not cars, capital must find something else to sell. Computers and mobile phones became big-ticket items, requiring minerals produced in destructive ways and toxic chemicals, for example in semiconductor manufacture. They epitomise practices of built-in obsolescence (Cato 2013) and more subtle problems of waste disposal and its cost determination (Herod 2018). Capital's imperatives also mean that greater efficiency in the extraction and use of natural resources can increase their demand. Even in Europe, with the strictest regulation, and where material consumption grew more slowly than GDP, it still grew (Levidow 2014). Only those good environmental practices which pay are likely to be practised.

If this points towards the need for state intervention, it also suggests that the idea of the state acting with capital to achieve green objectives becomes problematic. There are likely to be more vested interests opposed to radical redirection than in favour, with recent experiences giving little indication of any diminution of corporate influence on policy. In practice the idea of '"sustainability" was used as a pretext for the implementation of selective, targeted developmental programmes' (Szalavetz 2015: 75). Perhaps the most egregious examples were the effective subsidies which rich-country stimulus packages gave to car companies through schemes to replace older cars (Aşici and Bünül 2012). But a range of ostensibly green measures could actually harm the environment. The commodification of nature is encouraged by carbon pricing models, deepening the financialised model of capitalism, while the models allow carbon credits to be awarded for planting damaging crops like palm (oil) trees. Nuclear power is supported because of its gains in one dimension, but at the neglect of its costs in others (Levidow 2014). Korea could be seen as having the greenest of stimulus packages despite measures including a 'controversial project to dam and dredge four major rivers, putting a number of endangered species at serious risk' (Tienhaara 2014: 191). It is acknowledged that it is the competitive edge which stimulates apparently new green investments in both China and Korea (Barbier 2011).

This also points to analogous problems of competition at the international level. Emission levels improved for many rich-country economies, particularly in Europe, which had tougher environmental regulation than

most other parts of the world, but that could neglect the impact of dein-
dustrialisation, which effectively meant off-shoring much of the dirty work
(Cato 2013, Levidow 2014). Ciplet and Roberts (2019) draw out some
important tensions. Many developing countries make demands to prioritise
development over environmental protection and for compensation to enable
them to make any such protections. The G77 (a group of poorer countries
grown to 134) also fractured. OPEC states and India remained committed
to resisting any taxes on carbon emissions. But the Alliance of Small Island
States (AOSIS) also remained vocal advocates of meaningful change. 'While
they develop, we die', as Grenadian delegate Karl Hood is quoted as saying
(Ciplet and Roberts 2019: 285). Even amongst the poorest and most vulnerable countries, there could be 'intensified infighting over designations of
vulnerability in order to access the scarce existing public funds' (Ciplet and
Roberts 2019: 293). As one of the principal promotors of a Green New Deal
acknowledges, '[h]ow tax revenues are to be apportioned between national
and international spending priorities may be difficult to resolve' (Barbier
2011: 241).

All this again raises questions of how the left should engage with Keynes
and Keynesianism, and points to a 'yes-but-but' approach. Yes, it is right to
point to the failures of existing capitalism and the need for resistance and
change. State action to reduce or outlaw destructive practices, getting rid
of fossil fuels, or at the very least getting rid of the current fossil fuel subsidies, and encouraging sustainable practices, is welcome. Thinking about
Keynesian responses to the environmental crisis also usefully directs attention
to some profound problems in conventional economic accounting and the
need not to distinguish between 'growth' per se and strategies of de-growth,
as deeper-green ecologists would have it, but to think about those activities which are unsustainable 'and those that can expand over time without
negative environmental consequences. The latter would include large areas
of health, education, cultural activity, and resource- and energy-conserving
investment' (Harris 2013: 5). No doubt there is much to be done on the
science of transformation (O'Brien 2012), working out exactly what can be
done sustainably, but the fundamental obstacles are the vested interests, and
the challenge of overcoming them is therefore a political one. And, as the
green Keynesian thinking insists, there is scope for political change, there
are alternatives, and states manifestly have the power to act even if forcing
such action requires reinvigorated social movements whose ambitions soon
go beyond supporting reforms to the need for a fundamental reorganisation
of society (Schwartzman 2011).

But the environmental Keynesian or Green New Deal strategy is too
limited, while the limits of the strategy also potentially disorient. The
limits have been mentioned above. Emissions reduction targets are both

insufficient and insufficiently enforced. Some elements of the reform agenda can be counterproductive: support for biofuels and nuclear power, subsidies to slightly less destructive types of car production. What is done can also be undone by capital's logic if it is not challenged more fundamentally. More efficient production stimulates more production. Bans on one form of destructive behaviour fail to deter the next innovation in another destructive domain. Capital is mobile, in the literal, geographical sense able to arbitrage over regulatory laxity but more fundamentally in its ability to shift from one activity to the next. National regulations are undermined by capital's mobility but also by inter-state competition. China and the US (with Xi and Obama directly involved) ensured that the 2009 Copenhagen agreement abandoned any meaningful commitments (Ciplet and Roberts 2019). As the climate catastrophe deepens, it becomes increasingly clear that many of the measures being proposed are far too little and too late. It is at least necessary to go further.

But also, as Goldstein and Tyfield (2018: 77) describe, the 'middle paradigm' of Green New Deal proposals 'can be and often is pulled towards the right'. The potential disorientation stems from entrusting power to corporate and state bureaucracies which are part of the problem rather than the solution. 'The Green New Deal takes the present conditions of industrial capitalism as its point of departure. It does not question the basic functioning of capitalist production and reproduction' (Bauhardt 2014: 65). It fails to challenge fundamental productivist assumptions, not least that green investment should be directed towards male-dominated industries (Bauhardt 2014). Some of the best-known proposals can be directly counterproductive: for example, advocating the more accurate pricing of nature perpetuates the problem. Other proposals can compete with each other, and the more acceptable, moderate claims can displace the more radical. The lowest common denominator in terms of emissions reductions may be all that is politically achievable if the corporate and state interests are to be kept on-side. Encouragement of the right sort of investment can displace 'proposals for more stringent environmental regulation' (Levidow 2014: 3). Meanwhile, as Goldstein and Tyfield write, '[p]erhaps the most alluring aspect of a return to Keynesianism is the idea that the state will be able to function primarily in the public interest' (2018: 88). This points to the fundamental problem with Keynesian assumptions of the need to work with private enterprise and of the perfectibility of governments which are built into much of the reform thinking, and which can misdirect and disarm the movement for change.

Keynesianism's return and Keynes's political philosophy

This finally comes back to the impossible question of the prospects of a return to Keynes. It is impossible both because there are many versions of Keynes and because we live in a changed world. Any reapplication requires at least some creative reinterpretation. Keynes's vision was one in which states could intervene to provide some stability where the market was unstable, and in which states could encourage investment and growth where the private sector proved reluctant. In a world in which stability looks distant, perhaps more distant than ever, and in which rates of investment in rich-country economies continue to fall, the case for a return to Keynes seems compelling. But in another sense, the instability and stagnation put Keynes further out of reach. The social and economic constituency for nationally based solutions weakens while, for decades, states have been deeply implicated in the processes which have reshaped the global economy, creating new forms of instability, redistributive rather than dynamic growth and environmental destruction.

In terms of ideas, of course there can and should be a recovery. New generations can and should read Keynes, learn from him and criticise him. However, if we take Keynes's own avowed political philosophy seriously, the difficulty of implementing Keynesian policies becomes particularly stark. Chapter 2 described the Burkean basis of Keynes's political philosophy. This allowed at most cautious and gradual change, allowed changes not least to avoid anything more substantial. From this perspective, as the gap between where we are and where we might like to be increases, it becomes harder to justify the reforming leap of faith. To achieve even relatively modest reform, it may be necessary to risk more, to attempt more radical change, than Keynes would have countenanced.

Already three decades ago, Radice could write that '[t]he growth in trade as a proportion of national income, the internationalization of industrial and banking capital, the disorder in the world economy since the demise of the Bretton Woods system, have all undermined the efficacy of the conventional Keynesian policy tools' (1988: 153). There is an enduring appeal, and consistency with Keynes's own political approach, in still attempting to win intellectual arguments and to affect a governmental change of heart. In some areas, as suggested above, Keynesian practices and institutions persist and reinforcing them seems entirely practicable. But there would appear to be greater institutional obstacles to major reorientation and vested interests opposed to reorientation even than in Keynes's own times. There is a long history of hopes frustrated, of reformist plans withering in the face of economic and political opposition. But recent experiences, notably in the aftermath of the economic crisis of the 2000s, have reinforced the lesson very starkly. The uncertainty involved in attempting bolder reform, whether erecting trade barriers, resurrecting national bases of industry, or euthanising rentiers, continues to rise, and in terms of Keynes's own political philosophy, might well imply unacceptable risks.

It was also argued in Chapter 2, however, that Keynes's ideas of uncertainty, the Burkean argument and the principle of prudence can be spun in a more radical direction. If present horrors should not be contemplated in the name of only uncertain future gains, present horrors should not be suffered in the name of only uncertain future losses. A logic like this seems to have lain behind Keynes's acceptance of the rationale for state intervention. But it might more broadly allow ending current horrors, the consequences of austerity policies and environmental destruction, even if this involved governments accumulating debts or implementing new economic trajectories bearing unknowable long-term consequences. The means and the ends, though never separable, would appear to be in tension.

This returns to questions of agency and the limits of Keynes's state-centred political vision discussed in Chapter 3. It recalls that while elite opinion in the 1930s and 1940s did shift, the post-WWII Keynesian transformation was substantially achieved as the unintended consequence of a unique conjuncture of class struggle, capital accumulation and international competition which had little place in Keynes's schema. Again, the disappearance of such a conjuncture might augur pessimism about the prospects of a return to Keynes. But as capitalism continues to throw up new horrors, it fosters new struggles whose outcomes are unknowable. It creates new possibilities and difficult strategic choices.

An economics that Keynes thought 'moderately conservative in its implications' now itself throws up the need for radical change. And this raises questions about the possibilities of reaching further, pointing back to Marx and the Marxist understanding which informed this book's critique of Keynes. Remembering Marx should not suggest ready-made alternative economic analyses and solutions. On the contrary, it has been argued that many of Keynes's insights about unemployment and investment, about money and the state, need to be incorporated, if sometimes in reworked form, into any adequate modern Marxism. Nor should remembering Marx imply that the reforming impulse of Keynes is conceived only in the negative, as the antithesis of revolution; rather, it should also be conceived in terms of the questions it raises about how to fight for a better world, where and how to struggle and where and why to stop. Indeed Mann (2017a) suggests that Keynesianism is always informed by the threat of revolution. Mann also reasonably warns that the experiences of many revolutions have been sobering. It would seem that we must, as Keynes wrote in a different context, 'believe and disbelieve, and mingle faith with doubt' (CWXVII: 448). But it seems hard to imagine recovering even the precarious Keynesian middle ground without recovering the revolutionary impulse.

References

Aglietta, M. (2018) *Money: 5,000 years of debt and power*. London: Verso.

Aldcroft, D.H. (1993) *The European Economy 1914–1990*, 3rd edition. London: Routledge.

Alexander, S.S. (1940) 'Mr Keynes and Mr Marx', *The Review of Economic Studies*, 7(2): 123–35.

Allen, C.S. (1989) 'The Underdevelopment of Keynesianism in the Federal Republic of Germany', in Hall, P.A., ed., *The Political Power of Economic Ideas: Keynesianism across nations*. Princeton NJ: Princeton University Press.

Allen, H.C. (1968) *A Concise History of the U.S.A.* London: Ernest Benn.

Anderson, P. (1979) *Lineages of the Absolutist State*. London: Verso.

Arestis, P. (1996) 'Introduction', in Arestis, P., ed., *Keynes, Money and the Open Economy*. Cheltenham: Edward Elgar.

Arestis, P. and Howells, P. (2001) 'The 1520–1640 "Great Inflation": an early case of controversy on the nature of money', *Journal of Post Keynesian Economics*, 24(2): 198–203.

Arestis, P. and Pelagidis, T. (2010) 'Absurd Austerity Policies in Europe', *Challenge*, 53(6): 54–61.

Arestis, P. and Sawyer, M.C. (2002) '"New Consensus" New Keynesianism, and the Economics of the "Third Way"', Levy Economics Institute Working Paper No. 364.

Armstrong, P., Glyn, A. and Harrison, J. (1984) *Capitalism Since World War II*. London: Fontana.

Arrighi, G. (1994) *The Long Twentieth Century*. London: Verso.

Arrow, K.J. (1994) 'Methodological Individualism and Social Knowledge', *The American Economic Review*, 84(2): 1–9.

Arthur, C.J. (2005) 'Value and Money', in Moseley F., ed., *Marx's Theory of Money: modern appraisals*. Springer ebook.

Aşici, A.A. and Bünül, Z. (2012) 'Green New Deal: a green way out of the crisis?', *Environmental Policy and Governance*, 22(5): 295–306.

Backhouse, R.E. (2006) 'The Keynesian Revolution', in Backhouse, R.E. and Bateman, B.W., eds, *The Cambridge Companion to Keynes*. Cambridge: Cambridge University Press.

Backhouse, R.E. and Bateman, B.W. (2006) 'A Cunning Purchase: the life and work of Maynard Keynes' in Backhouse, R.E. and Bateman, B.W., eds, *The Cambridge Companion to Keynes*. Cambridge: Cambridge University Press.

Backhouse, R.E., and Bateman, B.W. (2011) *Capitalist Revolutionary: John Maynard Keynes*. Cambridge, MA: Harvard University Press.

Baldwin, T. (1993) 'Editor's Introduction', in Moore G.E., *Principia Ethica*. Cambridge: Cambridge University Press.

Balogh, [T.] (1976) 'Keynes and the International Monetary Fund', in Thirlwall, A.P., ed., *Keynes and International Monetary Relations*. London: Macmillan.

Banaji, J. (2010) *Theory as History*. Chicago: Haymarket.

Baragar, F. (2003) 'Joan Robinson on Marx', *Review of Political Economy*, 15(4): 467–82.

Baran, P.A. and Sweezy, P.M. (1968) *Monopoly Capital*. Harmondsworth: Penguin.

Barbier, E. (2010) 'How is the Global Green New Deal Going?', *Nature*, 464(7290): 832–3.

Barbier, E. (2011) 'The Policy Challenges for Green Economy and Sustainable Economic Development', *Natural Resources Forum*, 35(3): 233–45.

Barker, C. (1978) 'A Note on the Theory of Capitalist States', *Capital and Class*, 4: 118–26.

Bateman, B.W. (1987) 'Keynes's Changing Conception of Probability', *Economics and Philosophy*, 3(1): 97–119.

Bateman, B.W. (2006) 'Keynes and Keynesianism', in Backhouse, R.E. and Bateman, B.W., eds, *The Cambridge Companion to Keynes*. Cambridge: Cambridge University Press.

Bateman, M. and Chang, H.J. (2012) 'Microfinance and the Illusion of Development: from hubris to nemesis in thirty years', *World Economic Review*, 1: 13–36.

Bauhardt, C. (2014) 'Solutions to the Crisis? The Green New Deal, Degrowth, and the Solidarity Economy: alternatives to the capitalist growth economy from an ecofeminist economics perspective', *Ecological Economics*, 102: 60–8.

Benanav, A. (2015) 'A Global History of Unemployment: surplus populations in the world economy, 1949–2010', PhD thesis, UCLA.

Benanav, A. and Clegg, J. (2010). 'Misery and Debt', *Endnotes*, 2: 20–51.

Berend, I.T. (2006) *An Economic History of 20th Century Europe: economic regimes from laissez-faire to globalization*. Cambridge: Cambridge University Press.

BIS (2017) 'Annual Report 2017', Bank of International Settlements.

BIS (2019) 'Annual Economic Report 2019', Bank of International Settlements.

Blaug, M. (1994) 'Recent Biographies of Keynes', *Journal of Economic Literature*, 32(3): 1204–15.

Blaug, M. (1997) *Economic Theory in Retrospect*, 5th edition. Cambridge: Cambridge University Press.

Bludnik, I. (2009) 'The New Keynesianism: proclamation of a consensus?' *Poznan University of Economics Review*, 9(1): 5–24.

Blyth, M. (2013) *Austerity: the history of a dangerous idea*. Oxford: Oxford University Press.

Boyer, R. (1986) 'The Influence of Keynes on French Economic Policy: past and present', in Wattel, H.L., ed., *The Policy Consequences of John Maynard Keynes*. Basingstoke: Macmillan.

Boyer, R.O. and Morais, H.M. (1977) *Labor's Untold Story*. New York: UE (United Electrical, Radio and Machine Workers of America).

Brandis, R. (1985) 'Marx *and* Keynes? Marx *or* Keynes?', *Journal of Economic Issues*, 19(3): 643–59.

Braudel, F. (1974) *Capitalism and Material Life: 1400–1800*. Glasgow: Fontana/Collins.

Braudel, F. (1985) *Civilization and Capitalism 15th–18th Century, Vol. III: The Perspective of the World*. London: Fontana.

Brenner, R. (1998) 'The Economics of Global Turbulence', *New Left Review*, 229.

Brenner, R. (2003) *The Boom and the Bubble*. London: Verso.

Brittan, S. (2006) 'Keynes's Political Philosophy', in Backhouse, R.E. and Bateman, B.W., eds, *The Cambridge Companion to Keynes*. Cambridge: Cambridge University Press.

Brothwell, J. (1988) 'The *General Theory* after Fifty Years: why are we not all Keynesians now?', in Hillard, J., ed., *J.M. Keynes in Retrospect: the legacy of the Keynesian revolution*. Aldershot: Edward Elgar.

Broz, L. (2000) 'The Domestic Politics of International Monetary Order: the Gold Standard', in Frieden, J. and Lake, D., eds, *International Political Economy: perspectives on global power and wealth*. New York: St Martin's Press.

Bryan, D. and Rafferty, M. (2005) *Capitalism with Derivatives: a political economy of financial derivatives, capital and class*. London: Palgrave Macmillan.

Burczak, T.E. (2013) 'Interest, Theories of', in Cate, T. ed., *An Encyclopedia of Keynesian Economics*. Edward Elgar ebook.

Burke, E. (1955) *Reflections on the Revolution in France*. Indianapolis: Bobbs-Merrill.

Cagan, P. (1987) 'Monetarism', in Eatwell, J., Milgate, M. and Newman, P., eds, *The New Palgrave Dictionary of Economics, Vol. 3*. London: Macmillan.

Cahill, D. (2014) *The End of Laissez-Faire? On the durability of embedded neo-liberalism*. Cheltenham: Edward Elgar.

Callinicos, A. (1989a) *Making History*. Cambridge: Polity.

Callinicos, A. (1989b) *Against Postmodernism*. Cambridge: Polity.

Callinicos, A. (2014) *Deciphering Capital*. London: Bookmarks.

Campbell, M. (2005) 'Marx's Explanation of Money's Functions: overturning the quantity theory', in F Moseley, ed., *Marx's Theory of Money*. Springer ebook.

Carruthers, B.G. and Ariovich, L. (2010) *Money and Credit: a sociological approach*. Cambridge: Polity.

Caspari, V. (2019) 'Consumption and Saving', in Dimand, R.W. and Hagemann, H., eds, *The Elgar Companion to John Maynard Keynes*. Edward Elgar ebook.

Cato, M.S. (2013) *The Paradox of Green Keynesianism*. Weymouth: Green House.

Cerny, P. (1996) 'International Finance and the Erosion of State Policy Capacity', in Gummett, P., ed., Globalization and Public Policy. Cheltenham: Edward Elgar.

Cerny, P.G. (2000) 'Structuring the Political Arena: public goods, states and governance in a globalizing world', in Palan, R., ed., *Global Political Economy: contemporary theories*. London: Routledge.

Chandavarkar, A. (2000) 'Was Keynes Anti-Semitic?' *Economic and Political Weekly*, 35(19): 1619–24.

Chick, V. (1983) *Macroeconomics after Keynes*. Cambridge, MA: MIT Press.

Chick, V. (1992) 'The Evolution of the Banking System and the Theory of Saving, Investment and Interest', in Arestis, P. and Dow, S.C., eds, *On Money, Method and Keynes: selected essays [by] Victoria Chick*. Basingstoke: Macmillan.

Chick, V. (2019) 'Liquidity Preference', in Dimand, R.W. and Hagemann, H., eds, *The Elgar Companion to John Maynard Keynes*. Edward Elgar ebook.

Chow, Y.S. and Teicher, H. (2012) *Probability Theory: independence, interchangeability*. New York: Springer.

Chowdhury, A. (2009) 'Microfinance as a Poverty Reduction Tool: a Critical Assessment', UN, DESA Working Paper No. 89 ST/ESA/2009/DWP/89.

Chown, J.F. (1994) *A History of Money: from AD800*. London: Routledge.

Ciplet D. and Roberts J.T. (2019) 'Splintering South: ecologically unequal exchange theory in a fragmented global climate', in Frey R., Gellert P. and Dahms H., eds, *Ecologically Unequal Exchange*. Cham, Switzerland: Palgrave Macmillan.

Clarke, P. (1988) *The Keynesian Revolution in the Making, 1924–1936*. Oxford: Clarendon.

Clarke, S. (1988) *Keynesianism, Monetarism and the Crisis of the State*. Aldershot: Edward Elgar.

Clarke, S. (1994) *Marx's Theory of Crisis*. Basingstoke: Macmillan.

Coates, D. (2005) *Models of Capitalism: growth and stagnation in the modern era*. Cambridge: Polity.

Coddington, A. (1983) *Keynesian Economics: the Search for first principles*. London: George Allen & Unwin.

Cohen, B.J. (1998) *The Geography of Money*. Ithaca, NY, and London: Cornell University Press.

Cohen, G.A. (1978) *Karl Marx's Theory of History: a defence*. Oxford: Oxford University Press.

Cohen, G.A. (1982) 'Reply to Elster on "Marxism, Functionalism, and Game Theory"', *Theory and Society*, 11(4): 483–95.

Colander, D. (2013) 'IS/LM Model and Diagram', in Cate, T., ed., *An Encyclopedia of Keynesian Economics*. Edward Elgar ebook.

Conrad, J.W. (1963) *An Introduction to the Theory of Interest*. Berkeley: University of California Press.

Cottrell, A. (2012) 'Keynes's Vision and Tactics', in Davis, J.B., ed., *The State of Interpretation of Keynes*. Boston: Kluwer Academic Publishers.

Cox, R.W. (1996) *Approaches to World Order*. Cambridge: Cambridge University Press.

Darrell, J. (1937) 'The Economic Consequences of Mr. Keynes', *Science and Society*, 1: 194–211.

Davidson, P. (1978) *Money and the Real World*, 2nd edition. London: Macmillan.

Davidson, P. (2007) *Interpreting Keynes for the 21st Century, Vol. 4: The Collected Writings of Paul Davidson*. Basingstoke: Palgrave Macmillan.

Davidson, P. (2009) *John Maynard Keynes*. Basingstoke: Palgrave Macmillan.

Davidson, P. (2010) 'Keynes's Revolutionary and "Serious" Monetary Theory', in Dimand, R.W., Mundell, R.A. and Vercelli, A., eds, *Keynes's General Theory After Seventy Years*. London: Palgrave Macmillan.

Davies, G. (1996) *A History of Money: from ancient times to the present day*. Cardiff: University of Wales Press.

Davis, A.E. (2010) 'Marx and the Mixed Economy: money, accumulation, and the role of the state', *Science & Society*, 74(3): 409–28.

Davis, J.B. (1992) 'Keynes on the Socialization of Investment', *International Journal of Social Economics*, 19(10/11/12): 150–63.

Davis, J.B. (1994) *Keynes's Philosophical Development*. Cambridge: Cambridge University Press.

Davis, J.B. (2019) 'G.E. Moore', in Dimand, R.W. and Hagemann, H., eds, *The Elgar Companion to John Maynard Keynes*. Edward Elgar ebook.

De Angelis, M. (2000) *Keynesianism, Social Conflict and Political Economy*. Basingstoke: Macmillan.

De Brunhoff, S. (1976) *Marx on Money*. New York: Urizen.

De Carvalho, F.J.C. (1988) 'Keynes on Probability, Uncertainty, and Decision Making', *Journal of Post Keynesian Economics*, 11(1): 66–81.

De Carvalho, F.J.C. (1996) 'Paul Davidson's Rediscovery of Keynes's Finance Motive and the Liquidity Preference Versus Loanable Funds Debate', in Arestis, P., ed., *Keynes, Money and the Open Economy*. Cheltenham: Edward Elgar.

De Cecco, M. (1989) 'Keynes and Italian Economics', in Hall, P.A., ed., *The Political Power of Economic Ideas: Keynesianism across nations*. Princeton, NJ: Princeton University Press.

De Vroey, M. (2011) 'The Marshallian Roots of Keynes's General Theory', in Arnon, A., Weinblatt, J. and Young, W., eds, *Perspective on Keynesian Economics*. Springer ebook.

De Vroey, M. and Hoover, K.D. (2004) 'Introduction: seven decades of the IS–LM model', *History of Political Economy*, 36(Annual Supplement): 1–11.

Dean, J.W. (1980) 'The Dissolution of the Keynesian Consensus', *National Affairs*, 10(Special Issue): 19–34.

Dillard, D. (1980) 'A Monetary Theory of Production: Keynes and the institutionalists', *Journal of Economic Issues*, 14(2): 255–73.

Dillard, D. (1984) 'Keynes and Marx: a centennial appraisal', *Journal of Post Keynesian Economics*, 6(3): 421–32.

Dillard, D. (1986) 'The Influence of Keynesian Thought on German Economic Policy', in Wattel, H.L., ed., *The Policy Consequences of John Maynard Keynes*. Basingstoke: Macmillan.

Dimand, R.W. (2019a) 'The Economic Consequences of Mr Churchill', in Dimand, R.W. and Hagemann, H., eds, *The Elgar Companion to John Maynard Keynes*. Edward Elgar ebook.

Dimand, R.W. (2019b) 'A Tract on Monetary Reform', in Dimand, R.W. and Hagemann, H., eds, *The Elgar Companion to John Maynard Keynes*. Edward Elgar ebook.

Dimand, R.W. (2019c) 'The Multiplier', in Dimand, R.W. and Hagemann, H., eds, *The Elgar Companion to John Maynard Keynes*. Edward Elgar ebook.

Ditchburn, D. and MacKay, A. (2007) 'Financial Centres in Western Europe', in Ditchburn, D., Maclean, S. and MacKay, A., eds, *Atlas of Medieval Europe*. Abingdon: Routledge.

Dobb, M. (1956) 'Foreword', in V.B. Singh, ed., *Keynesian Economics: a symposium*. Delhi: People's Publishing House.

Dos Santos Ferreira, R. (2019) 'Imperfect Competition', in Dimand, R.W. and Hagemann, H., eds, *The Elgar Companion to John Maynard Keynes*. Edward Elgar ebook.

Dostaler, G. (1996) 'The Formation of Keynes's Vision', *History of Economics Review*, 25(1): 14–31.

Dostaler, G. (2007) *Keynes and his Battles*. Cheltenham: Edward Elgar.

Dow, S. (1996) *The Methodology of Macroeconomic Thought: a conceptual analysis of schools of thought in economics*. Cheltenham: Edward Elgar.

Dow, S. (2019) 'Risk and Uncertainty', in Dimand, R.W. and Hagemann, H., eds, *The Elgar Companion to John Maynard Keynes*. Edward Elgar ebook.

Dowd, D. (2004) *Capitalism and Its Economics*. London: Pluto.

Dumenil, G. and Levy, D. (2004) *Capital Resurgent*. Cambridge, MA: Harvard University Press.

Dumenil, G. and Levy, D. (2011) *The Crisis of Neoliberalism*. Cambridge, MA: Harvard University Press.

Dunkley, G. (2004) *Free Trade: myth, reality and alternatives*. London: Zed.

Dunn, B. (2009) 'Myths of Globalisation and the New Economy', *International Socialism*, 121: 75–97.

Dunn, B. (2011) 'Value Theory in an Incomplete Capitalist System: reprioritizing the centrality of social labor in Marxist political economy', *Review of Radical Political Economics,* 43(4): 488–505.

Dunn, B. (2014) 'Making Sense of Austerity: the rationality in an irrational system', *The Economic and Labour Relations Review*, 25(3): 417–34.

Dunn, B. (2017) 'Against Neoliberalism as a Concept', *Capital and Class*, 41(3): 435–54.

Dunn, B. (2018) 'On the Prospects of a Return to Keynes: taking Keynes's political philosophy seriously', *Global Society*, 32: 302–23.

Eaton, J. (1951) *Marx against Keynes*. London: Lawrence & Wishart.

Eatwell, J. (1986) 'Keynes, Keynesians, and British Economic Policy', in Wattel, H.L., ed., *The Policy Consequences of John Maynard Keynes*. Basingstoke: Macmillan.

Eichengreen, B. (1984) 'Keynes and Protection', *The Journal of Economic History*, 44(2), 363–73.

Eichengreen, B. (2007) *The European Economy since 1945: coordinated capitalism and beyond*. Princeton, NJ: Princeton University Press.

Eichengreen, B. and Cairncross, A. (1983) *Stirling in Decline*. Oxford: Blackwell.

Elster, J. (1982) 'Marxism, Functionalism, and Game Theory', *Theory and Society*, 11(4), 453–82.

Elster, J. (1985) *Making Sense of Marx*. Cambridge: Cambridge University Press.

Ereira, A. (1981) *The Invergordon Mutiny*. London: Routledge & Kegan Paul.

Fan-Hung (1939) 'Keynes and Marx on the Theory of Capital Accumulation, Money and Interest', *Review of Economic Studies*, 7: 28–41.

Fetter, F.W. (1977) 'Lenin, Keynes and Inflation', *Economica*, 44(1): 77–80.

Fine, B. (2010) 'Locating Financialisation', *Historical Materialism*, 18: 97–116.

Fine, B. and Harris, L. (1979) *Rereading Capital*. London: Macmillan.

Fine, B. and Milonakis, D. (2009) *From Economics Imperialism to Freakonomics*. London: Routledge.

Fisher, I. (1907) *The Rate of Interest*. New York: Macmillan.

Fitzgibbons, A. (1988) *Keynes's Vision: a new political economy*. Oxford: Clarendon Press.

Fitzgibbons, A. (1991) 'The Significance of Keynes's Idealism', in Bateman, B.W. and Davis, J.B., eds, *Keynes and Philosophy*. Aldershot: Edward Elgar.

Flanders, M.J. (2019) 'Before and after Bretton Woods', in Dimand, R.W. and Hagemann, H., eds, *The Elgar Companion to John Maynard Keynes*. Edward Elgar ebook.

Flaschel, P. (2009) *The Macrodynamics of Capitalism*. Bielefeld: Springer.

Folbre, N. (1982) 'Exploitation Comes Home: a critique of the Marxian theory of family labour', *Cambridge Journal of Economics*, 6(4): 317–29.

Foley, D. (1986) *Understanding Capital: Marx's economic theory*. Cambridge, MA: Harvard University Press.

Forder, J. (2019) 'The Phillips Curve', in Dimand, R.W. and Hagemann, H., eds, *The Elgar Companion to John Maynard Keynes*. Edward Elgar ebook.

Foster, J.B. (2000) *Marx's Ecology*. New York: Monthly Review Press.

Foster, J.B. and McChesney, R.W. (2012) *The Endless Crisis: how monopoly-finance capital produces stagnation and upheaval from the USA to China*. New York: Monthly Review Press.

Fratianni, M. and Spinelli, F. (2006) 'Italian City-States and Financial Evolution', *European Review of Economic History*, 10(3): 257–78.

Frieden, J.A. (1991) 'Invested Interests: the politics of national economic policies in a world of global finance', *International Organization*, 45(4): 425–51.

Friedman, M. (1962) *Capitalism and Freedom*. Chicago: University of Chicago Press.

Friedman, M. (1987) 'Quantity Theory of Money', in Eatwell, J., Milgate, M. and Newman, P., eds, *The New Palgrave Dictionary of Economics, Vol. 4*. London: Macmillan.

Fukuyama, F. (1992) *The End of History and the Last Man*. London: Hamish Hamilton.

Galbraith, J[ames].K. (1996) 'Keynes, Einstein and Scientific Revolution', in Arestis, P., ed., *Keynes, Money and the Open Economy*. Cheltenham: Edward Elgar.

Galbraith, J[ohn].K. (1986) 'Keynes, Roosevelt, and the Complementary Revolutions', in Wattel, H.L., ed., *The Policy Consequences of John Maynard Keynes*. Basingstoke: Macmillan.

Galbraith, J[ohn].K. (1995) *Money: whence it came, where it went*. Harmondsworth: Penguin.

Gallagher, K.P. (2008) 'Introduction: international trade and the environment', in Gallagher, K.P., ed., *Handbook on Trade and the Environment*. Cheltenham: Edward Elgar.

Garrett, G. (2000) 'Shrinking States? Globalization and national autonomy', in Woods, N, ed., *The Political Economy of Globalization*. Basingstoke: Macmillan.

Gereffi, G., Humphrey, J. and Sturgeon, T. (2005) 'The Governance of Global Value Chains', *Review of International Political Economy*, 12(1): 78–104.

Gerrard, B. (1988) 'Keynesian Economics: the road to nowhere?', in Hillard, J., ed., *Keynes in Retrospect: the legacy of the Keynesian revolution*. Aldershot: Edward Elgar.

Giddens, A. (1981) *A Contemporary Critique of Historical Materialism*. London: Macmillan.

Glyn, A. (1977) 'Inflation', in Green, F. and Nore, P., eds, *Economics: an anti-text*. London: Macmillan.

Glyn, A. (2006) *Capitalism Unleashed: finance, globalization, and welfare*. Oxford: Oxford University Press.

Goldstein, J. and Tyfield, D. (2018) 'Green Keynesianism: bringing the entrepreneurial state back in (to question)?' *Science as Culture*, 27(1): 74–97.

Goldstein, J.P. (2009) 'A Keynes-Marx Theory of Investment', in Goldstein, J.P. and Hilliard, M.G., eds, *Heterodox Macroeconomics: Keynes, Marx and globalization*. Abingdon: Routledge.

Goldstein, J.P. and Hillard, M.G. (2009) 'Introduction: a second-generation synthesis of heterodox macroeconomics principles', in Goldstein, J.P., and Hillard, M.G., eds, *Heterodox Macroeconomics: Keynes, Marx and globalization*. Abingdon: Routledge.

Goodwin, R.M. (2014) 'A Growth Cycle', paper presented at the First World Congress of the Econometric Society, Rome.

Gordon, R.J. (2000) 'Does the "new economy" measure up to the great inventions of the past?', National Bureau of Economic Research Working Paper No. 7833.

Gourevich, P.A. (1989) 'Keynesian Politics: the political sources of economic policy choices', in Hall, P.A., ed., *The Political Power of Economic Ideas: Keynesianism across nations*. Princeton, NJ: Princeton University Press.

Gray, J. (2011) 'A Point of View: the revolution of capitalism', BBC News, available at www.bbc.com/news/magazine-14764357 (accessed 14 December 2020).

Greenspan, A. (2008) *The Age of Turbulence*. London: Penguin.

Hadley, E.M. (1989) 'The Diffusion of Keynesian Ideas in Japan', in Hall, P.A., ed., *The Political Power of Economic Ideas: Keynesianism across nations*. Princeton, NJ, Princeton University Press.

Hagemann, H. (2019) 'Say's Law', in Dimand, R.W. and Hagemann, H., eds, *The Elgar Companion to John Maynard Keynes*. Edward Elgar ebook.

Halevi, J. and Kriesler, P. (1992) 'An Introduction to the Traverse in Economic Theory', in Halevi, J., Laibman, D. and Nell, E.J., eds, *Beyond the Steady State*. London: Palgrave Macmillan.

Hall, P.A. (1989a) 'Introduction', in Hall, P.A., ed., *The Political Power of Economic Ideas: Keynesianism across nations*. Princeton, NJ: Princeton University Press.

Hall, P.A. (1989b) 'Conclusion: the politics of Keynesian ideas', in Hall, P.A., ed., *The Political Power of Economic Ideas: Keynesianism across nations*. Princeton, NJ: Princeton University Press.

Hall, P.A. ed. (1989c) *The Political Power of Economic Ideas: Keynesianism across nations*. Princeton, NJ: Princeton University Press.

Hansen, A.H. (1953) *A Guide to Keynes*. New York: McGraw Hill.

Harcourt, G.C. (2004) 'The Economics of Keynes and Its Theoretical and Practical Importance', Centre for Alternative Economic Policy Research Discussion Paper No. 3, June.

Harcourt, G.C. and Sardoni, C. (1996) 'The General Theory of Employment, Interest and Money: three views', in Arestis, P., ed. *Keynes, Money and the Open Economy*. Cheltenham: Edward Elgar.

Hardeen, I. (2019) 'Lydia Vasilievna Lopokova', in Dimand, R.W. and Hagemann, H., eds, *The Elgar Companion to John Maynard Keynes*. Edward Elgar ebook.

Harman, C. (1984) *Explaining the Crisis*. London: Bookmarks.

Harman, C. (2009) *Zombie Capitalism*. London: Bookmarks.

Harris, J.M. (2013) *Green Keynesianism: beyond standard growth paradigms*, GDAE Working Paper No. 13-02, Tufts University, available at https://ideas.repec.org/p/dae/daepap/13-02.html (accessed 1 May 2020).

Harris, S.E. (1953) 'Foreword', in Hansen, A.H., *A Guide to Keynes*. New York: McGraw Hill.

Harrod, R.F. (1939) 'An Essay in Dynamic Theory', *The Economic Journal*, 49(193): 14–33.

Harrod, R.F. (1951) *The Life of John Maynard Keynes*. London: Macmillan.

Harvey, D. (2005) *A Brief History of Neoliberalism*. Oxford: Oxford University Press.

Hayek, F.A. (1947) *The Road to Serfdom*. Sydney: Dymock's Book Arcade.

Hayek, F.A. (1976) *Choice in Currency: a way to stop inflation*. London: Institute of Economic Affairs.

Heilbroner, R. (1999) *The Worldly Philosophers*. Harmondsworth: Penguin.

Helburn, S. (1991) 'Burke and Keynes', in Bateman, B.W. and Davis, J.B., eds, *Keynes and Philosophy*. Aldershot: Edward Elgar.

Helleiner, E. (1994) *States and the Reemergence of Global Finance*. Ithaca, NY: Cornell University Press.

Henwood, D. (1998) *Wall Street*. London: Verso.

Henwood, D. (2003) *After the New Economy*. New York: New Press.

Herod, A. (2018) *Labor*. Cambridge: Polity.

Hicks, J.R. (1937) 'Mr. Keynes and the "Classics"; a suggested interpretation', *Econometrica: Journal of the Econometric Society*, 5(2): 147–59.

Hillard, J. (1988) 'J.M. Keynes: the last of the Cambridge economists', in Hillard, J., ed., *J.M. Keynes in Retrospect: the legacy of the Keynesian revolution*. Aldershot: Edward Elgar.

Hodgson, G. (1982) *Capitalism, Value and Exploitation: a radical theory*. Oxford: Martin Robertson.

Hodgson, G.M. (2004) 'Is It All in Keynes's General Theory?' *Post-Autistic Economics Review*, 25: 21–4.

Hollander, S. (2011) 'Making the Most of Anomaly in the History of Economic Thought: Smith, Marx-Engels, and Keynes', in Aman, A, Weinblatt, J. and Young, W., eds, *Perspectives on Keynesian Economics*. Heidelberg: Springer.

Hollander, S. (2019) 'Thomas Robert Malthus', in Dimand, R.W. and Hagemann, H., eds, *The Elgar Companion to John Maynard Keynes*. Edward Elgar ebook.

Homer, S. and Sylla, R. (2005) *A History of Interest Rates*. Hoboken, NJ: Wiley.

Hoover, K.D. (2012) *Applied Intermediate Macroeconomics*. Cambridge: Cambridge University Press.

IMF (2011) 'Tensions from the Two-Speed Recovery: unemployment, commodities, and capital flows', World Economic Outlook, 11 April, IMF.

IMF (2020) 'International Financial Statistics', available at https://data.imf.org/regular.aspx?key=61545869 (accessed 14 December 2020).

Ingham, G. (2004) *The Nature of Money*. Cambridge: Polity.

Itoh, M. (2005) 'The New Interpretation and the Value of Money', in Moseley F., ed., *Marx's Theory of Money: modern appraisals*. Springer ebook.

Itoh, M. and Lapavitsas, C. (1999) *Political Economy of Money and Finance*. Basingstoke: Macmillan.

Jayawardena, L. (1990) 'Preface', in Marglin, S.A. and Schor, J.B., eds, *Reinterpreting the Postwar Experience*. Oxford: Clarendon.

Jevons, W.S. (1957) *The Theory of Political Economy*, 5th edition. New York: Sentry Press.

Johnson, C. (1982) *MITI and the Japanese Miracle: the growth of industrial policy, 1925–1975*. Stanford, CA: Stanford University Press.

Jones, P. (1997) *The Italian City-State*. Oxford: Clarendon.

Kahn, R.F. (1931) 'The Relation of Home Investment to Unemployment', *The Economic Journal*, 41(162): 173–98.

Kahn, [R.F.] (1976) 'Historical Origins of the International Monetary Fund', in Thirlwall, A.P., ed., *Keynes and International Monetary Relations*. London: Macmillan.

Kalecki, M. (1943) 'Political Aspects of Full Employment', *The Political Quarterly*, 14(4), 322–30.

Kalecki, M. (1971) 'Outline of a Theory of the Business Cycle', in *Selected Essays on the Dynamics of the Capitalist Economy 1933–1970*. Cambridge: Cambridge University Press.

Kenwood, A.G. and Lougheed, A.L. (1992) *The Growth of the International Economy: 1820–1990*. London: Routledge.

Keohane, R.O. (2005) *After Hegemony*. Princeton, NJ: Princeton University Press.

Keynes, J.M. (1921) *A Treatise on Probability*. London: Macmillan and Co.

Keynes, J.M. (1923) A Tract on Monetary Reform, available in Keynes, J.M. (1978, online 2012) *The Collected Writings of John Maynard Keynes*, ed. E. Johnson and D. Moggridge. London: Royal Economic Society.

Keynes, J.M. (1973 [1936]) *The General Theory of Employment, Interest and Money*. London: Macmillan.

Keynes, J.M. (1978, online 2012) *Collected Writings of John Maynard Keynes, Vols I–XXX*, ed. E. Johnson and D. Moggridge. Cambridge: Cambridge University Press.

Keynes, J.M. (2011 [1930]) *A Treatise on Money*. Mansfield Center, CT: Martino.

Kicillof, A. (2018) *Keynes and the General Theory Revisited*. London: Routledge.

Kincaid, J. (2006) 'Finance, Trust and the Power of Capital: a symposium on the contribution of Costas Lapavitsas. Editorial introduction', *Historical Materialism*, 14(1): 31–48.

Kindleberger, C.P. (1973) *The World in Depression*. London: Allen Lane.

Kindleberger, C.P. (1984) *A Financial History of Western Europe*. London: George Allen & Unwin.

King, J.E. (2002) *A History of Post Keynesian Economics since 1936*. Cheltenham: Edward Elgar.

King, J.E. (2015) *Advanced Introduction to Post Keynesian Economics*. Cheltenham: Edward Elgar.

Klein, L.R. (1947) *The Keynesian Revolution*. New York: Macmillan.

Konings, M. (2010) 'Rethinking Neoliberalism and the Crisis: beyond the re-regulation agenda', in Konings, M., ed., *The Great Credit Crash*. London: Verso.

Kregel, J.A. (1976) 'Economic Methodology in the Face of Uncertainty: the modelling methods of Keynes and the post-Keynesians', *The Economic Journal*, 86(342): 209–25.

Krippner G.R. (2011) *Capitalizing on Crisis: the political origins of the rise of finance*. Cambridge, MA: Harvard University Press

Krugman, P. (1990) *Rethinking International Trade*. Cambridge, MA: MIT Press.

Krugman, P. (1993) *Geography and Trade*. Leuven, Belgium: Leuven University Press.

Krugman, P. (2012) 'Europe's Austerity Madness', *New York Times*, 27 September.

Laibman, D. (1992) *Value, Technical Change, and Crisis: explorations in Marxist economic theory*. Armonk, NY: M.E. Sharpe.

Laidler, D. (2006) 'Keynes and the Birth of Modern Macroeconomics', in Backhouse, R.E. and Bateman, B.W., eds, *The Cambridge Companion to Keynes*. Cambridge: Cambridge University Press.

Lapavitsas, C. (2006) 'Relations of Power and Trust in Contemporary Finance', *Historical Materialism*, 14(1): 129–54.

Lapavitsas, C. (2013) *Profiting without Producing: how finance exploits us all*. London: Verso.

Lapides, K. (1992) 'Henryk Grossmann and the Debate on the Theoretical Status of Marx's "Capital"', *Science & Society*, 56(2): 133–62.

Lavoie, M. (2009) *Introduction to Post-Keynesian Economics*. Basingstoke: Palgrave Macmillan.

Lawlor, M.S. (2006) *The Economics of Keynes in Historical Context: an intellectual history of the* General Theory. Basingstoke: Palgrave Macmillan.

Lawson, T. (1988) 'Probability and Uncertainty in Economic Analysis', *Journal of Post-Keynesian Economics*, 11(1): 38–65.

Lawson, T. (1997) *Economics and Reality*. London: Routledge.

Lazonick, W. (2012) 'The Financialization of the US corporation: what has been lost, and how it can be regained', *Seattle University Law Review*, 36: 857–908.

Lederer, E. (1936) 'Commentary on Keynes – II', *Social Research*, 3(4): 478–87.

Lee, B.A. (1989) 'The Miscarriage of Necessity and Invention: proto-Keynesian and democratic states in the 1930s', in Hall, P.A., ed., *The Political Power of Economic Ideas: Keynesianism across nations*. Princeton, NJ: Princeton University Press.

Leeson, R. (2013a) 'Phillips A.W.H.', in Cate, T., ed., *An Encyclopedia of Keynesian Economics*. Edward Elgar ebook.

Leeson, R. (2013b) 'Phillips Curve', in Cate, T., ed., *An Encyclopedia of Keynesian Economics*. Edward Elgar ebook.

Leijonhufvud, A. (2006) 'Keynes as a Marshallian', in Backhouse, R.E. and Bateman, B.W., eds, *The Cambridge Companion to Keynes*. Cambridge: Cambridge University Press.

Lekachman, R. (1967) *The Age of Keynes: a biographical study*. Harmondsworth: Penguin.

Lekachman, R. (1986) 'The Radical Keynes', in Wattel, H.L., ed., *The Policy Consequences of John Maynard Keynes*. Basingstoke: Macmillan.

Levidow, L. (2014) 'What Green Economy? Diverse agendas, their tensions and potential futures', IKD Working Paper No. 73, Open University.

Linder, M.C. (1977) *Anti-Samuelson, Vols 1–2*. New York: Urizen.

Lipietz, A. (1985) *The Enchanted World: inflation, credit and the world crisis*. London: Verso.

Littleboy, B. (2019) 'G.L.S. Shackle', in Dimand, R.W. and Hagemann, H., eds, *The Elgar Companion to John Maynard Keynes*. Edward Elgar ebook.

Lopez, J.G. and Assous, M. (2010) *Michael Kalecki*. Basingstoke: Palgrave Macmillan.

Lucarelli, B. (2011) *The Economics of Financial Turbulence*. Cheltenham: Edward Elgar.

Lyotard, J.F. (1984) *The Postmodern Condition: a report on knowledge*. Minneapolis: University of Minnesota Press.

MacIntyre, A. (1967) *A Short History of Ethics*. London: Routledge & Kegan Paul.

MacLean, J. (2000) 'Philosophical Roots of Globalization and Philosophical Routes to Globalization', in Germain, R.D., ed., *Globalization and Its Critics*. Basingstoke: Macmillan.

Maddison, A. (2003) *The World Economy: historical statistics*. Paris: OECD.

Magnus, G. (2011) 'Give Karl Marx a Chance to Save the World Economy', Bloomberg, 29 August, available at https://georgemagnus.com/give-karl-marx-a-chance-to-save-the-world-economy (accessed 14 December 2020).

Mandel, E. (1969) *Marxist Economic Theory*. London: Merlin.

Mandel, E. (1978) *The Second Slump*. London: NLB.

Mann, G. (2013) 'Keynes Resurrected? Saving civilization, again and again', available at http://ias.umn.edu/wp-content/upLoads/2013/11/Geoff-Mann-Paper-on-Keynes-and-Civilization.pdf (accessed 23 August 2016).

Mann, G. (2016) 'Keynes Resurrected? Saving civilization, again and again', *Dialogues in Human Geography*, 6(2): 119–34.

Mann, G. (2017a) *In the Long Run We Are All Dead: Keynesianism, political economy, and revolution*. London: Verso.

Mann, G. (2017b) *The General Theory of Employment, Interest and Money: a reader's companion*. London: Verso.

Marglin, S.A. and Bhaduri, A. (1990) 'Profit Squeeze and Keynesian Theory', in Marglin, S.A. and Schor, J.B., eds, *Reinterpreting the Postwar Experience*. Oxford: Clarendon.

Marshall, A. (2009) *Principles of Economics, 8th edition*. New York: Cosimo Classics.

Marx, K. (1970) *A Contribution to the Critique of Political Economy*. Moscow: Progress.

Marx, K. (1973) *Grundrisse*. New York: Random House.

Marx, K. (1975) *Early Writings*. Harmondsworth: Penguin.

Marx, K. (1976) *Capital: a critique of political economy, Vol. I*. Harmondsworth: Penguin.

Marx, K. (1978) *Capital: a critique of political economy, Vol. II*. Harmondsworth: Penguin.

Marx, K. (1981) *Capital: a critique of political economy, Vol. III*. Harmondsworth: Penguin.

Marx, K. and Engels, F. (1983) *Letters on 'Capital'*. London: New Park.

Marx, K. and Engels, F. (2010) *Marx and Engels Collected Works, Vols 1–49*. Lawrence & Wishart ebook.

Masterson, T. (1998) 'Household Labour, the Value of Labour-Power and Capitalism', paper prepared for the 1998 Eastern Economic Association Conference's International Working Group on Value Theory.

Matthews, R.C.O. (1968) 'Why Has Britain Had Full Employment since the War?', *The Economic Journal*, 78(311): 555–69.

Mattick, P. (1971) *Marx and Keynes: the limits of the mixed economy*. London: Merlin.

McCormack G. (2002) 'Breaking the Iron Triangle', *New Left Review*, 13.

McNally, D. (2011) *Global Slump*. Pontypool: Merlin.

Meek, R. (1956) 'The Place of Keynes in the History of Economic Thought', in Singh, V.B., ed., *Keynesian Economics: a symposium*. Delhi: People's Publishing House.

Meek, R. (1967) *Economics and Ideology and Other Essays*. London: Chapman and Hall.

Mehrling, P. (2012) 'A Money View of Credit and Debt', paper prepared for the 'Economics of Credit and Debt' session at the INET/CIGI False Dichotomies conference, Waterloo, Ontario, Canada, 18 November.

Melitz, J. (1976) *Primitive and Modern Money: an interdisciplinary approach*. Reading, MA: Addison-Wesley.

Milberg, W. and Winkler, D. (2010) 'Financialisation and the Dynamics of Offshoring in the USA', *Cambridge Journal of Economics*, 34: 275–93.

Milgate, M. (1987) 'Keynes's General Theory', in Eatwell, J., Milgate, M. and Newman, P., eds, *The New Palgrave Dictionary of Economics, Vol. 3*. London: Macmillan.

Miliband, R. (1983) 'State Power and Class Interests', *New Left Review*, 138: 57–68.

Minsky, H.P. (1986) *Stabilizing an Unstable Economy*. New York: McGraw Hill.

Minsky, H.P. (2008) *John Maynard Keynes*. New York: McGraw Hill.

Moggridge, D. (2019) 'World War II', in Dimand, R.W. and Hagemann, H., eds, *The Elgar Companion to John Maynard Keynes*. Edward Elgar ebook.

Moggridge, D.E. (1976) *Keynes*. London: Macmillan.

Moggridge, D.E. (1992) *Maynard Keynes: an economist's biography*. London: Routledge.

Moore, B.J. (1988) 'The Endogenous Money Supply', *Journal of Post Keynesian Economics*, 10(3): 372–85.

Moore G.E. (1993) *Principia Ethica*. Cambridge: Cambridge University Press.

Moran, M. (1991) *The Politics of the Financial Services Revolution*. Basingstoke: MacMillan.

Mott, T. (1989) 'Kaleckianism vs. "New" Keynesianism', Economics Working Paper Archive wp_25, Levy Economics Institute.

Murray, P. (2005) 'Money as Displaced Social Form: why value cannot be independent of price', in Moseley F., ed., *Marx's Theory of Money: modern appraisals*. Springer ebook.

Myrdal, G. (1957) *Economic Theory and Under-Developed Regions*. London: Gerald Duckworth.

Negri, A. (1988) *Revolution Retrieved: selected writings on Marx, Keynes, capitalist crisis and new social subjects 1967–1983*, transl. E. Emery and J. Merrington. London: Red Notes.

Niggle, C.J. (1991) 'The Endogenous Money Supply Theory: an institutionalist appraisal', *Journal of Economic Issues*, 25(1): 137–51.

O'Brien, K. (2012) 'Global Environmental Change II: from adaptation to deliberate transformation', *Progress in Human Geography*, 36(5): 667–76.

O'Brien, R. (1992) *Global Financial Integration: the end of geography*. London: Pinter.

O'Donnell, R.M. (1989) *Keynes. Philosophy, Economics and Politics: the philosophical foundations of Keynes's thought and their influence on his economics and politics*. Basingstoke: Macmillan.

O'Donnell, R.M. (1991) 'Keynes's Political Philosophy', in Barber, W.J. , ed., *Perspectives on the History of Economic Thought, Vol VI*. Aldershot: Edward Elgar.

OECD (2018) 'OECD Data', available at data.oecd.org (accessed 10 December 2018).

OECD (2020) 'Crude Oil Production (Indicator)', available at www.oecd-ilibrary. org/energy/crude-oil-production/indicator/english_4747b431-en (accessed 31 May 2020).

oica.net (2020) 'International Organization of Motor Vehicle Manufacturers', data, available at oica.net (accessed 3 May 2020).

Onuf, N. (1997) 'A Constructivist Manifesto', in Burch, K. and Denemark, R.A., eds, *Constituting International Political Economy*. Boulder, CO: Lynne Rienner.

Ormerod, P (1994) *The Death of Economics*. London: Faber and Faber.

Ortiz-Ospina, E. and Roser, M. (2018) 'Our World in Data', available at ourworldindata.org (accessed 10 September 2018).

Palley, T.I. (2015) 'Money, Fiscal Policy, and Interest Rates: a critique of modern monetary theory', *Review of Political Economy*, 27(1): 1–23.

Panico, C. (1987) 'Liquidity Preference', in Eatwell, J., Milgate, M. and Newman, P., eds, *The New Palgrave Dictionary of Economics, Vol. 3*. London: Macmillan.

Papadimitriou, D.B. and Wray, L.R. (2008) 'Introduction' in Minsky, H.P., *John Maynard Keynes*. New York: McGraw Hill.

Parboni R (1981) *The Dollar and Its Rivals*. London: New Left Books.

Parijs, P. van (1982) 'Functionalist Marxism Rehabilitated', *Theory and Society*, 11(4): 497–511.

Passmore, J. (1968) *A Hundred Years of Philosophy*. Harmondsworth: Penguin.

Patinkin, D. (1987) 'John Maynard Keynes', in Eatwell, J., Milgate, M. and Newman, P., eds, *The New Palgrave Dictionary of Economics, Vol. 3*. London: Macmillan.

Peden, G.C. (2006) 'Keynes and British Economic Policy', in Backhouse, R.E. and Bateman, B.W., eds, *The Cambridge Companion to Keynes*. Cambridge: Cambridge University Press.

Perry, G.L. (2008) 'Demand-Pull Inflation', in Durlauf, S.N. and Blume, L.E., eds, *The New Palgrave Dictionary of Economics*. London: Macmillan.

Phillips, A.W. (1958) 'The Relation between Unemployment and the Rate of Change of Money Wage Rates in the United Kingdom, 1861–1957', *Economica*, 25(100): 283–99.

Pigou, A.C. (1933) *The Theory of Unemployment*. London: Macmillan.

Piketty, T. (2014) *Capital in the Twenty-First Century*. Cambridge, MA: Belknap Press.

Pilbeam, B. (2003) 'Whatever Happened to Economic Liberalism?' *Politics*, 23(2): 82–8.

Pilling, G. (1986) The Crisis of Keynesian Economics, available at www.marxists.org/archive/pilling/works/keynes (accessed 24 June 2020).

Polanyi, K. (2001). *The Great Transformation*. Boston: Beacon Press.

Pollin, R. and Zhu, A. (2006) 'Inflation and Economic Growth: a cross-country non-linear analysis', *Journal of Post Keynesian Economics*, 28(4): 593–614.

Popper, K. (1944) 'The Poverty of Historicism, I', *Economica*, 11(42): 86–103.

Pradella, L. (2014) *Globalization and the Critique of Political Economy: new insights from Marx's writings*. London: Routledge.

Punnett, R.M. (1994) *British Government and Politics*, 6th edition, Aldershot: Dartmouth.

Radice, H. (1988) 'Keynes and the Policy of Practical Protectionism', in Hillard, J., ed., *J.M. Keynes in Retrospect: the legacy of the Keynesian revolution*. Aldershot: Edward Elgar.

Reddaway, W.B. (1964) 'The General Theory of Employment, Interest, and Money', in Lekachman, R., ed., *Keynes' General Theory: reports of three decades*. New York: St Martin's Press.

Reynolds, P.J. (1987) *Political Economy; a synthesis of Kaleckian and post Keynesian economics*. Sussex: Wheatsheaf.

Ricardo, D. (1951) *Principles of Political Economy*. Cambridge: Cambridge University Press.

Rivot, S. (2019) 'Unemployment', in Dimand, R.W. and Hagemann, H., eds, *The Elgar Companion to John Maynard Keynes*. Edward Elgar ebook.

Robinson, J. (1964) *Economic Philosophy*. Harmondsworth: Pelican.

Robinson, J. (1966) *An Essay on Marxian Economics*, 2nd edition. London: Macmillan.

Robinson, J. (1978) *Contributions to Modern Economics*. Oxford: Blackwell.

Robinson, J. and Eatwell, J. (1973) *An Introduction to Modern Economics*. London: McGraw Hill.

Rochon, L.P. and Rossi, S. (2013) 'Endogenous Money: the evolutionary versus revolutionary views', *Review of Keynesian Economics*, 1(2): 210–29.

Roemer, J.E. (1982) 'Methodological Individualism and Deductive Marxism', *Theory and Society*, 11(4): 513–20.

Rosanvallon, P. (1989) 'The Development of Keynesianism in France', in Hall, P.A., ed., *The Political Power of Economic Ideas: Keynesianism across nations*. Princeton, NJ: Princeton University Press.

Rosdolsky, R. (1977) *The Making of Marx's Capital.* London: Pluto.

Rosenberg, J. (2006) 'Why Is There No International Historical Sociology?' *European Journal of International Relations* 12(3): 307–40.

Rotheim, R.J. (1988) 'Keynes and the Language of Uncertainty', *Journal of Post Keynesian Economics,* 11(1): 82–99.

Rotta, T.N. (2018) 'Unproductive Accumulation in the USA: a new analytical framework', *Cambridge Journal of Economics,* 42: 1367–92.

Roubini, M. (2011). 'Marx was Right', *Wall Street Journal,* 12 August.

Runciman, D. (2014) *The Confidence Trap: a history of democracy in crisis.* Princeton, NJ: Princeton University Press.

Rupert, M. (1995) *Producing Hegemony.* Cambridge: Cambridge University Press.

Russett, B. (1985) 'The Mysterious Case of Vanishing Hegemony; or, is Mark Twain really dead?', *International Organization,* 39(2): 207–31.

Salant, W.S. (1989) 'The Spread of Keynesian Doctrines and Practices in the United States', in Hall, P.A., ed., *The Political Power of Economic Ideas: Keynesianism across nations.* Princeton, NJ: Princeton University Press.

Samuelson, P.A., Hancock, K. and Wallace, R. (1973) *Economics.* Sydney: McGraw Hill.

Sardoni, C. (1987) *Marx and Keynes on Economic Recession: the theory of unemployment and effective demand.* New York: New York University Press.

Sawyer, M. (1996) 'Money, Finance and Interest Rates: some post Keynesian reflections', in Arestis, P., ed., *Keynes, Money and the Open Economy.* Cheltenham: Edward Elgar.

Sawyer, M. (2019) 'Michael Kalecki', in Dimand, R.W. and Hagemann, H., eds, *The Elgar Companion to John Maynard Keynes.* Edward Elgar ebook.

Say, J.B. (1827) *A Treatise of Political Economy.* Philadelphia: John Grigg.

Schumpeter, J.A. (1954a) *History of Economic Analysis.* London: Routledge.

Schumpeter, J.A. (1954b) *Capitalism, Socialism, and Democracy,* 4th edition. London: Unwin University Books.

Schumpeter, J.A. (2003) 'John Maynard Keynes 1883–1946', *The American Economic Review,* 36(4): 495–518.

Schwartzman, D. (2011) 'Green New Deal: an ecosocialist perspective', *Capitalism Nature Socialism,* 22(3): 49–56.

Shackle, G.L.S. (1972) *Epistemics and Economics: a critique of economic doctrines.* Cambridge: Cambridge University Press.

Shaikh, A. (2016) *Capitalism: competition, conflict, crises.* Oxford: Oxford University Press.

Sheehan B. (2009) *Understanding Keynes' General Theory.* Basingstoke: Palgrave Macmillan.

Shionaya, Y. (1991) 'Sidgwick, Moore and Keynes: a philosophical analysis of Keynes's "My Early Beliefs"', in Bateman, B.W. and Davis, J.B. ,eds, *Keynes and Philosophy.* Aldershot: Edward Elgar.

Sjöberg, O. (2000) 'Unemployment and Unemployment Benefits in the OECD 1960–1990 – and empirical test of neo-classical economic theory', *Work, Employment and Society,* 14(1): 51–76.

Skidelsky, R. (1968) 'When They Realised the Game Was Up', *The Times,* 4 December: 27.

Skidelsky, R. (1983) *John Maynard Keynes, Vol. I: Hopes Betrayed, 1883–1920.* London: Macmillan.

Skidelsky, R. (1992) *John Maynard Keynes, Vol. II: The Economist as Saviour 1920–1937*. London: Macmillan.

Skidelsky, R. (2000) *John Maynard Keynes, Vol. III: Fighting for Freedom, 1937–1946*. New York: Viking Penguin.

Skidelsky, R. (2009) *Keynes: the return of the master*. London: Allen Lane.

Skidelsky, R. (2013) 'The Influence of Burke and Moore on Keynes', in Cate, T., ed., *An Encyclopedia of Keynesian Economics*. Edward Elgar ebook.

Skidelsky, R. (2014) 'The Origins of Keynesian Economics', in Forstater, M. and Wray, L.R., eds, *Keynes for the Twenty-First Century: the continuing relevance of the general theory*. New York: Palgrave Macmillan.

Skidelsky, R. (2019) 'The General Theory of Employment, Interest and Money', in Dimand, R.W. and Hagemann, H., eds, *The Elgar Companion to John Maynard Keynes*. Edward Elgar ebook.

Skocpol, T. (1979) 'State and Revolution', *Theory and Society*, 7(1–2): 7–95.

Sloman, J. and Norris K. (1999) *Economics*. Sydney: Prentice Hall.

Smith, A. (1997) *The Wealth of Nations, Books I–III*. Harmondsworth: Penguin.

Smith, A. (1999) *The Wealth of Nations, Books IV–V*. Harmondsworth: Penguin.

Smithin, T. (2016) 'Endogenous Money, Fiscal Policy, Interest Rates and the Exchange Rate Regime: a comment on Pally, Tymoigne and Wray', *Review of Political Economy*, 28(1): 64–78.

Soderberg, S. (2014) *Debtfare States and the Poverty Industry*. London: Routledge.

Solt, F. (2020) 'The Standardized World Income Inequality Database, Versions 8–9', available at https://dataverse.harvard.edu/dataset.xhtml?persistentId=doi:10.7910/DVN/LM4OWF (accessed 10 March 2020).

Soros, G. (2013) 'Fallibility, Reflexivity, and the Human Uncertainty Principle', *Journal of Economic Methodology*, 20(4), 309–29.

Steedman, I. (1977) *Marx after Sraffa*. London: NLB.

Stewart, M. (1972) *Keynes and After*, 2nd edition. Harmondsworth: Penguin.

Stiglitz, J. (2002) *Globalization and Its Discontents*. London: Penguin.

Stiglitz, J.E. (2010) *Freefall: America, free markets, and the sinking of the world economy*. New York and London: WW Norton & Company.

Stigum, M. and Crescenzi, A. (2007) *Stigum's Money Market*, 4th edition. New York: McGraw Hill.

Stockhammer, E. (2008) 'Is the NAIRU Theory a Monetarist, New Keynesian, post Keynesian or a Marxist Theory?' *Metroeconomica*, 59(3), 479–510.

Strange, S. (1986) *Casino Capitalism*. Oxford: Oxford University Press.

Strange, S. (1998) *The Retreat of the State: diffusion of power in the world economy*. Cambridge: Cambridge University Press.

Sweezy, P.M. (1956) 'John Maynard Keynes', in Singh, V.B., ed., *Keynesian Economics: a symposium*. Delhi: People's Publishing House.

Sweezy, P.M. (1964) 'John Maynard Keynes', in Lekachman, R., ed., *Keynes' General Theory: reports of three decades*. New York: St Martin's Press.

Szalavetz, A. (2015) 'Post-Crisis Approaches to State Intervention: new developmentalism or industrial policy as usual?' *Competition & Change*, 19(1): 70–83.

Tabb, W.K. (1999) *Reconstructing Political Economy*. London: Routledge.

Tarshis, L. (1947) *The Elements of Economics*. Boston: Houghton Mifflin.

Taylor, A.J.P. (1965) *English History 1914–1945*. Oxford: Clarendon Press.

Thirlwall, A.P., ed. (1976) *Keynes and International Monetary Relations*. London: Macmillan.

Tienhaara, K. (2014) 'Varieties of Green Capitalism: economy and environment in the wake of the global financial crisis', *Environmental Politics*, 23(2): 187–204.

Tily, G. (2007) *Keynes Betrayed*. Basingstoke: Palgrave Macmillan.

Tily, G. (2019) 'Keynesianism in the United Kingdom', in Dimand, R.W. and Hagemann, H., eds, *The Elgar Companion to John Maynard Keynes*. Edward Elgar ebook.

Tobin, J. (1972) 'Inflation and Unemployment', *American Economic Review*, 62(1): 1–18.

Tobin, J. (1986) 'Keynes's Policies in Theory and Practice', in Wattel, H.L., ed., *The Policy Consequences of John Maynard Keynes*. Basingstoke: Macmillan.

Toporowski, J. (2015) 'Neologism as Theoretical Innovation in Economics', in O'Sullivan, P., Allington, N.F.B. and Esposito, M., eds, *The Philosophy, Politics and Economics of Finance in the 21st Century: from hubris to disgrace*. Abingdon: Routledge.

Trautwein, H.-M. (2019) 'Bertil Ohlin', in Dimand, R.W. and Hagemann, H., eds, *The Elgar Companion to John Maynard Keynes*. Edward Elgar ebook.

Tsuru, S. (1994) *Economic Theory and Capitalist Society*. Aldershot: Edward Elgar.

Tullock, G (1987) 'Public Choice', in Eatwell, J., Milgate, M. and Newman, P., eds, *The New Palgrave: A Dictionary of Economics*. London: Macmillan.

Turner, C.B. (1969) *An Analysis of Soviet Views on John Maynard Keynes*. Durham, NC: Duke University Press.

USGS (2018) 'Minerals Information', available at https://minerals.usgs.gov/minerals/pubs/commodity/gold (accessed 14 November 2018).

Vane, H.R. (2013) 'Inflation', in Cate, T., ed., *An Encyclopedia of Keynesian Economics*. Edward Elgar ebook.

Varoufakis, Y., Halevi, J. and Tehocarakis, N.J. (2011) *Modern Political Economics*. London: Routledge.

Venugopal, R. (2015) 'Neoliberalism as a Concept', *Economy and Society*, 44(2): 165–87.

Vilar, P. (1984) *A History of Gold and Money 1450–1920*. London: Verso.

Wattel, H.L. (1986) 'Introduction', in Wattel, H.L., ed., *The Policy Consequences of John Maynard Keynes*. Basingstoke: Macmillan.

Weber, M. (1930) *The Protestant Ethic and the Spirit of Capitalism*. London: Unwin.

Weeks, J. (1988) 'Value and Protection in the *General Theory*', in Hillard, J., ed., *J.M. Keynes in Retrospect: the legacy of the Keynesian Revolution*. Aldershot: Edward Elgar.

Weeks, J. (2011) 'Neoclassical Inflation: no theory there', Research on Money and Finance Discussion Paper No 33, available at https://core.ac.uk/download/pdf/6258880.pdf (accessed 2 November 2017).

Weir, M. (1989) 'Ideas and Politics: the acceptance of Keynesianism in Britain and the United States', in Hall, P.A., ed., *The Political Power of Economic Ideas: Keynesianism across nations*. Princeton, NJ: Princeton University Press.

Weir, M. and Skocpol, T. (1985) 'State Structures and the Possibilities for "Keynesian" Responses to the Great Depression in Sweden, Britain, and the United States', in Evans, P.B., Rueschemeyer, D. and Skocpol, T., eds, *Bringing the State Back In*. Cambridge: Cambridge University Press.

Williams, M. (2000) 'Why Marx Neither Has Nor Needs a Commodity Theory of Money', *Review of Political Economy*, 12(4): 435–51.

Williamson, J. (1985) 'On the System in Bretton Woods', *The American Economic Review*, 75(2): 74–9.

Winch, D. (1989) 'Keynes, Keynesianism and State Intervention', in Hall, P.A., ed., *The Political Power of Economic Ideas: Keynesianism across nations*. Princeton, NJ: Princeton University Press.

Woolley L (1963) 'The Beginnings of Civilization', in Hawkes, J. and Woolley, L., eds, *History of Mankind: cultural and scientific development, Vol I*. London: George Allen & Unwin.

World Bank (various dates) 'World Development Indicators', available at http://databank.worldbank.org (accessed 14 December 2020).

Wray, L.R. (1992) 'Alternative Approaches to Money and Interest Rates', *Journal of Economic Issues*, 26(4): 1145–78.

Wray L.R. (2008) 'The Commodities Market Bubble: money manager capitalism and the financialization of commodities', Public Policy Brief No 96, Levy Economics Institute of Bard College.

Wray, L.R. (2014) 'Introduction: the continuing legacy of John Maynard Keynes', in Forstater, M. and Wray, L.R., eds, *Keynes for the Twenty-First Century: the continuing relevance of the general theory*. New York: Palgrave Macmillan.

Index

Milton Keynes UK
Ingram Content Group UK Ltd.
UKHW052112240624
444664UK00023B/405